MANAGING AND LEADING TODAY'S POLICE

CHALLENGES, BEST PRACTICES, & CASE STUDIES

FOURTH EDITION

MANAGING AND LEADING TODAY'S POLICE

CHALLENGES, BEST PRACTICES, & CASE STUDIES

Kenneth J. Peak
University of Nevada, Reno

Larry K. Gaines
California State University, San Bernardino

Ronald W. Glensor
Reno, Nevada, Police Department

 Pearson

330 Hudson Street, NY NY 10013

Vice President, Portfolio Management: Andrew Gilfillan
Portfolio Manager: Gary Bauer
Editorial Assistant: Lynda Cramer
Field Marketing Manager: Bob Nisbet
Product Marketing Manager: Heather Taylor
Director, Digital Studio and Content Production: Brian Hyland
Managing Producer: Jennifer Sargunar
Content Producer: Rinki Kaur
Manager, Rights Management: Johanna Burke
Operations Specialist: Deidra Smith
Creative Digital Lead: Mary Siener

Managing Producer, Digital Studio: Autumn Benson
Content Producer, Digital Studio: Maura Barclay
Full-Service Management and Composition: Integra Software Services Pvt. Ltd.
Full-Service Project Manager: Gowthaman Sadhanandham
Cover Designer: StudioMontage
Cover Art (or Cover Photo): Stefano Venturi/123RF, Greg Browning/Shutterstock
Printer/Binder: LSC Communications, Inc.
Cover Printer: Phoenix Color/Hagerstown
Text Font: Times LT Pro

Library of Congress Cataloging-in-Publication Data
Names: Peak, Kenneth J., 1947- author. | Gaines, Larry K., author. | Glensor, Ronald W., author.
Title: Managing and leading today's police: challenges, best practices, & case studies / Kenneth J. Peak, University of Nevada, Reno, Larry K. Gaines, California State University, San Bernardino, Ronald W. Glensor, Reno, Nevada, Police Department.
Other titles: Police supervision and management
Description: Fourth edition. | Upper Saddle River, New Jersey: Pearson Education, [2019]
Identifiers: LCCN 2017031189 | ISBN 9780134701271 | ISBN 0134701275
Subjects: LCSH: Police—Supervision of.
Classification: LCC HV7936.S8 P39 2019 | DDC 363.2/20973—dc23
    LC record available at https://lccn.loc.gov/
                                            2017031189

8 2021

ISBN 10:   0-13-470127-5
ISBN 13: 978-0-13-470127-1

DEDICATIONS

Robert Browning wrote that "[There] are...two points in the adventure of the diver: one—when a beggar, he prepares to plunge. Two—when a prince, he rises with his pearl." (Paracelsus, Part I: "Paracelsus Aspires," 1835); I dedicate this fourth edition to those persons who aspire to "plunge" into criminal justice leadership positions—which today are surely the most challenging and difficult roles our society has to offer.

—K. P.

To my wife Jean, my children Ashley, Courtney, and Cody; and to my grandchildren Braedon, Luke, Deaken, Chloe, Kai, Ashton, and Cezanne. Projects such as this have stolen valuable time from them.

—L. K. G.

To my wonderful and supportive family: wife Kristy, daughter Breanne and son Ronnie, their spouses Derek and Katie, and grandchildren Addison, Chloe, Claire and Heidi. And to my ever-caring parents Charles and Helga, whose passing this year we all mourn.

—R. W. G.

CONTENTS IN BRIEF

EXPANDED TABLE OF CONTENTS

PREFACE

NEW TO THIS EDITION

In general, this textbook represents a nearly complete revision of the previous (third) edition, which was authored nearly eight years earlier. During these intervening years, many new strategies, technologies, challenges, and methods have come to pass that have changed the field to a major degree; these elements of policing demand that today's leaders possess the kind of knowledge that can best be obtained in a single, consolidated source such as that which this book represents.

Furthermore, the order of chapters has been substantively re-aligned (and several completely new chapters added) so as to provide what is believed to be optimal flow. We also note that dozens of new case studies, exercises, exhibits, discussion questions, and "Internet Investigations" (i.e., links to related topics or organizations) have been added.

In sum, with the obvious exceptions of long-standing theories and practices, following are other revised, new, or updated additions to this fourth edition:

Chapter 1: An overview of police leadership and management, to include intelligence-led policing, evidence-based policing, predictive policing; police goals, mission statements, strategic plans; the Black Lives Matter movement and the problem of police shootings; police legitimacy and procedural justice, militarization of the police; body-worn cameras

Chapter 2: Updates on organizational theories and operational units, generally

Chapter 3: Updates on personnel management theories and leading in today's policing environment, generally

Chapter 4: Updates on communication and media relations, generally; police and social media, the art of negotiating, coping with conflict

Chapter 5: Contemporary challenges of human resources, including affirmative action; recruitment, hiring, and training; community policing and performance appraisals; sexual harassment; testing for promotions; risk management

Chapter 6: Officers' rights; policy needs with legalization of recreational marijuana; dealing with complaints; Early Intervention System; liability

Chapter 7: Police unions today; role of union and management leaders; negotiation of contracts; addressing grievances and appeals

Chapter 8: Enhancing budgets and financial stewardship; knowing what the job entails and what the competition is doing; grants; civilianization; mobilizing stakeholders, strategically planning

Chapter 9: Creating a culture of integrity; are police "guardians" or "soldiers"?; constitutional policing and legitimacy; procedural justice; inappropriate police behaviors;

Chapter 10: Judicious use of policing jargon; community policing and academy preparation; implementation and preservation; challenges of measuring results; role of local police in homeland security; cybercrime and community policing; applying science to policing

Chapter 11: Police wellness programs; transitioning from wartime soldier to peacetime officer; a safety plan and change of agency culture; need for training, policy, technology; OSHA and policing; federal and task force efforts; selected case studies

Chapter 12: Defining and improving police productivity; use of citizen surveys, Compstat and crime analysis; specialized tactical units; criminal investigation units; traffic units

Chapter 13: Homeland security and the terrorist threat; lone wolf terrorists; weapons of mass destruction; Department of Homeland Security; homeland security at the local level—intelligence-led policing and threat assessment, fusion centers, critical infrastructure identification, partnering with private security

Chapter 14: Five types of core policing technologies; sensor and surveillance technology (body cameras, drones); identification technology; determining which IT tools to use based on type of task involved; employing social media; updates on uses of robots; using apps for crime-fighting, solving cold cases; some legal, moral, practical considerations; the Internet of Things

PREFACE **xvii**

INTRODUCTION

This is an exciting point in time to be studying (or working in) law enforcement at any jurisdictional or hierarchical level, as evidenced by the fact that, since this book's previous edition appeared, the new strategies (smart policing, intelligence-led policing, predictive policing, and so on), technologies, and methods that have come into being have changed the field to a major degree. Added to the already challenging philosophy and strategies of community- and problem-oriented policing, these even newer strategies challenge the intellect and ability of today's police officers to address crime and disorder in ways that are more stimulating and exhilarating than ever before.

Famed educator John Dewey advocated the "learning by doing" approach to education or problem-based learning. This fourth edition is written, from start to finish, with that philosophy in mind and is reflected in the book's subtitle, *Challenges, Best Practices, & Case Studies*. And, as with its three predecessors, this book benefits from the authors' more than 100 years of combined practical and academic experience. Its chapters contain a real-world, applied flavor not found in most such textbooks and reflect the changing times in which we live and the tremendous challenges facing federal, state, and local agents and officers every day. And, also like its three preceding editions, this edition continues to represent our best attempt to allow the reader, to the fullest extent possible, to vicariously experience what one must know and do when occupying a leadership position in policing by providing a highly practical, comprehensive worldview of the challenging occupation.

TERMS USED THROUGHOUT THE BOOK

Although the terms *administration*, *management*, and *supervision* are often used synonymously, it should be noted that each is a unique concept that occasionally overlaps with the others. **Administration** is a process whereby a group of people are organized and directed toward achievement of the group's objective. The exact nature of the organization will vary among the different types and sizes of agencies, but the general principles used and the form of administration are often similar. Administration focuses on the overall organization and its mission and its relationship with other organizations and groups external to it. Administrators are often concerned with the department's direction and its policies and with ensuring that the department has the resources to fulfill its community's expectations. Police administrators generally include the chief, assistant chiefs, and high-ranking staff who support the chief in administering the department.

Management, which is also a part of administration, is most closely associated with the day-to-day operations of the various elements within the organization. For example, most police departments have a variety of operational units such as patrol, criminal investigation, traffic, gang enforcement, domestic violence, or community relations. Each of these units is run by someone who is most aptly described as a manager. In most cases, these managers are captains or lieutenants. These managers ensure that their units fulfill their departmental mission and work closely with other units to ensure that conflict or problems do not develop. They also attend to planning, budgeting, and human resource or personnel needs to ensure that the unit is adequately prepared to carry out its responsibilities.

Although the book's primary focus is on the two above levels of leadership, occasionally we will discuss **supervision**, which involves the direction of officers and civilians in their day-to-day activities, often on a one-to-one basis. Supervisors ensure that subordinate officers adhere to departmental policies, complete tasks correctly and on a timely basis, and interact with the public in a professional manner. Supervisors often observe their subordinates completing assignments and sometimes take charge of situations, especially when a deployment of a large number of officers is needed. They also work closely with managers to ensure that officers' activities are consistent with the unit's mission and objectives.

Captains and lieutenants (called middle managers) also supervise, but they supervise persons who are also supervisors, and are more concerned with a unit's activities rather than with an individual officer's activities. In actuality, all ranking personnel from the chief to the sergeant supervise, but this text is concerned with supervision by sergeants and mid-level managers.

Finally, the terms *police officer*, *law enforcement officer*, and *peace officer* are also generally interchangeable. The primary difference is that peace officer refers to anyone who has arrest authority and usually includes correctional officers, probation officers, parole officers, and persons with special police powers. Correctional officers have specific police powers in their correctional facility workplace, and investigators of welfare or Medicaid fraud have limited peace officer powers. In this text, we are primarily concerned with the following: local police (including municipal police officers and county deputy sheriffs); state police and highway patrol troopers; and others holding local, state, or federal law enforcement officer status. For the purpose of this text, the term *police officer* will generally be used to refer to all the positions noted.

ORGANIZATION OF THE BOOK

This fourth edition's 14 chapters have been revised and reorganized to better provide the reader with an understanding of the key elements of police leadership from both the theoretical and applied perspectives.

Part I, "Organizations as Living Entities," generally introduces how and why police agencies are formally organized and behave in general. Chapter 1 defines an organization and its leadership roles, and why goals, mission statements and strategic planning are important therein. Chapter 2 will explain scientific management and how it applies to organizing work and several major theories as they have been found to contribute to organizational administration and management. Chapter 3 continues that theme, focusing on theories as they relate to personnel motivation, how leadership skills are developed, empowering employees, and the major roles of police executives. Chapter 4 explains the very important concept of communications as it exists within police organizations, to include formal and informal communication, barriers, jargon and codes, negotiation and conflict resolution.

Part II, "Managing Human Resources," obviously focuses on several aspects of police leadership as they relate to personnel. Chapter 5 provides an explanation of how police human resource systems operate; also discussed are the impact of affirmative action laws and requirements; police recruitment, testing, and training; an overview of how new officers are evaluated; promotional systems; specialized units; and risk management. Chapter 6 begins with an overview of the Peace Officers' Bill of Rights and several areas in which their constitutional rights are limited under the U.S. Constitution and federal court decisions; included is the spreading legalization of marijuana and policing, the nature and handling of police complaints, early intervention systems for use with problem officers, and police liability. Chapter 7 will explain how and why police unions were created, the three collective bargaining models, union contracts, and leaders' tips for navigating the waters of collective bargaining. Finally, Chapter 8 covers financial administration, to include methods of enhancing budgets, types and formats of budgets, and grants and uses of civilians.

Part III, "Managing the Work of Police," approaches the police leader's role in the workplace from several perspectives. Chapter 9 discusses police ethics and what managers and their first-line supervisors can and must do to maintain a culture of integrity; also discussed are constitutional policing, legitimacy, procedural justice, bias-based policing, and workplace harassment. Chapter 10 considers several facets of the community policing and problem-solving philosophy and strategy, including officer training and education, adapting organizational culture and roles under this strategy, and several related concepts (i.e., CompStat, smart policing, intelligence-led policing, and predictive policing). Chapter 11 considers the essential topics of police wellness and stress, to include officers' dangers, maintaining a wellness program, and employee assistance programs. Chapter 12 considers several means of evaluating police productivity, including use citizen surveys, different methods of patrol; the implications of the Kansas City patrol study; directed patrol; when saturation patrols, crackdowns, stop-and-frisk, and tactical units should be used; employing follow-up investigations; and traffic functions. Chapter 13 considers the very important topic of homeland security, including international groups that are involved in terrorism, how Americans become radicalized, weapons of mass destruction and armaments, agencies of the Department of Homeland Security, the National Infrastructure Protection Plan, critical infrastructure, fusion centers, working with private security agencies, and how the National Incident Management System operates.

Finally, Part IV, entitled "In the Police Toolkit: Essentials for the Tasks," explains how technologies serve as a support system for methods and practices discussed in most if not all of the preceding chapters. Its Chapter 14 looks at core technologies for police; how to determine which technologies to use; technologies in crime analysis, mapping, problem-solving, real-time crime centers, crime management, and fingerprinting; the debate surrounding body-worn cameras and license plate readers; and the status of selected technologies, including drones, social media, facial recognition, robots, apps for crime-fighting, and the Internet of Things.

The book concludes with an appendix that includes related wisdom of the ages—advice from Lao-Tzu, Confucius, and Machiavelli.

Also, note the following enhancements for each chapter:

- At the beginning of each chapter are "Key Terms and Concepts" and "Student Learning Outcomes" sections, affording readers an idea of the chapter's content as well as the major concepts and points to be drawn from it.
- In keeping with this book's emphasis on the applied, practical approach, each chapter includes several case studies—which we term "You Decide" exercises—that allow you to contemplate the kinds of problems that are routinely confronted by police supervisors and managers, and apply the chapter's materials to the problem at hand.
- Discussion questions and "Internet Investigations" sections are provided at the end of each chapter, to assist the reader to further understand the information contained therein and to engage in independent study of the chapter's materials via the World Wide Web.

With a fundamental knowledge of the criminal justice system and these chapter enhancements, the reader should be in a position to engage in some critical analyses—and even, it is hoped, some spirited discussions—of the issues involved and arrive at several feasible solutions to the problems presented.

INSTRUCTOR SUPPLEMENTS

Instructor's Manual with Test Bank. Includes content outlines for classroom discussion, teaching suggestions, and answers to selected end-of-chapter questions from the text. This also contains a Word document version of the test bank.

TestGen. This computerized test generation system gives you maximum flexibility in creating and administering tests on paper, electronically, or online. It provides state-of-the-art features for viewing and editing test bank questions, dragging a selected question into a test you are creating, and printing sleek, formatted tests in a variety of layouts. Select test items from test banks included with TestGen for quick test creation, or write your own questions from scratch. TestGen's random generator provides the option to display different text or calculated number values each time questions are used.

PowerPoint Presentations. Our presentations are clear and straightforward. Photos, illustrations, charts, and tables from the book are included in the presentations when applicable.

To access supplementary materials online, instructors need to request an instructor access code. Go to **www.pearsonhighered.com/irc**, where you can register for an instructor access code. Within 48 hours after registering, you will receive a confirming e-mail, including an instructor access code. Once you have received your code, go to the site and log on for full instructions on downloading the materials you wish to use.

ALTERNATE VERSIONS

eBooks. This text is also available in multiple eBook formats. These are an exciting new choice for students looking to save money. As an alternative to purchasing the printed textbook, students can purchase an electronic version of the same content. With an eTextbook, students can search the text, make notes online, print out reading assignments that incorporate lecture notes, and bookmark important passages for later review. For more information, visit your favorite online eBook reseller or visit **www.mypearsonstore.com.**

ACKNOWLEDGMENTS

This fourth edition, and our collaborative effort in bringing it to fruition, was made possible with the input, counsel, guidance, and moral support of several people. First, the authors wish to acknowledge the following people at Pearson Education: Gary Bauer, Product Manager; Gowthaman Sadhanandham, Project Manager; Rinki Kaur, Program Manager; and Sunila, Copyeditor.

We are also grateful to the book's reviewers, who provided their insights and guidance and contributed a great deal toward making this a better effort (of course, we bear sole responsibility for any shortcomings in the final product). They were as follows: Vicki Lindsay, Troy University; Marshall Roache, Chemeketa Community College; and Bryan Wauke, Honolulu Community College.

ABOUT THE AUTHORS

Ken Peak is professor and former chairman of the Department of Criminal Justice, University of Nevada, Reno, where he was named "Teacher of the Year" by the university's Honor Society. He entered municipal policing in Kansas in 1970 and subsequently held positions as a nine-county criminal justice planner in Kansas; director of a four-state Technical Assistance Institute for the Law Enforcement Assistance Administration; director of university police at Pittsburg State University (Kansas); acting director of public safety, University of Nevada, Reno; and assistant professor of criminal justice at Wichita State University. He has published 33 textbooks (on introductory criminal justice, general and community policing, criminal justice administration, police supervision and management, and women in law enforcement), two historical books (on Kansas temperance and bootlegging), and more than 60 additional journal articles and invited book chapters. He served as chairman of the Police Section of the Academy of Criminal Justice Sciences and president of the Western and Pacific Association of Criminal Justice Educators. He received two gubernatorial appointments to statewide criminal justice committees while residing in Kansas, and holds a doctorate from the University of Kansas.

Larry K. Gaines currently is a professor and chair of the Criminal Justice Department at California State University at San Bernardino. He received his doctorate in criminal justice from Sam Houston State University. He has police experience with the Kentucky State Police and the Lexington, Kentucky, Police Department. Additionally, he served as the executive director of the Kentucky Association of Chiefs of Police for 14 years. Dr. Gaines is also a past president of the Academy of Criminal Justice Sciences. His research centers on policing and drugs. In addition to numerous articles, he has coauthored a number of books in the field: *Police Operations*; *Police Administration*; *Managing the Police Organization*; *Community Policing: A Contemporary Perspective*; *Policing Perspectives: An Anthology*; *Policing in America*; *Drugs, Crime, and Justice*; *Criminal Justice in Action*; and *Readings in White Collar Crime*. His current research agenda involves the evaluation of police tactics in terms of their effectiveness in reducing problems and fitting within the community policing paradigm. He is also researching the issue of racial profiling in a number of California cities.

Ronald W. Glensor is an assistant chief (retired) of the Reno, Nevada, Police Department (RPD). He has accumulated more than 36 years of police experience and commanded the department's patrol, administration, and detective divisions. In addition to being actively involved in RPD's implementation of community-oriented policing and problem-solving since 1987, he has provided such training to thousands of officers, elected officials, and community members representing jurisdictions throughout the United States as well as Canada, Australia, and the United Kingdom. He is also a judge for the Herman Goldstein International Problem Oriented Policing Awards held annually throughout the nation. Dr. Glensor was the 1997 recipient of the prestigious Gary P. Hayes Award, conferred by the Police Executive Research Forum, recognizing his contributions and leadership in the policing field. Internationally, he is a frequent featured speaker on a variety of policing issues. He served a six-month fellowship as problem-oriented policing coordinator with the Police Executive Research Forum in Washington, DC, and received an Atlantic Fellowship in public policy, studying repeat victimization at the Home Office in London. He is coauthor of *Community and Problem-Oriented Policing: Effectively Addressing Crime and Disorder* (seventh edition) and was coeditor of *Policing Communities: Understanding Crime and Solving Problems*; Dr. Glensor has also published in several journals and trade magazines, is an adjunct professor at the University of Nevada, Reno, and instructs at area police academies and criminal justice programs. He holds a doctorate in political science and a master's of public administration from the University of Nevada, Reno.

Organizations as Living Entities

CHAPTER 1

Leading and Managing Today's Police: Challenges and Opportunities

STUDENT LEARNING OUTCOMES

After reading this chapter, the student will:

■ understand what an organization is and how police departments meet the criteria to be called an organization

■ describe why leadership and management are key components in a police organization and why they are important

■ understand how and why night watches were created and how they evolved into police departments

■ know the history of the London Metropolitan Police Department and how it contributed to modern policing in the United States

■ distinguish between the different phases or periods of American policing

■ be able to define goals, mission statements, and strategic planning and why they are important to police organizations

■ list the challenges to police departments and identify other challenges that may be facing law enforcement

■ know the opportunities that police departments have and why they are opportunities

KEY TERMS AND CONCEPTS

• Accountable
• Act for Improving the Police in and near the Metropolis
• Black Lives Matter
• Bureaucratic policing
• Catalyst for change
• Community-oriented policing and problem solving
• Community relations units
• Community relationships
• Consciously coordinated
• Evidence-based policing
• Frankpledge system
• Goals
• Henry Fielding
• Intelligence-led policing
• Law enforcement
• Leadership
• Leges Henrici

• Magna Carta
• Management
• Militarization of the police
• Mission statement
• Night watches
• Omnibus Crime and Safe Streets Act
• Order maintenance
• Organization
• Police legitimacy
• Predictive policing
• Provision of services
• Procedural justice
• Problem
• Relatively identifiable boundary
• Sir Robert Peel
• Social entity
• Strategic plan
• Value-driven

INTRODUCTION

Leadership and management are extremely important factors in determining whether or not an organization achieves its mission and goals. Every organization must contain leaders who can manage for results, be it a private company or a police department. Police departments are organizations, and as such they are charged with accomplishing a number of tasks and goals in our society. Police departments, for most people, are the most visible government agency in our society. Many people see police officers every day, and numerous citizens come into contact with police officers daily, weekly, or at some point during their lives. They may come into contact with police officers as a suspect, traffic violator, witness, victim, or a citizen needing assistance. Police departments must effectively deal with the challenges and problems in their community.

Although there are principles that guide how the police should lead and manage, as discussed in more detail in later chapters, some police officers and departments possess these skills, while others do not possess them at the level that they are effective. Moreover, there is a mix of skill levels in most police departments with some officers who are able-bodied leaders and managers, while others are deficient. Leadership and management are activities that constantly must be improved, and this responsibility rests primarily with a department's administrators.

We compare leadership and management here to develop a better understanding of these concepts.[1] First, leadership envisions change and introduces it to the department, while management is responsible for implementing the change and transforming the department. Second, good leadership requires vision to determine the direction the department should move. Management, on the other hand, is about dedication, dedication to changing the department and ensuring that operational units remain true to the envisioned organizational arrangements. Third, good leaders are able to explain direction, while managers must teach subordinates how it is operationalized. Fourth, leadership requires that the leader have a firm understanding of the environment so that direction can be visualized. Managers must understand the work at hand and ensure that it gets done. Finally, leadership is forward thinking while management is the here and now. Police administrators, commanders, and even supervisors must have leadership and management skills. They must envision and apply the tenets of good police work.

Leading and managing a police department today is much more challenging as compared to the past; today's environment is much more uncertain.[2] There are always events that complicate police leadership and management. As an example, the United States experienced its worse recession beginning in 2008 since the Great Depression. The recession effectively slashed police budgets nationwide; police departments had to do more with much less. Today, we see globalization, immigration, and technology affecting the fiber of many communities. The 9/11 attacks on New York and Washington, DC, resulted in the creation of new federal agencies and changed the direction of many others. State and local police departments, especially in our larger cities, had to develop policies and new operational units to ferret out possible terrorists and be prepared to respond to possible attacks. The 2014 police shooting of Michael Brown by a Ferguson, Missouri, police officer resulted in riots in that city, and it raised acute awareness of the police use of deadly force throughout the nation. Many cities remain on edge as marches and riots have occurred in other cities in the aftermath of police shootings. Police departments have had to prepare for possible civil disobedience. American law enforcement from the federal level to the local level is constantly changing and evolving. This means that police leaders must constantly refocus their management priorities and their department's activities.

This chapter provides an introduction to leadership and management, which are critical components for an effective police department. This chapter examines some of the challenges and opportunities that police departments encounter. Police organizations, like all organizations, exist within an environment that presents challenges and opportunities. Before examining these challenges and opportunities, it is important to understand the dynamics of a police department. The first section of this chapter provides an overview of some of the organizational attributes that are central to effective policing.

THE CONCEPT OF ORGANIZATIONS

In their simplest form organizations are entities consisting of two or more people who cooperate to accomplish an objective or objectives. In that sense, certainly the *concept* of organization is not new. Undoubtedly, the first organizations were primitive hunting parties. Organization and a high degree of coordination were required to bring down huge animals, as revealed in fossils from as early as 40,000 B.C. Organizations today are much more complex, often involving thousands of people. The New York City Police Department has more than 34,500 officers who must be supervised and managed.[3] Most organizations, however, are much smaller. The majority of police departments in the United States have 10 or fewer officers. Regardless of size, all organizations are organized, led, and managed. As police departments grow and become larger, its leaders and supervisors must have better leadership and management skills as a result of organizational complexity. The chief of the New York City Police Department has an inherently more complex and difficult job as compared to a police chief in a small town with 10 or 15 officers.

An **organization** may be formally defined as "a consciously coordinated social entity, with a relative identifiable boundary, that functions on a relatively continuous basis to achieve a common goal or set of goals."[4] The term **consciously coordinated** implies leadership and management. That is, organizations consist of many pieces that must be coordinated. For example, large and medium-sized police departments will have patrol, traffic, detective, training units, and so on. All of these units must be coordinated so that they work together ensuring that the department effectively achieves its goals and objectives. When there is inadequate coordination, a police department likely will not be effective.

This principle also applies to working with and coordinating with agencies outside the police department. There are numerous situations where police departments must work with other agencies, for example, when police officers investigate a domestic violence call that involves children. Here, social workers specializing in children's services are called to the scene. There are a variety of agencies that the police must coordinate with, including probation, parole, fire, emergency services, community action organizations, building inspection, and so on. Police departments must also coordinate with other criminal justice agencies such as prosecutors and other local, state, and federal agencies. For example, the federal Drug Enforcement Administration often works with local departments to investigate drug trafficking. There are many problems that are best addressed when there is a response from several agencies.

Social entity refers to the fact that organizations are composed of people who interact with one another and with people outside the organization. As noted earlier, police officers interact with all sorts of citizens whether they are suspects or people in need of assistance. Additionally, police officers, especially at the executive level, interact with city governing officials and other government agencies, be they at the local, state, or federal levels. They also interact with private and parochial entities such as corporations or community action groups. These interactions or demands have an impact on police departments in that they affect or alter the police organization's activities.

Relatively identifiable boundary alludes to the organization's goals and the public served. Organizational goals, to a large extent, dictate what an organization does. For example, robbery detectives investigate robberies. If these detectives engage in other activities, the department likely will not solve as many robberies as they cannot spend the necessary time investigating the robberies. Within police

FOCUS ON: "TUCSON POLICE DEPARTMENT REORGANIZATION"

Police departments periodically alter their organizational structure. This is due to changing problems in the community, changing priorities for the department, or changes in the number of officers. Police organizational structures become stale over time, which necessitates change. Recently, the Tucson Police Department announced a reorganization plan. It was motivated by the city having a significant budget deficit. The department was authorized 992 officers, had been operating with about 900 officers, and the new reorganization placed the authorized strength at 830 officers, a significant reduction in the number of officers. The reduction would be accomplished by not filling vacant positions as opposed to layoffs. The department reduced special assignment pay, another cost savings move, by moving some officers from the street interdiction unit, gang unit, property crime surveillance unit, and domestic violence tactical unit back to patrol. Other detectives were moved

out of headquarters and began working out of the patrol districts. The traffic unit was decentralized and officers were assigned to traffic duties out of the districts. The number of officers was reduced in a number of other units.

When police departments make major changes in their structures, they must ensure that they continue to provide the same level of services or improve the level of services. Consequently, department reorganization can be risky. Also, when departments make major changes, especially when they involve personnel, police unions oppose the changes and bring public attention to the possible pitfalls. Tucson demonstrates how budgets can affect a police department's organization.

Source: Based on C. Duarte "Tucson Chief's Plans Include Reducing Officers, Reorganization." http://tucson.com/news/local/tucson-chief-s-plans-include-reducing-officers-reorganization/article_158e92bc-264b-583d-a77b-6ccf0d345f96.html Accessed February 15, 2017.

departments, officers and units have boundaries. The same is true for police departments in general. Although police departments' primary responsibilities are to prevent and solve crimes and to reduce disorder, they are also expected to provide services to the public. As the number of service calls and types of services demanded by the public increase, police officers will not be able to devote as much time to their primary responsibilities. It is important for police departments to stay on task and refrain from venturing beyond their primary responsibilities.

A second police department boundary is its jurisdictional borders. Police departments are created and funded to serve specific jurisdictions. For example, the Kansas City Police Department serves the residents of Kansas City, and the department's police activities, for the most part, are limited to the city's limits. Of course, this can be problematic as criminals do not adhere to jurisdictional boundaries when they commit crimes. This results in police departments having to coordinate their activities with adjoining or nearby departments.

POLICE LEADERSHIP AND MANAGEMENT: AN OVERVIEW

This book focuses on leadership and management in the police organization. Too often people fail to comprehend the complexity of these two activities. When this occurs, the police department is less effective. Administrators and managers, from the chief to the police officer on the street, must possess these skills to some extent. This section provides an overview of leadership and management.

Leadership

Simply stated, **leadership** is getting things done through other people. Leaders ensure that tasks are accomplished and goals are reached. The administrators, managers, and supervisors are responsible for ensuring harmonious coordination in the police department. Supervisors are concerned with tasks and human resources. Supervisors are responsible for ensuring that subordinate officers attend to their duties in a manner that is consistent with departmental and community expectations. They see that officers do their jobs the best way possible. The term human resources refers to the fact that supervisors are responsible for people who, especially in the workplace, often have problems and difficulties. Supervisors attempt to solve these problems and difficulties through training and the provision of direction.

Managers generally are lieutenants and captains who are responsible for units within a police department. Examples of managers would be a captain in charge of a patrol district or precinct or a lieutenant in charge of a robbery squad. They essentially have the same responsibilities as sergeants, only at a higher level. They also are concerned with a larger picture. A sergeant may be responsible for a squad of patrol officers, while the sergeant's captain is concerned with how well police services are delivered in the sergeant's precinct. In addition to being concerned with tasks and human resources, managers must ensure that the efforts of supervisors and officers collectively fulfill the unit's departmental responsibilities. Police management is discussed more below.

Finally, administrators guide and lead the department by setting an overall direction and are at the highest levels within a police department. Administrators by working with governing officials and citizens identify priorities or goals. This contributes to the department being responsive to the community it serves. Once goals are identified, administrators lead the department toward their accomplishment. Essentially, leaders at all levels in the police department move the department forward (Figure 1-1).

Management

Whereas leadership is getting things done through other people, **management** consists of tools by which to put leadership into action. These tools include decision making, planning, providing direction, making decisions about staffing, communicating, organizing, and budgeting. Police chiefs are the primary conduits for the public to provide input into a police department. This is generally done through a political process where citizens communicate with their council members and other elected officials. In some cases, police chiefs receive direct input from the community. Police chiefs consider this input and ultimately make decisions on how their departments should respond. This may involve the development of new programs such as special patrols in a high-crime area or directing a lieutenant in charge of a domestic violence unit to review officers' cases to ensure that they are following the law and making arrests when they are mandated by law.

Middle managers are also involved in managing; they manage their individual units to ensure that their officers' activities contribute to accomplishing the goals as set by the department's administrators. When administrators develop programs to address specific problems, the programs generally are assigned to specific units. The unit commanders then ensure that those programs are implemented. They will observe officers'

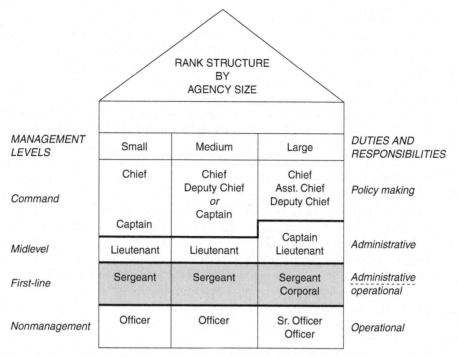

FIGURE 1-1   Rank Structure by Agency Size

performance and consult with supervisors to monitor activities. For example, a robbery unit commander will closely monitor the number of cases that are cleared and review individual detectives' reports. A traffic unit commander will examine where accidents occur and direct traffic officers to write citations where traffic crashes are occurring in an effort to reduce the number of crashes. These middle managers are the interface between administrative policy making and the actual work in the field.

Supervisors, generally sergeants, manage their officers by monitoring their subordinate's activities on a regular basis. This is especially important for new officers or for veteran officers who have been transferred to a different unit. Supervisors manage by ensuring that subordinates perform their work correctly. This entails supervisors reviewing their officers' reports. Reports are important as they document what occurs at a call or crime scene. Supervisors are able to identify a number of problems and take corrective action as a result of reviewing reports. Supervisors back up their officers on calls or investigations, allowing the former to determine if officers are following department procedures or are making mistakes when engaging in police activities. This also allows for problems to be identified and corrected.

Finally, police officers are to some extent managers. For example, a traffic officer while investigating a traffic crash involving multiple vehicles often will have to deal with several citizens, those involved in the crash and witnesses, as well as taking a report and clearing the scene. The same can be said of detectives while investigating crimes. Detectives must effectively manage their investigations in order to solve cases. Although officers and detectives are not considered managers, they nonetheless must possess good management skills in order to effectively do their jobs.

Leadership and management are key ingredients in a police department. They are qualities that every officer must possess. When police personnel at all levels have leadership and management skills, the department functions more effectively. Police administrators must ensure that personnel have these important skills.

POLICE LEADERSHIP AND MANAGEMENT: AN HISTORICAL PERSPECTIVE

Police history is rather revealing. John Skinner advises that history repeats itself.[5] Perhaps the best example is **community-oriented policing and problem solving**, which to some extent mirrors policing in the early 1900s. History provides us with an understanding of how we arrived at our current policing philosophies and arrangements. It provides us with a template by which to better understand the inter-workings of police departments, and it informs us about what the future might bring. This section provides a brief history of policing with an emphasis on leadership and management.

Early Policing Efforts

Governments have always had to have some mechanism by which to control its citizens and outsiders who would attempt to harm citizens or overthrow the existing government. For example, in early Roman Empire times this was accomplished by the Roman army. The army's primary objective was to protect the Roman emperor and the empire. The army was not concerned with the populace, and citizens' reaction to crime was often vigilantism or revenge. Noblemen often hired bodyguards to protect them and their families. If a significant problem occurred that threatened the empire, the army was dispatched to quell any disturbances, and this generally was accomplished in a brutal manner. There was an absence of police authority and actions. This method of operation was typical for early cultures and civilizations.

Modern policing began or has its roots in England. There were several important historical events that led up to the creation of the first modern police department in London in 1829. The first policing system to evolve in England was the **frankpledge system**, which was present in medieval England. Here, the men in each village were divided into groups of 10, and then 10 of these groups were combined into a "hundred." These groups were then charged with bringing offenders to justice. Although there was an element of formality or management, it remained a vigilante system. Shire-reeves were later appointed by the king who were responsible for collecting taxes and presiding over the king's courts.[6] The shire-reeves were the forerunner of today's sheriffs.

In 1116, the king issued the **Leges Henrici**, which identified offenses against the crown or state. The state became involved in dealing with criminal behavior. Previously, crimes were considered offenses against persons that were handled by citizens, not government. The Leges Henrici is the foundation of our modern legal system. Today, crimes are offenses against the state or federal government as defined by statutes. In 1215, King John of England was forced to sign the **Magna Carta**. This document essentially guaranteed people certain civil and political rights. The Magna Carta served as the foundation of our Constitution. The Leges Henrici and Magna Carta are important since they are at the foundation of our legal system.

Early Policing in England

As a result of the Industrial Revolution, cities in England became heavily populated with thousands of people coming from the countryside in search of work. This substantial increase in population and unemployment created high levels of crime, particularly in London. The people of London were essentially defenseless. The government responded by creating night watches. The early **night watches** involved citizens who patrolled the streets at night to deter and observe for crime. In order to staff these night watches, all adult male citizens had

Modern English police officers walking a beat.
Source: betty finney/Alamy Stock Photo

to periodically serve as a watchman. Many citizens paid others to serve their times as watchmen. They often hired drunks, vagabonds, and criminals to serve in their place. Consequently, the watchmen did little watching and had little effect on the crime problem. The night watch system was totally ineffective since there was a total absence of leadership and management.

Although there were several early English reformers who attempted to improve policing in London, one of the most notable was **Henry Fielding**.[7] Fielding was appointed as a magistrate in the Bow Street area of London. He made two important contributions to policing. First, he was an excellent writer and he wrote about crime and poverty in London in an effort to draw attention to the crime problem. Second, he employed a group of "thief takers" who investigated crimes in the area and brought criminals to justice. The thief takers were the forerunners of today's police detectives.

A second early reformer was **Sir Robert Peel**. Peel was England's home secretary, and was concerned with the crime problem in London and recognized that stronger actions had to be taken. In 1829, he introduced a bill in Parliament, the **Act for Improving the Police in and near the Metropolis**. This bill created the first modern police department. Initially, 1,000 officers were hired and organized into divisions. The police department was organized around 12 principles:[8]

1. The police must be stable, efficient, and organized along military lines.
2. The police must be under government control.
3. The absence of crime will best prove the efficiency of police.
4. The distribution of crime news is essential.
5. The deployment of police strength by both time and area is essential.
6. No quality is more indispensable to a policeman than a perfect command of temper; a quiet, determined manner has more effect than violent action.
7. Good appearance commands respect.
8. The securing and training of proper persons are at the root of efficiency.
9. Public security and training of proper persons are at the root of efficiency.
10. Police headquarters should be centrally located and easily accessible to the people.
11. Policemen should be hired on a probationary basis.
12. Police records are necessary to the best distribution of police strength.

Peel determined that the police should be organized using military principles. He believed that the military provided the best management structure. It provided a level of control by which to ensure that officers were performing in an effective manner. It is notable that these principles remain a part of modern police management.

Early Policing in America

Large cities in America such as New York, Boston, and Philadelphia followed London's lead and created watchman systems. Like London, American cities found the watchman systems to be ineffective; they did little to curtail crime. The watchman systems slowly evolved into police departments. In 1844, a police force was created in New York, and Boston created a police force in 1854. Additionally, states began to create state police organizations. Pennsylvania, Massachusetts, and Texas were the first states to do so.

These early police departments were inefficient and rife with corruption. The problem was they were controlled by local politicians who used the police as a force to ensure political order. The police often were told who to arrest or not to arrest; they allowed prostitution and illegal liquor sales to occur when proprietors were aligned with the dominant politicians; and they minimally addressed crime problems. Leadership and management were present only when it was advantageous to the dominant politicians. This model continued into the 1950s.

YOU DECIDE...

As we note, Sir Robert Peel was the father of modern policing. He shaped the London Metropolitan Police Department into a fairly effective police organization at the time. Policing and social conditions before Peel were deplorable. Many of Peel's 12 principles apply today. Thus, it appears that policing has not changed very much in some ways, but has changed drastically in other ways.

Questions for Discussion

1. Which of Peel's principles are still relevant in today's police department and why?
2. How are today's police departments different from the London Metropolitan Police Department?
3. Which of Peel's principles are not important in modern American police departments and why?

Professional Policing

There were many efforts to professionalize American policing during the early twentieth century, and they crystalized in the 1950s. These reform efforts emanated from two directions: citizens and citizen groups who were concerned with the quality of policing and police reformers who aspired to have professional police organizations. The citizen reformers were often propelled by police scandals. For example, from 1894 through 1993, there were six commissions that examined police corruption in New York City alone.[9] The scandals often resulted in reform political candidates to be elected and brought changes to the police departments.

Reform police chiefs used a variety of methods to wrestle control from the corrupt politicians. After World War II and the Korean War, police departments were able to hire a number of veterans as officers. These veterans were accustomed to discipline and fit the professional model of policing. A strong sense of duty was at their core. Police departments began to create training units to inoculate officers from political corruption and to instill professionalism. Specialized units such as vice were created to reduce politicians' control on officers. Chiefs created additional administrators such as majors and assistant chiefs to exert more control over their police forces. This reduced the influence of local politicians since there were more administrators guiding the departments. Police departments began to establish minimum hiring standards to prevent derelict officers from being hired. These efforts had a profound impact on policing.[10] Essentially, police executives were beginning to manage and lead their departments.

By the 1950s, American policing could be characterized as **bureaucratic policing**. After decades of corruption, police chiefs were committed to eliminating graft and corruption. There were two general methods these police chiefs used to eliminate corruption and to instill professional effectiveness. First, chiefs attempted to exert maximum control over their officers. This was accomplished though close supervision and strict rules and regulations. In terms of close supervision, sergeants were assigned to guide officers and to ensure that they performed their duties in a prescribed manner. Close supervision was supplemented by internal affairs units. These units investigated officers to ensure compliance with departmental expectations. Police chiefs wanted to stop any inappropriate behavior as quickly as possible to avoid scandals or criticism of their departments.

Second, they attempted to isolate officers from the public. Many police chiefs believed that close relations with the public led to corruption. There were many undesirables such as gamblers, prostitutes, or thieves who would corrupt officers in order to facilitate their crimes. Police chiefs attempted to minimize the contact that officers had with citizens. Their prescribed demeanor was to be standoffish and professional; they responded to

Police officer stop circa 1950s.
Source: National Motor Museum/Heritage Image Partnership Ltd/Alamy Stock Photo

calls and crimes with minimum interaction with the public. Although this reduced opportunities for police officers to be corrupted, it ultimately presented public relations problems for officers. The reduction of corruption was more important than working with the community.

Community Relations Policing

The 1960s was a period of great unrest in the country. The Vietnam War and the civil rights movement resulted in riots and protests in many of America's cities and on college campuses. The civil rights movement and poverty spawned riots in cities such as Los Angeles, Detroit, and Washington, DC, and resulted in substantial property damage and, in some cases, deaths. College students protested the Vietnam War by conducting marches and campus sit-ins. Police departments across the nation initially were not prepared to handle the disturbances.

Many police departments created **police-community relations units** to help deal with the disorder. These units implemented programs that were designed to foster better relations with the neighborhoods and communities. These programs included police youth athletic leagues, crime prevention programs, community meetings with citizen groups and neighborhoods, and youth programs such as taking disadvantaged juveniles on outings such as fishing, sporting events, and amusement parks. Efforts were made to develop better relations with communities. The police came to understand that working with the community could contribute to reducing crime and disorder.

The relationship between the police and the community was bifurcated. On the one hand, the police worked to develop better relations with the community. On the other hand, the police adhered to a law-and-order perspective, and in many cases crime reduction was substantially more important than better relations with the community. The law-and-order tactics often would erase successes made in developing more positive relations. The move into community relations complicated police executives' management and leadership responsibilities as they had to guide their departments in both directions.

As a result of the national disorder problem, in 1968, Congress passed the **Omnibus Crime Control and Safe Streets Act**. The Act was recognition by Congress that the police needed assistance, and it was the first time that large amounts of federal monies were given to local and state police agencies. The Act funded many of the police-community relations programs that police departments implemented. The Act also provided funding to the states to create police training programs. Prior to the Act, many police officers did not receive adequate training. The Act funded police officers' higher education in the form of tuition assistance, which resulted in the establishing of college criminal justice programs across the nation. Police departments were able to hire and train better-qualified officers, which enabled police departments to more effectively deal with crime and disorder problems.

Community Policing

Community policing, which is discussed in more detail in Chapter 10, was the first substantive change in American policing since the professional model was implemented in the 1950s.[11] **Community policing** consists of two distinct qualities.[12] First, the police must work to improve **community relationships**. Philosophically, the police should not police the community but work with the community to prevent and solve crimes and to alleviate conditions causing crime and disorder. This partnership helps to build communities and neighborhoods and inoculate them against crime. When building communities, the police work directly with neighborhood citizens and other government and social agencies to improve the quality of life, which contributes to the reduction of crime and disorder.[13]

The second attribute of community policing is problem solving. Historically, police officers responded to calls for service and would intervene in situations that they observed while patrolling or investigating crimes. They responded to situations, not problems. A **problem** is an event, occurrence, or location that generates crime or disorder. For example, a nightclub could serve alcohol to inebriated patrons that results in a large number of fights and assaults. The fights and assaults are the situations requiring police intervention, but the nightclub is the problem because it generates the incidence of disorder. If the police crackdown on the nightclub, a number of fights and assaults are avoided in the future. Problem solving is where causes or instigators of crime and disorder are addressed and eliminated.

Intelligence-Led Policing

Intelligence-led policing (ILP) became prevalent as a result of the 9/11 attacks on New York and Northern Virginia. There was a realization that local law enforcement was on the front line battling terrorism and acts of terrorism, and the police needed more tools to be more effective. ILP is a collaborative effort that encompasses community engagement and problem solving from community policing and heightened intelligence operations.[14] It focuses on risk management. Whereas problem solving involved identify problems and clusters of crime, ILP goes deeper. That is, police officers collect intelligence about places, people, and activities in an attempt to identify possible or impending problems. A variety of sources of information are used when collecting intelligence

Police crime prevention presentation.
Source: Halfdark/Getty Images

such as informants, ownership of homes and other buildings, sales of guns and materials that could be used as explosives and so on. Information from other sources such as businesses and social agencies is collected to supplement police information. Information is collected on gangs, organized criminal groups and potential terrorists. ILP is more proactive because it attempts to identify conditions before they become problems.

Once intelligence information is collected, it must be analyzed and collated into a useable product. All information from all sources about an event, person, place, or activity is compiled and analyzed to determine if an actionable problem exists. If so, decision makers develop a strategy to counter the potential problem. Strategies are evaluated to ensure that they produce the desired results.[15] ILP is discussed in more detail in Chapter10.

Evidence-Based Policing

According to Lawrence Sherman, **evidence-based policing** is a method where decisions about practices and strategies are based on what works or is effective and efficient. Historically, police administrators made strategic decisions based on tradition and assumptions.[16] Whereas community policing and ILP are strategies with which to combat crime and disorder, evidence-based policing provides a framework for identifying the strategies and tactics to deploy once a problem has been identified. In other words, strategies should "work"; they should effectively and efficiently reduce crime and disorder. It is not enough to implement strategies; the strategies must be effective in reducing the problem.

As an example, Weisburd and his colleagues examined a number of cases where problem solving was used to tackle crime problems. They found that problem solving generally contributed to reducing crime.[17] The departments in their study used a variety of tactics to confront the problems that were encountered. When police departments tailor their responses to the problem, they often are successful in dealing with problems. There are numerous possible responses to any problem, and the tactic used to confront the problem should be based on *what works*. This means that officers should constantly monitor the situation to determine if the response or strategy produces the desired results. Evidence-based policing is discussed in more detail in Chapter 10.

Predictive Policing

Predictive policing is a process where mathematical models or algorithms are combined with geospatial information to predict future crime and disorder. According to the National Institute of Justice, it is "taking data from disparate sources, analyzing them and then using results to anticipate, prevent and respond more effectively to future crime."[18] Private corporations and businesses have been using "big data" for years; now police departments are using data to predict crime much like Walmart or some other business will use data to predict the kinds of products that interest their customers.

The Richmond, Virginia, Police Department used predictive policing to reduce random gunfire. Every New Year's Eve the city experienced a substantial increase in random gunfire. In 2003, the police examined the gunfire data for several years on New Year's Eve. Consequently, they were able to anticipate the time, location, and nature of the random incidents. The department assigned officers to the locations where gunfire had previously occurred. They reduced the gunfire by 47 percent and significantly increased the number of weapons seized.[19] In another example, the Arlington, Texas, Police Department used predictive policing to attack a burglary problem. Here, they found a direct relationship between burglaries and building code violations. Physical decay was contributing to the conditions that resulted in the burglaries. The police department began working with other city departments to improve neighborhood conditions and reduce the incidence of burglaries.[20]

Today, predictive policing is in its infancy, and it is expected to become more sophisticated and be adopted by more departments in the years to come. Police departments have a wealth of data with which to make predictions about crime and disorder. Predictive policing is discussed in more detail in Chapter 10.

POLICE GOALS: WHAT DO POLICE DEPARTMENTS DO?

The previous section briefly examined the history of the police and how different periods affected police leadership and management. We can better understand police leadership and management by examining police departments' functions or activities. Organizations generally establish goals to guide their operations and activities. **Goals** are specific results or achievements toward which police departments direct their efforts.[21] In other words, goals delineate what needs to be accomplished. They guide behavior. All activities in a police department should be directed toward the accomplishment of a goal.

Police departments are public agencies and as such serve the public. As such, there are three general categories of police activities: law enforcement, provision of services to the community and citizens, and maintaining order in the community. **Law enforcement** consists of those activities where police officers deter crimes, investigate crimes, and arrest offenders whether for misdemeanors or felonies. The **provision of services** refers to officers engaging in activities such as looking for missing children, providing motorists assistance, and engaging in crime prevention activities. Finally, **order maintenance** is where officers intervene in fights, family disturbances, protests, and other activities to keep the peace. The mix of these activities varies from one community to another as different communities have different needs and problems.

Mission Statements

One of the ways to clarify a department's goals is to examine its mission statements. A **mission statement** is a statement of a department's commitment to the community, and provides information about how the department will accomplish. For example, the Los Angeles Police Department's (LAPD) mission statement is

…to safeguard the lives and property of the people we serve, to reduce the incidence and fear of crime, and to enhance public safety while working with diverse communities to improve their quality of life.[22]

The LAPD's mission statement establishes broad goals for the department. Administrators then develop programs and tactics to achieve these goals. The mission statement also reassures the public about what the department is attempting to achieve.

YOU DECIDE...

Today, most police departments have webpages as a way to provide citizens information about the department. These webpages generally contain the department's mission statement. Assume you are a sergeant in a 30-officer police department. A new chief has been hired by the city council. The old chief retired under pressure because many people in the community believed that he was not doing a good job. The news media had attacked him accusing the department of only being concerned with writing traffic tickets. The new chief wants to dispel this perception. The chief has decided to create a webpage for the department and wants to include a mission statement. The chief has asked you to write a mission statement for the department paying particular attention to the community's impression that the department is only concerned with writing tickets.

Questions for Discussion

1. Who would you talk with when deciding on what to include in the mission statement?
2. What elements would you include in the mission statement?
3. How would you address the need to better explain what the department does?

Mission statements help police executives to better manage their departments. It is a statement that is transmitted to citizens and officers about what the police department intends to accomplish in the community. It helps to ensure that everyone in the department is on the same page in terms of expectations.

Strategic Plans

Another way to identify a police department's goals is to examine its strategic plan. A **strategic plan** is a document that details specific goals that a police department is committed to accomplish and the specific strategies the department deploys to accomplish the goals. In some cases, the department will establish benchmarks such as reducing burglaries by 10 percent as a part of the plan. The plan represents a roadmap for police activities. It often advises specific units in the department of the operational format and what they should accomplish.

For example, the Tucson, Arizona, Police Department developed a strategic plan that contained six primary goals:

1. Reduce, Solve, and Prevent Crime
2. Improve Quality of Life Issues
3. Embrace and Integrate Technology throughout the Agency
4. Strengthen Communication
5. Achieve Organizational Excellence and Provide Superior Services
6. Develop Employee Competency and Capabilities[23]

Notice that goals 1 and 2 (and to some extent goal 5) target direct services to the public. The remaining goals focus on improving the department's efficiency and effectiveness. In some cases, departments fail to consider strengthening their organizational and operational capabilities in their strategic plans, but these areas should not be neglected.

The Tucson Police Department's goals are general in nature. However, once goals are established, specific objectives are assigned to each goal. For example, the objectives for Tucson's goal 1—Reduce, Solve, and Prevent Crime—included the following:

1. Establish Effective Enforcement Initiatives
2. Enhance Investigative Initiatives
3. Engage the Community in Joint Problem-Solving and Crime Prevention Activities[24]

Finally, to complete the strategic planning process, each objective is assigned action items. Action items consist of statements that describe more precise language about what is to be accomplished. Each action item is also assigned to a specific unit or commander and given a time line for accomplishment. The action items for the objective Establish Effective Enforcement Initiatives include the following:

1. Research and implement methods to reduce violent crime
2. Conduct educational outreach campaign
3. Implement the data-driven approaches to crime and traffic safety
4. Develop and implement crime prevention strategies based on targeted operational planning and other data-driven approaches
5. Establish a unit dedicated to metal theft
6. Modernize and enhance the capability of the division crime response units; expand to two squads per division, each with 8–10 unmarked vehicles, surveillance, and recording equipment
7. Establish/renew the crime prevention unit
8. Research and develop a plan to work with victims to reduce repeat victimization
9. Establish a unit dedicated to graffiti
10. Establish a vice unit[25]

The action items in the Establish Effective Enforcement Initiatives objective are far reaching, addressing a number of crime problems. Several new units are established. These units will address specific crime problems. In some cases, the action items are designed to enhance the equipment needs of current operational units.

Strategic plans represent an excellent vehicle that assists in leading and managing a police organization. In terms of leadership, a strategic plan advises the organizational members about what the department is attempting to accomplish and the department's priorities. From a management perspective, it provides unit commanders with responsibilities and priorities. The plan helps to coordinate the activities within the department as it ensures that all departmental responsibilities are assigned to specific individuals or persons.

American police departments are presented with a number of challenges and opportunities that affect their efficacy. The following section examines some of these challenges and opportunities.

CHALLENGES AND OPPORTUNITIES

We see that leadership and management are key ingredients to a successful police organization. Police departments are government agencies that exist and function within society, and as such, various elements within society affect the department and what it does. In other words, police departments do not exist in a vacuum. Police executives and their officers must face these challenges and react to them in a way that minimizes their problematic nature. On the other hand, when opportunities avail themselves, police departments should embrace them and use them to build a more effective police department.

Challenges to American Policing

We see challenges as situations, conditions, or events that affect policing in terms of creating a problem or adverse situation. They frequently make it more difficult for a department to police its community. Some of these challenges are extremely problematic from the perspective that they make policing much more difficult. Nonetheless, police departments must consider and respond to these challenges.

Black Lives Matter and the Problem of Police Shootings

Black Lives Matter is a national movement that is a reaction to the police shooting black men. It likely has its origin in the shooting of Trayvon Martin, who was killed in 2012 by George Zimmerman, who was a member of a neighborhood watch. The number of police shootings of black men has raised the specter of police racism. According to a *Washington Post* study, 24 percent of those killed by police officers are black, while blacks constitute only 13 percent of the population.[26] In 2015, 991 people were shot dead by the police. The increase in smart phones with video capability and body worn cameras by police has resulted in the sensationalism associated with the many police shootings that have occurred, and they occur rather frequently. Any shooting is likely to be picked up by the media and covered nationally. This national attention results in many Americans believing that all or many police officers are racists and do not refrain from shooting people. Social media adds to the problem. Information about the shooting is quickly spread throughout a community, and unfortunately in many cases, much of the information is false. For example, in September 2016, police officers in Charlotte, North Carolina, shot and killed Keith Scott, which led to violent protects in Charlotte. During the confrontation with police and its aftermath, Scott's wife maintained that Scott did not have a gun, which was broadcast repeatedly in social media. However, upon investigation, it was determined that Mr. Scott did have a gun.[27]

A black lives matter protest.
Source: Todd Bannor/Alamy Stock Photo

A reaction to Black Lives Matter in police circles has been *blue lives matter*. This call is an effort to point out that dozens of police officers are murdered each year. Police work is increasingly more dangerous. Blue lives matter should not be seen as a method to lessen the problematic nature of the police shootings. Both types of shootings are separate problems that must be reduced. Police departments must take action to ensure that the number of both types of shootings is minimized. This should be a high priority for police leaders.

Police Legitimacy and Procedural Justice

Police legitimacy essentially is the right for officers to use power to enforce the law. This premise is accepted by almost everyone at least to some degree. However, some people and some neighborhoods question police officers' legitimate right to exercise police powers. This largely stems from their perceptions of how they or their acquaintances have been treated in the past. This may have been where they perceive that they were treated unfairly or where they believe that the police did not provide them with an adequate level of service or protection. The police have not met their standard of acceptable behavior. When citizens view the police as illegitimate, they are less likely to abide or obey the police.[28] Police leaders must work to increase the perceptions of police legitimacy and acceptance in all neighborhoods.

Procedural justice, on the other hand, is how citizens evaluate police performance. Do they see the police treating them in a fair and just manner?[29] Singular encounters with the public matter; they can cumulatively and over time negatively affect people's perception of the police. Procedural justice can be enhanced when police officers listen and explain their actions to citizens, treat them in a fair manner, show them dignity and respect, and have a trustworthy motive when dealing with citizens.[30] In other words, when police officers give someone a citation or place them under arrest, they can do so in a professional manner. This in many cases is difficult since police officers have so many negative encounters with citizens, but officers can make an effort to treat citizens with dignity and fairness.

Jim Bueermann has identified three principles that police departments should adopt in order to enhance their legitimacy in the community.[31] First, a department must be **value-driven**; a department must adopt, articulate, and abide by values such as community collaboration, ethics, excellence, and respect for all community constituents. Second, a police department must be a **catalyst for change** not only within the department but also within the community. The department must solve community problems and collaborate with segments within the community to adopt progressive reforms to mediate problems. Finally, departments must train and hold officers **accountable** to ensure all officers respond to all segments of the community in highly legitimate ways. Police legitimacy and procedural justice should always be important goals for police leaders.

Militarization of the Police

Militarization of the police refers to when the police use military equipment and tactics to carry out their duties, and the adoption of a military culture when policing certain problems.[32] This has its roots in special weapons and tactics (SWAT) teams. Initially, militarized police units were used to intervene in dangerous situations such as barricaded persons, serving drug search and arrest warrants, and so on. However, the services of these units have expanded over time in many police departments, and they now are deployed in an array of situations. It is not uncommon to see police officers masked and dressed in military garb when the news media covers a situation. Some police departments have obtained armed personnel carriers from the military and use them on city streets.

Militarization affects the culture of a police department. It often results in a mentality that is antithetical to police legitimacy. Police officers tend to take a hard-nosed approach to citizen interactions that otherwise require a level finesse. It also affects public attitudes as perceived over-reactions by the police affect citizens' perceptions of procedural justice. There are circumstances where SWAT types of operations are appropriate. They should be managed by developing policies that dictate when military types of operations can be used. When used, unit commanders should complete after action reports (AARs) that document operations. This will ensure accountability and allow for the evaluation of such operations.

OPPORTUNITIES FOR AMERICAN POLICING

Police Body-Worn Cameras

One result from the controversy surrounding Black Lives Matter is that many police departments are now deploying body-worn cameras. The police were opposed to them for many years, because they felt the videos would be used in disciplinary actions or otherwise in court against them. They also believed that the body-worn cameras violated their privacy and the privacy of citizens. These attitudes have changed as more citizens are

FOCUS ON: POLICE BODY-WORN CAMERAS

Police departments across the country are issuing body-worn cameras to their officers. These cameras capture interactions between police officers and citizens that they encounter; they provide documentation to these encounters. The impact of these cameras has been studied in a number of departments. The Mesa, Arizona, Police Department equipped 50 officers with body-worn cameras and compared their activities to 50 officers who were not issued cameras. The officers equipped with the cameras had a 40 percent decrease in complaints and a 75 percent decrease in use-of-force incidents during the one-year study period.[35] Similarly, the Phoenix Police Department equipped 56 officers with body-worn cameras and compared their activities with 50 officers who were not equipped with the cameras. Police officers equipped with the cameras reported that they were comfortable with the cameras as well as their interactions with citizens.[36] Over the years, the police have adamantly opposed the use of body cameras. Contemporary research shows that body-worn cameras are now receiving more acceptance in police circles. Moreover, it appears that body-worn cameras are a tool that improves the quality of police work, and they improve police-community relations.

videotaping police encounters with their smart phones. Now the police see body cameras as a tool to counter criticism and better document their interactions with the public. The cameras often validate police officers' actions when there is a citizen complaint.

There are a number of benefits to using body-worn cameras. They increase transparency and citizens' views of procedural justice, and along these lines, they can have a calming effect on citizens and officers during an encounter. Video has evidentiary benefits when resolving complaints and in court. They also provide training opportunities by providing real-life situations.[33] Research has shown that body-worn cameras have a positive impact. Barak Ariel and his colleagues found that they resulted in officers using less force during citizen encounters, and they reduced the number of complaints filed against officers.[34] Police leaders should implement this innovation as it has positive results not only in the department but also in the community. Body-worn cameras will be discussed in more detail in Chapter 14.

Enhanced Technology

The technology revolution is an ongoing phenomenon that advances in leaps and bounds and there is no end in sight. Today, we are seeing driverless cars, thinking computers, a wealth of methods by which to communicate, and many other advances that assist us in our daily lives. Recent innovations in law enforcement include body cameras, facial recognition, drones, license plate readers, advances in DNA analysis, and so on. Police departments are increasingly using Facebook, Twitter, and other forms of communications to interact with the public. Crime mapping is becoming more sophisticated with some departments using geospatial information to predict crimes. In five years, there will be even more advances, and the process will continue. It is important for police leaders to evaluate and embrace new technology in the future to more effectively deal with the many and varied problems facing law enforcement.

Police Research and Evidence-Based Policing

As noted earlier, evidence-based policing in decisions about practices and strategies are based on what works or is effective and efficient. When confronted with crime and other problems, police managers should implement strategies that most effectively deal with them. It means that the police should tailor responses to the intricacies associated with the problem. This means that two similar problems may require different responses as a result of the environment or other intervening conditions. It is not good enough to "do what we have done in the past"! It means that police leaders and managers must thoroughly analyze problems and search for new solutions.

Since the Kansas City Preventive Patrol Experiment in 1972, researchers have been examining police operations. Today, there is a substantial body of research to inform police leaders about what works when confronting police problems. For example, Cody Telep and David Weisburd recently reviewed the police literature and identified studies that showed positive effects for hot spot policing, focused deterrence strategies, problem-oriented policing, disorder policing, illegal firearms possession, DNA, and drug enforcement.[37] Thus, there is a wealth of programs from which police leaders can select to counter problems. Moreover, studies not only describe the strategies but also describe the conditions surrounding the problems that resulted in program implementation. These types of information can substantially assist police leaders and managers to reduce crime and disorder in their communities.

Summary

This chapter started with an overview of organizations, which will be explored in more detail in Chapter 2. Police departments are organizations that must provide services to the public in an effective and efficient manner. Organization theory and structure play an important role in policing. As a part of this discussion, we examined the meaning of leadership and management, two key ingredients in organizations. We provided some context to police leadership and management by briefly examining policing from an historical framework. History is useful in that it provides us with information about how we arrived at our current organizational arrangements.

This chapter briefly examined the concept of police goals. Goals are important as they establish standards for performance. We demonstrated how goals often are enumerated in police department mission statements and strategic plans. Finally, we briefly discussed some of the challenges and opportunities confronting American law enforcement. It is important for police leaders to confront the challenges and take advantage of the opportunities.

The environment of policing is constantly changing, and police leaders must be forward-thinking and ensure their departments continue to move forward in an effective manner.

Discussion Questions

1. What is leadership and how does it affect the police organization?
2. What is management and what are the levels of management in a police department?
3. Explain how English policing affected the creation of policing in the United States.
4. What are police legitimacy and procedural justice? Explain how they affect policing and why they are important.
5. What is an organization? How do police departments meet the three criteria that describe an organization?
6. Explain why evidence-based policing is important. Provide an example of evidence-based policing.
7. Why are mission statements important? What do you think is the primary mission of police departments?

Internet Investigations

National Institute of Justice, "Police Leaderships Challenges in a Changing World"
https://www.ncjrs.gov/pdffiles1/nij/238338.pdf

Oakland, California Police Department, "Strategic Plan 2016"
http://www2.oaklandnet.com/oakca1/groups/police/documents/webcontent/oak056503.pdf

National Institute of Justice, "Research on Body-Worn Cameras and Law Enforcement"

https://www.nij.gov/topics/law-enforcement/technology/pages/body-worn-cameras.aspx

Office of Community Oriented Policing Services, "The State of Policing in the United States, Volume 1"
https://ric-zai-inc.com/ric.php?page=detail&id=COPS-W0815

Bureau of Justice Statistics, "Local Police Departments, 2013: Personnel, Policies, and Practices"
https://www.bjs.gov/content/pub/pdf/lpd13ppp.pdf

CHAPTER 2

The Dynamics of Police Organizations: Structure and Theories

STUDENT LEARNING OUTCOMES

After reading this chapter, the student will:

- understand scientific management and how it applies to organizing work
- be able to describe POSDCORB and discuss its components
- know Max Weber's contribution to administration and management
- understand the three ways in which police tasks are organized
- be able to describe the Hawthorne experiments and their impact on management
- distinguish between theory X and theory Y
- be able to explain Maslow's hierarchy of needs and apply it to motivation
- describe how culture affects police management
- know what the informal organization is and how it can affect police departments
- know what the linking pin system is and how it would apply to police hierarchy
- know what a matrix structure is and how it could be used in police departments
- be able to compare human relations theory with traditional police management
- know how chain of command, specialization, and unity of command are applied in police departments
- understand the relationship between delegation of authority and chain of command

KEY TERMS AND CONCEPTS

- Administration
- Administrative theory
- Bureaucracy
- Chain of command
- Community policing and problem solving
- Culture
- Delegation of authority
- Employee-centered management
- Excessive layering
- Function
- Functional supervision
- Geography
- Hawthorne experiments
- Hierarchy of authority
- Hierarchy of needs
- Human relations theory
- Inertia
- Informal organization
- Linking pin system
- Management
- Matrix structure
- Max Weber
- Organization
- Organizational theory
- Policies
- POSDCORB
- Procedures
- Rules and regulations
- Scientific management
- Span of control

- Special operations
- Specialization
- Systems theory
- Theory X

- Theory Y
- Time
- Unity of command

INTRODUCTION

We touched on the subject of organizations in Chapter 1. Here, we explore organizations, especially police organizations, in more detail. Organizations to some extent are living entities in that they are constantly changing. Police executives often change their departments' structure to meet the changing needs of the community; they must be adaptive. They also can be considered to be living in that they have a nervous system—a chain of command where communications such as orders, policies, strategies, and decisions flow throughout the organization to control and coordinate activities. Police leaders and managers play key roles in these processes; they move the organization in the right direction.

Generally speaking, here we are referring to police administration. **Administration** refers to the cumulative processes that direct and move the department. Police chiefs, sheriffs, and their executive staffs are considered to be administrators. They make decisions about what problems to address and how the departments should respond to them. Administration often is seen as the overall management of a department. Administration basically consists of two primary elements, organization and management.[1]

Organization, as discussed in Chapter 1, refers to the structure of a department. Large police departments with hundreds of officers can structure their departments in a variety of ways. Structure is dictated by the demands made upon the police department. Structuring essentially concerns the decision about which operational units will be created in the department and the assistant chiefs or other executives will be responsible for them. For example, if a city has a gang problem, the chief may consider forming a gang unit. The decision will be predicated on (1) the extent of the gang problem, (2) the number of officers that would have to be moved from other units to staff the gang unit and the effect on the other units, and (3) the presence of more pressing policing problems that must be addressed. Organization is important since a poorly organized department may not effectively meet the community's needs.

Again, **management** concerns the processes that occur within the structure. These processes include decision making, communications, staffing, command and control, planning, and budgeting. Management refers to the activities of the leaders and managers when directing the department. There are different kinds of managers in a police department. There are ranks such as assistant chief, major, captain, lieutenant, and sergeant. These managers will be assigned to different units in the department, requiring some of them to have different duties and responsibilities. Nonetheless, all of them will be involved in the management processes.

THE DEVELOPMENT OF ORGANIZATIONAL THEORY AND ITS APPLICATION TO POLICING

The following sections examine the development of **organizational theory**, which explains how an organization operates and provides the background for understanding leadership and management. It begins with early organizational thought and finally examines more contemporary organizational models. This section provides an historical perspective of organizational theory, which is important to understanding how organizations operate.

Scientific Management

Frederick Taylor, whom many consider to be the "father of **scientific management**," sought to refine management techniques by studying how workers might become more complete extensions of machines.[2] Taylor was primarily interested in discovering the best means for getting the most out of employees. He believed that work could be studied and procedures implemented to make work more efficient. He studied workers at Bethlehem Steel in Pennsylvania where he worked as chief engineer in 1898. Taylor maintained that management knew little about the limits of worker production and was the first to introduce time and motion studies to test his argument.

Taylor believed that by observing workers in action, wasted motions could be eliminated and production increased. He began by measuring the amount of time it took workers to shovel and carry pig iron. Taylor then standardized the work into specific tasks, improved worker selection and training, established workplace rules, and advocated close supervision of workers by a foreman. In doing so, he made sure that workers were not overworked—tired workers were not productive.

The results were incredible; worker productivity soared. The total number of shovelers needed dropped from about 600 to 140, and worker earnings increased from $1.15 to $1.88 per day. The average cost of handling a long ton (2,240 pounds) dropped from $0.072 to $0.033. His application of scientific management reduced labor costs and benefited the employees.

Although criticized by unions for his management-oriented views, Taylor nonetheless proved that administrators must know their employees and their work. He proved that work should be designed, not haphazard. His views caught on and soon emphasis was placed on the formal administrative structure; later, such terms as *authority*, *chain of command*, *span of control*, and *division of labor* (discussed later) became part of the workplace vocabulary.

Taylor's work also spawned the idea of functional supervision, which is applicable to policing. In Taylor's time, supervisors were assigned to jobs but did not always have the technical expertise to adequately supervise their subordinates. **Functional supervision** entailed having several different supervisors on a job so that each one oversaw a particular aspect or part of the job—a part he or she had expertise in and could provide adequate supervision over. Functional supervision is important in policing. For example, a sergeant supervising criminal investigations must have expertise in investigations, while a sergeant in traffic must have expertise in accident investigation and selective enforcement techniques. Police executives attempt to make patrol work more efficient by designing patrol beats so that officers have the time to respond to all the calls that occur in each beat.

Bureaucratic Management

Police departments without question are organizations. They have policies and procedures that restrict behavior and are guided through a process of supervision and management. Work is further controlled by dividing it across units or offices. They are very rigid in terms of how they deal with the public and the organization's members. Police agencies certainly fit the description of a bureaucracy. They are managed by being organized into a number of specialized units. Administrators, managers, and supervisors exist to ensure that these units work together toward a common goal; each unit working independently would lead to fragmentation, conflict, and competition and would subvert the entire organization's goals and purposes. Also, police agencies consist of people who interact within the organization and with external organizations, and they exist to serve the public.

The development of an organization requires careful consideration, or the agency may be unable to respond efficiently to community needs. For example, the creation of too many specialized units in a police department (e.g., street crimes, bicycle patrol, media relations, or domestic violence) may obligate too many officers to these functions and result in too few patrol officers. As a rule of thumb, at least 55 percent of all sworn personnel should be assigned to patrol.[3] One national study found that the percentage of police officers assigned to patrol ranged from 54 to 96 percent of the total officers in departments.[4] Patrol is the backbone of a police department, and there must be enough officers assigned to patrol to respond to calls, prevent crime, and mediate disorder situations.

Police administrators, through a mission statement, policies and procedures, a proper management style, and direction, attempt to ensure that the organization maintains its overall goals of crime suppression, order maintenance, and investigation, and that it works amicably with other organizations and people. As the organization becomes larger, the need becomes greater for people to cooperate to achieve organizational goals. (Formal organizational structures, which assist in this endeavor by spelling out areas of responsibility, lines of communication, and the chain of command, are discussed later.)

As noted, police organizations in the United States are also bureaucracies, as are virtually all large organizations in modern society, such as the military, universities, and corporations.[5] In popular terms, a **bureaucracy** has often come to be viewed in a negative light, as slow, ponderous, routine, complicated, and composed of "red tape," which frustrates its members and clients.[6] This image is far from the ideal or pure bureaucracy developed by Max Weber, the German sociologist, who claimed in 1947 that a bureaucratic organization,

> ...from a purely technical point of view, [is] capable of attaining the highest degree of efficiency and is the most rational known means of carrying out imperative control over human beings. It is superior to any other form in precision, in stability, in the stringency of its discipline, and in its reliability, and is formally capable of application to all kinds of administrative tasks.[7]

The administration of most police organizations is based on the traditional, pyramidal, quasi-military organizational structure containing the elements of a bureaucracy: specialized functions, adherence to fixed rules, and a hierarchy of authority. This pyramidal organizational environment is undergoing increasing challenges, especially as a result of the implementation of community policing by departments.

A simple structure indicating the hierarchy of authority or **chain of command** is shown in Figure 2-1.

To a large extent, police agencies are similar in their structure and management process. The major differences between agencies exist between the large and the very small agencies; the former will be more complex, with much more specialization, a more complex hierarchical structure, and a greater degree of authoritarian style of command. This bureaucratic model is especially prevalent in large police organizations.[8]

In the 1970s, experts on police organization, such as Egon Bittner,[9] contended that the military-bureaucratic organization of the police was a serious handicap that created obstacles to the development of a truly professional police system. The reasons for this disillusionment include the quasi-military rank and disciplinary structures within police organizations; the lack of opportunity of management to match talent and positions; the organizational restrictions on personal freedom of expression, association, and dress; communication blockage in the tall structure; the organizational clinging to outmoded methods of operation; the lack of management flexibility; and the narrowness of job descriptions in the lower ranks of police organizations.[10] This criticism continues as proponents of community policing advocate that bureaucratic police departments should be decentralized so that decisions are made at lower levels of the department, allowing operational units to better meet citizen demands.[11]

Notwithstanding this growing disenchantment with the traditional bureaucratic structure of police organizations, this structure continues to prevail; for many administrators, it is still the best structure when rapid leadership and division of labor are required in times of crises. It also remains the most effective format to manage large organizations like the New York City Police Department or the Chicago Police Department.[12] A number of agencies have experimented with other approaches, and the results have been mixed. Most departments have elected to retain the classical police structure or portions of it.[13]

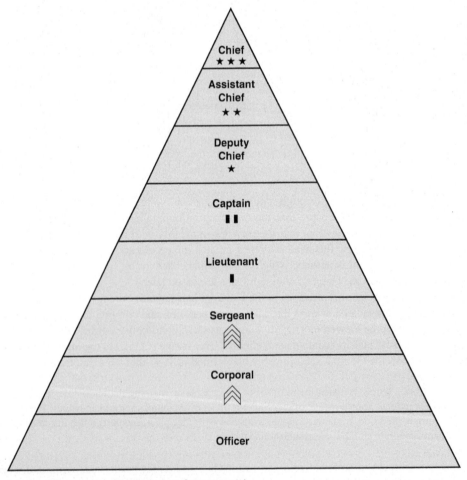

FIGURE 2-1 Traditional Pyramidal Chain of Command

ADMINISTRATIVE THEORY

Administrative theory seeks to identify generic or universal components or activities associated with administration. It is the search for those activities that allow the organization to better reach its goals. There are numerous ways by which an organization can be operated, and finding the right ones is important. The following section examines classical organizational theory. Classical organizational theory is the first cohesive set of principles used to manage organizations, and it is associated with bureaucracy in that classical organizational theory is very rigid and controlling, giving workers little discretion or latitude in how they do their jobs. Key contributors to this school are Luther Gulick, and Lyndall Urwick[14] and Max Weber.[15] Gulick and Urwick's contribution was POSDCORB, which is an acronym that identifies the management processes in an organization. Weber, on the other hand, studied successful organizations and identified the attributes that led to their successes.

POSDCORB

As noted, Gulick and Urwick (1937) examined the role of administration and identified several key management functions. They articulated these functions using the acronym **POSDCORB** (for *p*lanning, *o*rganizing, *s*taffing, *d*irecting, *co*ordinating, *r*eporting, and *b*udgeting), as noted in Figure 2-2. Gulick and Urwick were most interested in how organizations might be structured and the role of managers within them. POSDCORB identified the key administrative activities that occupy the majority of a manager's time, and they remain important activities for police leaders and managers.

Weber's Principles of Management

Max Weber identified the attributes of successful organizations. He studied the Catholic Church and the Prussian Army, two organizations that at the time were considered effective and efficient. As such, he identified several principles that when applied to an organization resulted in a measure of managerial effectiveness.

Hierarchy of Authority or Chain of Command

Weber's first principle is **hierarchy of authority** or chain of command. The chain of command is a hierarchy of authority because officers at higher ranks have more authority to make decisions and issue commands as compared to those under them in the chain of command. A police chain of command is displayed in Figure 2-1. The chain of command provides consistency in an organization in that every officer reports to a superior officer and allows for coordination and communication. For example, a patrol sergeant may receive orders from a lieutenant about priorities or goals. The sergeant then will provide officers with specific orders or assignments. The lieutenant likely had been given orders or direction from the captain. The captain issues orders to all the lieutenants that allow them to cohesively address a problem.

An important question when organizing a police department concerns how many levels a department should have in its chain of command. One study found that large American police departments averaged from nine to thirteen levels of rank or hierarchy.[16] A common problem is **excessive layering**. This refers to when there are too many levels of rank, and when this occurs the department often becomes more bureaucratic. It results in orders and information having to flow through too many subordinate managers and leaders, and this results in the department being too slow to act in some cases. There is no formula when determining the levels of rank in a department. However, ranking personnel should have ample responsibilities, but at the same time not be overburdened with work to the point that they cannot adequately supervise their subordinates and manage their responsibilities.

Planning—working out in broad outline the things that need to be done and the methods for doing them to accomplish the purpose set for the enterprise.

Organizing—establishment of the formal structure of authority through which work subdivisions are arranged, defined, and coordinated for the defined objective.

Staffing—the whole personnel function of bringing in and training the staff and maintaining favorable conditions at work.

Directing—the continuous task of making decisions, embodying them in specific and general orders and instructions, and serving as a leader of the enterprise.

Coordinating—the all-important duty of interrelating the various parts of the work.

Reporting—keeping those to whom the execution is responsible informed about what is going on, which includes keeping himself and his subordinates informed through records, research, and inspection.

Budgeting—all that goes with budgeting in the form of fiscal planning, accounting, and control.

FIGURE 2-2 POSDCORB

Span of Control

Span of control is the key factor when deciding on the levels of rank in a chain of command. **Span of control** refers to the number of officers or civilian employees that a superior officer can effectively supervise. At the top of the organization the limit is small, normally three to five. This small span of control is because problems and issues addressed by chiefs and their staffs normally are complex, involving several units and large numbers of officers in the department. Complex problems require a reduction in the span of control.

Larger numbers of officers can be supervised at the lower levels of the organization depending on factors such as the capacity of the supervisor and those persons supervised, the type of work performed, the complexity of the work, the geographical area covered, the time needed to perform the tasks, and the type of persons served. Normally, a patrol sergeant will supervise six to ten officers. Sergeants can supervise a limited number of officers because the officers typically are assigned across a large geographical area, several beats. Patrol lieutenants may have four or five sergeants reporting to them. This distribution of supervisors and managers applies to most of the units in a police department.

Some advocate for larger spans of control to reduce excessive layering. It is believed that larger spans of control reduce such problems as the distortion of information as it flows through the organization; slow, ineffective decision making and action; increased functional roadblocks and "turf protection"; emphasis on controlling the bureaucracy rather than on customer service; higher costs due to the larger number of managers and management support staff; and less responsibility assumed by subordinates for the quality of their work. Some also argue that rank-and-file employees favor larger spans of control because they receive less detailed and micromanaged supervision, greater responsibility, and a higher level of trust from their supervisors.[17]

There potentially is a major disadvantage to having a larger span of control. A large span of control means there is less time for any one supervisor to spend with any one subordinate. This limited time is reduced even more if a supervisor has to spend more time with a few new or problem employees. Thus, when designing a department's chain of command, careful consideration must be given to the span of control.

Specialization

Specialization is another important organizational principle, and it refers to grouping similar tasks into specialized units to facilitate productivity. There are three methods by which to implement specialization: (1) function, (2) geography, and (3) time.[18] Police departments organize tasks or activities by **function**—patrol, traffic, criminal investigation, training, domestic violence, gangs, drugs, and so on. For example, a detective unit will be responsible for criminal investigations. In large departments there may be specialization within the detective unit. Figure 2-3 shows the criminal investigation organization in the Omaha Police Department.

As shown in the Omaha example, detectives assigned to the robbery unit investigate all the robberies, and the same is true for the detectives assigned to the other units. This specialization increases detectives' proficiency. They come to understand the criminals who commit crimes; they know the types of evidence that likely will be at a crime scene; and they know various criminals' modus operandi. Specialization by function increases the ability of officers to do their jobs. Moreover, there is enough work in Omaha to keep the detectives in these units occupied.

FOCUS ON: SEATTLE POLICE DEPARTMENT REFORMS ITS BEAT STRUCTURE

Recently, the Seattle Police Department reorganized its beat structure. Many police departments reorganize their beats because crime, disorder, and calls for service patterns will change over time. This is due to population shifts, the construction of new housing and roadways, and a number of economic factors. Prior to the change, the department had 51 beats. The new beat boundaries are more consistent with the city's neighborhoods. This allows the department to provide better information about crime in their neighborhoods. They are also consistent with the census tracts (census tracts are geographical areas that are used by the census to gather demographic information in a community). This will allow the department to monitor population growth and demographic changes and their impact on crime.

Source: Based on Seattle Police Department, http://spdblotter .seattle.gov/2015/01/27/spd-adds-supervisors-shifts-police -beats-as-part-of-reform-efforts/

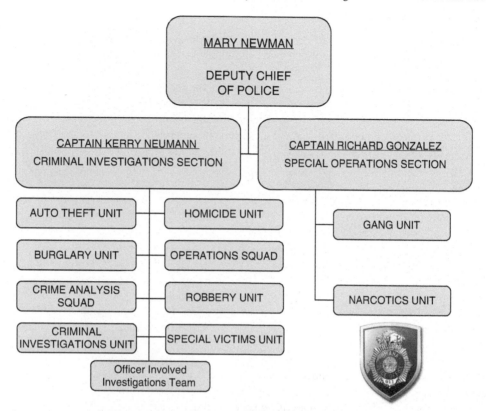

FIGURE 2-3   Omaha Police Department Criminal Investigation Unit Organization
Source: Omaha Police Department, *Criminal Investigations Bureau.* http://police.cityofomaha.org/images/Annual
_Reports/2015-Annual-Report-.pdf. Used with permission by Omaha Police Department, Criminal Investigations Bureau.

Specialization by **geography** refers to organizing tasks by different areas. For example, Figure 2-4 shows the beat structure for the Seattle Police Department. Notice that there are five precincts and each precinct is divided into several patrol beats. Seattle, like other large cities and counties, must make geographical divisions like precincts. Operating from one centralized location such as a headquarters would be ineffective given the number of officers in the department and the large geographical area policed by the department. The beats allow the department to divide work among the patrol officers. Each beat should represent the number of calls that a patrol officer can handle during a patrol shift while having enough time to patrol. In some cases, a large department will assign detectives to these precincts, especially when a department has a large number of detectives. This allows the detectives to work more closely with patrol officers who are familiar with activities that occur on their beats.

Finally, specialization by **time** refers to organizing work by shifts. Most police departments will have three or four shifts, with the fourth shift overlapping during peak periods when there are large numbers of calls for service. Each shift may be commanded by a lieutenant or captain depending on the size of the department. The lieutenant or captain is responsible for all activities during the shift. Traffic and investigative units often have multiple shifts, but in many cases they will have only two shifts (days and evenings) as early morning hours may not require the personnel. The number of shifts is driven by activity.

Specialization allows for more control in a police department. The patrol shift commanders can be held accountable for problems that occur during their shifts. This motivates them to monitor activities and make adjustments when necessary. The same is true for detective supervisors and managers. If the clearance rate for homicides declines precipitously, the chief can discuss the problem with the homicide unit commander. Specialization is an important vehicle for police executives to exert control over their departments. When there is a problem, the chief or other staff member knows who to contact to investigate the situation.

Delegation of Authority

Delegation of authority is another management principle associated with classical organizational theory. **Delegation of authority** essentially is the assignment of tasks and responsibilities to subordinate managers and supervisors and holding them accountable for their accomplishment. Police chiefs and sheriffs delegate many operational

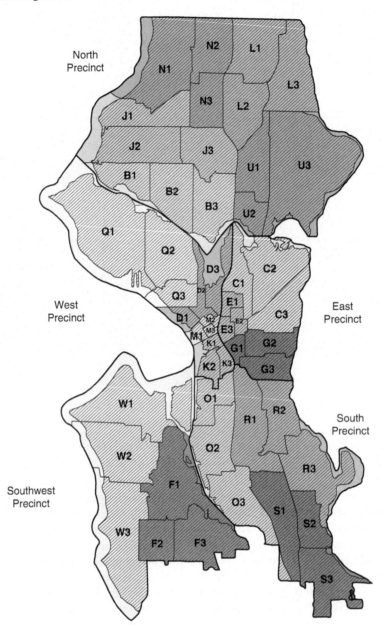

FIGURE 2-4   Beat Structure for the Seattle Police Department
Source: Beat Structure for the Seattle Police Department, Seattle Police Department retrieved from http://www
.seattle.gov/police/maps/precinct_map.htm

responsibilities to their managers. For example, the commander of a traffic unit is responsible for reducing accidents and expediting the traffic flow, and in some jurisdictions, for generating revenue. If the traffic commander does not adequately attend to these responsibilities, he or she may be replaced or otherwise held accountable.

An important caveat associated with delegation of authority is that when responsibilities are delegated, the people being held accountable must have commensurate authority. They must have supervisory power to guide their subordinates toward the objective. Too often police managers are given responsibilities, but are not free of interference from their commanders. Good leadership entails that leaders trust and support their subordinate managers and supervisors.

Unity of Command

Unity of command is another important principle. **Unity of command** refers to placing one officer in command or in control of every situation and officer, and every officer should report to one and only one superior (following the chain of command). The unity of command principle applies to administrators and managers as well.

Police officers receiving guidance from their superior.
Source: Alex Segre/Alamy Stock Photo

That is, they do not skip over a sergeant or other supervisor and give commands directly to an officer. This ensures that everyone in the chain of command is aware of priorities and actions that subordinates take.

Ambiguity over authority occurs frequently in police organizations. Detectives and patrol officers often dispute who has authority over a criminal case; officers in two different patrol beats may disagree over who has responsibility for a call for service that is located on a beat boundary. Numerous situations result in conflict because the lines of authority are sometimes unclear. As departments become larger and more complex, the extent of conflict naturally increases.

The unity of command principle also ensures that multiple and/or conflicting orders are not issued to the same police officers by several supervisors. For example, a patrol sergeant might arrive at a hostage situation and deploy personnel and give all the appropriate orders, only to have a shift lieutenant or captain come to the scene and countermand the sergeant's orders or give new orders. This type of situation would obviously be counterproductive for all persons concerned, and it would confuse officers at the scene. It is also important that all officers know and follow the chain of command at such incidents. In this example, the shift lieutenant or captain normally should consult with the sergeant before taking charge of the situation or giving any orders. This allows for consistency of leadership at the scene.

Policies, Procedures, and Rules and Regulations

In policing, policies, procedures, and rules and regulations are important for defining role expectations for officers. In essence, they specify how officers should do their jobs. The department relies on these directives to guide or control officers' behavior and performance. Because police agencies are intended to be service-oriented in nature, they must work within well-defined, specific guidelines designed to ensure that all officers conform to behavior that will enhance public protection.[19] Police supervisors must control officer behavior, but it is hoped that officers have the initiative and dedication to perform up to departmental standards.

Police agencies normally distribute their policies, procedures, and rules and regulations in the form of General Orders. Larger agencies may have as many as a hundred General Orders, covering topics such as code of conduct, use of force, and pursuit driving. The General Order normally begins with a policy statement about the subject and then follows with detailed procedures concerning how the order will work in practice. Figure 2-5 is an example of a police agency's General Order. Notice how the General Order provides fairly specific guidelines. Such orders provide officers specific guidance about various tasks and responsibilities.

POLICE DEPARTMENT GENERAL ORDER

| Legal Advisor: | Approving Deputy Chief: | Chief of Police: |

General Order No: 3/254.000
DOMESTIC VIOLENCE

| Date Issued: November 4, 2007 | Last Review: NOV/08 |

I. POLICY

The Anywhere USA Police Department recognizes that domestic violence has serious consequences to the family involved and necessitates prompt and thorough investigation. The Anywhere USA Police Department will investigate all calls for service involving domestic violence, recognizing that an aggressive policy of arresting domestic violence assailants leads to the reduction of domestic violence crimes and domestic homicides.

II. PROCEDURES

Officers will adhere to the arrest requirements as set forth under State Law PC 170.137:

170.137 Domestic violence: When arrest required; report required; compilation of statistics.

1. Except as otherwise provided in subsection 2, whether or not a warrant has been issued, a peace officer shall, unless mitigating circumstances exist, arrest a person when he has probable cause to believe that the person to be arrested has, within the preceding 24 hours, committed a battery upon his spouse, former spouse, any other person to whom he is related by blood or marriage, a person with whom he is or was actually residing, a person with whom he has had or is having a dating relationship, a person with whom he has a child in common, the minor child of any of those persons or his minor child.
2. If the peace officer has probable cause to believe that a battery described in subsection 1 was a mutual battery, he shall attempt to determine which person was the primary physical aggressor. If the peace officer determines that one of the persons who allegedly committed a battery was the primary physical aggressor involved in the incident, the peace officer is not required to arrest any other person believed to have committed a battery during the incident. In determining whether a person is a primary physical aggressor for the purposes of this subsection, the peace officer shall consider:
    (a) Prior domestic violence involving either person;
    (b) The relative severity of the injuries inflicted upon the persons involved;
    (c) The potential for future injury;
    (d) Whether one of the alleged batteries was committed in self-defense;

FIGURE 2-5 Example of a Police Agency's General Order

Police officers have a great deal of discretion when answering calls for service or performing investigations.[20] The task for the supervisor is to find the middle ground between wide discretionary authority possessed by the police and total standardization. The police role is much too ambiguous and complex to become totally standardized, but it is also much too serious and important to be left completely to the total discretion of officers. Officers will often seek a supervisor's opinion and guidance in discretionary matters. This requires that a supervisor is well informed about all policies, procedures, and rules and regulations. In some cases, the supervisor must seek clarification from his or her manager, especially in abnormal situations.

Policies are quite general and serve as guides to thinking, rather than action. Policies reflect the purpose and philosophy of the organization and help interpret those elements to the officers. An example of a policy might be that when answering calls at locations with a history of multiple calls, officers should attempt to identify the cause of the problems and take remedial action. A number of departments today are expanding on the idea of policies or guides and developing mission statements and value statements for officers. These mission and value statements are overarching guides that attempt to provide direction to officers as they perform their various job duties.

Procedures are more detailed than policies and provide the preferred methods for handling matters pertaining to investigation, patrol, booking, radio procedures, filing reports, roll call, use of force, arrest, sick leave, evidence handling, promotion, and many more job elements. Procedures describe how officers are to complete a specific task. This allows for consistency and control as officers do their jobs. For example, a department's policy on how evidence is handled ensures that all evidence is handled in the same manner, and this ensures that the evidence can be admitted in court.

Rules and regulations are specific guidelines that leave little or no latitude for individual discretion. Some examples are requirements that police officers not smoke in public, check the operation of their vehicle and equipment before going on patrol, not consume alcoholic beverages within a specified number of hours of going on duty, arrive in court or at roll call early, or specify the type of weapons that officers carry on or off duty. Rules and regulations are not always popular, especially if perceived as unfair or unrelated to the job. Nonetheless, it is the supervisor's responsibility to ensure that officers perform these tasks with the same degree of professional demeanor as other job duties. As Thomas Reddin, former Los Angeles police chief, stated:

> Certainly we must have rules, regulations and procedures, and they should be followed. But they are no substitutes for initiative and intelligence. The more a [person] is given an opportunity to make decisions and, in the process, to learn, the more rules and regulations will be followed.[21]

This section described the principles of organization that are rooted in the classical model of organizations. They fairly effectively divided work into groups and allowed leaders to closely monitor and control activities. When adhered too closely they mirror a military model with lower-level personnel having little discretion or input into how work is conducted. They, to some extent, are present in all large organizations.[22] When excessively followed, they can negatively affect morale and productivity. This problem resulted in the creation of new models, particularly the human relations organizational model.

The Emergence of Human Relations Theory

Dissatisfaction with classical organizational theory began to develop in the 1930s. The emergence of labor unions had begun to put pressure on management to develop more humane and effective ways of managing and supervising workers. The human relations school of management evolved as a result of this dissatisfaction as well as from the Hawthorne experiments in the early 1930s.

Hawthorne Experiments

The **Hawthorne experiments** provided the first glimpse of **human relations theory**. The Western Electric Company conducted a number of scientific management studies at its Hawthorne facilities in Chicago from 1927 through 1932. The experiments were an attempt to determine the level of illumination (light) and pattern of employee breaks that produced the highest levels of worker productivity. The researchers segregated a group of workers in an area and made numerous and varied changes in the levels of illumination and the length and number of work breaks. It was believed that if the optimal level of illumination and number and duration of work breaks could be discovered, employees would be more productive. Productivity increased as these two variables were manipulated. Ultimately, however, no consistent pattern in the changes in production relative to the changes in lighting and work breaks emerged. Productivity increased when work breaks were increased, and it increased when work breaks were reduced. The same pattern occurred when illumination was increased and

YOU DECIDE...

You are a lieutenant in the Pleasantville Police Department, a small suburban community outside a large metropolitan city. Three days ago one of the officers was involved in a pursuit that ended badly. The officer was involved in a crash with a vehicle that was not involved in the pursuit, and the crash resulted in the death of two civilians. Your department did not have a pursuit policy. The local newspaper as well as the media in the metro area has given the incident a massive amount of coverage. The media has pointed out that thousands of innocent people have died as a result of wayward police pursuits, and that professional police departments have policies that restrict them. Some reporters suggested that the Pleasantville Police Department should not even get involved in pursuits and should leave them to the sheriff's department. The crash and the negative news coverage have led the city council to demand that the police take action.

The chief, realizing that she must take action, asks you to develop a pursuit policy for the department. She instructs you to make sure that it is comprehensive and will better ensure the safety of motorists in the city.

Questions for Discussion

1. Would you prevent officers from engaging in any pursuits?
2. If you allowed pursuits, for which crimes and offenses would it be permissible for officers to engage in a pursuit?
3. What restrictions would you place on officers if they became involved in a pursuit?
4. If there are pursuits, how would you ensure that they were properly supervised?

reduced. Given the inconsistencies, the researchers could not discern why productivity was changing. Finally, the increases in productivity were attributed to worker job satisfaction from increased involvement and concern on the part of management. In essence, management's displayed concern for the workers, as evidenced in the experiment itself, resulted in higher morale and productivity.[23]

Prior to the Hawthorne experiments, employers were not concerned with employees or their feelings. It was assumed that employees followed management's dictates. The Hawthorne experiments spurred a significant change in the relationship between management and employees. Management realized that individual workers and the work group itself could have just as much impact on productivity as management. The experiments signaled a need for management to harness worker energy and ideas so that management and workers could mutually benefit.

Theoretical Foundation for Human Relations Organizational Theory

The move to a human relations model of organization was also fueled by a number of theorists. Maslow's **hierarchy of needs**, discussed more thoroughly in Chapter 3, demonstrated that people were motivated by things other than money or material rewards. Maslow postulated that once material needs were met, needs such as belongingness and esteem became the principal motivators.[24]

Douglas McGregor (1966) was a proponent of a more humanistic and democratic approach to management. His work was based on two basic assumptions about people: **Theory X**, which views employees negatively and sees the need for structured organizations with strict hierarchal lines and close supervision; and **Theory Y**, which takes a more humanistic view toward employees, believing that they are capable of being motivated and productive. A further explanation of the assumptions about human nature and behavior that emerges from these divergent theories follows:

THEORY X

- The average employee dislikes work and will avoid it whenever possible.
- People are lazy, avoid responsibility, and must be controlled, directed, and coerced to perform their work.
- People are inherently self-centered and do not care about organizational needs.
- People will naturally resist change.

THEORY Y

- The average employee does not inherently dislike work.
- People will exercise self-control and are self-directed when motivated to achieve organizational goals.
- People are capable of learning and will not only accept but seek responsibility.
- People's capacity for imagination, ingenuity, and creativity is only partially utilized.

Theory X portrays a dismal view of employees and their motivation to work and supports the traditional model of direction and control, bureaucracy or classical theory. In contrast, Theory Y is more optimistic and leads one to believe that motivated employees will perform productively. Also, Theory Y postulates that managers assume some responsibility to create a climate that is conducive to learning and achieving organizational goals.

Although it may appear that Theory X managers are bad and Theory Y managers are good, McGregor did not support one style over the other. Administrators may need the flexibility of employing one or both theories, depending on the personnel involved and the situation. For example, a supervisor dealing with an officer resisting attempts to remediate unacceptable behavior may need to rely on a Theory X approach until the officer is corrected. On the other hand, a self-motivated and skilled officer given the task of developing a briefing training lesson plan may require limited supervision and therefore can be guided through the task by employing Theory Y.

As a general rule, the police field found bureaucratic management to be more acceptable. In the first half of the last century, police managers were strongly influenced by the reform movement that swept the nation. Corruption was rampant and the key words for resolving the problems were "efficiency" and "control." The goals of progressive chiefs were to gain control of their departments and to reduce political influence. The term human relations was viewed as vague in its meaning, and the military model with its rank and structure was viewed as almost a perfect panacea for resolving the problems of police managers.[25] Moreover, police departments and police chiefs were accountable to the public. One method for the chief to ensure that people and units were operating as envisioned was to enact controls, which were best facilitated by the principles of classical management.

During the 1940s and 1950s, this research led to both private and public organizations recognizing the strong effect of the working environment and informal structures on the organization. In policing, attention was being paid to job enlargement and enrichment techniques to generate interest in the profession as a career. **Employee-centered management** approaches such as participative management began to appear in policing. By the 1970s, there was also a move away from the traditional pyramid-shaped organizational structure to a more flattened structure with fewer mid-levels of management.[26] This resulted in an increase in responsibilities for managers and first-line supervisors as more responsibilities were delegated downward in the department.

A good example of the application of human relations theory can be found in Rensis Likert's **linking pin system** of participative management where small work groups conduct tasks, and each group was linked together with a manager or supervisor.[27] Figure 2-6 shows how the linking pin system is organized.

Since the linking pin system consists primarily of small work groups, it results in more interaction between group members and supervisors and their superiors. Leadership is participative in that each group is assigned a geographical area or a set of tasks, and group members openly discuss how to best accomplish tasks and objectives. It results in the discussion of potential tactics when responding to a problem, and it results in better decision making. The supervisor stays in contact with his or her superior so that the information is discussed at the next higher level in the chain of command. The superiors also keep their supervisors abreast on discussions and activities. This ensures that information freely flows throughout the organization. Officers at the lowest levels have some input into decisions that are made at higher levels in the chain of command. A number of departments use this format when implementing community policing since community policing activities delve into problems and community building.

The Systems Approach

By the mid-1950s, it was apparent that classical organizational theory and the human relations approach were inadequate to ensure a productive organization.[28] Consequently, a new theory, systems theory, began to evolve. **Systems theory** has its roots in biology. An organization is similar to a living organism. It absorbs energy, processes the energy into some kind of output such as services, and attempts to maintain an equilibrium with its environment.

The systems approach emphasizes the interdependence and interrelationship of each and every part to the whole. "A system is composed of elements or subsystems that are related and dependent upon one another. When these subsystems are in interaction with one another, they form a unitary whole."[29] Each unit affects other units and the whole. For example, if patrol officers are deficient in completing the preliminary crime investigations, it will make investigators' jobs more difficult. These interrelationships are present throughout police organizations.

The main premise of the theory is that to fully understand the operation of a department, the department must be viewed as a system or as a whole. The system can be modified only through changes in its parts. A thorough knowledge of how each part functions and the interrelationships among the parts must be present before modifications can be made, because any change in one police unit can and most certainly will affect other units.[30]

This view opposes the way law enforcement agencies traditionally have been organized and have functioned. For example, detective units often work separate and apart from the remainder of the police department. It is not uncommon for other specialized units such as gangs, traffic, and street crimes to work in isolation as well. Functionally, what often occurs is that there are isolated subsystems with limited interrelationships. The systems approach to management attempts to deal with this problem, trying to unify the various parts of the organization into a functioning whole. If these different units communicate and work more closely, they likely will be more productive.

A systems-oriented manager and other leaders must look at the big picture and continually analyze and evaluate how the entire organization is performing with respect to its mission, goals, and objectives. For

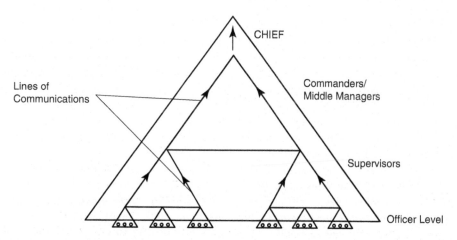

FIGURE 2-6 Likert's Linking Pin System

example, in the case of a new policy regarding police pursuits, a systems-oriented supervisor would be conscious of how the new policy would affect all the organizational divisions, including patrol, investigations, administration, and training. A systems approach also takes into account the potential impact of decisions on external factors, such as the general public, political environment, and other criminal justice agencies. The goal is that all agencies and their units work together to resolve problems.

This section provided a brief introduction to organizational theory. Over time, three different schools of organizational thought have evolved: classical, human relations, and systems. Although various parts of human relations and systems theory can be applied to police organizations, most departments today still use classical theory as the basis for organizing.[31] One study found that 61 percent of police administrators in the study reported that there was no need to change the organizational structure of their departments.[32] Thus, it appears that many police administrators are content with current arrangements.

RATIONALES AND PURPOSES OF POLICE ORGANIZATIONAL DESIGN

All organizations have an organizational structure, be it basic or highly complex. Administrators, managers, and supervisors use their organizational chart as a blueprint for action. The size of the organization depends on the demand placed on it and the resources available to it. Growth precipitates the need for more people, greater division of labor, specialization, written rules, and other such administrative elements. Police administrators modify or design the structure of their organization to fulfill its mission.

An organizational chart reflects the formal structure of task and authority relationships determined to be most suited to accomplishing the police mission. The major concerns in organizing are as follows:

1. Identifying what jobs need to be done, such as conducting the initial investigation, performing the follow-up investigation, and providing for the custody of evidence seized at crime scenes.
2. Determining how to group the jobs, such as those responsible for patrol, investigation, and the operation of the property room.
3. Forming levels of authority, such as officer, detective, corporal, sergeant, lieutenant, and captain.
4. Equalizing responsibility—if a sergeant has the responsibility to supervise seven detectives, that sergeant must have sufficient authority to discharge that responsibility properly or he or she cannot be held accountable for any results.[33]

Perhaps the best way to understand police supervision and management is to examine a police organization. Figure 2-7 shows the organizational chart for the Portland Police Department, including the division of labor and responsibilities common to a fairly large department. Notice that each of the three major branches in the department contains a number of units. The Investigations Branch has six major divisions:

- Family Services Division
- Drugs and Vice Division
- Forensic Evidence Division
- Property/Evidence Division
- Tactical Operations Division
- Detective Division

Each of these divisions is further divided into different activities or units. For example, investigators and other leaders and managers are given responsibility for different crimes and other activities. Different crimes and activities are grouped together within the various units. This results in the individual units investigating similar crimes. Each of those divisions has a set of distinctive goals and objectives and is commanded by a manager.

What distinguishes the higher-ranking officers from supervisors is that they also perform planning, organizing, staffing, and other managerial functions for the sections. Higher-ranking managers have executive as well as supervisory responsibilities. They are responsible for both organization-wide functions and the supervision of their immediate subordinates.

Since all managers, regardless of their level in the organization, must supervise their subordinates, they are all responsible for directing and controlling. Higher-level managers, because of their other responsibilities, generally are unable to devote as much attention as sergeants to these two important tasks. Thus, the brunt of direction and control in most organizations, including police departments, usually falls on the shoulders of supervisors. Managers cannot neglect supervision, however, because they ultimately are responsible for the operation of larger units in the organization.

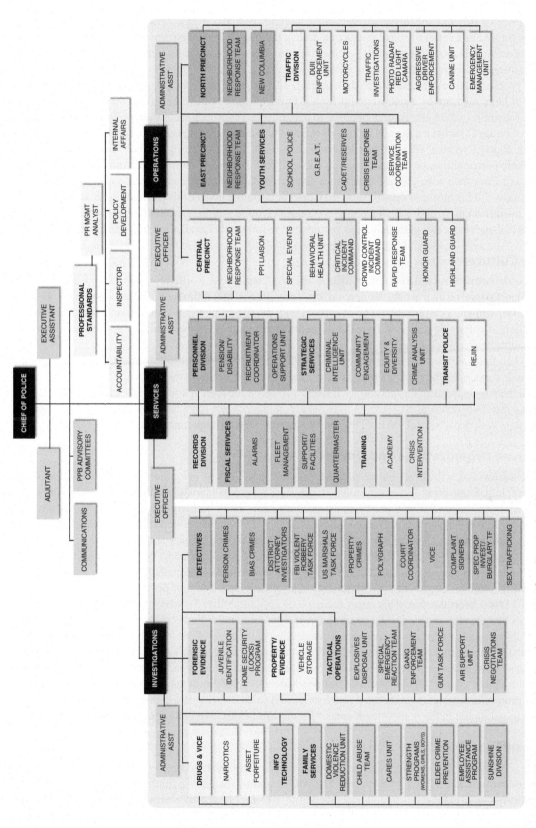

FIGURE 2-7 Organizational Structure for the Portland, Oregon, Police Department

Source: Portland Police Bureau, *Organizational Chart January 2014.* retrieved from: https://www.portlandoregon.gov/police/article/548323. Used with permission from Portland Police Bureau.

FACTORS THAT INFLUENCE ORGANIZATION

The Informal Organization

Existing side by side with the formal organizational structure of a police organization is the **informal organization**, which is formed as a result of social interaction among the people in the department, particularly at the unit level. The informal organization for the most part overlays the formal organization, but the informal organization often exerts influence over personnel and activities. For example, a new officer may consult with a senior patrol officer about a problem before consulting with the sergeant. The structure and functions of a police organization will be shaped in large measure by these powerful forces. Officers oftentimes will perform their duties adhering to the norms of the informal organization as opposed to departmental expectations or even policies and procedures.

Police agencies have a life and culture of their own. Within any organization, some people emerge as leaders, regardless of whether they are in a leadership position. They are recognized as leaders because of having charismatic personalities, or because they are recognized for some of their past accomplishments. In addition, people will form their own groups, which may operate without official recognition and may influence agency performance.[34] This informal organization may help or harm the goals of the formal organization and can carry gossip, misinformation, and malicious rumors (communication within organizations is discussed in Chapter 4). Therefore, supervisors and managers must recognize the informal organization that exists within their agency.

Police Culture

A police department's **culture** consists of the officers' collective worldview, values, and norms. It defines how officers perceive their work, the department, and citizens, and ultimately it affects how they do their jobs. A police department's culture should be congruent with the department's overall mission and goals. When there is variation, it causes deviation in how the department responds to the community and its problems. In other words, culture affects behavior.[35]

When there are vast differences between a department's culture and management, it affects organizational structure. For example, the department has to have more well-defined policies and procedures to better ensure that offices adhere to departmental expectations. It likely will affect the span of control since officers may require closer and more direct supervision. At the same time, leaders and managers must take steps to alter the culture so that it is consistent with departmental values. This can be accomplished through training and participative management.

Employee Organizations and Unions

Another factor that will affect police organization and practices is unionization, and their impact has been considerable. Unions do in fact result in fewer administrative and management prerogatives; at the bargaining table, they have shaped the way policy decisions have been made in many ways. They have thwarted the creation of civilian review boards, advocated the election of "law and order" candidates, resisted the replacement of two-officer patrol cars with one-officer cars, litigated against disciplinary actions, lobbied for increased budgets, and caused the removal of chiefs and other high-ranking administrators. When the objectives of the union and the police leaders are the same, the union can be a powerful ally. Nonetheless, unions often compete with the administration for control of the department; many chiefs have left their posts in order to move to an agency that has a less powerful union. This raises the issue of accountability: To what extent can police executives and managers be held responsible for the operation of the department?

Police executives have two strategies when dealing with unions. First, they must try to work with the union to ensure that the tenants of the union contract do not impede management's prerogatives on how the department is operated. This includes using participative management and negotiation. Second, the police executive must work with city or county administrators to not negotiate away important management prerogatives such as shift design, promotions, assignments to specialized units, and so on. Whenever a contract is negotiated, the union will attempt to gain more in the management areas. Unions will be discussed in more detail in Chapter 7.

Departmental Inertia

Inertia is where an organization will continue down the same path and is resistant to change. Changing the path often requires substantial intervention. The willingness to change is a fundamental requirement for today's police leaders and managers, especially considering the importance of **community policing and problem-solving**, changes in technology, the Black Lives Matter movement, budgetary constraints, and other community expectations. In order for police agencies to change, they must modify their culture from top to bottom, and obtain a commitment from personnel to change. Change is never easy because there is so much uncertainty accompanying it. It is much easier to proceed with the status quo, because "we've always done it this way."

Indeed, probably the most common characteristic of change is people's resistance to it. Adapting to a new environment or methods often results in feelings of stress or other forms of psychological discomfort. Resistance to change is likely when employees do not clearly understand the purpose, mechanics, or consequences of a planned change because of inadequate or misperceived communication.

Those who resist change are sometimes coerced into accepting it. Change in police agencies, particularly a major change, is frequently characterized by the use of centralized decision making and coercive tactics. Through the use of task forces, ad hoc committees, group seminars, and other participatory techniques, employees can become more directly involved in planning for change. By thoroughly discussing and debating the issues, a more accurate understanding and unbiased analysis of the situation is likely to result. To some extent, change must be sold, not enacted.

CONTEMPORARY ORGANIZATIONAL STRATEGIES

The previous sections described the traditional police organizational structure that is rooted in Gulick and Urwick's POSDCORB and Weber's principles of management. Larry Gaines and Charles Swanson have pointed out that the principles, as discussed above, remain the primary mode of police administration.[36] This is because accountability remains a key consideration when organizing a police department. Nonetheless, police departments have modified their organizational structures at least partially. The following sections describe some of these innovations.

Community Policing

Community policing, discussed more thoroughly in Chapter 10, has been a part of policing for several decades and has expanded across the United States. It consists primarily of community relationships and problem-solving. Community policing means that officers should increase the communications, especially positive communications, with citizens. This means decentralizing the organizational structure so that officers have time and the authority to interact with citizens and the ability to deal with their problems.[37] Departments have used different tactics to accomplish this goal. Some have assigned community policing officers to geographical areas who handle all community policing activities. Others have trained all patrol officers in an effort to implement community policing more comprehensively, while other departments have created a separate organizational unit devoted to community policing.

It also means that police officers and their supervisors are vested with greater decision-making responsibility (decentralization). In the end, officers need to be able to tailor responses or tactics to meet the needs of problems. Also, citizens should have substantial input into what the police are doing in their neighborhoods in

Community policing officer on bike patrol.
Source: Fotomaton/Alamy Stock Photo

terms of problems, goals, and objectives. Police departments and officers do not always understand or recognize the problems facing citizens in a particular neighborhood. In order to adequately adopt community policing, the department's structure must be altered to facilitate community relationships and problem solving.

Matrix Structure

A **matrix structure** is a form of decentralization where personnel from different units are merged together to focus on a specific problem. A police department may create such a unit to combat elevated levels of crime in a specific geographical area, or when the jurisdiction is experiencing an increase in a specific crime. For example, a department may assign a group of detectives and patrol officers to respond to an increase in convenient store robberies. The patrol officers would enhance patrols of the stores while the detectives would perform undercover stakeouts. They could identify the most possible targets by examining past robberies of convenient stores.

In some cases, officers could team up with officials from other agencies. A number of cities have created gang task forces consisting of police officers and probation officers.[38] Generally, the terms of probation allow probation officers to search probationers' homes and stop them while they are driving or riding in a vehicle; police officers must have a warrant or probable cause to conduct such searches. The police probation teams are able to more effectively investigate gang members. *Operation Ceasefire*, which has been implemented in a number of cities, took this concept further. In some cases, prosecutors were part of the team. In cities like Chicago and Baltimore, the police worked with community groups and community activists and former gang members and went into areas with high levels of gang activity to work with at-risk youths. In many cases, the programs reduced the levels of gang and juvenile homicides.[39] The matrix structure allows departments to react to a variety of problems by selecting officers from different units that match the problem at hand.

Matrix structures provide departments with a great deal of flexibility. It allows departments to analyze problems and then formulate a strategy that best meets the problem. The matrix structure expands a department's ability to deploy more effective measures.

Special Operations Units

The organizational structure for the Portland Police Department, as displayed in Figure 2-7, has a rapid response team in their Operations Branch. A number of departments are creating special operations or tactical units. These units are designed to respond to emerging crime or disorder problems. Essentially, the department can send these officers into a high-crime or disorder area to tamp down problems, and the unit can respond to a variety of problems. These units generally are assigned to a problem or area on a short-term basis and move from one problem to another. Such units give a department the ability to quickly move large numbers of officers to a

Police tactical unit breaching a house.
Source: Mikael Karlsson/Alamy Stock Photo

YOU DECIDE...

You are a captain in the Wetherbee Police Department. Wetherbee has a large police department and therefore has numerous specialized units. You recently were assigned to head the special operations or tactical unit. The unit has 20 officers divided into three teams and each is supervised by a sergeant. You were appointed to manage the unit because the chief thought that the previous commander was not doing a good job. He believed the unit had not been responsive enough and could do more to attack the crime and disorder problems in Wetherbee. Crime has increased slightly over the past two years, and there is a gang problem in two areas in the city.

You understand that the chief expects you to manage the unit and produce results. The first thing you should do is develop a plan of action.

Questions for Discussion

1. As the commander, what will be your unit's priorities?
2. How will you identify the neighborhoods or areas where you need to assign your officers?
3. How will you decide on the unit's organization?

problem area. They can use different tactics, including patrol, undercover or stakeout operations, enhanced traffic enforcement, and so on. Special operations units can substantially enhance a department's ability to respond to problems.

Police leaders and managers must maintain a degree of flexibility in their departments. It allows them to address different problems that may present themselves. Moreover, as we learned from community policing, authority to select tactics when dealing with problems should be decentralized to the units involved in countering the problem.

Summary

This chapter has set the stage for the study of police leadership and management, defining organizations generally, then placing police agencies within the context of organizational theories and structures. Included were several important facets of leadership and management, including the evolution of organizational theory, several major administrative theories, and selected factors that influence organizations, such as culture and employee unions. We also examined some of the more flexible organizational forms that police departments can use to mitigate problems.

It is important to note that organizations, especially police organizations, are organized according to traditional or bureaucratic organizational principles. These principles include chain of command, policies and procedures, specialization, delegation of authority, and unity of command. Police departments, especially large departments, require a considerable amount of organization. These principles guide how departments should be organized. They also infer that police departments can be organized in a variety of ways, and the police executive must find the way that best meets the needs of the department and community.

Discussion Questions

1. The backbone of any police department is patrol. Patrol officers answer calls for service and respond to and prevent crime. Smaller departments may have no specialized units or only a few. How would you determine if a department needs to form a specialized unit?
2. We have discussed several organizational theories in this chapter. How do these theories affect the department and police officers on the street?
3. We examined POSDCORB in this chapter. How do each of the elements in POSDCORB apply to a police organization?
4. Police departments have a system of policies and procedures. What are the areas that you think are most important for these regulations to cover?
5. Use the Internet to find two comparable-sized police departments' organizational structure. How are they different? How are they the same?

Internet Investigations

Office of Community Oriented Police Services, "Foot Patrols Crime Analysis and Community Engagement to Further the Commitment of Community Policing" https://cops.usdoj.gov/html/dispatch/February_2009/foot_patrol.htm

Riverside, California Police Department, "Policy Manual" https://riversideca.gov/rpd/ChiefOfc/manual.pdf

Governing: The States and Localities, "The Culture of Management that Police Departments Need" http://www.governing.com/gov-institute/voices/col-culture-management-police-departments-need.html

Los Angeles Police Department, "Management Principles of the LAPD" http://www.lapdonline.org/inside_the_lapd/content_basic_view/846

CHAPTER 3

Leadership and Motivation: What Works

STUDENT LEARNING OUTCOMES

After reading this chapter, the student will:

- comprehend what is involved in transforming a "good" police organization into one that is "great"

- know the basic leadership theories, and how leadership skills are developed

- have a working knowledge of motivating personnel in the workplace, and how motivational strategies may be applied in the police agency

- understand the difference between leading and managing

- understand empowerment—its importance for today's policing and its levels and stages

- be aware of the major roles of police executives, using the Mintzberg model of chief executive officers

- be able to explain the basic precepts of strategic thinking and planning for strategic management

- explain what is meant by adaptive change, and how it applies to police leaders

- be able to discuss how leadership can fail in a police department

- know which leadership styles are best for the police agency

KEY TERMS AND CONCEPTS

- Active sergeants
- Argyris's maturity–immaturity theory
- Authority
- Coercion power
- Conceptual skills
- Consideration
- Contingency theory
- Content theories
- Decision-making role
- Empowerment
- Engel's supervisory styles
- Equity theory
- Expectancy theory
- Force field analysis
- Expertise power
- Herzberg's motivation-hygiene theory
- Human skills
- Informational role
- Initiating structure
- Innovative sergeants
- Interpersonal role
- Likert's leadership styles
- Leadership

- Leadership styles
- Legitimate power
- Managerial grid
- Maslow's hierarchy of needs
- McClelland's achievement, power and affiliation theory
- Motivation
- Ohio State University studies
- Planning cycle
- Power
- Process theories
- Reward power
- Situational leadership
- Strategic management
- Strategic planning
- Supportive sergeants
- Sustainable leadership
- Technical skills
- Traditional sergeants
- Transformational leadership
- Trait theory
- University of Michigan studies
- Zone of indifference

INTRODUCTION

Previous chapters provided a backdrop to police leadership and management. Chapter 1 provided an overview of the importance of these two administrative concepts and how they fit within the overall police organization. It is important to remember that leadership is a trait that all police officers must possess regardless of their rank or assignment in the department. Obviously, the chief or sheriff must lead the department toward the accomplishment of the department's mission and goals. Unit commanders or managers must lead their officers in a similar fashion; they must ensure that their subordinates capably perform their duties and complete the mission of their units. Individual officers such as patrol officers, detectives, and other sworn officers lead by handling situations and ensuring that these situations are managed in a fashion that results in a positive outcome.

Whereas **leadership** is a process where superiors interact with subordinates to motivate them to complete tasks and responsibilities, management principles, as discussed in Chapter 2, provide a roadmap for accomplishing this important task. Police chiefs, managers, and supervisors must ensure that subordinates follow departmental policies and procedures; they plan strategies and tactics for reaching objectives; they ensure they have the resources to implement their strategies and tactics; they organize their units by issuing personnel assignments that meet the needs of objectives; and they provide supervision by observing subordinates' actions and issuing orders and direction when necessary. Thus, management and leadership are interrelated. One cannot be a good leader without being a good manager, and the opposite is also true.

This chapter examines motivation as well as leadership. **Motivation** is an innate quality within people to work, be productive, or to accomplish some objective. All police officers must be motivated to effectively carry out their assignments. Police work is not like an assembly line where work is strictly controlled and monitored. Police officers have immense discretion, and we depend on them to accomplish their assignments effectively. As discussed below, leaders have the ability to motivate subordinates, and must do so if the department is effective.

It is important to remember that behind every good practice lies a good theory. Theory and practice are inextricably intertwined. Thus, we look at the primary theories behind employee satisfaction, motivation, and leadership. We might also point out that many books examine leadership theories in length; thus, in this chapter we limit our coverage to comparatively brief overviews of related theories for policing.

POLICE OFFICIALS AS LEADERS

A Problem of Definition

Leadership is the heart and soul of any organization. The idea of leadership has been with us for quite a long time, yet widespread debate and disagreement as to its characteristics and meaning continue. As Bennis and Nanus observe, there has been long-standing difficulty in defining leadership: "Like love, leadership … is something everyone knew existed but nobody could define." It is clear that leadership is elusive, and everyone in a supervisory or managerial position must make every attempt to possess it.[1]

Early ideas about leadership assumed that it was a matter of birth: the so-called *Great Man* theory of leadership. Leaders were born into leadership positions (e.g., monarchs). History has shown, however, that many of these born leaders were actually ineffective. When this view failed to explain leadership, it was replaced by the notion that great events made leaders because they excelled in extraordinary situations. Moses, Julius Caesar, Martin Luther, Abraham Lincoln, Winston Churchill, Harry Truman, Gandhi, Martin Luther King, Jr., and many others sought to assert their influence when time and social events intersected to make them great leaders. This definition is also inadequate, because there have been many instances requiring a leader, but one has failed to materialize. For example, one might conjecture that police executives failed to exert proper leadership during the riots that have occurred in the aftermath of police shootings or during crime sprees. Still others postulated that great leaders possessed traits such as intelligence, had specific personalities, were political savvy, and so on. However, one can conjure an extensive list of traits or qualities, and in the end, few people will possess all the traits that can be envisioned.

The word leadership is widely used and has resulted in as many definitions as there have been studies of the subject. Some commonly used definitions include the following:

- "Leadership is the process of directing the behavior of others toward the accomplishment of some objective."[2]
- "The process of influencing the activities of an individual or a group in efforts toward goal achievement in a given situation."[3]
- "The process of directing and influencing the task-related activities of group members."[4]

Police officers must show leadership in many types of situations.
Source: Michael Matthews/Police Images/Alamy Stock Photo

An examination of these definitions reveals a set of consistent elements. First, there is a *leader* who is charged with leading or directing. Second, there are *followers* or people who are led. Third, there are *tasks* or *goals* that must be accomplished. Leadership consists of an intricate relationship between these three elements. They must be in synchronization if leadership is to be effective.

Another leadership perspective that must be considered is subordinate acceptance of leadership. Bernard notes that followers must respect and accept a leader's orders and directives if they are to be followed.[5] This entails that the leader develop relationships with followers, and directives must be within the boundaries of organizational norms and established policies. It means that leaders must sometimes sell their instructions to subordinates to gain compliance. Too often there is a **zone of indifference** in which subordinates do not respect their leader or they question his or her directives. When this occurs, compliance is, at best, minimal. This means, as Bernard notes, that a leader's authority is delegated upward, not downward.

Superior officers use various methods for motivating subordinates. There is no one best way to manage and lead people in every situation. Leader style is largely dependent on the situation and the capabilities of those being led. In fact, people in leadership positions may need to rely on a combination of strategies to be effective leaders. A number of leadership and motivation theories are addressed in this chapter, and an effective leader will need to rely on several of them, depending on the situation at hand.

DEVELOPING LEADERSHIP SKILLS

Katz identified three essential skills that leaders should possess: technical skills, human skills, and conceptual skills.[6] Figure 3-1 illustrates these skills and how they apply to managers and supervisors. Notice that technical skills are most important at the lower supervisory ranks while conceptual skills preoccupy the higher ranks in an organization. Katz defined a *skill* as the capacity to translate knowledge into action in such a way that a task is accomplished successfully. Each of these skills, when performed effectively, results in the achievement of objectives and goals, which is the primary thrust of management and supervision.

Technical Skills

Technical skills are those a manager needs to ensure that specific tasks are performed correctly. They are based on proven knowledge, procedures, or techniques. A supervisor's technical skills may involve knowledge in areas such as high-risk tactics, law, and criminal procedures. The police sergeant usually depends on training and departmental policies for technical knowledge. The areas in which managers need technical skills include computer applications, budgeting, strategic planning, labor relations, public relations, and human resources

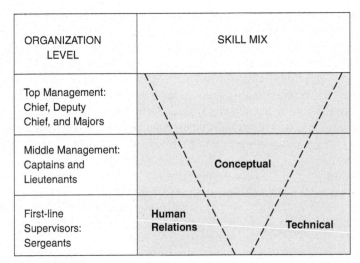

FIGURE 3-1 The Leadership Skill Mix in a Police Department
Source: SWANSON, CHARLES R.; TERRITO, LEONARD J.; TAYLOR, ROBERT W., POLICE ADMINISTRATION: STRUCTURES, PROCESSES, AND BEHAVIOR, 8th Ed., © 2012. Reprinted and Electronically reproduced by permission of Pearson Education, Inc., New York, NY.

management. The manager must also have knowledge of the technical skills required for the successful completion of tasks that are within his or her command. Finally, top management must understand how technology can enhance a department's ability to accomplish its mission and goals.

Human Skills

Human skills involve working with people and include being thoroughly familiar with what motivates employees and how to utilize group processes. Katz visualized human skills as including "the executive's ability to work effectively as a group member and to build cooperative effort within the team he leads."[7] Katz added that the human relations skill involves tolerance of ambiguity and empathy. Tolerance of ambiguity means that the manager is able to handle problems when insufficient information precludes making a totally informed decision. Empathy is the ability to put oneself in another's place or to understand another's plight. The practice of human skills allows a manager to provide the necessary leadership and direction, ensuring that tasks are accomplished in a timely fashion and with the least expenditure of resources. Sergeants need more human relations skills since they are constantly dealing with a number of subordinates as well as citizens interacting with their officers. Middle managers require a lower level of human relations skills as their focus is more on programs and unit activities; they have less involvement in dealing with human relations problems. Finally, chiefs are more involved with conceptual skills, running the department.

Conceptual Skills

According to Katz, **conceptual skills** involve "coordinating and integrating all the activities and interests of the organization toward a common objective."[8] Katz considered such skills to include "an ability to translate knowledge into action" and emphasized that these skills can be taught to actual and prospective managers and supervisors. Thus, good managers and supervisors are not simply born but can be trained to assume their responsibilities.

All three of these skills are present in varying degrees for each management level. As one moves up the hierarchy, conceptual skills become more important and technical skills less important. The common denominator for all levels of management is human skills. In today's unionized and litigious environment, it is inconceivable that a manager or supervisor could neglect the human skills.

AUTHORITY, POWER, AND LEADERSHIP

While considering the nature of leadership, it is important to remember that organizations exist to accomplish missions and goals that citizens cannot achieve alone. Within police organizations, employees are granted the authority and power to morally and legally accomplish their tasks. Authority and power are related but separate concepts, however. **Authority** is a grant made by the formal organization to a position, which the person occupying that position wields in carrying out his or her duties. For example, a lieutenant has more authority than a sergeant, and a captain or higher-ranking officer has more authority than a lieutenant. This does not mean that the person in an authority position is automatically able to influence others to perform. As Bernard suggested, subordinates must accept a superior's authority for maximum efficacy.

Power is the foundation of leadership, and it consists primarily of the ability to sanction others for inadequate performance. It is a necessary ingredient in influencing others to act or perform. While the leader whose subordinates refuse to follow is not totally without power (subordinates may be reprimanded, suspended, terminated, fined, and so on), such power must be used judiciously; both invoking it without just cause or failing to invoke it when necessary may contribute to a breakdown in discipline and performance, morale problems, and other negative side effects.

Power also arises in the informal side of an organization; members of a work group give one or more of their members power by virtue of their willingness to follow them on the basis of that person's charisma, experience, or heroism. For example, new patrol officers may seek advice from a veteran peer officer as opposed to going to their sergeant. Within any organization people can exhibit different types of power.

Types of Power

Power is not static. Its use will vary over time, and a superior officer may use different types of power depending on the situation. Essentially, power is used to influence others. The following are the types of power that can be used.

1. **Reward power** is the ability to provide subordinates something of value for their exemplary services, for example, salary increase, high performance appraisals, new equipment, desired days off, compliments, and so on. Reward power is not a bribe, but is given for extraordinary performance. It serves to motivate.
2. **Coercion power** is the opposite of reward power. It is the ability to punish someone for inadequate service. When **coercion power** is used it generally entails using a department's disciplinary system.
3. **Legitimate power** comes from an individual's authority or position in the organization. For example, a police captain as a consequence of his or her position is vested with a level of power. In other words, position results in recognition and power.
4. **Expertise power** comes with someone's familiarity and ability to perform some task or function. For example, evidence technicians are lower-level employees, but they derive power at crime scenes as a result of their knowledge of evidence. Expertise power is distributed throughout the police organization.
5. **Referent power** comes from people having personal relationships with others who have power. For example, if the mayor's son is a police officer, he likely would receive more deference as compared to other police officers. Many police officers attempt to develop personal relations with higher-ranking officers to gain referent power, which can be used for promotions, specialized assignments, and so on.

FOCUS ON: THE AURORA POLICE DEPARTMENT'S YOUTH EMPOWERMENT PROGRAM

Generally, when we think of empowerment, we consider various employee groups within the police organization. For example, we might want to empower patrol officers to make better decisions when dealing with a crime or disorder problem. However, we may want to empower citizens so they can be more responsible citizens. The Aurora Police Department (Colorado) developed a unique program to empower the youths in the city. Essentially, the department developed a booklet that provided youths with guidance on a number of topics, including their rights, why people get pulled over, dating advice, understanding traffic laws and criminal laws, and preventing suicide.

We know that many citizens are not knowledgeable about the police and the law. If we educate them, we are less likely to have problems with them. Hopefully, the booklet will help youths to understand the various problem circumstances that they find themselves in. In the same vein, we need to educate to empower our police officers. When they know what a police department is doing and why it is doing it, they are more likely to abide by the policies.

Source: Based on Aurora Police Department, "Empowering" https://www.auroragov.org/UserFiles/Servers/Server_1881137/ File/Residents/Public%20Safety/Police/Aurora%20For%20 Youth/Empowering%20booklet_police%20web.pdf

Empowerment

Today, much is being written about the importance of **empowerment,** which is also known as participative management or dispersed leadership. Today's officers are more highly trained and educated in a variety of subjects and have learned to think independently. Therefore, today's policing—particularly in this community policing and problem-solving era—demands the self-initiated thinking, innovation, and freedom that result from employee empowerment.[9] Certainly, the greater acceptance of community policing by the rank and file may directly hinge on officers having greater latitude and authority.[10]

Officers at all levels, top management, middle management, and supervisors, should recognize that empowering employees offers the benefits of decreased work-related stress, increased job satisfaction, higher employee involvement and contributions, and positive outcomes. Empowerment may range from the delegation of power (such as allowing officers flexibility to change work hours, meeting with citizen groups, selecting equipment for a particular function, or serving on a temporary crime task force) to simply having more communication, goal setting, and feedback. But with greater empowerment comes greater accountability; skilled supervisors must carefully balance both and not vest too much attention to one, thus tipping the scale and causing problems; excessive freedom may cause workers to feel alienated or confused, while too much oversight can lead to micromanagement and thus foment low morale.[11] Leaders must pursue a balance when empowering subordinates.

According to Gove, those police leaders striving to empower their employees will find guidance from the **situational leadership** model (discussed below).[12] In its most basic framework, the model details a continuum of leader and follower actions that progresses through four cycles, shown in Figure 3-2. Figure 3-2 shows the process beginning with the "telling" supervisor, who provides specific instructions and closely monitors the performance of his or her subordinates; the supervisor then moves into a "selling" phase, where communication becomes more open, leaders seek ideas from subordinates, employees are granted more "buy-in" with decision making, and praise and recognition are used. The third phase, "participating," involves officers becoming more confident and sharing ideas; joint decision making becomes more frequent, and supervision is not invasive. Finally, the delegating phase involves very little supervisory oversight (while employees are held accountable for their actions and decisions); trust and accountability are balanced properly. The end result involves much more than merely delegating tasks; it culminates in a more confident, self-directed, and motivated officer.[13]

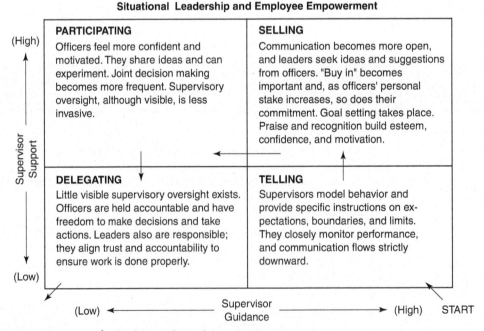

FIGURE 3-2 Situational Leadership and Employee Empowerment

APPLYING MINTZBERG'S VIEW OF LEADERS

Police leadership actually encompasses many roles. Police chief executives, many middle managers, and supervisors practice behaviors and tasks as set forth by Henry Mintzberg. Following is an overview of the roles assumed and tasks performed by the leaders of the police agency using the Mintzberg model's *interpersonal*, *informational*, and *decision-maker* roles as an analytic framework.[14]

The Interpersonal Role

The manager's **interpersonal role** includes *leadership* and *liaison* or *human relations* duties. The *leadership* function requires the manager to motivate and coordinate workers while attaining different goals and needs within the department and the community. For example, a chief or sheriff may have to urge the governing board to enact a code or ordinance that, whether popular or not, is in the best interest of the jurisdiction. The chief executive also serves as a liaison with all elements in the community. Middle managers must lead their subordinates to accomplish goals. This entails the development of interpersonal relations with subordinates and superiors. Here, middle managers serve as linking pins between top management and subordinate units. Finally, supervisors must lead their officers daily to ensure that tasks are performed and contribute to the department's mission. This entails developing a positive relationship with subordinates so that sergeants' authority and assignments are accepted and followed.

The Informational Role

The **informational role** involves the monitoring/inspecting and disseminating information and acting as spokesperson. In the *monitoring/inspecting* function, managers constantly examine the workings of the department and its various units to ensure that they are operating effectively. Many police chiefs monitor their departments by reviewing reports about police activities, such as crime rates, crime clearance rates, response time to calls for service, conviction rates, and so on. They also will conduct daily or weekly staff meetings where unit commanders discuss how their units are performing. Middle managers operate in the same ways. They periodically will meet with their supervisors to discuss operations and monitor many of the same statistics that top executives receive. Supervisors are more hands on. They will observe officers in the field and monitor statistics that are relevant to their units

The *dissemination* tasks involve disseminating vital information to members of the department. This may include e-mails, special orders, general orders, policies, or direct orders. Everyone in the department must know what is expected of them and how they are to perform their responsibilities. Every detail must be clearly communicated. The informational role is best accomplished when all units are linked together.

The Decision-Maker Role

The **decision-making role** occurs at all levels in the police organization. Chiefs and sheriffs make decisions about policies, priorities, and budgets. For example, if a chief decides to implement a new crime prevention program, he or she must decide how it is to be implemented and how it will be staffed or funded. Middle managers then must make decisions about the responsibilities of the units under their command, and finally, supervisors must make decisions about individual officers' responsibilities. Moreover, situations within the community constantly arise that require decisions at some level, whether it is a tactical situation such as a barricade person or neighborhood community group demanding a greater police presence. Every response to situations requires decisions.

STRATEGIC THINKING AND PLANNING FOR STRATEGIC MANAGEMENT

Today, it is not enough for police leaders to think in terms of the "current circumstances." The world is changing rapidly, and people who think solely in contemporary terms will quickly find themselves out of date and sync with society. They must think, plan, and manage in what are called *strategic* terms; current and future perspectives and potential changes must be considered.

In order for chiefs to engage in strategic management, they must first be a strategic *thinker* and *planner*. This means seeing both emerging trends and their operational implications. Strategic thinking refers to a creative, divergent thought process. It is a mode of strategy making that is associated with reinventing the future.[15] It means that police departments must be proactive; they must anticipate impending changes and respond to them before they become problematic. Concentrating exclusively on the present ultimately places the police at a disadvantage.

Police officers receive tactical information about gangs.
Source: ZUMA Press, Inc/Alamy Stock Photo

Strategic thinking is a prerequisite to strategic planning. Both are required in any thoughtful strategy-making process and strategy formulation. The creative, groundbreaking strategies emerging from strategic thinking still have to be operationalized through convergent and analytical thought (strategic planning). Thus, both strategic thinking and strategic planning are necessary, and neither is adequate without the other for effective strategic management.[16]

Strategic planning involves more people than the chief executive; critical transformation within an organization should be guided by teams under the direction of strategic managers—command and support staff members who have the expertise, credibility, and competence to move the department in a new and pertinent direction.[17] Officers at lower-ranking levels often have intimate knowledge about impending problems and trends and can provide valuable input into the planning and decision-making processes.

Strategic planning is both a leadership tool and a process. It is primarily used for one purpose: to help an organization do a better job—to focus its energy, ensure that members of the organization are working toward the same goals, and assess and adjust an organization's direction in response to a changing environment. Strategic planning is therefore a disciplined effort to produce fundamental decisions and actions that shape and guide what an organization is, what it does, and why it does it, with a focus on the future. Its aim is to achieve competitive advantage.

Strategic planning also includes the following elements:

- It is oriented toward the future and looks at how the world could be different five to ten years in the future. It is aimed at creating the organization's future.

- It is based on thorough analysis of foreseen or predicted trends and scenarios of possible alternative futures.

- It thoroughly analyzes the organization, both its internal and external environment and its potential.

- It is a qualitative, idea-driven process.

- It is a continuous learning process.

- When it is successful, it influences all areas of operations, becoming a part of the organization's philosophy and culture.[18]

For police leaders, strategic planning holds many benefits. It can help an agency anticipate key trends and issues facing the organization, both currently and in the future. The planning process explores options, sets directions, and helps stakeholders make appropriate decisions. It facilitates communication among key stakeholders who are involved in the process and keeps organizations focused on outcomes while battling daily crises. Planning can be used to develop performance standards to measure an agency's efforts. Most important, it helps leaders facilitate and manage change (which is the subject of the following chapter).

Planning Cycle

A **planning cycle** is used for strategic planning—the initial steps to be taken in the process—with appropriate involvement by all stakeholders. The process is not fixed, however; it must be flexible enough to allow rapid revision of specific strategies as new information develops. The first step is to identify the planning team, which should include the involvement of the following key stakeholders, both internal and external to the organization:

a. *Department and city leadership.*   Police chief and sheriff executives and other officeholders should be involved.
b. *Department personnel.*   Supervisors, officers, non-sworn staff members, and all members of the department should be included.
c. *The community.*   The plan must be developed in partnership with the community it is designed to serve.
d. *Interagency partners.*   These include both staff and other government agencies and representatives of key social welfare agencies.

Once strategic information is collected from all stakeholders, the information should be compiled into a strategic planning document. When compiling the information it is critical that the input from the various quarters is collated into a coherent, workable plan. Too often strategic plans consist of pieces that are hobbled together, which inhibits implementation.

Strategic Management

Strategic management is therefore a systems management approach that uses the proper thinking and planning approaches that are discussed above. Community policing, external and internal environments, political influences, homeland security, and new technologies are molding the profession into a highly complex structure. To be successful in this environment, executives need to set their course.

Leaders in the organization move change across organizational boundaries. A small team of personnel is assembled to analyze operational functions, identify inefficiencies, review systems integration, and detect gaps in management communications that hinder performance. Major transformation within an organization cannot rest with one person, but should be guided by teams under the direction of strategic managers—command and support staff members who have the expertise, credibility, and competence to get the job done.

FOCUS ON: PHOENIX POLICE CHIEF HAS TROUBLES WITH UNION

The Phoenix police chief experienced difficulties with the union in 2017. The chief began to redeploy detectives and sergeants to cover some of the city's patrol beats. The city increased sales tax over the years, with a substantial portion going to public safety. However, over the last few years city spending as well as an increase in the population has resulted in a reconsideration of the budget. Since 2000, the police department's budget has increased by 118 percent. Also, the number of officers has declined 10 percent, but calls for service declined by 11 percent and the number of reported major crimes declined by 35 percent since 2008.

The union complained that the city had not hired enough police officers even though the department was in the process of hiring additional officers, but the union had issues with the reassignment of the detectives and sergeants to patrol. The chief in making the reassignments was attempting to ensure that the city's beats were covered to maintain response times.

This demonstrates the difficult situations that many police chiefs face. City councils make demands on the police that are counter to the needs of the rank-and-file officers. These situations highlight the need for leadership in the police department.

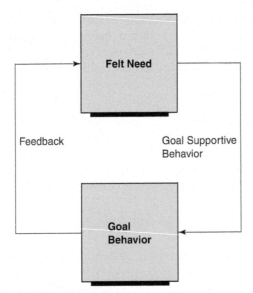

FIGURE 3-3 The Needs–Goal Model of Motivation
Source: CERTO, SAMUEL C.; CERTO, TREVIS, MODERN MANAGEMENT: CONCEPTS AND SKILLS, 12TH, © 2012. Printed and Electronically reproduced by permission of Pearson Education, Inc., Upper Saddle River, New Jersey.

MOTIVATION THEORY

Motivation generally refers to "the set of processes that arouse, direct, and maintain human behavior toward attaining some goal."[19] This definition implies that motivation consists of several areas. First, "arousal" refers to getting subordinates interested in performing some action. Some people are self-motivated and do not require a stimulus from a supervisor. Others, however, require direction or prodding. Second, this definition implies that people make choices about their behavior, such as about the amount and quality of their work. Management, through policies, direction, and consultation, can assist employees in making the correct choices. Finally, motivation is about maintaining productive behavior. Leaders must strive to have their subordinates work constantly to achieve goals. At its most fundamental level, motivation involves a *needs–goal model,* in which an individual seeks to fulfill a need (see Figure 3-3). The need is then transformed into some behavior that is directed toward satisfying that need. For example, police officers as a result of their commitment to the profession have an innate need to successfully combat crime and disorder; the police department must facilitate the satisfaction of this need by providing an organization that assists them in satisfying this need. If a person is unable to satisfy a need, he or she becomes frustrated. This frustration may lead to withdrawal and mediocre productivity. When subordinates cannot achieve their goals, problems may arise.

Motivating employees on the job is not so simplistic. Therefore, motivation theory helps us understand the why of people's behavior. It is often misunderstood as something that supervisors do to employees. In reality, it is more internal and relates to an individual's needs, wants, and desires. But what exactly sparks an employee's desire to achieve a higher level of performance is not easily identified. What is clear, however, is that what motivates one employee to perform may not motivate another employee.

Motivation theories may be divided into two general categories: content theories and process theories. **Content theories** focus on the individuals' needs, wants, and desires and attempt to explain internal needs that motivate people's behavior. **Process theories** attempt to explain how people are motivated and focus on the interplay of the individual with forces in the workplace.

CONTENT THEORIES: MASLOW, ARGYRIS, HERZBERG, AND MCCLELLAND

Maslow's Hierarchy of Needs

Abraham Maslow founded the humanistic school of psychology during the 1940s. Maslow's work focused on human needs and wants. He viewed people as perpetually *wanting* in nature and described their needs as insatiable. According to Maslow, people's needs are not random but progress in a "hierarchy of needs" from survival to security, social, ego-esteem, and self-actualization needs, as shown in Figure 3-4.[20]

Maslow asserted that people are motivated by their lowest level of unsatisfied need. Once a lower need is satisfied, higher needs are sought. An important implication to motivation theory is understanding that a satisfied need is no longer a motivator of behavior. Simply stated, people who have their security needs met can be motivated only by higher needs.

Self-actualization Needs	Job-related Satisfiers
Reaching Your Potential	Involvement in Planning Your Work
Independence	Freedom to Make Decisions Affecting Work
Creativity	
Self-expression	Creative Work to Perform
	Opportunities for Growth and Development

Esteem Needs	Job-related Satisfiers
Responsibility	Status Symbols
Self-respect	Merit Awards
Recognition	Challenging Work
Sense of Accomplishment	Sharing in Decisions
Sense of Competence	Opportunity for Advancement

Social Needs	Job-related Satisfiers
Companionship	Opportunities for Interaction with Others
Acceptance	
Love and Affection	Team Spirit
Group Membership	Friendly Coworkers

Safety Needs	Job-related Satisfiers
Security for Self and Possessions	Safe Working Conditions
Avoidance of Risks	Seniority
Avoidance of Harm	Fringe Benefits
Avoidance of Pain	Proper Supervision
	Sound Company Policies, Programs, and Practices

Physical Needs	Job-related Satisfiers
Food	Pleasant Working Conditions
Clothing	Adequate Wage or Salary
Shelter	Rest Periods
Comfort	Labor-saving Devices
Self-preservation	Efficient Work Methods

FIGURE 3-4   Maslow's Hierarchy of Needs
Source: A. H. Maslow, *Motivation and Personality,* 2d ed. (New York: Harper & Row, 1970).

What are the implications of this theory for the police organization? According to Maslow's hierarchy, a supervisor will better understand officers' performance and what motivates them by identifying their unfulfilled needs. There must also be a recognition that different officers may be at various levels in the hierarchy of needs and, therefore, are not necessarily motivated by the same wants. For example, a rookie officer may be most concerned with successfully completing the probationary period; therefore, security is that officer's primary concern and motivator. The veteran officer may be interested in promotion; motivation may derive from the esteem and status level. The supervisor may be successful in motivating this officer by delegating team leader duties and assisting the officer in preparing for the sergeant's exam.

For most police officers, their physical, safety, and social needs are satisfied by the job. Their employment or salary satisfies their physical needs. Police officers generally have civil service or union protection, so their safety needs are satisfied. Their social needs are satisfied by their membership in cohesive police units and the informal organization. Police leaders and managers generally must focus on subordinates' esteem needs. This often is best accomplished by implementing some form of participative management and getting subordinates involved in decision making. It also involves recognizing officers' exemplary performance.

Argyris's Maturity–Immaturity Theory

Argyris's **maturity–immaturity** continuum also furnishes insight on human needs. According to Argyris, people naturally progress from immaturity to maturity.[21] They develop needs for more activity and relative independence. They also have deeper interests, consider a relatively long-term perspective, and show more awareness of themselves and more control of their own destiny. Argyris viewed an effective organization as one requiring employees to be responsible, self-directed, and self-motivated. He argued that motivation can be maximized when each employee pursues goals and experiences psychological growth and independence. He noted that the organization has a responsibility to structure the work environment so that employees can grow and mature. Police leaders and managers must design work so that subordinates can progress throughout their careers.

Herzberg's Motivation-Hygiene Theory

In 1968, Frederick Herzberg developed a motivation theory based on a study of 200 engineers who were queried about when they were satisfied and dissatisfied with their jobs. The findings led Herzberg to identify two vital factors that are found in all jobs: (1) items that influence the degree of job dissatisfaction, called maintenance or *hygiene* factors, which relate mostly to the work environment, and (2) factors that influence the degree of job satisfaction, called *motivators,* which relate to the work itself. The items that comprise Herzberg's hygiene and motivator factors are shown in Figure 3-5.[22]

Herzberg distinguished between job satisfaction and motivation. Indeed, using his scheme, an officer can be dissatisfied and motivated at the same time. If negative hygiene factors are present in a job, workers will become dissatisfied. Addressing these factors, such as by increasing salary, generally will not motivate people to do a better job, but it will keep them from becoming dissatisfied. In contrast, if motivating factors are high in a particular job, workers generally are motivated to do a better job. People tend to be more motivated and productive as more motivators are built into their job situation.[23]

The process of incorporating motivators into a job situation is called *job enrichment.* Subordinates are given more responsibilities, allowed to be involved in more complex cases, and have the opportunity to provide input into those decisions that directly affect them. The most productive employees are involved in work situations with desirable hygiene factors and motivating factors. This relates to **Maslow's hierarchy of needs** as well; for example, hygiene factors (such as a pay raise) can help to satisfy physical, security, and social needs, while motivating factors (e.g., an award for outstanding performance) can satisfy employees' esteem and self-actualization needs.

According to Herzberg, hygiene factors may attract people to join an organization, but they do not provide the intrinsic satisfaction in the work itself that motivates people to perform at higher levels. Intrinsic motivation can come only from what the individual does through job responsibilities and subsequent satisfaction gained from job accomplishment. It appears that people are influenced more by intrinsic motivators than by hygiene factors. Put more simply, job satisfaction appears to be more important to most people than pay and benefits.

Dissatisfaction: Hygiene or Maintenance Factors	Satisfaction: Motivating Factors
1. Company policy and administration	1. Opportunity for achievement
2. Supervision	2. Opportunity for recognition
3. Relationship with supervisor	3. Work itself
4. Relationship with peers	4. Responsibility
5. Working conditions	5. Advancement
6. Salary	6. Personal growth
7. Relationship with subordinates	

FIGURE 3-5 Herzberg's Hygiene Factors and Motivators

A supervisor who conducts frequent team meetings to keep officers informed about departmental matters and to dispel rumors, who delegates additional duties to those officers ready to accept new challenges and compliments their work, and who solicits officers' participation in decision making whenever possible is enhancing and appealing to their intrinsic motivators.

McClelland's Achievement, Power, and Affiliation Motives

McClelland, another humanistic theorist, believed that individual needs were acquired over time and as a result of experience. From his studies, he identified three motives or needs that are important to an individual within an organizational environment:

1. *Need for achievement*—the need to succeed or excel. Some individuals must have standards or benchmarks to separate success from failure, and they have an internal force (motivation) that drives them toward accomplishment.
2. *Need for power*—the need to exert control over one's environment. Some individuals have an internal desire to make decisions and ensure that others abide by those decisions.
3. *Need for affiliation*—the need to establish and maintain friendly and close interpersonal relationships (social need).[24]

Individuals who have a compelling drive to succeed are more interested in personal achievement than the rewards for their success. Such people have a desire to do things better; they seek situations in which they can attain greater personal responsibility; and they quickly volunteer for complex, challenging assignments. As they work through an assignment, they must have immediate and continuing feedback on their performance.

McClelland notes that power and affiliation needs are closely related to success. Successful leaders and managers have a greater need for power and a lower need for affiliation. Such individuals are willing to take charge of a situation and act without undue regard for the social implications of decisions. If the need for power overshadows the affiliation need to a significantly greater extent, however, leaders and managers may become Machiavellian types who concentrate on their own success rather than on that of the organization or its personnel.

McClelland's theory has broad implications. The administrator should identify the high achievers and place them in positions where their attributes would best meet the department's needs. Some positions call for affiliation-oriented people, while others require achievers. When there is a crisis situation, a problem area within the department, or a new program is being developed and implemented, planning and operations are best handled by a high achiever. This internally motivated individual will take charge and exert all his or her energy toward ensuring that the assignment is completed successfully.

PROCESS THEORIES: EQUITY THEORY AND EXPECTANCY THEORY

In reality, the motivation process is much more complex than is depicted by the needs–goal model, shown in Figure 3-3, as advocated by the content theorists. Content theories focus solely on the individual and what the individual has internalized and, to a great extent, neglect the effects of the work environment on the individual. They place the bulk of responsibility for motivation with the individual worker. They tend to neglect that the police organization has a responsibility for facilitating motivation.

Adams' Equity Theory

Adams perceived that an element of motivation is equity. He explained his **equity theory**:

> Evidence suggests that equity is not merely a matter of getting a "fair day's pay for a far day's work," nor is inequity simply a matter of being underpaid. The fairness of an exchange between employee and employer is not usually perceived by the former and simply as an economic matter. There is an element of relative justice involved that supervenes economics and underlies perceptions of equity or inequity.[25]

Essentially, employees examine the rewards they receive in relation to the rewards and efforts of others in the organization. If an officer perceives that another officer who is less productive or not a good officer receives greater or similar rewards, the officer may perceive inequity. Similarly, if one officer is not promoted while another officer who is less qualified is promoted, the officer will perceive inequity. Police leaders and managers must consider their reward systems and ensure that rewards are equitable.

| Motivation strength | = | Perceived value of result of performing behavior | × | Perceived probability that result will materialize |

FIGURE 3-6 Vroom's Expectancy Model of Motivation in Equation Form

Vroom's Expectancy Theory

Vroom's **expectancy theory** was developed in the 1960s and addresses some of the complexities related to motivation. This theory holds that people are motivated primarily by a felt need that affects behavior; however, Vroom's theory adds the issue of motivation *strength*—an individual's degree of desire to perform a behavior.[26]

Vroom's expectancy model is shown in equation form in Figure 3-6. According to this model, motivation strength is determined by the perceived value of performing a task or job and the perceived probability that the work performed will result in an appropriate reward. That is, an individual is motivated if he or she perceives that the effort will be rewarded and if the value of the reward is equal to or greater than the amount of effort or work. Generally, individuals tend to perform the behaviors that maximize rewards over the long term.

Expectancy theory suggests that officers who experience success will feel more competent and therefore will be more willing to take risks in improving performance levels. When officers know that certain behaviors will produce anticipated departmental rewards, they are motivated. For example, an officer may be motivated to participate in a community policing project knowing that it could result in a higher performance rating, departmental letter of commendation, or improved promotional prospects. If such rewards are not forthcoming, the officer will be less enthusiastic when participating in similar projects in the future.

This discussion of motivation theories demonstrates that motivation is complex. We frequently fail to provide the support and setting to motivate police officers. We too often depend solely on subordinates' innate drive. Leaders should constantly monitor the level of motivation of their subordinates and provide the support to ensure that they are highly committed.

LEADING VERSUS MANAGING

Leading is related to managing. In this chapter, however, we maintain that effective leadership goes well beyond the basic management functions described at the beginning of the chapter. Bennis and Nanus (1985: 21) distinguish between management and leadership: "To be a manager is to bring about, to accomplish, to have charge of, responsibility for, to conduct. Leading, on the other hand, is influencing, guiding in direction, course, action, opinion."[27] They go on to say that managers are people who *do things right*, and leaders are people who *do the right things*. Managers are more efficiency-driven and focus on mastering routine activities, while leaders are driven by vision and judgment. Managers tend to be bean counters, while leaders focus on achieving desired results.

Another clear distinction between the leader and the manager is organizational consensus on overall goals—having a vision. According to Bennis and Nanus, by focusing attention on a vision, the leader operates on the *emotional* and *spiritual resources* of the organization—on its values, commitment, and aspirations.[28] The manager, by contrast, operates on the *physical resources* of the organization—its capital, human skills, raw materials, and technology. As they put it,

> Any competent manager can make it possible for people to earn a living [and] see to it that work is done productively and efficiently, on schedule, and with a high level of quality. It remains for the effective leader, however, to help people in the organization know pride and satisfaction in their work.[29]

They added: "The essential thing in organization leadership is that the leader's style *pulls* rather than *pushes* people on. Leading is a responsibility, and the effectiveness of this responsibility is reflected in the attitudes of the led."[30]

We concur that a successful police leader must be a good manager. As Whisenand and Ferguson explained, "If you're a competent manager, you are getting the most out of your resources. If you're a competent leader, you are pointing their energy in the right direction."[31] It is therefore important that the supervisor manage departmental resources in as efficient a manner as possible, while also motivating and inspiring employees to perform to the best of their ability. Therein lies the influential art of leadership that instills the sense of esprit de corps or common purpose that imbues successful cohesive teams.

FOCUS ON: THE STATE POLICE ACADEMY

An academy trainee reported that trainees in an Iowa police academy recently were passing a study guide around that contained the actual exam questions. There was no information on how many of the recruits saw the study guide. Nonetheless, the commander of the academy immediately announced that all exams were considered compromised, and all the recruits were required to retake all the exams in order to graduate.

The incident raises several questions. Did the academy staff provide the exam to the recruits? If so, it shows a lack of leadership on the

part of the staff. It also shows a lack of understanding about the knowledge and skills that are important in police work, knowledge and skills that must be obtained in the academy. Second, what does it say about the integrity of those recruits who had access to the exams? Integrity is an important part of leadership, and these recruits failed the test.

Source: Based on The News Tribune, Cheating at the police academy a leadership failure, http://blog.thenewstribune.com/bluebyline/2013/10/31/cheating-at-the-police-academy-a-leadership-failure/

LEADERSHIP THEORIES

We now discuss trait, behavioral, and situational theories that attempt to explain leadership behavior. Whereas trait theories are based on the intrinsic qualities a leader possesses, behavioral theories explain leadership by examining what the leader does. Situational theories maintain that effective leadership is a product of the fit between the leader's traits or skills and the situation in which he or she exercises leadership. Finally, contingency theories, to a degree, merge and extend trait and behavioral theories by examining how the environment or workplace affects leadership and the leader.

TRAIT THEORY

Early leadership studies of the 1930s and 1940s focused on the individual and assumed that some people were born leaders, and that good leaders could be studied to determine the special traits that leaders possess. From an organizational standpoint, this **trait theory** had great appeal. For example, in the police field it was assumed that all that was needed was for leaders with these special traits to be identified and promoted to managerial positions within the department.

For more than 50 years researchers attempted to identify those special traits that separate successful leaders from poor leaders. For example, Davis found 56 different characteristics or traits that he considered important. While admitting it was unlikely that any manager would possess all 56 traits, he said the following 9 traits were required for executive success: intelligence, experience, originality, receptiveness, teaching ability, knowledge of human behavior, courage, tenacity, and a sense of justice and fair play.[32]

The age-old assumption that leaders are born and develop their technical, human, and conceptual skills was completely discredited, because researchers have been unable to agree or present empirical evidence to support its claims.[33] There are too many traits that a good leader must possess, and some good leaders possess some of the traits, while other good leaders possess a different set of traits. Additionally, there are traits that both good leaders and bad leaders possess. Consequently, it is now believed that certain traits and skills increase the *likelihood* that a given person will be an effective manager. There are no guarantees, however.

BEHAVIORAL THEORIES

The *behavioral* approach focuses on a leader's behavior in relation to the environment. Studies at the University of Michigan and Ohio State University and Blake and Mouton's "managerial grid" led the early research of behavioral theories leadership. These studies were important because they studied leadership in real-life situations.

University of Michigan Studies

The University of Michigan conducted a series of studies of leadership behavior in relation to job satisfaction and productivity in business and industrial work groups. The researchers determined that leaders must have a sense of the task to be accomplished as well as the environment in which the followers worked. They found the following to be the beliefs of a successful leader:

1. The leader assumes the leadership role is more effective relative to managers who fail to exhibit leadership.
2. The closeness of supervision will have a direct bearing on the production of employees. High-producing units had less direct supervision; highly supervised units had lower production. To conclude, employees need some area of freedom to make choices. Given this, they produce at a higher rate.
3. Employee orientation is a concept that involves managers taking an active interest in subordinates. It is the leader's responsibility to facilitate employees' accomplishment of goals.[34]

The University of Michigan studies definitively demonstrated the differences between leadership and management. Even though leadership consists of a different set of activities, it is no more important than management. Effective leadership and management must be present in the effective police department.

The Ohio State University Studies

Ohio State University began its study of leadership in 1945 and identified leadership behavior in two dimensions: initiating structure and consideration. **Initiating structure** referred to supervisory behavior that focused on the achievement of organizational goals and included characteristics such as assigning subordinates to particular tasks, holding subordinates accountable for following rules and procedures, and informing subordinates of what is expected of them. **Consideration**, on the other hand, consisted of a manager's concern for subordinates. This included behaviors such as a superior's openness concerning subordinates' ideas and respect for their feelings as persons and also characteristics such as listening to subordinates, being willing to make changes, and being friendly and approachable. It was assumed that high consideration and moderate initiating structure yielded higher job satisfaction and productivity than did high initiating structure and low consideration.[35]

The Managerial Grid

The managerial grid, developed by Robert Blake and Jane Mouton (1962), has received a great deal of attention since its appearance and is based on and expands the research conducted at the Ohio State University and the University of Michigan.

The **managerial grid** (Figure 3-7) has two dimensions: concern for production or productivity and concern for people. Each axis or dimension is numbered from 1, meaning low concern, to 9, indicating a high concern. The horizontal axis represents the concern for production and performance goals, and the vertical axis represents the concern for human relations or empathy. The way in which a person combines these two dimensions establishes a leadership style in terms of one of the five principal styles identified on the grid.

The points of orientation are related to styles of management. The lower left-hand corner of the grid shows the 1,1 style (representing a minimal concern for task or service and a minimal concern for people). The lower right-hand corner of the grid identifies the 9,1 style. This type of leader would have a primary concern for the task or output and a minimal concern for people. People are seen as tools of production. The upper left-hand corner represents the 1,9 style, often referred to as country club management, with minimum effort given to output or task. The upper right, 9,9, indicates high concern for both people and production—a team management approach of mutual respect and trust. In the center, a 5,5, middle-of-the-road style, the leader has a give a little, be fair but firm philosophy, providing a balance between output and people concerns. It represents a mediocre or unexceptional commitment to people and productivity.

These five **leadership styles** can be summarized as follows:

1. Authority-compliance management (9,1)
2. Country club management (1,9)
3. Middle-of-the-road management (5,5)

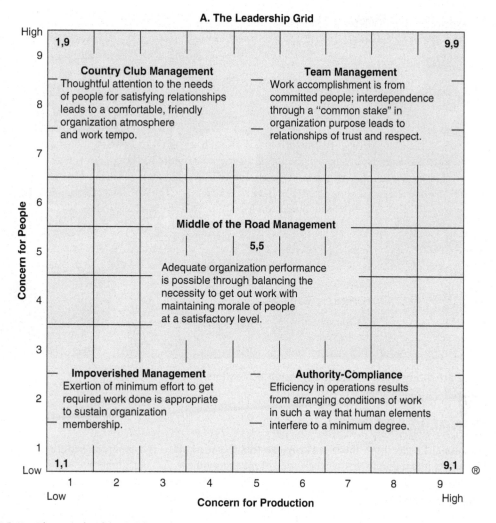

FIGURE 3-7   The Leadership Grid

Source: The Leadership Grid figure, Paternalism Figure and Opportunism from Leadership Dilemmas—Grid Solutions, © Grid International, Inc. Used with permission.

4. Impoverished management (1,1)
5. Team management (9,9)

Swanson and Territo attempted to investigate the extent to which Blake and Mouton's various styles are utilized by police managers. They surveyed managers from 166 different departments and found that almost 40 percent of the participants reported that they primarily used the team style of leadership. Twenty-nine percent reported the task or middle-of-the-road style as their primary form of leadership, 15 percent reported using the impoverished style, 11 percent reported using the authority-compliance form, and only 9 percent said they were country club managers.[36] Swanson and Territo's research indicates a variety of styles being used by police leaders. The predominant style they found was the team style. The leaders who were not team leaders need to move in that direction.

William Bratton, the former police chief in New York City and Los Angeles, was able to increase the departments' productivity by focusing on both concern for productivity and concern for people. He "... displayed a job centered style by carefully monitoring police officers' performance and providing rewards or punishment based on performance, he also demonstrated an employee centered style by decentralizing authority and opening communications channels with the department."[37] Emphasizing and balancing productivity and people in a police department can result in increased effectiveness.

There are many types of situations requiring leadership.
Source: B Christopher/Alamy Stock Photo

SITUATIONAL LEADERSHIP

Situational Leadership® theories recognize that the workplace is a complex setting subject to rapid changes. Therefore, it is unlikely that one best way of managing these varying situations would be adequate. Simply, the best way to lead depends on the situation. Hersey and Blanchard presented a model of Situational Leadership® that has been used in training by many major corporations and the military services. Their model emphasizes the leader's behavior to a great extent should be dictated by the actions and behavior of those being led as well as the situation.

Situational Leadership® takes into account worker maturity; *maturity* is defined as the capacity to set high but attainable goals, the willingness to take responsibility, and the education and/or experience of the individual or the group. Hersey and Blanchard have identified four levels of worker maturity. First, some workers or followers are unable or unwilling to take responsibility for accomplishing work (high level of immaturity). They are content with their current work environment and do not want to change. A second type of subordinate is one who is willing to take responsibility for the tasks, but for some reason, such as lack of training or experience, cannot take responsibility for completing the task or work. Officers who are transferred to a new unit often have the willingness to do a good job, but are unfamiliar with how all the work is performed. A third type of subordinates are those who have the ability to complete the task, but are unwilling to do so. For example, when police departments initiate new programs or policies, officers often are resistant to them. Finally, there are subordinates who are willing and able to perform—mature subordinates.

The four types of task behavior, described here, are based on their maturity. Each type or level of maturity must be handled differently. Four basic styles of leadership are associated with maturity and task accomplishment. They operate similarly to those on the managerial grid. First is telling. This style of leadership is most appropriate for subordinates who are unwilling to take responsibility for accomplishing tasks—they must be told what to do. Second is selling. Here, the leader can sometimes overcome resistance explaining the benefits or importance of accomplishing tasks. Selling is always preferable to depending only on direct orders. The third style of leadership is participating where the leader and subordinates participate or jointly discuss issues and decisions. Finally, mature subordinates can be led by delegation. They have the willingness and capacity to accomplish the assigned tasks.

As the maturity level of followers develops from immaturity to maturity, the appropriate style of leadership moves in a corresponding way. Hersey and Blanchard asserted that leaders could reduce their close supervision and direction of individuals and increase delegation as followers' readiness to complete tasks increased. The difficulty of this style of leadership is its dependence on leaders' ability to diagnose follower ability and then adjust their leadership style to the given situation. This is often easier said than done.

YOU DECIDE...

Officer Maria Sanchez has 17 years of experience, mostly as a detective in undercover narcotics and vice. She is a capable officer with numerous departmental commendations and awards for her work. As a result, Sanchez was selected to be a member of an elite multiagency vice and narcotics task force. On the first day of her new assignment, Sanchez met with her new supervisor, Sgt. Webster. He is from a neighboring agency and does not know Sanchez outside the selection interview process and review of her personnel file. Sgt. Webster was also recently assigned to the unit from patrol division where he gained the reputation of being somewhat of a perfectionist and detail person. Webster assumed responsibility for breaking in all new team members to ensure they knew exactly what, when, where, and how they should perform their tasks. Webster had developed a four-week orientation for all new members. After two weeks of basic orientation, including an elementary review of drug law, raid procedures, vice laws, and so on, Sanchez becomes extremely frustrated with Sgt. Webster and asks why she is not being allowed to participate in drug and vice raids with the rest of her team. She argues that

she has worked with the task force on many occasions, is very familiar with operational procedures, and could demonstrate her abilities if Webster would only allow her to work with the rest of the team. Webster denies her request, saying she has to finish the orientation just the same as everyone else does. The next day, Sanchez submits a memo to the lieutenant in charge of the task force, requesting to be reassigned back to her agency. In the memo, Sanchez states that she believes Sgt. Webster is treating her differently from other people in the unit and does not have any respect for her past experience and work. She does not believe she can work under these conditions, in which she is being treated like a child.

Questions for Discussion

1. Could this problem have been avoided? If so, how?
2. What situational style of leadership was Sgt. Webster employing?
3. How would you assess the maturity level of Officer Sanchez?
4. What style of situational leadership would be more appropriate for this situation?

CONTINGENCY THEORY

Whereas situational leadership is based on the capabilities of subordinates, **contingency theory** focuses on the capabilities of subordinates, job responsibilities, and the work environment. All of these factors interplay and ultimately require adjustments in a manager's leadership style.

Several researchers attempted during the late 1950s and early 1960s to show that no one leadership style was appropriate for all job situations.[41] Some jobs require one type of leadership, while another may require a different one. For example, a leader's style in a barricaded person situation would be different from that of the same leader working with officers confronting a burglary problem. Therefore, contingency theories of leadership are based on the concept of leader flexibility: Successful leaders must change their leadership style as they confront different situations. But can leaders be so flexible as to employ all major styles? Obviously, not all leaders are capable of such flexibility. It may be that leaders are locked into a particular style as a result of their personalities and job experiences.

Fiedler developed one strategy for overcoming these obstacles, which is to change the organizational situation to fit the leader's style, and not vice versa.[42] According to Fiedler, leader–member relations (the degree to which the leader feels accepted by the followers), task structure (the degree to which the work to be done is outlined clearly), and power of the leader (discussed above) should be considered when assigning leaders. Police departments commonly move sergeants with investigative experience into detective units to capitalize on their knowledge. It likely is disadvantageous to move a new sergeant who does not have investigative experience into a detective unit. According to Fiedler, it may be just as important to evaluate the potential manager's leadership style and ability to ensure that it matches the leadership situation. The head of a special weapons and tactics (SWAT) unit must be decisive, and, on the other hand, the captain in charge of community policing in a department must have the ability to decentralize decision making and use participative management techniques.

The basic components of **contingency theory** then are that (1) among people's needs is a central need to achieve a sense of competence, (2) the ways that people fulfill this need vary from person to person, (3) competent motivation is most likely to occur when there is a fit between task and organization, and (4) a sense of competence continues to motivate people even after competence is achieved.[43] It seems that not only are subordinates unhappy when they have a leader whose style does not match the job but the leader may also be just as unhappy and unmotivated. Contingency theory argues that authoritarian leaders are more effective in performing structured and organized tasks. Human relations–type leaders are best suited for performing unstructured and uncertain tasks. Understanding this distinction requires that managers and supervisors tailor jobs to fit people or give people the skills, knowledge, and attitudes they will need to become competent.[44]

TYPOLOGIES OF LEADERSHIP STYLES

Several researchers have attempted to develop typologies of leadership styles. A typology attempts to identify all the possible types or styles within a general category. Here, researches attempted to identify all the different styles of leaders that could be found in an organization. We can discern how organizations function by examining the different styles of leadership that occur in the organization. Here, we examine different typologies of leadership.

Likert's Leadership Systems

Likert examined a number of industrial plants in an attempt to discover the style of leadership used by various managers. He was primarily interested in determining those leaders who were successful and why. Likert identified four distinct leadership types: exploitive-authoritarian, benevolent-authoritarian, consultative, and participative.[45] Figure 3-8 shows these types in a continuum from low employee involvement to high involvement and interaction.

- *Exploitive-Authoritarian Leadership:* The exploitive-authoritarian leader has no confidence or trust in subordinates, and subordinates are not allowed to provide input into decisions. Policies and decisions are formulated by top management and filter down the chain of command. There is little superior–subordinate interaction, and when there is, it is usually negative or directive in nature. Superiors generally attempt to motivate subordinates through fear, threats, and punishment. Employees become frustrated and join together in informal groups to protect themselves from top management and to oppose unpopular policies. The exploitive-authoritarian style of leadership thwarts motivation and causes officers to concentrate only on attaining minimum productivity levels. This style of leadership is obviously inappropriate in policing, because police officers' activities cannot be highly or easily controlled as a result of the types of activities performed and the high degree of discretion officers must have when dealing with crime and calls for service. Moreover,

Operating Characteristic	Exploitive Authoritarian System	Benevolent Authoritarian System	Consultative	Participative
Motivation	Economic security marked with fear & threats	Economic and occasionally status rewards coupled with some punishment	Economic, ego, and desire for new experiences. Occasional punishment	Economic, ego, and full involvement in the organization and shared power
Communication Processes	Very little and downward	Little and mostly downward	Quite a bit, up and down the organization	Substantial throughout the organization
Character of interaction-influence	Little interaction, usually distrustful	Some interaction with caution on the part of subordinates	Moderate interaction and a moderate level of trust and confidence	Extensive collegial interaction with a high degree of trust and confidence
Decision making	Centralized with top administrators	Policy dictated by top administrators with some decisions resting with mid-level managers	Broad policies made at top with lower level echelons having input into programs	Decisions made throughout the organization with lower level subordinates having input in all decisions
Goal setting	Goals set by top administrators and orders issued by administrators. Directives resisted by subordinates	Goals set by top administrators and orders issued by administrators with some discussion by subordinates	Goals and orders issued after discussion with subordinates. Goals and orders have some level of acceptance by subordinates	Goals established through group participation with high levels of acceptance by work group
Control Processes	Formalized controls established by top management which are resisted by subordinates	Control rests primarily at the top with resistance from subordinates	Moderate delegation of authority and responsibility with subordinates having some input in performance expectations	Concern for performance throughout the organization coupled with collegiality
Productivity	Mediocre productivity	Fair to good productivity	Good productivity	Excellent productivity

FIGURE 3-8 Likert's System Organizational Characteristics

first-line supervisors seldom provide close supervision of officers, which is a key component of the exploitive-authoritarian style.

Here, police officers tend to neglect problem solving and community policing. If this style of leadership exists in law enforcement, it exists only in a few isolated cases.

- ***Benevolent-Authoritarian Leadership:*** The benevolent-authoritarian style is somewhat more positive than the exploitive-authoritarian style. In this style, most policies and decisions are made by top management and are distributed through the chain of command, but sometimes managers and supervisors listen to subordinates' problems. More interaction takes place between managers and supervisors and line employees than in the exploitive-authoritarian style. Superiors frequently are willing to listen, but they continue to make all the decisions. Subordinates still view superiors with caution and distrust, but not to the point that they oppose organizational goals. They feel somewhat frustrated because they have little input into daily activities, especially those that directly affect them. This style of leadership permeates many traditionally organized police departments and is responsible for many of the motivational problems in these departments. A possible reason for the existence of authoritarian leaders in police work is that the enforcement aspect of policing is, to a great extent, authoritarian, thereby attracting this type of individual. Many officers working under this leadership style concentrate on accomplishing their assigned tasks, but they seldom go beyond them because of the lack of encouragement and the possibility of getting into trouble with their superiors. Hence, there is little motivation to succeed, which is a necessary part of a successful police agency. No statistics are available on the extent to which particular leadership styles exist in police organizations, but many police leaders likely are benevolent-authoritarian or consultative.

- ***Consultative Leadership:*** **Consultative leadership** involves management's establishment of goals and objectives for the department with subordinates making some of the decisions on methods of goal achievement (i.e., strategic and tactical decisions). A more positive relationship exists between superiors and line personnel as problems and possible solutions are discussed openly and freely. Employees are encouraged to become involved by providing input into some decisions and unit goals. Positive rewards are emphasized and punishment is used to motivate only in extreme cases. Whole or parts of police departments formally or informally adhere to this leadership style. This is especially true in larger police departments in which operational units have a great deal of autonomy.[46] For example, the leadership style in drug units often is consultative. Officers in these units likely have substantial discretion in how they attack an area's drug problem. This style of leadership tends to emphasize involvement and esteem rewards and leads to a more positive motivational climate.

- ***Participative Leadership:*** The **participative leadership** style involves subordinates having input not only into tactical decisions but also into policy formulation. It is a team approach whereby everyone has input in the organization's goals and objectives and operational strategies and tactics. The participative style implies that police officers provide direct input into what the department should be doing. Witte, Travis, and Langworthy found that officers at all levels within police departments favored the use of participatory management, but that only those officers in administrative positions believed that they were allowed an adequate level of participation.[47] All other officers believed that they were not allowed adequate participation in decision making and strategic planning. Managers sometimes are given objectives that are counter to the expectations of officers. Such disagreements on policy usually center on law enforcement versus service roles. If there is a high degree of trust within the police organization, however, this may be only a minor problem. In the vast majority of cases, subordinates should be allowed to have some level of input into decisions. An open discussion of such matters generally brings about compliance and cooperation.

Police organizations must move toward the latter two styles of leadership. Approximately 80 percent of any police department's budget is devoted to salaries for personnel, and personnel represent an important resource in police agencies. These resources must be used to their maximum advantage. The consultative and participatory styles of leadership create a positive motivational atmosphere in which officers are more likely to be concerned about doing an excellent job in accomplishing objectives.

Engel's Supervisory Styles

Engel developed a typology of street sergeants by studying lieutenants and sergeants' styles of supervision in Indianapolis and St. Petersburg. She identified four different styles: traditional, innovative, supportive, and active.[48] **Traditional sergeants** believed their officers should make large numbers of arrests and issue large numbers of citations. They essentially are *bean counters*. Further, they do not see community policing and community engagement as important; such activities cannot be quantified. They focus on calls for service, but not problem solving. **Innovative sergeants** are the opposite of traditional sergeants. They focus on community policing and community building. They want to have an impact on the community and the conditions that cause crime and disorder. **Supportive supervisors** have a need to be liked and tend to provide their subordinates with little direction. They see one of their roles as protecting their subordinates from management. They are largely ineffective. Finally, **active sergeants** tend to write large numbers of citations and make large numbers of arrests. They are glorified police officers, not supervisors. They should not have been promoted. Obviously, the ideal supervisor for today's police department is the innovative supervisor.

Engel has identified several dysfunctional supervisors as well as innovative supervisors who are functional and more effective. Police managers must ensure that their supervisors are leaders, leading their subordinates toward goal accomplishment that includes a variety of services to their communities. We need innovative managers and supervisors who will solve problems and work with the community.

LEADING IN TODAY'S ENVIRONMENT

Thus far, we have discussed traditional and innovative ways to lead and manage police organizations. In order to be more responsive to community problems, police leaders and managers must decentralize decision making and innovate to effectively serve communities. This often means that police departments must depart from the status quo. To accomplish this change, Heifetz suggests what he terms *adaptive change*, which he calls for when a problem cannot be solved with one's existing knowledge and skills and requires people to make a shift in their expectations, attitudes, or habits of behavior.[49] To clarify his intended meaning, let us consider how Heifetz describes differences in adaptive problems and technical problems. There are problems, he says, that are *technical* only—purchasing a new computer system, installing body-worn cameras, providing officers with less than deadly force weapons, and so on. Such problems are fixable by technical expertise. On the other hand, there are problems that technicians cannot fix, and that require people in the community or department to change their values, behavior, and attitudes.

Technical fixes alone will not work with drug, gang, and other police problems. Rather, our leaders must call for adaptive change, which is engaged collaboratively through the conferred authority of those being led. Heifetz proposes four principles for bringing about adaptive change:

1. Be able to recognize when the challenge requires adaptive work for resolution; understand the values and issues at stake in the situation.
2. Remember that adaptive change will cause distress in the people being led. The leader should keep the distress in the tolerable range (too much stress can be defeating, and too little stress does not motivate people).
3. Keep the focus on the real issue—do not get sidetracked by denial, scapegoating, and so on, as these are "work avoidance mechanisms."
4. Ensure that the people who need to make the change take the responsibility for doing the work of change themselves.[50]

When problematical situations arise that cannot be resolved through old tried and true methods, this approach will help to provide the leader with a perspective to help people resolve it

When leaders and managers decide to adapt their units, they will use transformational leadership. **Transformational leadership** is where the leader or manager attempts to change direction to broaden the

Force Field Analysis

Forces in Support of Change		Resistance to Change
=====>	Equal	<====
=====>	More support for change	<====
=====>	More resistance for change	<====
	Nature of balance	

FIGURE 3-9 Lewin's Force Field Analysis

interests and horizons of subordinates and move to a new direction. It requires maximum engagement with the work group that needs to change.[51] Schermerhorn has identified six traits that a leader must possess in order to effectively transform a unit or work group.

1. Vision. The leaders must have a clear and detailed understanding of where and how the unit needs to change. What does the unit do and look like after change has been implemented.
2. Charisma. The leader must have personality and skills to effectively engage and motivate subordinates. The leader must inspire and sell new goals or operational strategies to subordinates.
3. Symbolism. The leader must establish a reward system for subordinates who successfully fulfill the new mission. This can consist of ceremonies, special awards, or congratulatory conversations.
4. Empowerment. Subordinates must be given truly challenging work assignments. This facilitates change and subordinates' commitment to the new arrangements.
5. Intellectual stimulation. Foster an atmosphere where subordinates begin to think about the problems at hand and provide input into possible solutions. This also engenders support for the new arrangements.[52]
6. Integrity. The leader or manager must be totally honest with subordinates at all times. A high standard of ethics and morality will further motivate subordinates.

An analytical tool that can assist a leader in facilitating change is Lewin's force field analysis.[53] **Force field analysis** is a process where the leader or manager who is attempting to implement change specifies the change (organizational arrangements and behavior), and then identifies the forces that support or facilitate the change as well as the forces that impede the change as depicted in Figure 3-9. When the forces in support of the change are greater than the forces opposed to the change, the leader is more likely to be successful. On the other hand, if the forces are fairly equal or there is more resistance than support, it is difficult to effect the change.

Obviously, there must be ample support for change in order for the change to be implemented. Change can be facilitated by increasing or strengthening the forces for the change and mitigating the resistance. The leader must identify the forces and develop a strategy for dealing with them. For example, if a patrol captain wants to change the patrol beats in his or her area, he or she can explain how the new beat configuration will provide better patrol coverage. This should strengthen support and reduce resistance. The patrol captain must sell the change to subordinates to elicit support.

Proper transformational leadership requires that leaders and managers exhibit strong leadership skills. Moreover, leaders and managers must engage their subordinates and move them in a new direction. This means that all leaders and managers in the organization must have a commitment to the changes, and a firm strategy to implement the change.

Transformational leadership is used to implement change in the organization. However, what about leadership when change is not the primary objective? Here, sustainable leadership should be used. **Sustainable leadership** is where the leader or manager attempts to maximize unit effectiveness through continued oversight and motivation. Leadership sometimes is episodic, or leaders only exert their leadership skills when a problem exists or when change is necessary. However, leadership should be a constant force applied on a daily basis. When leadership occurs periodically or episodically, it is much less effective and a unit's productivity can diminish over time. In sustainable leadership, the manager will exhibit some of the same transformational leadership traits but with the intent to maximize current organizational arrangements and objectives. It also entails that subordinates know and accept objectives and operational strategies. Subordinates also need to understand superiors' expectations and leaders and managers must when possible reward positive behavior.

WHY LEADERS FAIL

The previous discussion of theories and methods of leadership—some of which were developed decades ago—is intended to help managers and supervisors avoid failure. In today's stop-and-go, ever dangerous, litigation-vulnerable world of policing, the price paid for incompetent leadership is too high; there is little room for error. Moreover, it means that we must not depend on on-the-job-training but must develop our leaders before they are placed in leadership positions. This means we must implement promotion systems that identify those who can assume the duties of leaders and managers. It also means that we need to continually increase and broaden their responsibilities so that they can learn. Finally, it means that we must constantly provide our leaders training so that they can assume new responsibility when they are promoted.

Some of the above sections described typologies of leaders, executives, and sergeants. It is obvious as a result of this discussion that there are some styles of leadership that are inappropriate in law enforcement. Again, we must select leaders and managers who can and will do the job.

Finally, Steven Brown provided a list of 13 fatal errors that can erode a leader's effectiveness:[54]

1. Refuse to accept personal accountability
2. Fail to develop people in the absence of the leader
3. Try to control results instead of activities
4. Join the wrong crowd
5. Manage everyone in the same way
6. Forget the importance of service
7. Concentrate on problems rather than objectives
8. Be a buddy, not a boss
9. Fail to set standards
10. Fail to train subordinates
11. Condone incompetence
12. Recognize only top performers
13. Try to manipulate people

A number of pitfalls are waiting for the police supervisor or manager. Being a good leader entails a great deal of hard work. The best leaders are those who are actively involved with their subordinates and the department. They have a vision of where they are going, and they adhere to a set of values to guide their actions.

Summary

This chapter has examined several management theories that are of interest to leaders and managers, including what motivates employees, theories of leadership, and quality leadership. In addition to covering these theories, we discussed the importance of empowering employees, how to think and act strategically. Leadership is not simple; it is a complex and ongoing endeavor. Many leaders fail to display proper or proven leadership skills on a continuous basis. Leadership is an organizational constant and should never be neglected.

It should be remembered that all of these elements and issues of leadership and management revolve around one very important feature of the workplace: people. The major point being emphasized in this chapter may well be that leaders and managers must know their people, and how to motivate them. To be effective in the labor-intensive field of policing, superior officers should first learn all they can about this most valuable asset, just as much as they must learn about agency policies and procedures and new technology. Effective leaders are made, not born; thus, they must also receive the requisite training and education for performing well. An educated approach is far better than simply marching the new leader off the plank, to either sink or swim.

Discussion Questions

1. What is the zone of indifference and why is it important?
2. Contrast what is meant by "leader" versus "manager."
3. Describe situational leadership and how it applies to the police leader.
4. Review some of the ways in which a manager can increase his or her personal power.
5. Explain how and why a police leader would empower his or her subordinates.
6. How would Mintzberg's model for chief executives apply to chiefs of police, sheriffs, and their middle managers?
7. Review how one must first think strategically in order to manage the organization in a strategic manner.
8. There are a number of theories of motivation. How might these theories be applied in the police setting?
9. Explain what Heifetz meant by "adaptive change," including its four principles, and how it applies to police supervision and management.
10. Delineate several ways in which a leader can fail, and how failure can be avoided.

Internet Investigations

Police Executive Research Forum, "Future Trends in Policing"
http://www.policeforum.org/assets/docs/Free_Online_Documents/Leadership/future%20trends%20in%20policing%202014.pdf

National Institute of Justice, "How Police Supervisory Styles Influence Patrol Officer Behavior"
https://www.ncjrs.gov/pdffiles1/nij/194078.pdf

FBI, "Improving Motivation and Productivity of Police Officers"
https://leb.fbi.gov/2015/august/improving-motivation-and-productivity-of-police-officers

International Association of Chiefs of Police, "Strategic Planning"
http://www.theiacp.org/portals/0/pdfs/bp-strategicplanning.pdf

University of San Diego, "What Style of Police Leadership Is Most Effective?"
https://onlinedegrees.sandiego.edu/what-style-police-leadership-most-effective/

CHAPTER 4

Communication, Negotiation, and Conflict Resolution

STUDENT LEARNING OUTCOMES:

After reading this chapter, the student will:

- understand the communication process, including types of formal and informal communication
- know the major barriers to effective communication, including problems with electronic methods of communicating
- better understand the unique nature of police communications, specifically their jargon and codes
- know how police use negotiations to effectively communicate ideas and information in order to gain greater compliance to orders and directives
- understand the nature of organizational and group conflict
- be able to effectively mediate conflict when it occurs

KEY TERMS AND CONCEPTS

- Accommodation
- Ambiguity over authority
- Annual report
- Assertiveness
- Avoidance
- Collaboration
- Communication
- Communications channel
- Competition
- Competition over resources
- Compromise
- Conflict resolution
- Cooperativeness
- Decode
- Distrust
- Encode
- Failure to properly communicate
- Faulty attributes
- Feedback
- Formal communications
- Grapevine
- Grudge
- Informal communications

- Internet homepage
- Intergroup conflict
- Interorganizational conflict
- Interpersonal conflict
- Intrapersonal conflict
- Media relations
- Medium
- Negotiation
- Noise
- Organizational conflict
- Organizational reward system
- Perceptual problems
- Personal characteristics
- Physical barriers
- Power differential
- Pre-negotiation stage
- Public information officer
- Semantic problems
- Social media
- Status
- Stereotyping
- Value judgments

INTRODUCTION

Communication is obviously very important in every segment of our society, including law enforcement. Police officers, especially less experienced officers, do not understand the importance of communications, especially written communications skills necessary in report writing. They see writing traffic citations and making arrests as being more important. They do not understand that a conviction of a felon often depends on the quality of the crime or arrest report; prosecutors, defense attorneys as well as judges often scrutinize these reports, and a bad or poorly written report can be used to impeach an officer's testimony.

All of police work is coordinated and conducted through some form of communication, be it verbal or written. Police officers, regardless of rank, spend a significant portion of a workday communicating with citizens, other officers, other government agencies, or superiors. Essentially, police departments run on information and communications. It is also critical that officers learn communications skills in light of the importance of working with the community and understanding and solving problems. Police officers are at a significant disadvantage when they cannot communicate effectively.

A companion process to communication is **negotiation**. A good police leader must be skilled in negotiations. When we think of negotiations, we think of people attempting to work out a problem when there is appreciable disagreement. However, negotiation actually occurs in most communications, be it negotiating with a police union or a police chief negotiating with another city agency such as child protection services to have social workers available to assist police officers when they deal with domestic violence involving children. Moreover, a police chief can issue an order, but it will not necessarily be followed unless it is accepted and understood. Negotiation legitimizes the order, while communications skills transmit it clearly to subordinates. Therefore, to some extent, negotiation is the art of gaining compliance or selling people on an idea.

The chapter opens with a general look at the communication process, including barriers to effective communication. We then look at police communications specifically. Next, we examine the art of negotiating, including various approaches and tactics, and then turn to conflict—its nature, levels, and sources, and how to cope with it. We also provide a discussion on employee counseling, which is a form of negotiation.

THE ACT OF COMMUNICATING

A Large Part of the Workday

Communication is a complex process. Indeed, communications, formal or informal, written or verbal, serve to link people and activities. We use a variety of technologies and social media to communicate, including smart telephones, fax machines, the Internet, texting, Facebook, Twitter, and police computers and radios. The power of these tools was demonstrated in the most recent presidential election by candidate Donald Trump, who utilized Twitter to battle the media and communicate with the public at large. These new tools for communications are being used by police agencies to enhance their crime control and prevention efforts as well as inform and educate the public about police events and availability of resources. Yet, people seldom give much thought to how they communicate and the content of their communications. When there are errors in communication, or when information is not communicated effectively, a greater probability exists that those receiving the information will not fully grasp the meaning of the communication. Proper communication essentially serves to make a group of workers into a team and provides a means to coordinate people and work.

Several studies have examined the amount of communications in the police department. Mayo found that police executives spent about 70 percent of their time communicating, with the overwhelming majority of their communication occurring in meetings.[1] A substantial amount of communication occurs at all levels of the organization. Supervisors communicate with a variety of people at all levels of the department. More and Wegener reported that about 55 percent of supervisors' communications is with subordinates. Approximately 26 percent of their communications is with superiors in the department, while only 4 percent is with other supervisors. Only 15 percent of a supervisor's communications is with the public. They also examined the tasks performed by sergeants and found that 51 percent of the tasks involved some form of communication. Their statistics indicate that sergeants spend most of their time working with and supervising subordinates.[2]

Another study of supervisors found that they spent about 80 percent of their time communicating. The various types of communication in which they engaged are as follows: 45 percent listening, 30 percent talking, 16 percent reading, and 9 percent writing.[3] It appears that about 39 percent of the time supervisors are communicating to others, and 61 percent of the time someone is communicating to the supervisor. Supervisors spend more time receiving information than providing it. This study indicates that police supervisors are extensively involved in the communication process, and that they communicate with an array of people.

Police officers communicate with individuals in a variety of situations.
Source: Marmaduke St. John/Alamy Stock Photo

THE COMMUNICATION PROCESS

Communication has been defined as "the process by which the sender—a person, group, or organization—transmits some type of information (the message) to another person, group, or organization (the receiver)."[4] Lussier expands this definition by noting that communications occur with the intent to (1) influence, (2) inform, or (3) express feelings or opinions.[5] The act of communicating is a complicated transaction between two or more parties that occurs with the intention of having an impact. In reality, communicating is a complicated process wrought with pitfalls that can lead to mistakes or ineffective communications. Figure 4-1 provides a detailed schematic for communicating and shows how complicated communications really are.

The process begins with the communicator or *sender* wishing to communicate an idea or information to another person(s) or organization. The first step in the communication process is that the sender must **encode** the idea or information—translate it into a form such as writing, language, or nonverbal communication. The encoding process can be difficult, especially if the sender is attempting to communicate complex ideas. Although people may have little difficulty conceptualizing complex ideas, they sometimes have trouble putting them into the proper words or language so that others can understand the full meaning of their ideas. In other

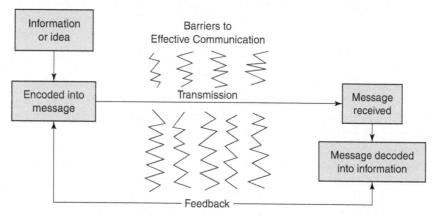

FIGURE 4-1   The Communication Process

instances, the communicator may have difficulty in communicating. That is, some people are restricted by a limited vocabulary or their understanding of language.

Once a message has been encoded, the sender must select a **communications channel** through which a message is transmitted or sent to the recipients. The primary communications channels are formal and informal. Within these two channels, communications can be written, verbal, and nonverbal. **Formal communications** are the official transmissions of information in the organization, and they generally follow the police department's chain of command or organizational chart. Formal communications generally are written in the form of letters, memoranda, e-mails, or orders. **Informal communications** are usually oral and are used to convey a variety of official and unofficial information throughout the department. Formal and informal communications are discussed below.

When deciding on the channel to use, the communicator also selects a medium. **Medium** refers to the manner in which the message is sent. It may be written and sent in the form of an e-mail or policy, or it may be verbal at a meeting, on the telephone, or through a one-on-one conversation. It is important to select the proper medium when communicating. For example, if a lieutenant wants to discuss staffing problems with his or her sergeants, a face-to-face meeting would be more effective than an e-mail or a telephone call.

Once information is transmitted to *a recipient*, the recipient must **decode** the message, or conceptually translate the information into meaningful knowledge. When people receive new information, they typically give it meaning by comparing it with past experiences and knowledge, which can be either a help or a hindrance. The receiver may have difficulty internalizing its full implication or, in the worst case, may reject it entirely.

It is important that the receiver have the same conceptual impression of the information as that envisioned by the individual transmitting the message. If inconsistencies occur, then the desired information has not been fully internalized. One way of ensuring full internalization is **feedback**: the process whereby the sender initiates additional two-way communications to test the receiver's comprehension and understanding of the information communicated. Feedback serves to ensure that everyone received the correct information. The level of feedback should increase (1) as the content of messages becomes more complex, (2) when it is critical that receivers have the information, (3) when the information is drastically different from past information or operating procedures, and (4) when there are disruptions in the communication process itself. The police leader has the responsibility for ensuring that information is properly exchanged.

Formal and Informal Communications

Formal and informal communications, discussed briefly earlier, can be written or verbal. Generally, however, formal communications are written, while informal communications are verbal. Written communications allow all participants to have a permanent record of the communication. This may be important at a future time when the people involved in the communications must refresh their recollection of the transaction. Also, as an official document, written communications have weight or authority requiring a measure of action or response. The problem with written communication is that it is sometimes difficult for people to reduce complex issues into writing, and there is no two-way communication or feedback to ensure that the message was fully comprehended.

Formal communications generally flow downward, although feedback and information about problems and issues are sometimes transmitted upward by subordinates. Katz and Kahn found that downward communications fall into one of five categories: (1) job instructions, (2) rationale or explanations about jobs, (3) procedures, practices, and policies, (4) feedback on individual performance, and (5) efforts to encourage a sense of mission and dedication toward departmental goals.[6] Police agencies operate on policies and procedures that guide officers in how to properly perform their duties and responsibilities. In the past, these policies and procedures were voluminous and filled several large binders for which each officer was responsible. Today, officers can access all the agency policies and procedures via a computer, mobile data terminal in their vehicle, or smart phone. Official communications serve a variety of purposes for managers and supervisors. An example would be a patrol division captain who observes problems with offense reports being submitted late by officers; the captain then writes an e-mail to his lieutenants and sergeants informing them that all such reports must be turned in to and reviewed by a supervisor by the end of the shift.

Informal communications are generally accomplished via conversations and informal notes. For example, a supervisor on a shift may leave a note for a supervisor on the following shift to have the officers check a residence because of reports of prowlers or suspicious persons. In this example, although the note is an informal communication, it is being used in an official capacity. By leaving a note, the supervisor is able to communicate rapidly and effectively without going through the chain of command. Instead of leaving a note, the supervisor

FOCUS ON: SEATTLE POLICE DEPARTMENT'S SOCIAL MEDIA POLICY

Seattle Police Chief Kathleen Toole announced on February, 20, 2015, a new social media policy that clearly identifies her expectations for professional conduct on social media. Department Directive 15-00007, 5.125—Social Media provides guidance regarding the department's official use of social media as well as employees' personal use of social media. It specifically addresses a number of digital communication platforms, including social networking sites, microblogging sites, photo

and video-sharing sites, wikis, blogs, and news sites. Social media apps include Facebook, Twitter, Instagram, YouTube, Reddit, Tumbler, and others. The policy outlines the agency's use of social media for public affairs, investigations, and employee personal use.

Source: Based on Seattle.gov, Seattle Crime News: SPD Blotter http://spdblotter.seattle.gov/2015/02/20/chief-otoole -announces-new-social-media-policy/

could have waited for the next shift supervisor to tell him or her directly about the problem. This face-to-face conversation would have allowed the sergeant to fully explain what had happened and what actions the sergeant took. In essence, informal communications can be used for formal or informal purposes. They allow officers to communicate rapidly.

Informal communications typically consist of "interpersonal networking"[7] and quasi-formal exchanges of information between coworkers occurring most frequently in the informal organization or work group. Such exchanges typically use verbal and nonverbal communications. Oftentimes, members of an organization find that formal communications are inadequate for accomplishing communications activities. When this occurs, people tend to use informal networks through which they contact others to obtain official information, or they work unofficially with others to solve problems. For example, officers will use informal communications to get information about a new commander and his or her priorities and dealings with subordinates.

Informal communications essentially allow information to flow more freely and rapidly. In a study of excellent organizations, increased levels of informal communications were associated with organizational success.[8] Indeed, managers and supervisors who can rapidly gain information or discuss problems with subordinates and other managers throughout the police department have an important advantage.

Another type of informal communications is rumors, or the **grapevine**, so termed because it zigzags back and forth across organizations like a grapevine. There is probably *no* type of organization in our society that has more grapevine information than that found in police agencies. Policing is a 24-hour per day, 7-day per week occupation, so rumors are easily carried from one shift to the next as officers discuss issues such as pay raises, assignments, new policies or procedures, and other matters that affect them at work or at home.

Although it may carry many falsehoods, cynicism, and employee malice, the grapevine has several potential benefits, including that it is fast; it operates mostly at the place of work; and it supplements regular, formal communication. It can be a tool for management to get a feel for employees' attitudes, to spread useful information, and to help employees vent their frustrations. Without a doubt, the grapevine is a force for supervisors to reckon with on a daily basis. Some officers initiate false information in the grapevine to cause dissension or disruptions in the formal organization. Efforts should be made to monitor the information being communicated informally in the work group and take measures to ensure that false information does not result in problems in work group performance.

BARRIERS TO EFFECTIVE COMMUNICATION

The act of communicating occurs under a variety of circumstances. For example, a lieutenant may be coordinating a crime scene where he or she must communicate to subordinates while maintaining the integrity of the scene, keeping witnesses separated, and providing assistance to injured persons. It is extremely difficult for the lieutenant to effectively communicate to all the sergeants, officers, and civilians in this situation. The lieutenant must ensure that everyone receives the appropriate orders or directions.

Many distractions can occur in any type of situation. Such distractions are commonly referred to as **noise**, which is anything that disrupts the communication process.[9] The different types of noise that the supervisor should be aware of when communicating are discussed in the following sections.

Perceptual Problems

Perceptual problems occur when either the sender's or the receiver's perception of the other affects how the message is sent or received. One such perceptual problem is **status**. To a great extent, people judge the significance and accuracy of information by the status and ability of the sender. Information from an assistant chief will be received differently from information that is given by a lieutenant, even though both officers provide their receivers with accurate information. All information should be evaluated on its own merits. Another perceptual problem is **stereotyping**: Judgments are made about communications because of the sender's traits or qualities. For example, it is assumed that a police union leader and a police captain would likely interpret the same information differently, because of their relative orientations about the department. The information should be given due consideration, regardless of from where it emanated.

A third perceptual problem is the **value judgments** people make about information. If the information is consistent with old information or values, it generally is given more credibility. If it is not, receivers sometimes have difficulty accepting or internalizing it. Police managers should take extra precautions when attempting to communicate new or radically different information. Accuracy of the receiver's understanding of the information can best be evaluated via feedback.

A fourth perceptual problem involves semantics. **Semantic problems** refer to instances when the receiver improperly decodes a message because symbols or verbiage used by the sender is interpreted differently by the receiver. A simple comma can change the meaning of a sentence or communication. Consider these two sentences and differences in their meaning. Let's eat, mom or Let's eat mom. The second sentence is certainly direr for mom. Certain words have different meanings to different people. Semantic problems can be overcome through the feedback process or by restating the same information several times. Semantic problems perhaps are the most difficult problems to detect in the communication process, especially when there is no feedback.

Physical Barriers

Physical barriers to communication are those attributes and activities in the immediate environment that interfere with or detract from the communication process. If police officers are spread over a wide area, it is more

Police officers are faced with an assortment of situations in which they communicate with the public.
Source: David Grossman/Alamy Stock Photo

difficult to communicate effectively with them. It is distracting when a sergeant tries to counsel subordinates in an office while answering the telephone. Officers may experience difficulty in accurately receiving a radio message while operating their police vehicle. Every effort should be made to ensure that communications are free of barriers. When barriers do exist, the sender should delay communicating or take special precautions to ensure that receivers obtain information correctly.

This discussion illustrates that communicating is a complicated process and that the person communicating a message should give careful consideration to how to convey the message. The following elements should be considered prior to communicating:

1. The sender's purpose
2. The sender's and receiver's positions in the department, perceptions, and listening skills
3. The content of the message
4. Available methods for sending the message
5. Possible interpretations of the message and its content
6. The sender's desired results

COMMUNICATING VIA TEXTING AND E-MAIL

Certainly, the ubiquitous text messaging and e-mail systems of communication can and does present a barrier to effective communications, a problem that is greatly exacerbated by persons trying to operate a motor vehicle while sending a text message, which is illegal in many states. For the most part, radio communications is safer and more effective as compared to electronic communications when communicating to officers in vehicles since the radio allows for feedback. This is especially true when communicating to officers who are operating police vehicles.

These shortcomings become potentially more critical in police work, where people's lives—both inside and outside the department—stand to be seriously affected by poor communications. People in policing must remember, therefore, to express themselves very carefully in e-mail and text messages. It is important that police officers should select the proper medium when communicating.

Police officials frequently hold press conferences to inform the public.
Source: ZUMA Press, Inc/Alamy Stock Photo

MEDIA RELATIONS

Communicating in a police department is critical to controlling and coordinating all activities performed by the department's members. These communications travel up and down the chain of command. They also travel horizontally from one unit to another or to individual officers. Another important constituency is the news media. **Media relations** are defined as the information provided to the news media and the relationship between the police department and the news media.

News dissemination is a delicate undertaking for the police; news organizations, especially the television and print media, are highly competitive businesses that seek to obtain the most complete news in the shortest amount of time, which often translates to wider viewership and therefore greater advertising revenues for them. The media must appreciate that a criminal investigation can be seriously compromised by premature or excessive coverage. On the other hand, the public has a right to know what is occurring in the community, especially as it concerns crime. Therefore, it is prudent to have an open and professional relationship with the media in which each side knows and understands its responsibilities. It is therefore also important that someone in the agency—either the chief executive, his/her designee, or a trained **Public Information Officer** (PIO)—knows how to perform public speaking and what kinds and how much information they should divulge to media outlets.

Unfortunately, many police executives can speak of the results of failing to develop an appropriate relationship with the media. Negative relations often result in criticism of the police chief and the department. One example is a former police chief in a medium-sized western city who sported a bumper sticker on his vehicle stating "I don't trust the liberal media." This action obviously did not endear him to the local newspaper, nor did it help him in editorials and articles when an issue concerning his involvement in a sexual harassment allegation became public, and he ultimately resigned. This chief obviously did not recognize the power of the pen, and that you "Don't argue with someone who buys his ink by the barrel!"

Certainly every police agency, large or small, should have a written media policy that is grounded on certain basic precepts:

- Never lie or embellish a story; do not refuse to talk with media representatives.
- Never slowly release details of a story in tiny scraps, because the media may assume that the police are hiding something.
- Do not lash out at the press; it only makes matters worse.
- Do not try to shift the blame unnecessarily; if the agency was responsible for something going wrong, assume accountability for it.
- Look at the big picture; avoid making bad news bigger by dwelling on scandals, faults, mistakes, and other embarrassments.
- Honor your promises. For example, if you tell a reporter "I'll get back to you," be sure to do so.
- Remember that the best news is that bad news really will pass, and soon there are sunny days.[10]

A media policy should stress to the individual officers that their interaction with an individual reporter, either positive or negative, will affect how the entire agency is viewed by the reporter, and possibly the public. A good relationship will help the agency to control what information the public receives and can also help to alleviate the problem of the media hounding detectives and others for updates and information.

Because it is important to "speak with one voice," the agency should also explain to all personnel the proper steps for referring reporters up the chain of command, what the chain is, and where they are on the chain. There are five basic approaches: (1) only the agency head speaks, (2) anyone can speak, (3) the senior ranking officer at the scene can speak, (4) only designated personnel can speak, (5) and only the PIO can speak. Note, too, that the normal chain of command may not be the chain of command when dealing with the media; a rank-and-file officer may be designated as the PIO and can be the next step in the chain as opposed to a detective or higher-ranking officer.[11]

Police departments are not at the mercy of the media when the media unfairly and incorrectly spins a story to criticize the police. The police need the media to provide information to the public, but at the same time, the media needs the police since crime news is a primary driver of local news. Police departments, through the police chief or PIO, should hold the media accountable and push back when stories are incorrect. Reporters and their superiors should be contacted and called out when this occurs. There have been instances where police chiefs have denied reporters from a media outlet access to the department when reporting was unfair. This is dramatic, but a police department should not tolerate unfair attacks from a media outlet.

Nowhere is it written on the officer's badge or pocket Miranda card that dealing with the press will always be easy or that the news they have to share will always be positive. However, in adhering to the above guidelines, the specter of agency "bad press" will hopefully be held at bay.

YOU DECIDE...

You are a sergeant in a small police department that has 30 sworn personnel. The department has a new chief who wants to work more closely with the community. When she was hired, she advised the city council that she was going to be transparent and provide more information to the community. Once a week she goes on the local radio station for a call in show. As a result of the call in show, she sees that many people in the community do not understand what the police department does or the services it provides. She also found that many people believe that the crime rates are much worse in the city and are climbing, a fact that is not born out in the actual crime statistics. Consequently, she has decided that the department needs a webpage to better inform the public. She has assigned the responsibility for designing the webpage to you. She wants the webpage to inform the public and improve public relations. More importantly, she wants to have material on the webpage that will reduce the fear of crime in the community. She has someone who will develop the webpage, but you must provide them with the materials.

Questions for Discussion

1. What kinds of general information will you post on the new webpage?
1. How will you address the crime issues?
2. What kinds of materials will you post in an effort to develop better relations with the community?

POLICE DEPARTMENTS AND SOCIAL MEDIA

Today, **social media** plays an important, extensive role in society. As noted above, there are numerous platforms by which people now communicate, including Facebook, Twitter, Instagram, LinkedIn, Tumblr, YouTube, Snapchat, and so on. Social media is deeply embedded in our culture. Countless people constantly monitor and communicate on their multiple social media accounts. Large, medium, and many small police departments now use social media accounts to communicate with the public. Social media now assists police departments in numerous ways. Particularly, departments can use social media to advise the public about new departmental programs, emerging crime problems, what the department is doing about problems in the jurisdiction or in neighborhoods.

The most common social media tool used by police departments is an **Internet homepage,** and they are an excellent medium by which to communicate with the public. Homepages potentially reach more people as compared to traditional media outlets. These homepages contain all sorts of information. Figure 4-2 provides a listing of some on the information commonly found on police homepages.

Rosenbaum and his colleagues examined police homepages. They found that 42 percent of the departments in their national study had homepages. These homepages emphasized providing information to the public

Department Information
    History of the department
    Department organization
    Command staff and other key personnel
    Precinct and beat configuration
    How to contact the department
    How to apply for job with the department
Crime Information
    Crime maps for neighborhoods
    Police blotter or arrestee information
    Information on crime trends
    How to report a crime
    Crime prevention tips
    Information about wanted persons
Police–Public Relations
    Human interest stories about police officers
    Human interest stories about victims and heroes in the community
    Department mission statement and value statements
    Public safety information
    Changes in the department

FIGURE 4-2   Content of Police Homepages

FOCUS ON: FARGO POLICE DEPARTMENT'S USE OF EMOJI'S IN TWEETS

The Fargo North Dakota police department found the use of popular emojis depicting police cars, telephone, smiley police faces, and keys as an innovative way to tweet crime prevention tips and other information to the public. Overuse led the police department to suspend its use of emojis in most tweets.

Source: Based on Fargo Police Department will scale back on emojis in social media posts by Kevin Wallevand Dec 23, 2016. Retrieved from http://www.wday.com/news/4186234-fargo-police-department-will-scale-back-emojis-social-media-posts

---

and to a lesser extent to allow the public to provide the departments with information. This transparency helps to keep the public informed, which encourages better relations with the community.

They found that cities that were committed to community policing were more transparent as opposed to departments that were not community policing oriented. The community policing agencies also used their homepages to solicit information from the public as compared to non-community policing departments.[12] Feedback from citizens through a department's homepage allows departments to develop a better understanding of community problems and attitudes. This trend demonstrates that a commitment to community policing can filter throughout a department.

Another important information tool is the department's **annual report** that is generally posted on a department's homepage. Annual reports provide a comprehensive view of departments. They contain most of the information outlined in Figure 4-2, but they often are more exhaustive, providing in-depth stories about department staff and the department. For example, when a department includes a section on its drug unit, it may include information about the unit's commander, types of operations, the number of arrests, quantities of drugs that the department seized, types of drugs that are present in the community, tips about preventing drug abuse, and so on. These reports often have a wealth of information that is of interest to the community.

Many police departments are now using social media to inform the public. In one recent study, it was reported that 75 percent of the largest departments used at least one social media platform.[13] Some departments are using it sparingly as a result of the department's conservative culture, and when they do use it, Twitter is used to reinforce traditional methods of communications.[14] Twitter and similar platforms allow a department to have instant communications with the public, providing information on crimes, crime trends, and wanted persons.

The Boston Police Department's use of Twitter during the Boston Marathon bombing in 2013 shows how useful a medium like twitter can be. The police department used twitter to inform the public about the ongoing investigation, calm nerves and request assistance, correct mistaken information reported by the press, and ask for public restraint. These actions assisted the police in locating the suspects, and they helped calm Boston's citizens during this traumatic event.[15] Social media can be an extremely useful tool especially when there is a major event such as the marathon bombing, floods, tornados, and other natural or man-made disasters. Departments can use social media to inform the public of lesser problems such as road closures, accidents, and crimes in progress. When police departments provide useful information to the public, more people join the department's social network.

Police departments, where possible, should monitor social media. Social media can provide valuable feedback about problems in the community. For example, if a particular incident is receiving significant coverage on social media, the department can more rapidly respond and defuse the situation. In some cases, specific crime or traffic problems can be identified. Social media is a valuable resource to get input from the public about the department and its operations.

THE ART OF NEGOTIATING

Negotiation is a form of communicating, and is defined as "the collaborative pursuit of joint gains and a collaborative effort to create value where none previously existed."[16] The ability to effectively negotiate with others is an important characteristic, and it essentially consists of effectively communicating with other people. Negotiations play a key role when management and employees attempt to agree on a new contract or working conditions; when the police chief negotiates a new budget with the city council; or when a detective captain and a patrol captain attempt to improve working relationships. Negotiations require that the two sides communicate until an agreement is reached. When the two sides negotiate effectively, they are more likely to arrive at a mutually acceptable or win-win agreement.

When a group of people discuss an issue, there likely will be conflict or disagreement. For example, officers often disagree with departmental policies regarding pursuit driving, arrest procedures, or dealing with citizens. Racial profiling is a primary example. Police agencies often examine officers' actions in terms of their effects on public relations and community support, while officers tend to emphasize their law enforcement role.

Officers resent that their patrol stops and citations are being reviewed for racial profiling patterns. The inability of leadership to successfully resolve these concerns can devastate officer morale. Communication and negotiations are sometimes necessary to ensure that policies and actions are properly balanced. Situational leadership, as discussed in Chapter 3, plays a key role in getting things done, and managers and supervisors must learn to apply various leadership styles to different situations. This is a key part of negotiating.

One can easily see the need for negotiation skills when dealing with the public. For example, when a police officer encounters a domestic violence situation or a barroom fight, the situation is best handled when the officer can talk or negotiate the combatants into submission. Negotiation is an important tool that is used in a variety of situations.

Effective negotiations occur when issues of substance are resolved and the working relationships among the negotiating parties are improved or at least not harmed.[17] Because negotiations sometimes occur over an extended period of time, it is critical that the parties attempt to maintain good working relationships. It is not in the interest of a particular side to decimate the other side, because they likely will meet again in a similar situation. All parties should attempt to achieve a win-win outcome where all parties are at least satisfied with the outcome.

The Pre-Negotiation Stage

Negotiation is a process that occurs in steps; the first is the **pre-negotiation stage**. Negotiators must prepare themselves in advance. Three important elements comprise the pre-negotiation stage. First, the negotiator must fully understand what is at issue. In some cases, this is rather simple, such as whether or not space is available in the training schedule for personnel to receive training. But when the issues are complex, as is often the case in collective bargaining, it may be a fairly difficult task to come to some understanding about what is at stake. The successful negotiator is able to ferret out the real issues when conflict occurs.

Second, it is important for the negotiator to be empathetic and understand the other side's position. In some cases, officers may be making demands that are unachievable, or they may not be feasible because of budget constraints or personnel limitations. In other cases, however, officers may be making demands as a result of a problem that adversely affects their ability to perform their assigned duties. For example, officers may complain about how beats are configured. Some officers may be overworked as a result of beat boundaries, while others have too little to do. Thus, it is important for the patrol commander to be thoroughly familiar with officers' concerns before attempting to address them.

Third, the successful negotiator understands all the options before sitting down to negotiate. For example, if a chief is aware that officers are upset about a particular policy, then the chief should research the issues prior to discussing it. A new departmental policy may prohibit officers from eating meals outside their beats. For officers working early morning hours or in a rural area, this policy might pose a major problem, especially if there are no restaurants on their beat and their home is outside the beat area. A thorough understanding of all the issues is a critical part of negotiating.

Personal Factors Affecting Negotiations

Cohen examined successful negotiations and identified three important factors that identify a successful negotiator: power, time, and information.[18] *Power* refers to the negotiator's ability to influence or have an impact on the other side. Power can be used in a positive or negative way. Rewards often are greater motivators than the threat of punishment. Further, power in negotiations does not necessarily refer to the power derived from one's position. Other sources of power include technical expertise or association with other powerful individuals in the department, as discussed in Chapter 3.

Time is also an important factor in that extended negotiations can exacerbate conflict. Sometimes it is best to extend negotiations, however. This allows tempers to cool. For example, if some officers are upset over a new policy, it is perhaps best to discuss it with them after they have had time to think about it. In some cases, the issue becomes less important over time. The good negotiator understands time and uses it to his or her advantage.

Finally, *information* is the most important tool when negotiating. When people are knowledgeable about an issue, they are in a better position to negotiate. Often knowledge disarms adversaries since a great deal of conflict often is the result of misunderstandings or misinformation. Knowledge also allows parties to consider more alternatives or solutions to an issue.

Guidelines for Conducting Negotiations

Although every negotiation will proceed differently, some general guidelines may be helpful. These are listed in Figure 4-3.[19]

These guidelines can assist the supervisor when negotiating with subordinates, peers, or superiors.

1. Have and understand your objectives. This includes the rationale for the objectives and their relative importance.
2. Do not hurry when negotiating. Information is far more important than time, and information is lost when negotiating is hastily done.
3. When there is doubt, consult others for the facts. It often is extremely difficult to break agreements that are the result of negotiations.
4. Ensure that you have access to supporting documentation and data as the negotiations become more formal.
5. Maintain some measure of flexibility in your position.
6. Attempt to discover the driving force behind the other side's request.
7. Do not become deadlocked over minutiae or some singular point.
8. Ensure that you allow room for your opponent to save face. Total defeat of an opponent leads to long-term resentment and future problems.
9. Focus on listening throughout the negotiating, and pay close attention to the other side.
10. Make sure that your emotions are controlled, regardless of how the negotiations proceed.
11. During the negotiations process, ensure that you listen and consider every word. Nail down statements into precise, understood language.
12. Try to understand your opponents.

FIGURE 4-3 Negotiation Guidelines

Negotiation by Police Managers and Supervisors

Police managers and supervisors must constantly negotiate with their subordinates and be able to ensure their maximum compliance with orders, directives, and assignments. In some cases, orders are clearly within the bounds of reason and the purview of the superior's authority. In these cases, the orders generally are unquestioned. In some cases, however, the superior may issue an order that is not understood or is outside the range of past practices, and the subordinate may come to question it. For example, while a sergeant can order an officer to perform certain tasks, it is generally more effective if a consensus is reached, and a consensus can normally be reached only through discussion and negotiation. A supervisor is better able to induce voluntary compliance when he or she is able to negotiate effectively. The exception would be emergencies or critical incidents, when the officer is expected to follow orders without delay.

Police supervisors also must often negotiate with their superiors and peers. They must argue their case when there are personnel shortages, when members of the unit are given too many responsibilities, or when the unit needs new equipment. Negotiation skills allow leaders to better present their case and ultimately be more successful.

Conflict between units over assignments sometimes occurs, resulting in managers and supervisors having to negotiate with peers about working conditions. For example, officers engaged in community policing projects may work contrary to patrol or investigative operations. Detectives and patrol officers sometimes have disputes over cases and arrests. When such conflicts occur, they must be negotiated and resolved.

It becomes even more evident that negotiation is important when we consider the nature of police work. Police officers are often called on to engage in activities that are perceived as being less important or not as prestigious as other tasks. For example, most police officers would rather investigate a homicide or robbery than direct traffic after a high school football game. Directing traffic is not as interesting, nor will it reap the same amount of prestige or publicity that a successful homicide investigation might bring to the officer. Nonetheless, directing traffic is a vital function to be performed by the police department. Indeed, there are many more mundane tasks for officers than there are exciting ones. Yet, all of these tasks must be performed effectively. Without a doubt, the efforts of superior officers, regardless of rank, must possess negotiation skills to increase the probability that officers will perform these tasks more effectively.

YOU DECIDE...

In recent months it has become increasingly apparent to your deputy chief of operations that the watch commanders (lieutenants) and, by extension, sergeants are not communicating, coordinating, or cooperating well toward meeting the organization's mission and goals. Specifically, three central issues are at the core of the matter:

1. Several patrol lieutenants have recently been attempting to improve the quality of officers' reports by rejecting those that are deemed unacceptable. Other lieutenants have taken the view that, with all of the other pressures on officers to perform, this concern about reports is far too "nitpicky."

2. Six months ago all patrol vehicles in the department were equipped with mobile data computers (MDCs)

to improve officer efficiency in the field and to relieve the burden on the communications section. Now, however, it is clear that differences of opinion exist about when it is practical and appropriate to use the MDCs; the deputy chief has learned that officers are in fact using them infrequently in the field, and practically never during traffic stops. This has naturally resulted in a heavy burden being placed again on communications. Some lieutenants have differences of opinion about when/how MDCs should be used.

3. Due to the above two issues, both sergeants and patrol officers, perceiving the differences in how lieutenants view the matters, have been "shopping" for lieutenants who are more "sensitive" to their side, and have them approve their reports.

These are just three examples of several where watch commanders are not communicating or working well together. This is the *overarching* problem, resulting in increased animosity between lieutenants and decreasing consistency between shifts. Clearly, the need exists for

greater strength and consensus among mid-level managers. In sum, each lieutenant is either part of the problem or a part of the solution.

Questions for Discussion

1. Using the information provided, follow the steps below to evaluate the problem and make suggestions for ways to resolve the problem. You are encouraged to think outside the box and include *all* levels of command in your assessment and suggestions.
   A. Evaluate the overall problem. Be specific and concise as to what are the causal factors.
   B. Write an impact statement. Tell how these specific problems if left unchecked can have wide-ranging negative consequences throughout the agency.
   C. Recommend change. Be explicit as to what you feel must be done to rectify the problems, especially as they relate to interaction between management, supervisory, and rank-and-file personnel.

COPING WITH CONFLICT

Thus far, we have discussed communications and negotiations. This section examines conflict and **conflict resolution**. Communication and negotiation skills are necessary to avoid and resolve conflict. Regardless of the efforts put forth by managers and supervisors, however, conflict erupts. This section describes how best to deal with it.

The Nature of Organizational Conflict

Conflict is a natural phenomenon, occurring in all organizations. **Organizational conflict** is a situation in which two or more people disagree over issues of organizational substance and experience some emotional antagonism with one another.[20] Conflict has four key elements: (1) individuals or groups with opposing interests, (2) acknowledgment that the opposing viewpoints or interests exist, (3) the belief by parties that the other will attempt to deny them their goal or objective, and (4) one or both sides of the conflict have overtly attempted to thwart the other's goals and objectives.[21] These elements require overt action on the part of superiors. In many cases, if conflict is left unresolved or managed, it will affect the productivity of the officers involved in the conflict.

Conflict should be viewed as a continuous process, occurring against a backdrop of relationships and events. Conflict is inevitable when there are people, relationships, and activities. Thus, conflict is not an isolated, short-term event, but rather it is something that managers and supervisors will encounter on a continuing basis. Conflict as a process also affects and involves a variety of people and activities within the organization. It tends to spread and cut across other activities. Finally, it can result from a variety of causes, ranging from personal to professional; personal conflict affects professional relationships just as professional conflict affects personal relationships.[22]

The nature of police work often leads to conflict. Few citizens are pleased when they encounter a police officer, regardless of the nature of the encounter. Such encounters often require intervention and negotiation. In other instances, the police supervisor is seen as the person in the middle who must mediate the impact of departmental policies on subordinate officers. Officers tend to expect supervisors to make policies realistic in their application, while managers expect supervisors to follow policies and procedures explicitly. There are many differences of opinion in a police department that can lead to conflict.

Levels of Conflict

Conflict can occur throughout an organization. For example, two precinct commanders may develop a conflict over resources. Both may need additional officers in order to properly staff their patrol beats. Specialized services such as detention, training, or crime prevention often compete with patrol and criminal investigation for officers. At another level, conflict may develop between detectives and patrol officers when both

The police are often involved in a variety of conflicts.
Source: David Bacon/Alamy Stock Photo

are attempting to solve the same case. Two officers may engage in conflict when they request to work in the same beat or shift. Managers and supervisors should be aware of the conflict swirling around them, since this conflict will likely have some impact on them or their units. With this in mind, conflict can occur at four levels within the agency:

1. *Intrapersonal:* An individual has a conflict within him- or herself.
2. *Interpersonal:* Individuals have a conflict with others in the unit or department.
3. *Intergroup:* Work groups within the organization develop a conflict.
4. *Interorganizational:* Different organizations are at odds as the result of some issue or event.

Intrapersonal conflict occurs when the individual is not content or satisfied with what is occurring in his or her life. The conflict may be work related, such as dissatisfaction with an assignment or potential for promotion. It may also be related to the individual's personal life. An officer may be experiencing problems at home or in some other part of his or her life (police officer stress and wellness). When a supervisor observes changes in a subordinate's demeanor or personality, the change should be investigated and support provided to the officer. Attempts should be made to prevent the problem from affecting work or resulting in overly aggressive behavior when dealing with the public.

Interpersonal conflict occurs when members of the work group have personal disagreements and conflicts with one another. Whenever several people work together, conflict is inevitable. Again, the conflict can be the result of the job or can be personal in nature. For example, some officers may become agitated because they perceive that their work schedule or assignments are not equitable relative to others. They may become threatened by other officers' productivity. Personality conflicts may develop and must be addressed. Often such conflict will not be dealt with by managers or supervisors, who hope that it will dissipate. In most cases, however, if not addressed, interpersonal conflict will only worsen and, ultimately, affect the productivity and collegiality of the work group.

Intergroup conflict occurs when officers in one unit have conflict with the officers in another unit. For example, officers assigned to a community policing unit may come into conflict with patrol officers who see community policing as being unimportant. A planning unit may draft new policies that restrict police officers' involvement in pursuits, which may raise concern by patrol. Decisive action is required when intergroup conflict occurs.

Finally, **interorganizational conflict** occurs when there are problems between the police department and other organizations. Unfortunately, law enforcement is not always the united, amicable, cooperative "family" that outsiders perceive it to be. It is not at all uncommon for a county sheriff's office and a municipal police department in the county to have problems or conflict because of "turf protection." For example, the city police department may resent deputies performing undercover operations in the city without coordinating their efforts. A police department may want to apply a broken windows strategy in a neighborhood and request that the sanitation department help by collecting garbage and trash to clean up the neighborhood, but the sanitation department fails to assist in the project. These interdepartmental problems can adversely affect a department's ability to respond to community needs.

SOURCES OF CONFLICT IN POLICE ORGANIZATIONS

Conflict can occur for a variety of reasons. Most often, it can be categorized as organizational or interpersonal. Greenberg and Baron (1995) have identified a number of causes of conflict, which are shown in Figure 4-4.[23]

Organizational Causes

One source of conflict is **competition over resources**, which occurs when units or sections within a police department compete for personnel, responsibilities, equipment, and other tangibles related to the job. Police departments also compete with other government agencies for these resources. When resources become available, everyone generally attempts to garner as much as possible. Competition for resources inevitably leads to conflict, especially when the parties resort to political measures to obtain their objectives. For example, a commander may go to a member of the city council to lobby for a particular program, bypassing the normal staff decision-making process concerning resource allocation in the department; while not acceptable, this often occurs.

A second source of conflict is **ambiguity over authority**, which refers to instances when two units or supervisors believe they have authority over a situation or personnel. It is similar to a breach in the span of control, discussed in Chapter 2. As an example, detectives will allow patrol officers to do as much work as possible on low-profile cases but immediately take control of high-visibility cases such as sex crimes, homicides, or large drug arrests.

Third, **organizational reward systems** cause conflict. Organizational reward systems consist of tangible and intangible benefits. Tangible benefits include extra pay in the form of overtime or specialists' pay, new equipment, and new vehicles. Intangible benefits include prestige and media exposure. Detectives frequently receive vast amounts of publicity when they solve a major case, while other units, even though they may have been central to the investigation, receive little if any recognition. Because of the nature of their work, some units have more equipment; and some units, such as traffic, may be afforded substantial amounts of overtime. As perceptions of *inequality* increase as a result of a department's reward system, so will job dissatisfaction and conflict. It is almost impossible to have all rewards distributed evenly within a police agency, because of the nature of the work. Efforts should be made, however, to ensure equity in a department's reward system.

Fourth, conflict results when there is a **power differential** within the police department. A power differential refers to some members having more power than others and usually occurs as a result of illegitimate power. For example, the chief may have spent most of his or her career in the traffic unit and

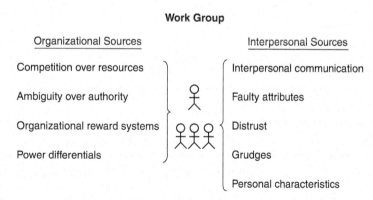

FIGURE 4-4 Causes of Conflict in Organizations

favors that unit over others. Individuals in the organization, because of their assignment, past work record, or personal relationships, may have closer ties with the chief or other high-ranking commanders, affording them higher levels of power and access. Each of these instances can cause conflict within the police organization.

Problems of power differential can occur at all levels of a department. When officers, regardless of rank, believe that they have little input in decisions and that they are not appreciated by the department, they may become frustrated and be more likely to engage in conflict. Power differentials can be negated by engaging all officers in decision-making processes.

Interpersonal Causes

The **failure to properly communicate** is a common interpersonal cause of conflict. The information or message may not be complete, may contain faulty information, or may be communicated in such a way as to antagonize the receiver. Managers and supervisors sometimes do not take the time to ensure that their message is complete or to obtain suitable feedback to ensure that their subordinates clearly understand the message. Managers sometimes fail to consider how a decision will affect their subordinate officers. In other cases, managers and supervisors may be curt or discourteous when communicating to subordinates. These examples show the importance of proper communications, and when effective communications are not used, subordinates may become frustrated, which ultimately leads to conflict.

A second interpersonal cause of organizational conflict is **faulty attributes**—the intentions or rationale for an action is misunderstood by someone who is directed to complete some task. In such cases, the assignment is seen as an act of malevolence rather than a legitimate request. For example, when a detective supervisor requests that a detective recontact some witnesses in a case, the detective may see the request as harassment, while the supervisor may believe that the detective's report contained insufficient information. Faulty communications often lead to faulty attributions in the workplace.

Third, **distrust** creates a great deal of conflict. For example, a substantial amount of distrust exists between some citizens and the police. At the organizational level, officers may distrust other officers or units within the department. Most officers, if not all, distrust officers assigned to the Internal Affairs Unit. Some officers may come to distrust officers working in the domestic violence unit, because at some point a domestic violence unit may have complained because an officer did not make an arrest in a mandatory arrest situation. Officers may come to distrust superiors. An officer may come to distrust a sergeant because the sergeant fails to communicate adequately, to back the officer when there is a problem, to keep a promise about an assignment, or imposes disciplinary action when the officer believes that he or she made an honest mistake. Innumerable situations may result in officers coming to distrust one another. Unfortunately, these situations are seldom addressed and resolved, which leads to festering conflict.

Fourth, people develop and tend to hold **grudges** against others in the department. Grudges can occur in a variety of situations. An officer may withhold information in a case so he or she can make the arrest, or one officer reports another officer's deviant or improper behavior to superiors. Grudges may occur for a variety of reasons. It is important to understand that they may last a number of years, and in some cases, officers never forgive the person toward whom they hold a grudge.

Finally, an officer's **personal characteristics** may lead to conflict. Personal characteristics refer to attributes such as curtness, inability to communicate clearly, a need to pry into others' business or affairs, or being unorganized and often failing to perform adequately. All sorts of people can be labeled as difficult or uncooperative. Generally, it is the nature of their personality that causes them to have difficulties with others. These people are frequently difficult to work with, and the reactions of others to them often antagonize them.

MANAGERS' AND SUPERVISORS' ROLES IN CONFLICT RESOLUTION

Managers and supervisors can choose to deal with conflict using a variety of strategies. Good senior police managers will constantly monitor the supervisors and managers within their command. This entails meeting with and talking with all of them periodically. The effective manager will maintain good communications so that he or she will know what is transpiring within the unit. At the same time, the manager should openly discuss problems with supervisors. In essence, managers should hold supervisors accountable and direct them to resolve problems. Supervisors sometimes avoid intervening in difficult situations. Good managers push supervisors into working with difficult situations.

There is no one way to deal with conflict because it manifests itself in many ways, and a different set of factors is always contributing to it. It is important, however, for the supervisor to be able to recognize conflict when it occurs and quickly take action. As noted earlier, negotiations skills play a key role in conflict resolution. The goal of conflict resolution is to eliminate the causes of conflict and reduce the potential for additional conflict in the future.

Intervention in conflict essentially involves two supervisory skills: cooperativeness and assertiveness.[24] **Cooperativeness** refers to a superior officer's attempts to cooperate with the conflicting parties and work toward a solution. **Assertiveness** is shown when the superior orders or directs combatants to behave in a certain manner, usually in accordance with departmental policies and procedures. Assertiveness does not attempt to alleviate the conflict; rather it attempts to remove its manifestations from the workplace.

Figure 4-5 shows the conflict management grid, which contains five means of addressing conflict, along with corresponding levels of cooperativeness and assertiveness. Perhaps, the most common reaction to conflict is **avoidance**; the superior refuses to recognize its existence and hopes that it simply will go away. Conflict is seldom resolved without intervention on a timely basis; however, and when it is left to its own designs, it will have a negative impact on the conflicting parties and their associates in the work group. Intervention in conflicts is generally difficult, personal, and uncomfortable and can be a highly emotional ordeal that can result in additional conflict between the negotiator and the parties involved. Thus, there is a natural tendency to avoid dealing with conflicts. This, of course, is a mistake since the problem likely will only worsen.

A second strategy for handling conflict is **accommodation**, or smoothing. Accommodation involves minimum intrusion on the part of the superior, who attempts to smooth over differences between those engaged in the conflict. Accommodation requires a high level of cooperativeness and a low level of assertiveness on the part of the superior. The superior does not attempt to assert his or her authority but tries to induce a higher level of cooperativeness. Actual differences are avoided so that harmony may be achieved. A sergeant involved in accommodation would attempt to work more closely with the officers engaged in the conflict. The sergeant would attempt to become more personable, engaging the officers in conversation about departmental and extra-departmental issues. Here, the sergeant would attempt to make the issues at the center of conflict a low priority.

A third conflict resolution strategy is **competition**. The superior intervenes and meets with the combatants, forcing them to present all the facts about the situation and then making a decision. The conflict becomes

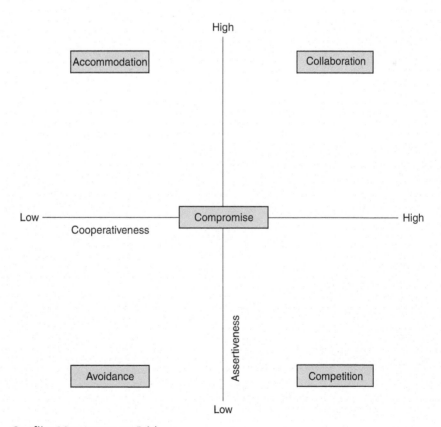

FIGURE 4-5 Conflict Management Grid

a competitive situation with a clear winner and loser. It involves a maximum degree of assertiveness with little or no cooperation on the part of the supervisor. Obviously, this strategy does not resolve the underlying cause of the conflict and may result in its reoccurring at a later time. It should be used only as a last resort.

An example of competition occurs when patrol officers and detectives dispute cases or arrests. On completing a preliminary investigation, patrol officers will generally turn the case over to detectives. When patrol officers make an arrest or are close to making an arrest in a high-profile case, however, they resent giving the case, and its inherent credit, to detectives. Thus, case assignment becomes a "winner take all" proposition unless other accommodations are made. Some departments have resolved this type of situation by allowing patrol officers to work with detectives throughout the follow-up investigation so that credit is shared. This arrangement also provides invaluable experience and training to patrol officers, which ultimately results in improved investigative skills.

A fourth strategy to resolve conflict is **compromise**, which involves a mix of cooperation and assertiveness. The intervening superior officer searches for a solution that satisfies all parties involved in the conflict. It is a process whereby everyone generally gains something, but at the same time it accommodates others. It is essentially a search for a middle ground. Sergeants frequently use compromise when they make the work schedule. They attempt to divide days off and hours worked so that everyone is accommodated to some extent. At the same time, few officers are totally happy with the arrangement.

Finally, conflict resolution can involve **collaboration**. Superior officers attempt to work through problems to fully address everyone's concerns. Sergeants should consult with or involve managers when attempting to solve problems. Managers often have to give their consent to solutions; therefore, it can be fruitful to have them involved in the beginning. Collaboration involves having all parties discuss the issues and look for solutions. Debate helps to clear any impediments and allows participants to understand the other side's issues. Once this occurs, people are more willing to work with one another toward a solution. Collaboration is akin to problem solving when the problem or cause of conflict is identified and removed or solved.

Whenever there is conflict, there likely will be winners and losers. Avoidance and accommodation generally result in lose-lose conflict resolution outcomes because the conflict is never really addressed, and no one really attains his or her objectives. If the conflict is allowed to continue, it will ultimately result in ill feelings that affect work relations for some time.

Competition and compromise strategies generally result in win-lose outcomes, where one side wins and the other side loses. Again, this ending will have negative effects on at least one side of the conflict. Competition and compromise fail to address the root causes of conflict, and even though a temporary solution

YOU DECIDE...

Sergeant "Spike" Jones was recently transferred back to the patrol division after three years in a street crimes unit, where he was involved with numerous high-risk arrests of dangerous offenders. He has built a reputation within the department as being a highly skilled tactical supervisor on the agency's special operations (SWAT) team, and he is also a trainer in special operations and tactics at the regional police academy. For these reasons, Jones's lieutenant was pleased to have him on a patrol team, to impart his knowledge and experiences to the officers and other team sergeants with less experience. Indeed, when Jones first came to the patrol team, the lieutenant praised his accomplishments in front of the other officers and supervisors during roll call briefings. Within a month, however, the lieutenant begins to notice a wide rift developing between Jones, his officers, and other team sergeants. Jones is overheard on several occasions discussing the menial work of patrol, saying it's not "real" police work. He is always trying to impress other supervisors with his experiences; he also says he cannot wait to get out of patrol and into another specialized, high-risk assignments. The other team sergeants complain to the lieutenant that Jones does not fit in.

Questions for Discussion

1. As the lieutenant concerned, how would you mediate the conflict that exists between Sgt. Jones and his team and other shift supervisors?

2. What kinds of strategies can the lieutenant employ to reduce or eliminate the rift?

3. What does the lieutenant need to do with Jones? What kinds of compromises or adjustments does Jones need to make in order to work well with his officers and peers?

can be found, the conflict will probably reoccur. Only collaboration attempts to seek solutions whereby all sides win. Collaboration attempts to impress on all the parties that it is mutually beneficial for a solution that is acceptable to everyone to be identified. Collaboration attempts to engage people in problem solving, and it encourages them to work out differences.

Managers and supervisors may use all of these strategies when dealing with conflict. Obviously, collaboration results in the best outcome, but in some cases the situation and the people involved in the conflict may prohibit the use of a collaborative strategy.

Summary

This chapter has addressed the interpersonal dynamics surrounding organizational communication, the unique forms of police communication, negotiation, and conflict resolution. These activities must be mastered if leaders and managers are to effectively oversee and direct subordinates and activities. Indeed, the chapter revealed that there are a number of barriers to, and problems with, communication that must be accounted for and dealt with. Leadership, to a great extent, involves superiors interacting with people, and the activities discussed in this chapter form a foundation for effective interaction. They allow the superior officer to translate departmental goals and objectives into action.

Communication is the effective transmittal of information, ideas, and directives to others. In order to interact and ensure that departmental goals are fulfilled, a leader must possess good communications skills. Communications, formal or informal, written or verbal, serve to link people and activities. In reality, tasks are accomplished in police organizations through communications.

Likewise, negotiations play an important role in a supervisor's success. To a great extent, successful policing involves reaching a consensus about police goals and objectives. Not everyone agrees with what should be done or how it should be done, however. Negotiation skills are often used to make officers accept or see the importance of following departmental procedures.

Finally, conflict is a natural phenomenon and occurs in all organizations. A substantial amount of conflict is the result of poor communications skills; oftentimes, effective negotiation skills are called on to resolve conflict. The supervisor must understand that conflict is almost always present; it is the nature of organizations and work groups. Steps must be taken to resolve conflict when it exists. This chapter identified a number to ways to accomplish this.

Discussion Questions

1. Describe the communication process. What are the key elements?
2. Explain the barriers to effective communications, including problems with communicating electronically.
3. As the supervisor concerned, how would you mediate the conflict that is developing within your team?
4. What are the types of organizational conflict and its levels and sources?
5. What kinds of strategies can a leader employ to reduce or eliminate the rift that has developed within the team?
6. What does the supervisor need to do with the other team members? What kinds of compromises or adjustments do the team members need to make in order to include Jones as part of their team?
7. What does the supervisor need to do with Jones? What kinds of compromises or adjustments does Jones need to make in order to become a team member?

Internet Investigations

The Law Enforcement Magazine, "Managing Conflict: Bridging the Gap"
http://www.policemag.com/channel/patrol/articles/2004/11/bridging-the-gap.aspx

Effective Justice Solutions, "Implementing Conflict Resolution Processes to Enhance Community-Police Relations: Lessons Learned in Convening Mediations and Dialogues"
http://effectius.com/yahoo_site_admin/assets/docs/Effectius_ImplementingConflictResolutionProcessesToEnhanceCommunity_MonyaKian_Newsletter13.150124543.pdf

University of San Diego, "Police Communication Skills Matter More than Ever: Here's Why"
https://onlinedegrees.sandiego.edu/police-communication-important-today/

Psychology Today, "Active Listening Techniques of Hostage & Crisis Negotiators"
https://www.psychologytoday.com/blog/beyond-words/201311/active-listening-techniques-hostage-crisis-negotiators

Managing Human Resources

CHAPTER 5

Human Resource Management: The Foundation for an Effective Police Department

STUDENT LEARNING OUTCOMES

After reading this chapter, you will:

- understand how police human resource systems operate
- understand the impact of affirmative action laws and requirements
- be familiar with police recruitment
- be able to list and understand the various tests and exercises used to select police officers
- know the various types of police training
- know the content and methods of recruit or academy training
- be familiar with how police officers are evaluated and the problems associated with performance systems
- know the various methods used by police departments to promote officers
- know the procedures used to select officers for specialized units
- understand the importance and operation of risk management in a police department

KEY TERMS AND CONCEPTS

- Academy training
- Americans with Disabilities Act
- Background investigation
- Basic certificate of completion
- Behaviorally Anchored Rating Scale (BARS)
- Constant error problem
- Criminal records
- Discretionary training
- Driving standards
- Drug use standards
- Education requirements
- Entry-level written test
- Equal employment opportunity
- Field Training Officer (FTO)
- Graphic rating form
- Halo effect

- Hostile work environment
- Human resource management
- In-service training
- Law enforcement liability
- Medical examination
- Numerical rating form
- Oral interview board
- Peace Officers Standards and Training (POST)
- Performance appraisal
- Physical agility standards
- Police auto liability
- Polygraph examination
- Promotion
- Psychological examination
- Quid pro quo
- Rater bias

- Rater errors
- Rating criteria
- Recentcy problems
- Residency requirements
- Recruitment
- Risk assessment
- Risk management
- Roll-call training
- Selection
- Sexual harassment

- Situational test
- Stress academies
- Technical training
- Title VII of the 1964 Civil Rights Act
- Unclear standards
- Vision requirements
- Workers' compensation
- Writing test
- Written promotional test

INTRODUCTION

Human resource management or personnel administration can be defined as "attract an effective workforce to the organization, develop the workforce to its potential, and maintain it over time."[1] When police departments make mistakes when hiring, promoting, and training officers, it can have disastrous effects; the department can be stuck with a mediocre police officer for 20 years or ill-trained officers can inadvertently violate a procedure, exposing the department to civil liability; wrong human resource decisions can significantly cost a police department. A police department, for the most part, is only as good as its human resource system. Therefore, it is important for police leaders to understand the proper functioning of human resource management.

HUMAN RESOURCE SYSTEMS

Cities and counties generally have established civil service guidelines, city or county policies or ordinances, or state laws that dictate how police human resource systems operate. These laws or procedures have been enacted to eliminate political interference in police personnel systems and to ensure that the best personnel decisions are made. Moreover, the standards established by statutes or ordinances vary from state to state, and jurisdictions in states may have different standards as passed by city or county governments. Typically, a city or county human resources department will oversee some of a police department's personnel operations. For example, a police department may be responsible for recruiting officers, but the city or county human resources department will administer selection tests, and in some cases establish hiring standards. Promotion testing also is frequently governed by the centralized human resources department.

In some cases, conflict will arise between the police department and the human resources department. The police department may prefer a different written test or performance evaluation system, and the human resources department may not allow any changes. City and county attorneys often interject burdensome restrictions to avoid any lawsuits. States have enacted minimum training standards for police departments. Police administrators' discretion is often limited in terms of how their human resource systems operate. The laws and procedures in a particular jurisdiction must be examined to determine how its police personnel system operates.

AFFIRMATIVE ACTION AND POLICE DEPARTMENTS

In addition to state and local statutes and ordinances guiding police personnel practices, there are a number of federal laws that apply. Most importantly, **equal employment opportunity** (EEO) laws provide important guidelines that ensure that employers, including police departments, do not discriminate against different protected classes of people. These laws are rooted in **Title VII of the 1964 Civil Rights Act**. The Act states that it is unlawful to

1. Fail, refuse to hire or discharge an individual, or otherwise discriminate against any individual with respect to his compensation, terms, conditions, or privileges of employment because of the individual's race, color, religion, sex, or national origin; or
2. Limit, segregate or classify employees or applicants for employment in any way that would deprive, or tend to deprive, any individual of employment opportunities or otherwise adversely affect his stature as an employee because of such individual's race, color, religion, sex, or national origin (Section 703a).

In 1971, the U.S. Supreme Court clarified the Act with the decision in *Griggs v. Duke Power Co.* First, the Court ruled that unintentional discrimination as well as intentional discrimination was illegal. Prior to *Griggs,*[2] a defense against discrimination complaints was that any discrimination was unintentional. Second, the Court ruled that when discrimination existed, the employers must prove that their employment or selection standards are of a business necessity. That is, any selection standard that adversely affects a protected class of individuals

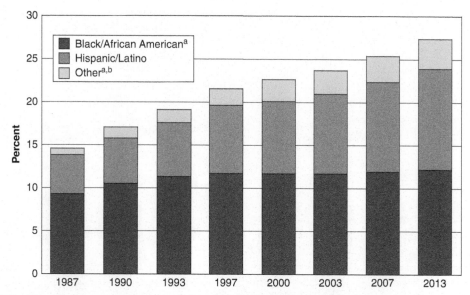

FIGURE 5-1   Minority Representation in Police Departments from 1987 to 2013.
Source: Reaves, *Local Police Departments, 2013: Personnel, Policies, and Practices* (Washington, DC: Bureau of Justice Statistics, 2015). https://www.bjs.gov/content/pub/pdf/lpd13ppp.pdf.

must be shown to predict job performance. If an employer cannot justify the selection standard and discrimination occurred, then the standard was deemed illegal.

The courts looked at the passing or selection rates of minorities and nonminorities or the composition of the community to determine if discrimination had occurred. For example, if a community has a large minority population, but there are not many minorities serving as police officers, the courts likely will recognize that discrimination is occurring, or if large numbers or minorities or women fail selection tests, the courts may attribute it to discrimination. In terms of hiring rates, the courts generally used the 80 percent rule where the selection rate for minorities should be at least 80 percent of the white selection rate. As noted, a finding of discrimination did not mean that a police department had to hire more minorities or women; it meant that the department had to prove that its selection standards predicted future job performance.

A good example of how the Act is applied is *Vanguard Justice Society v. Hughes* in 1979.[3] The court found that the Baltimore Police Department's 5 ft. 7 in. height requirement excluded 95 percent of female population but only 32 percent of the male population and therefore was discriminatory. Today, police departments have replaced height requirements with physical ability tests. Another interesting case was *Washington v. Davis (1976).*[4] Here, the Washington, DC, Metropolitan Police Department was found to discriminate against minorities in its written selection test. However, the police department showed that its selection test was job related or of a business necessity. The department demonstrated that the test scores were predictive of academy scores, and the academy scores were predictive of officer evaluations. This demonstrated that the test predicted future job performance.

The Act spurred police departments and other employers to recruit and hire more women and minorities and to develop better or more predictive selection procedures. Today, many police departments have affirmative action programs where they actively recruit women and minorities. A police department should be representative of the community it serves. For example, a police department serving a large Hispanic community must have bilingual officers to be effective. About 27 percent of full-time local police officers are members of a racial or ethnic minority.[5] Figure 5-1 shows how minority representation in policing has improved since 1987.

RECRUITMENT

White and Escobar advise that police departments must make an effort to promote diversity and college education in their recruitment campaigns.[6] A diverse police force better enables a police department to more positively interact with the community it serves. Better-educated police officers are more capable of understanding the issues facing today's police departments and carry out complicated police strategies such as community policing. Police departments' officers must be of the highest caliber.

Recruitment can be defined as attracting a sufficient pool of qualified applicants from which to select the needed number of new officers.[7] This is quite challenging as many applicants are not qualified or fail

Recruiting police officers at the recruitment fair.
Source: Jim West/Alamy Stock Photo

selection testing. For example, it was reported that the Suffolk County, New York, Police Department hired only 2 percent of the applicants in one of its applicant pool one year.[8] This is not unusual. The selection rate for many police departments is in the low single digits. This demonstrates that police departments must attract large numbers of applicants in order to fill vacant positions.

Essentially, police departments must pursue all avenues to recruit police officers. They should use media outlets such as radio, newspapers, and social media. They should visit college campuses, military bases, and other venues that may contain qualified applicants. A number of police recruiters from large cities will have to travel to distant cities and across state lines. Recruiters should emphasize the benefits of the job and why potential applicants should select their department. Police executives must ensure that recruitment efforts are maximized. This is best accomplished by requiring the commander in charge of recruitment to develop a recruitment plan. Once developed, it should be reviewed by the chief to ensure that recruitment efforts are extensive, and the chief or sheriff should ensure that there are adequate resources to implement it.

All applicants must be required to complete a comprehensive application that not only includes personal information but also information about drug history, past traffic violations, past employment information, criminal activity, and a list of references. This information is used to complete a background investigation and the polygraph examination.

POLICE SELECTION OR HIRING

Once the recruitment phase is completed, police departments will commence **selection**. Police departments use a variety of police officer hiring screening tools. Police officers can use deadly force and apply force when encountering citizens. They also constantly face dangerous situations. It, therefore, is critical that departments hire officers who can interact with the public and perform the job safely and effectively. Figure 5-2 shows the types of screening procedures and number of departments using them.

MINIMUM STANDARDS

Once the recruitment phase is completed, the department can begin the selection process. The selection process contains a number of steps. The first step is to ensure that applicants meet the minimum standards.

This is accomplished by reviewing their applications, and in some cases an initial interview. An initial review of qualifications is cost-effective in that unqualified applicants are eliminated from the selection process as soon as possible without a substantial cost. Figure 5-3 provides a list of the most common standards.

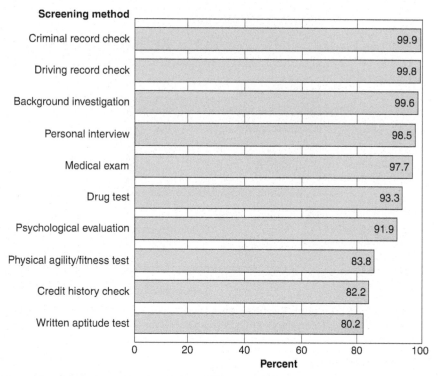

FIGURE 5-2   Screening Procedures Used to Select Officers and the Percentage of Departments Using Them
Source: B. Reaves, *Hiring and Retention of State and Local Law Enforcement Officers, 2008-Statistical Tables*
(Washington, DC, 2012), p. 11.

- Residency requirements
- Vision standards
- Educational standards
- Driving standards to include a valid driver's license and the absence of traffic violations
- Criminal behavior
- Drug usage

FIGURE 5-3   Minimum Standards for Hiring Police Officers

Police departments have adopted a variety of **residency requirements**. Some require applicants to reside in the city or county where the department is located, while other departments are more flexible in allowing the applicants to reside within a specific distance from the department, within the state, or anywhere in the United States. Strict residency requirements result in a more limited applicant pool, so they should not be too restrictive.

Police departments have **vision requirements**, and there is a great deal of variation in their restrictiveness. Each department establishes its own requirements. The justification for vision requirements is that if officers lose their glasses or contact lenses in a fight or traffic crash, it would impede their ability to defend themselves or provide assistance to citizens. Police executives must ensure that their officers can respond to all situations under any conditions.

There is a general consensus that college-educated officers potentially make superior officers as compared to those without a college education.[9] Only some of the smallest departments do not have an **education requirement**. Figure 5-4 shows the percentage of departments with an educational requirement.

Figure 5-4 shows that about 34 percent of departments had some college requirement upon entry. It is also noteworthy that a number of departments have college requirements for promotion. Many police departments may prefer college-educated officers, but keep their requirement at a high school diploma. The rationale is that many departments have difficulty hiring officers who otherwise are qualified. Nonetheless, these departments will still favor college-educated officers in the selection process.

Drug use standards refer to the amount of drugs that an applicant has consumed in the past. Different departments have varying standards. These standards focus on how recent the drug use was, the kinds of drugs used, and the amount of drugs used. Departments allow minor drug use as it is sometimes impossible to fill

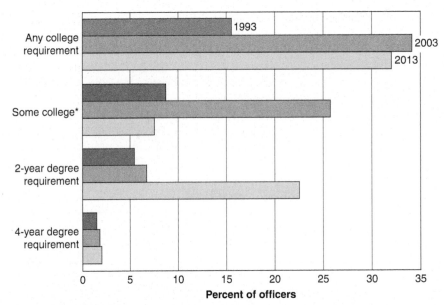

FIGURE 5-4 College Education Requirements for Entry-level Local Police Officers, 1993, 2003, and 2013.
Source: Reaves, *Local Police Departments, 2013: Personnel, Policies, and Practices* (Washington, DC: Bureau of Justice Statistics, 2015), p. 7.

positions when no prior drug use is the standard. One study showed that about half of departments considered applicants with prior marijuana use and a sixth of departments considered applicants with other types of drug use.[10] Most departments absolutely prohibit LSD and injectable drugs. Many departments allow minor marijuana use as long as it occurred years in the past. A number of departments have applicants submit to a drug test. This provides information about recent drug use.

Driving standards vary among different departments. Departments often consider when violations occurred, the number of violations, and the severity of violations such as driving under the influence (DUI), reckless driving, and so on. Numerous traffic violations, especially if they are recent, show poor judgment and a possible danger to the public and department.

Police departments should deny employment to applicants with **criminal records**. Such records show poor judgment. However, an applicant who has otherwise qualified and committed a minor misdemeanor years earlier could be considered if no other problems exist. It should be noted that anyone convicted of a domestic violence offense cannot be a law enforcement officer since federal law prohibits him or her from possessing a firearm.

The **entry-level written test** generally is the first step in the selection process after a review of minimum standards, and about 80 percent of departments use a written test. This identifies the candidates who have the aptitude to become police officers. It is first because it narrows the applicant pool. It would be cumbersome and expensive for a department to apply all the tests to all the applicants when the applicant pool may contain several hundred applicants, and the department is hiring 20 or so officers. Most departments grade the selection test pass-fail. Most departments purchase their selection tests from a company that specializes in police testing. These companies have validated their tests and have data showing that they are predictive of future police performance. Nonetheless, police managers should monitor the test outcomes to ensure that they serve the purposes of the department. In some cases, a separate human resources department will determine which exam is administered and oftentimes administer it for the police department.

Physical agility is an important part of a police officer's job. Although the job is often sedentary, officers sitting in a car or behind a desk, there are occasions where officers must exhibit extraordinary levels of physical strength and agility such as subduing a suspect, chasing a suspect, climbing fences, and so on. About 84 percent of departments require a physical agility test. **Physical agility testing** generally consists of a course with a variety of physical events, and applicants are timed while completing the events or they must exhibit some level of strength or agility. These events often consist of running, climbing, upper-body strength, climbing a wall, and so on. These tests generally examine strength and agility, and departments use a variety of tests to identify qualified applicants.

Police departments frequently have height-weight standards as part of the physical agility standards. These standards have replaced height standards and simply state that an applicant's height and weight must be proportionate. This standard eliminates applicants who are overweight and underweight. They are not discriminatory against women or other minority groups.

Once the written test and the physical agility test are concluded, the department will perform a **background** or character examination. Here, officers will contact applicants' references, former employers, neighbors, former teachers, and others who might know the applicants. The investigators try to find both positive and negative information about applicants. For example, they try to find out if the applicants were good employees; did they cause problems with their neighbors; were they good students; and so on. Such behaviors are predictive of future behaviors. Applicants should be responsible and good citizens. It is important for departments to do a comprehensive background investigation as they can provide valuable information in the selection process.

Generally, the polygraph examination follows after the background investigation. Information from the background investigation and the application is used to guide the polygraph examination. A **polygraph examination** essentially verifies the information on the application and investigates behaviors such as criminal behaviors, drug usage, and other deviant behaviors. Whereas the background investigation looks at and verifies the applicant's interaction with other people in a variety of settings, the polygraph examination focuses on negative behaviors. Moreover, since crime and drug use occur outside public view and may only be known by the applicant, it is important that a polygraph examination be used.

If applicants pass the above tests, many police departments will interview them using an oral interview board format. The **oral interview board** generally is composed of representatives of the police department and members of the community. The members of the board ask each candidate a standard series of questions and rate the applicants on their responses. The boards measure how applicants respond to questions about real situations, and they evaluate how applicants interact and communicate with people. Some of the common questions include:[11]

- Why do you want to be a police officer?
- Why did you select our department?
- What have you done to prepare yourself to be a police officer?
- If you see another officer committing a crime, what would you do?
- How do you deal with unreasonable people?
- Will working shifts and weekends be a problem?

There are an infinite number of different questions that can be asked. It is important that the questions and answers provide important information about the applicant's ability, commitment, and aptitude to be a police officer.

The oral interview board is often used to rank the acceptable applicants, and in some cases to disqualify applicants who do not do well in the oral interview board. The number of applicants being interviewed should exceed the number of positions that are to be filled as some of the applicants may drop out or otherwise be disqualified. The **Americans with Disabilities Act** requires that individuals who can perform the essential functions of the job cannot be denied employment due to a disability if they are otherwise qualified. The physical agility test is designed to ensure that applicants can complete the physical tasks of the job. Thus, applicants passing the oral interview board are then given a conditional job offer. This means that they are hired if they pass the remaining two hurdles: psychological examination and medical examination. These evaluations potentially can identify problems that can disqualify applicants—physical problems or mental issues that prevent them from performing the essential functions of the job.

The **medical examination** is conducted by a medical doctor who looks for physical or medical problems. If any are identified that would impede applicants' job performance, they are disqualified. The **psychological examination** is conducted by a psychologist or a psychiatrist. They generally use standardized tests such as the Minnesota Multiphasic Personality Inventory (MMPI), California Psychological Inventory (CPI), Rorschach Inkblot Test, and the Inwald Personality Inventory that were designed specifically to screen police candidates. If any problems are identified during the psychological examination, the applicant is disqualified irrespective of the conditional job offer.

A number of departments are now using a writing test. Many applicants cannot write using good grammar, sentence structure, or paragraph formation. This is critical since police officers must accurately and clearly document crimes and other problems when they complete reports. Poorly written crime reports can be used to impeach officers' testimony in court. The **writing test** often involves asking candidates to write about some topic. For example, several departments in Southern California ask candidates to write a short paper on what they did last summer. They really do not care what they did; they evaluate the papers on whether the candidates used proper English and could clearly explain what they did.

The police officer selection process is complicated, involving numerous steps. These steps are important since it is critical to select officers who can function effectively in our communities. A wrong hiring decision can create a number of problems for a police department.

TRAINING: PREPARING OFFICERS FOR THE STREETS

Adequate training is critical; officers must have the skills and abilities to perform the job. When departments fail to train their officers adequately, the departments can be liable. In *City of Canton v. Harris*,[12] the U.S. Supreme Court ruled that departments were liable under Title 42 U.S. Code Section 1983 when officers violated citizens' rights as a result of a failure to train. Ross examined about 1,500 of these lawsuits and found the following areas in which the police have been challenged as the result of inadequate training: use of force, false arrest or detention, search and seizure, failure to protect, detainee suicide, use of emergency vehicles, and the provision of medical assistance.[13] American police departments spend millions of dollars each year as a result of these lawsuits.

There are three types of training the chief or sheriff must implement and ensure that they are effective: academy or basic training, Field Training Officer (FTO), and in-service training. Generally, the chief will designate a captain or lieutenant the responsibility for managing the department's training program.

Academy or Basic Training

Newly hired police officers do not have the knowledge or skills to immediately serve as officers. Even though some officers will have college degrees in criminal justice or criminology, they will not know how their department functions or possess skills such as use of force, pursuit driving, and so on. **Academy training** fills this void. The content addressed in these academies is governed by Police Officer Standards Training (POST) bodies or other state laws. These laws or standards have been enacted to ensure that officers receive the training they need to perform the job effectively and safely. Figure 5-5 provides a breakdown of the training topics and the number of hours of training by topic in state and local police academies.

Police training has two important components: technical and discretionary. **Technical training** refers to providing officers with information about the procedures and laws for doing the job. Many of these procedures are outlined in departmental policies, and the laws refer to statutes as well as case law. The training also includes technology such as radios, weapons, evidence collection tools, and so on. **Discretionary training** refers to the training officers receive about how to apply procedures and law and the ramifications should the procedures and law be applied inappropriately. Training areas such as report writing, patrol procedures, defensive tactics, arrest procedures, and so on are technical training; they teach new officers how to do a job. Subjects such as ethics, communications, and professionalism are discretionary subjects and are just as important.

A criticism of police training is that it too often focuses too much on the technical or mechanical aspects of the job and does not adequately teach new officers how to deal with situations such as domestic violence, mentally ill suspects, belligerent suspects, and so on. Academy training should emphasize real-life situations.

Training area	Percent of academies with training	Average number of hours of instruction required per recruit*
Operations		
Report writing	99%	25 hrs.
Patrol procedures	98	52
Investigations	98	42
Traffic accident investigations	98	23
Emergency vehicle operations	97	38
Bask first aid/CPR	97	24
Computers/information systems	61	9
Weapons/defensive tactics/used of force		
Defensive tactics	99%	60 hrs.
Firearms skills	98	71
Use of force	98	21
Nonlethal weapons	88	16
Self-improvement		
Ethics and integrity	98%	8 hrs.
Health and fitness	96	49
Communications	91	15
Professionalism	85	11
Stress prevention/management	81	6
Legal education		
Criminal/constitutional law	98%	53 hrs.
Traffic law	97	23
Juvenile justice law/procedures	97	10

FIGURE 5-5 A Breakdown of the Training Topics and the Number of Hours of Training by Topic in State and Local Police Academies
* Excludes academies that do not include this instruction.
Source: Reaves, *State and Local Law Enforcement Training Academies, 2013* (Washington, DC: Bureau of Justice Statistics, 2016), p. 5

New police officers often do not have a real-world context to apply much of what they learn in the academy. Birzer advises that it is paradoxical that police officers function in a democratic society but are trained using paramilitary, authoritarian methods.[14] These methods frequently do not work when officers are confronting discretionary problems on the streets.

A number of academies across the country still use the paramilitary format for training. These academies are known as **stress academies**. Their proponents argue that this style of training is a time-proven and highly effective method of training that produces highly disciplined, fully functional, and physically fit police officers. Other observers, however, believe that discipline cannot be taught in the academy; a recruit already possesses it or not as a result of past socialization and education. A recruit's discipline level can best be measured through the background investigation and psychological screening. Violanti examined high-stress training and found that recruits tend to use a variety of maladaptive responses to this training, such as having difficulty making some decisions or needing close supervision. These responses inhibit the learning process and may also result in problems once the recruit is on the job.[15] Post in a study of police academies found that recruits actually learned better in non-stress academies.[16] Essentially, discipline cannot be taught. It is a quality that individuals possess or not. Application of knowledge in the real world is most important.

A national study of police academies showed that about 5 percent of graduates were not retained after probation.[17] This retention rate is due to a variety of trainee problems. It demonstrates that selection and training programs do not always result in the best outcomes.

State Certification

Once a recruit graduates from the academy, the state's commission or board of **Peace Officers Standards and Training** (POST) awards a **basic certificate of completion**. Many states require this certificate in order to be a law enforcement officer. Over the years, POSTs have also developed intermediate, advanced, managerial, and

Officers receive classroom training on tactical situations.
Source: PJF Military Collection/Alamy Stock Photo

executive certificates for police officers; these certificates, above the basic level, are generally categorized as "advanced" certificates. Each certificate requires a specified number of hours of training and/or higher education in various areas such as investigation, management, and operations.

The purpose of advanced certification programs is to enhance lifelong learning and career development for the officer. Over the years, advanced POST certification and higher education have become popular bargaining issues for police unions and associations. Some agencies offer as much as a 5 percent pay increase for an advanced certificate or a combination of advanced certificates and a four-year college degree. This system provides strong motivation for some officers to continue their education and training.

In some states, basic certification is tied to police discipline; that is, officers are required to have the certification in order to be a police officer. In some cases, if an officer's disciplinary infraction is substantial, the POST will revoke his or her certification. This means that the officer then is unable to obtain employment as an officer with any other department in the state.

The basic academy training has a number of implications for every level of the police department. Police commanders must ensure that new officers are prepared for the job. When new officers have problems, it generally falls on the sergeants to remedy any identified problems.

Field Training Officer Program

Following the completion of a basic academy, most departments assign their new officers to a **Field Training Officer (FTO)** program. The FTO program serves two primary functions. First, it has a training function. Some aspects of the job can be learned only through experience. These are demonstrated and taught by the FTOs. Second, the FTO program is an evaluation phase that determines if new officers have the ability to be police officers—whether or not the new officer can adequately apply the information he or she learned while in the academy. If not, the officer is terminated. A newly appointed police officer can be terminated at any time during the FTO process. Once an officer completes the FTO period, his or her file is reviewed and a decision is made to retain or dismiss the officer.

FTO programs are based on the San Jose, California, Police Department model of 1968. A typical FTO program, as shown in Figure 5-6, is divided into three phases and ideally takes 52 weeks, although many departments have shortened the program to about 14 weeks. Each phase is designed to help the recruit learn a particular set of tasks. It should be noted that when a department shortens the FTO program, it likely neglects important training and evaluation for the new officers.

> ***Phase I***   is the introductory phase. The trainee is taught certain basic skills, including officer safety and other areas of potential liability to the organization and officer. This phase serves as an orientation for the new officers; their demonstration of a willingness to learn from experienced officers is an important aspect of this phase.

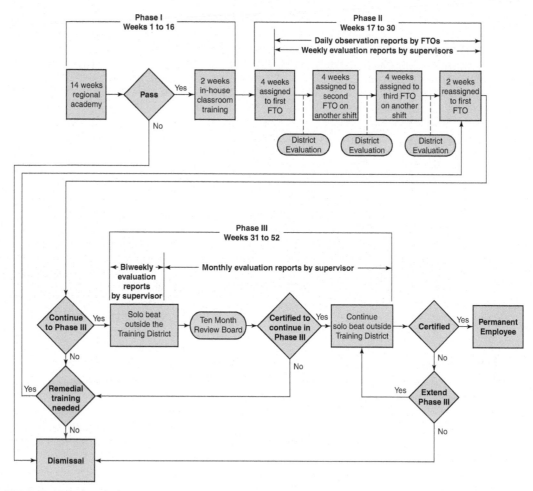

FIGURE 5-6 Schematic for FTO Program
Source: M. S. McCampbell, Field Training for Police Agencies: State of the Art. Washington, DC: U.S. Department of Justice, National Institute of Justice, 1997, pp. 4–6.

Phase II   is a continuation of Phase I; however, the training becomes more intense. The trainee begins to apply his or her mastery of basic skills. The routine activities of report writing, traffic enforcement, and crime scene investigations become routine for the trainee during this phase. Whereas Phase I consisted primarily of training, Phase II includes a larger measure of evaluation.

Phase III   is the last phase of directly supervised formal training. It is characterized by advanced skills training and polishing those skills already learned. This also provides an opportunity for the FTO to review those tasks previously accomplished and to ensure that the trainee is prepared for the final phase.

Field training programs are labor-intensive and require a great deal of leadership and management. FTOs complete a comprehensive daily observation report (DOR) form. An example of a DOR is shown in Figure 5-7. The DOR is a permanent record of the trainee's progress and includes remedial efforts and identified problems. The form shown in Figure 5-6 is composed of five major performance areas—appearance, attitude, knowledge, performance, and relationships—which are divided into 30 rating categories. FTO observes and evaluates the trainee in each applicable area during a shift, using a rating scale of 1 to 7. A narrative explanation is required in every area in which the trainee is rated below average (less than 2) or exceptional (more than 6).

Patrol supervisors play a vital role in the FTO program. It is the sergeant's responsibility to ensure that the standards and objectives of the agency's field training program are met. The supervisor must pay close attention to the training activities of the FTO and seek periodic feedback on the new trainees as the FTO program progresses. In essence, the sergeant must supervise the FTOs and the new officers. The supervisor should ensure that necessary corrective actions are taken so that the trainee has every opportunity to complete the program or that proper documentation exists in the case of a recommendation to terminate the trainee from employment. The sergeant should also observe the interaction between the trainee and the FTO to ensure that the FTO is

Date _____   Daily Observation Report No. _____
_____   _____
Trainee's Last Name First (MI) No.   FTO's Last Name First (MI) No.

RATING INSTRUCTIONS: RATE OBSERVED BEHAVIOR WITH REFERENCE TO THE SCALE BELOW.
COMMENT ON THE MOST AND LEAST STATISFACTORY PERFORMANCE OF THE DAY. A SPECIFIC
COMMENT IS REQUIRED ON ALL RATINGS OF "2" OR LESS AND "6" AND ABOVE. CHECK "N. O." IF NOT
OBSERVED. IF TRAINEE FAILS TO RESPOND TO TRAINING, CHECK "N. R. T." BOX AND COMMENT.

WATCH WORKED _____
FTO PHASE _____
ASSIGNMENT _____

	NOT ACCEPTABLE BY FTO STANDARDS			ACCEPTABLE LEVEL	SUPERIOR BY FTO STANDARDS					
	1	2	3	<4>	5	6	7			
R.T.								N.O.	N.R.T	

APPEARANCE

| [ ] [ ] 1. | 1 | 2 | 3 | 4 | 5 | 6 | 7 | [] [] | GENERAL APPEARANCE |

ATTITUDE

| [ ] [ ] 2. | 1 | 2 | 3 | 4 | 5 | 6 | 7 | [] [] | ACCEPTANCE OF FEEDBACK-FTO |
| [ ] [ ] 3. | 1 | 2 | 3 | 4 | 5 | 6 | 7 | [] [] | ATTITUDE TOWARDS POLICE WORK |

KNOWLEDGE

DEPARTMENT POLICIES AND
  PROCEDURES REFLECTED IN:

| [ ] [ ] 4. | 1 | 2 | 3 | 4 | 5 | 6 | 7 | [] [] | VERBAL/WRITTEN TESTING |
| [ ] [ ] | 1 | 2 | 3 | 4 | 5 | 6 | 7 | [] [] | FIELD PERFORMANCE |

CRIMINAL STATUTES REFLECTED IN:

| [ ] [ ] 5. | 1 | 2 | 3 | 4 | 5 | 6 | 7 | [] [] | VERBAL/WRITTEN TESTING |
| [ ] [ ] | 1 | 2 | 3 | 4 | 5 | 6 | 7 | [] [] | FIELD PERFORMANCE |

MUNICIPAL ORDINANCES REFLECTED IN:

| [ ] [ ] 6. | 1 | 2 | 3 | 4 | 5 | 6 | 7 | [] [] | VERBAL/WRITTEN TESTING |
| [ ] [ ] | 1 | 2 | 3 | 4 | 5 | 6 | 7 | [] [] | FIELD PERFORMANCE |

TRAFFIC ORDINANCES REFLECTED IN:

| [ ] [ ] 7. | 1 | 2 | 3 | 4 | 5 | 6 | 7 | [] [] | VERBAL/WRITTEN TESTING |
| [ ] [ ] | 1 | 2 | 3 | 4 | 5 | 6 | 7 | [] [] | FIELD PERFORMANCE |

PERFORMANCE

[ ] [ ] 8.	1	2	3	4	5	6	7	[] []	DRIVING SKILL: NORMAL CINDITIONS
[ ] [ ] 9.	1	2	3	4	5	6	7	[] []	DRIVING SKILL: STRESS CONDITIONS
[ ] [ ] 10.	1	2	3	4	5	6	7	[] []	ORIENTATION/RESPONSE TIME
[ ] [ ] 11.	1	2	3	4	5	6	7	[] []	ROUTINE FORMS: COMPLETE/ACCURATE

REPORT WRITING

[ ] [ ] 12.	1	2	3	4	5	6	7	[] []	ORGANIZATION/DETAILS
[ ] [ ] 13.	1	2	3	4	5	6	7	[] []	GRAMMER/SPELLING/NEATNESS
[ ] [ ] 14.	1	2	3	4	5	6	7	[] []	APPROPRIATE TIME USED
[ ] [ ] 15.	1	2	3	4	5	6	7	[] []	FIELD PERFORMANCE: NON-STRESS
[ ] [ ] 16.	1	2	3	4	5	6	7	[] []	FIELD PERFORMANCE: STRESS
[ ] [ ] 17.	1	2	3	4	5	6	7	[] []	INVESTIGATIVE SKILL
[ ] [ ] 18.	1	2	3	4	5	6	7	[] []	INERVIEW/INTERROGATION
[ ] [ ] 19.	1	2	3	4	5	6	7	[] []	SELF-INITIATED FIELD ACTIVITY
[ ] [ ] 20.	1	2	3	4	5	6	7	[] []	OFFICER SAFETY: GENERAL
[ ] [ ] 21.	1	2	3	4	5	6	7	[] []	OFFICER SAFETY: SUSPECTS/PRISONERS
[ ] [ ] 22.	1	2	3	4	5	6	7	[] []	VOICE COMMAND
[ ] [ ] 23.	1	2	3	4	5	6	7	[] []	PHYSICAL SKILL
[ ] [ ] 24.	1	2	3	4	5	6	7	[] []	PROBLEM SOLVING/DECISION MAKING RADIO
[ ] [ ] 25.	1	2	3	4	5	6	7	[] []	USE OF CODES/PROCEDURES
[ ] [ ] 26.	1	2	3	4	5	6	7	[] []	LISTEN AND COMPREHEND
[ ] [ ] 27.	1	2	3	4	5	6	7	[] []	ARTICULATION/TRANSMISSION

RELATIONSHIPS

[ ] [ ] 28.	1	2	3	4	5	6	7	[] []	CITIZENS IN GENERAL
[ ] [ ] 29.	1	2	3	4	5	6	7	[] []	ETHNIC GROUPS OTHER THAN OWN
[ ] [ ] 30.	1	2	3	4	5	6	7	[] []	OTHER DEPARTMENT MEMBERS

MINUTES OF REMEDIAL TIME

FIGURE 5-7 Daily Observation Report

properly doing his or her job, and conduct periodic informal meetings with the FTOs and trainees to discuss the progress of training.

Roll-Call Training

Roll call occurs during the 15 to 30 minutes prior to the beginning of a shift. This time is used by unit commanders to prepare officers for patrol. Roll-call sessions usually begin with a sergeant assigning officers to their respective beats. Information about wanted and dangerous persons and major incidents on previous shifts is usually disseminated. Other matters may also be addressed, such as issuing officers court subpoenas, explaining new departmental policies and procedures, and discussing shift- and beat-related matters.

Roll-call training during roll call affords an excellent opportunity for the department to update officers' knowledge and to present new ideas and techniques. For example, when the department changes a policy or adopts a new one, it is presented in roll call. Officers can then ask questions and clarify its meaning. Such two-way communication leads to a better understanding of the policy. It is also an opportunity for managers to point out crime and disorder problems and to assign officers to counter them. In some cases, members of other units can make presentations about their operations as they affect patrol. Roll-call training can be very productive.

In-Service Training

Changes in departmental policies and procedures, court decisions, and operational strategies and techniques demand that training be an ongoing process throughout a police officer's career. It is simply unreasonable to expect that the knowledge gained during academy training or specialized training can serve an officer for an entire career. **In-service training** is the most common method for maintaining and improving officer competency and may also reduce the likelihood of citizen complaints and future litigation. In-service training is also used to recertify, refresh, or provide new information to officers in the most critical areas of their job, including weapons qualification, driving, defensive tactics, first aid, and changes in the law.

Creating an effective in-service training program presents many challenges for the department. Larger police departments often provide officers with this training in-house while smaller departments rely on a state training agency. State agencies often offer a wide variety of courses addressing all aspects of policing such as accident investigation, criminal investigation, evidence, radar enforcement, and so on. Scheduling training can also be a problem as it takes officers off the street for a period of time. This training can result in units having personnel shortages, which will be extremely problematic for sergeants and unit commanders.

Today, many states and departments require officers who are promoted to sergeant and above to attend supervisory or management training. This training helps supervisors and managers to understand their new positions and assists them in performing at a higher level. We cannot expect an officer who is promoted to a higher level to automatically walk into the job and be proficient. Some of the topics taught in this training include scheduling, time management, conflict resolution, counseling, planning, and police tactics and operations.

PERFORMANCE APPRAISAL

According to Mathis and Jackson, **performance appraisal** is "the process of evaluating how well employees do their jobs compared with a set of standards and communicating that information to those employees."[18] Thus, in order for a department to have an effective performance evaluation system, it must have (1) performance standards, (2) a method of measuring performance, and (3) a way to provide officers with feedback relative to their performance. Generally, the performance appraisal is a formal process whereby supervisors examine subordinates' performance, rate their performance, and provide them with feedback about their behavior. It is a formal process because departments generally evaluate all officers at the same time using the same rating form and system. Once supervisors rate their subordinates, most departments require unit commanders to review and approve the ratings.

A department's formal performance appraisal process should coexist with and be parallel to the constant and informal evaluation of subordinates' behavior and performance by managers and supervisors. The informal process allows supervisors to collect information for the performance appraisal, and it allows them to take action and change subordinates' behavior that does not comply with the department's expectations. A captain should monitor the activities of his or her lieutenants and sergeants just as sergeants should constantly oversee the activities of their officers. Neither the formal process nor the informal process should supplant the other.

Police departments generally identify three reasons for a formalized performance appraisal:

1. To standardize the nature of the personnel decision-making process so that the rights of the job incumbent are fully represented.
2. To assure the public that the agency representatives are fully qualified to carry out their assigned duties.
3. To give the job incumbent necessary behavior modification information to maintain behaviors that are appropriate.[19]

Performance appraisal, in essence, is an accountability and control process. It is a system for ensuring accountability because the results can be used to evaluate individual officers and units within the police department, or the department as a whole. Administrators are able to make a number of comparisons by examining the results of performance appraisals. It is a control process because the results can be used by managers to direct and change subordinates' behavior. Supervisors can counsel individual officers who do not perform at expected levels and managers can discuss results with supervisors and unit commanders when unit productivity does not reach expected levels.

More specifically, the performance appraisal serves a number of organizational purposes: formalized feedback to employees, recruitment and selection, training, field training officer evaluation, horizontal job changes, promotions, compensation management, and discipline.

Formalized Feedback to Employees. Superior officers, regardless of rank, should constantly provide subordinates with feedback about their performance. This activity is the very essence of supervision. The quality and quantity of this feedback vary tremendously even within a given police department. Some supervisors will closely supervise their subordinates and constantly counsel them about their performance, while other supervisors may only discuss performance occasionally with their subordinates. Other supervisors may abdicate this responsibility altogether. The department should provide the structure—a minimum agenda—to guide the evaluation and the resulting feedback session. Also, the department should establish a policy that dictates the time and frequency of appraisals. A formal feedback session for subordinates is the most important purpose for performance appraisals, although formal feedback sessions should be supplemented with informal counseling on a continuous basis.

Recruitment and Selection. As a formal process, performance appraisal provides a structure whereby supervisors can collectively have input into recruitment and selection criteria. Personnel specialists should examine performance appraisals to identify personnel weaknesses or deficiencies. As problems are identified, they should be used to target pools of people for recruitment and to refine selection tests and criteria.

Training. The performance appraisal process should identify deficiencies or problems with officers' performance, especially those officers who recently graduated from the basic training academy. In some instances, these deficiencies are the result of improper training or the lack of training. The training staff should review the results of annual performance evaluations to identify training deficiencies. Adjustments can then be made in the recruit or basic training program as well as when veteran officers are provided with in-service training programs.

FTO Evaluation. Many police departments have an FTO program for their new officers, which represents a special type of performance appraisal. The program is designed to allow the department to determine whether officers should be retained. These field training evaluations are extremely important, because if the officer is retained after the probationary period, he or she can be dismissed only by showing cause. This creates a situation in which departments are forced to retain officers who are mediocre or who constantly cause minor problems. Below average or problem-causing officers should be dismissed during the probationary period. These evaluations can also serve to provide feedback to the training process.

Horizontal Job Changes. Many police departments have specialized units, such as traffic, criminal investigation, or planning, that require officers to have a variety of skills and different levels of job knowledge. Commanders of these units can review performance appraisal information to identify those officers who possess the best skills and productivity levels for these units. The performance appraisal can provide invaluable information when making decisions about transfers across units.

Promotions. The performance appraisal is one of the most common measures used in the promotion process. One survey showed that 32 percent of the departments surveyed used performance evaluations in their promotion system.[20] Only written tests and oral interview boards were used more frequently. The performance appraisal allows the department to consider officers' past behavior when making promotional decisions. Generally, past behavior is the best predictor of future behavior. When performance is used for promotions, police departments should use promotability ratings.[21] The difference between promotability ratings and performance appraisals is that promotability ratings concentrate on job dimensions or criteria that are important for the next level supervisory position while performance appraisals focus on important job behaviors for officers' current position. Officers should be evaluated on their performance relative to the new position rather than on how well they perform in the old position when performance is considered in the promotional process.

Compensation Management.   A number of departments base annual salary increments on the performance appraisal. If officers do not achieve a predetermined score on their annual performance appraisal, they do not receive their annual salary increment. Other departments provide merit raises for officers who receive high rankings. For example, the 10 officers who receive the highest performance appraisal scores for the department might receive an extra 5 percent merit raise. Performance appraisals are used extensively in determining raises for police officers.

Discipline.   In some instances, the performance appraisal can be to discipline officers. This is especially applicable when an officer fails to meet departmental expectations but does not do anything that violates policies or lies outside the bounds of acceptable behavior. Performance that is consistently below average or otherwise deficient can be documented on the performance appraisal form. If an officer fails to correct the behavior and receives several such deficient evaluations, the department might take disciplinary action. The performance appraisal formally documents unacceptable behavior and provides a record of the feedback to the officer.

Potential Problems

One of the problems with performance appraisals is that police managers attempt to use them for multiple purposes. The purpose of the ratings generally affects how supervisors rate their subordinates. For example, supervisors tend to be more lenient when ratings are used for promotions as compared to when they are used strictly for counseling and improvement. Consequently, when a department attempts to use a single set of ratings for multiple purposes, it tends to distort the ratings and create a variety of problems. Given that performance appraisal is such a critical part of supervision at all levels, police departments should consider developing a variety of rating schemes.

Defining Rating Criteria

Defining **rating criteria** is a three-step process. First, the job is studied in an attempt to identify what should be measured by the performance appraisal system. This includes reviewing job descriptions, job-task analysis information, and other job-related information, such as departmental policies and procedures, to identify the critical and most important activities associated with the position. This process ultimately should provide a listing of job activities and measures of their relative importance. Hence, the most important job components can be identified for measurement. The performance appraisal can also be

YOU DECIDE...

You are a captain in a medium-sized police department with 40 officers and serve as the assistant chief. The city recently hired a new police chief who came from a large department that had a number of community relations problems. She does not want to have problems in her new job. She has examined the department's performance appraisal system and found that it focused on police procedures and did not necessarily measure officers' performance with community residents. She has asked you to construct a new performance appraisal system that does a better job of appraising officers' work in the community.

Questions for Discussion

1. How would you approach this assignment?

2. Who would you consult with to get an idea of the new criteria that should be included on the new performance appraisal form?

3. What criteria would you include on the new form?

4. How would you sell the new form to the rank-and-file officers in the department?

used to change behaviors. For example, if the department is emphasizing community policing and problem solving, behaviors associated with this area can be included on the performance appraisal. Performance criteria should match the current job requirements; many rating systems do not include the current, important aspects of the job.[22]

Second, once this is accomplished, performance standards must be established. That is, at what level must subordinates perform these tasks or activities for their behavior to be deemed unacceptable, acceptable, or above average? When rating subordinates' work behavior, raters must have fairly specific standards to guide their decision making. Furthermore, subordinates, regardless of rank, must be made aware of standards so that they can evaluate their own work. These performance standards must then be captured on the performance appraisal rating form, the third step in the process.

Job criteria and performance standards must be articulated within the performance appraisal system. That is, the department must develop rating forms and guidelines. Every officer must be trained on the system prior to its implementation. Police administrators cannot expect subordinates to perform at acceptable levels unless subordinates have been informed of the standards.

Unfortunately, many performance ratings focus on mundane or bureaucratic activities or officer traits. One study examined over 1,400 rating dimensions used in police performance appraisals and found that the overwhelming majority of rating factors focused on internal procedures such as radio protocols, completing departmental forms, and dress code.[23] These types of rating dimensions actually relate to supervision and discipline rather than performance. Performance appraisals should focus on activities that are important in terms of accomplishing departmental objectives.

Finally, it should be noted that performance appraisal ratings represent unique measures of officer performance. Falkenberg, Gaines, and Cordner investigated the constructs or dimensions used in performance appraisals. They found that the measurements were distinctive from other psychological dimensions or scores on management tests. They concluded that performance appraisals provided productivity information that could not be obtained through other means.[24]

PERFORMANCE APPRAISAL FORMS

Police leaders have a variety of rating forms from which to choose when developing a performance appraisal system. Each form has its strengths and weaknesses. The following sections examine the various forms.

Graphic Rating Form

Perhaps the simplest rating form, the graphic rating form is that shown in Figure 5-8. The **graphic rating form** lists the job dimensions to be rated and provides a space for the rater to select a descriptive rating. When using the rating form in Figure 5-8, the supervisor would merely place an "X" or a checkmark in the box that best describes the officer's performance. For example, if the officer's performance in public relations skills was "good," it would be so noted. The supervisor would make this determination by considering the officer's behavior as well as citizen input (both complaints and commendations).

A variation on the graphic rating form is the **numerical rating form**. The only difference between these two forms is that the descriptive adjectives at the top of the form in Figure 5-8 are replaced by numbers, generally ranging from 0 to 10 or 50 to 100. When a numerical rating form is used, the rater has a wider range of possible scores. For example, the rating "fair" may be replaced by a range of 61 to 70.

DIMENSION	UNSATISFACTORY	FAIR	GOOD	SUPERIOR	EXCEPTIONAL
Relationship with Others					
Quantity and Quality of Work					
Communications Skills					
Attendance and Punctuality					
Public Relations Skills					

FIGURE 5-8 Graphic Rating Form for Rating Police Officers

DIMENSION: HANDLING DOMESTIC VIOLENCE SITUATIONS

Extremely good	+ 7	Uses good judgment in determining proper action. Always considers what performance is best for the victim. Will also attempt to discover a workable solution for the aggressor. Will consider actions for the short term as well as the long term.
Good performance	+ 6	Generally uses good judgment in determining proper action. Always considers what is best for the victim but does not necessarily take action that considers the aggressor or a long-term solution.
Slightly good performance	+ 5	Responds to calls. Generally collects information that is helpful in deciding what action to take. Sometimes considers both the victim and the perpetrator. Usually makes the correct decision.
Adequate performance	+ 4	Responds to calls. Attempts to collect information that is helpful in deciding what action to take. Attempts to help the victim but usually does not consider the perpetrator. Sometimes makes the correct decision.
Slightly poor	+ 3	Responds to the calls and takes information from the complainant and other witnesses. Usually will only do the minimum necessary action. Not interested in problem solving at all.
Poor performance	+ 2	Only interested in answering the call and takes the action that is the most expedient for the officer. Always does the absolute minimum. Sometimes takes action that escalates the situation.
Unacceptable	+ 1	Responds to calls because he or she has to. Sometimes becomes embroiled in the conflicts and too frequently leaves the situation worse than before police intervention.

FIGURE 5-9   Behaviorally Anchored Rating Scale

The rater can then give the officer a score within this range. The majority of police departments use a numerical rating form.

The foremost difficulty with graphic rating forms is that they lack reliability. Police departments generally have several people involved in rating. Sergeants from each shift or unit are responsible for rating their officers. The difficulty arises in interpreting the descriptive adjectives or numbers used in the scale. For example, one supervisor may rate a subordinate good on a dimension, while another supervisor will rate the same employee superior. As the number of supervisors involved in the rating process increases, so does the number of inconsistencies. The problem is that each supervisor has associated different meanings with the adjectives or numbers. The form does not provide the raters with information to assist in giving the ratings a meaning.

Behaviorally Anchored Rating Scale

Another variation of the graphic rating scale is the **Behaviorally Anchored Rating Scale (BARS)**. The BARS provides the rater with more information about performance standards and, therefore, leads to more accurate and reliable ratings. Figure 5-9 provides an example of a BARS for rating officers' handling of domestic violence situations. In addition to a numerical rating scale and an adjective rating scale, the form includes weighted descriptions of police officers' behavior or performance when handling these situations. The form contains "fixed standard" information. When rating a subordinate, the rater selects the description that best fits how the officer typically handles family disturbances. The primary advantage of BARS is that the descriptions assist the supervisor in making better and more consistent ratings.

COMMUNITY POLICING AND PERFORMANCE APPRAISALS

Although a majority of the police agencies in the United States have adopted community policing, a remaining problem has been that many officers and units at the lower levels of the police department are resistant to the strategy.[25] One way to facilitate acceptance is to adopt community policing activities into the performance appraisal system. This helps to identify the important aspects or activities associated with the strategy, and it provides a mechanism for rewarding officers who excel in community policing activities. Oettmeier and Wycoff noted that the Houston, Texas, Police Department used the performance appraisal to solidify that department's community policing efforts.[26] Figure 5-10 shows some of the criteria Houston used. Note that the performance objectives provide substantial guidance to officers in performing community policing.

Community Policing Performance Dimensions for the Houston Police Department

Tasks/Activities

Activities are listed beneath the tasks they are intended to accomplish.
Several activities could be used to accomplish a number of different tasks.

1. **Learn characteristics of area, residents, businesses**
   a. Study beat books
   b. Analyze crime and calls-for-service data
   c. Drive, walk area and make notes
   d. Talk with community representatives
   e. Conduct area surveys
   f. Maintain area/suspect logs
   g. Read area papers (e.g., "shopper" papers)
   h. Discuss area with citizens when answering calls
   i. Talk with private security personnel in area
   j. Talk with area business owners/managers

2. **Become acquainted with leaders in area**
   a. Attend community meetings, including service club meetings
   b. Ask questions in survey about who formal and informal area leaders are
   c. Ask area leaders for names of other leaders

3. **Make residents aware of who officer is and what s/he is trying to accomplish in area**
   a. Initiate citizen contacts
   b. Distribute business cards
   c. Discuss purpose at community meeting
   d. Discuss purpose when answering calls
   e. Write article for local paper
   f. Contact home-bound elderly
   g. Encourage citizens to contact officer directly

4. **Identify area problems**
   a. Attend community meetings
   b. Analyze crime and calls-for-service data
   c. Contact citizens and businesses
   d. Conduct business and residential surveys
   e. Ask about other problems when answering calls

5. **Communicate with supervisors, other officers and citizens about the nature of the area and its problems**
   a. Maintain beat bulletin board in station
   b. Leave notes in boxes of other officers
   c. Discuss area with supervisor

6. **Investigate/do research to determine sources of problems**
   a. Talk to people involved
   b. Analyze crime data
   c. Observe situation if possible (stakeout)

7. **Plan ways of dealing with problem**
   a. Analyze resources
   b. Discuss with supervisor, other officers
   c. Write Patrol Management Plan, review with supervisor

8. **Provide citizens information about ways they can handle problems (educate/empower)**
   a. Distribute crime prevention information
   b. Provide names and number of other responsible agencies; tell citizens how to approach these agencies

9. **Help citizens develop appropriate expectations about what police can do and teach them how to interact effectively with police**
   a. Attend community meetings/make presentations
   b. Present school programs
   c. Write article for area paper
   d. Hold discussions with community leaders

10. **Develop resources for responding to problem**
    a. Talk with other officers, detectives, supervisors
    b. Talk with other agencies or individuals who could help

11. **Implement problem solution**
    a. Take whatever actions are called for

12. **Assess effectiveness of solution**
    a. Use data, feedback from persons who experienced the problem, and/or personal observation to determine whether problem has been solved

13. **Keep citizens informed**
    a. Officers tell citizens what steps have been taken to address a problem and with what results
    b. Detectives tell citizens what is happening with their cases

FIGURE 5-10 Performance Dimensions for the Houston Police Department
Source: Oettmeier, T., and Wycoff, M. Personnel Performance Evaluations in the Community Policing Context. Washington, DC: Community Policing Consortium, 1997.

Even though community policing has been the primary strategy in many American police departments, community policing has not been integrated into police performance appraisals on a wide scale. Lilley and Hinduja report that community policing attributes have not been used in most community policing departments when measuring performance.[27] Departments still emphasize bean counting and adherence to police policies. Many performance appraisal systems remain mechanistic and fail to encourage or reinforce community policing activities. Departments must endeavor to include community policing and other important dimensions in departmental performance appraisals.

IMPROVING RATER PERFORMANCE

Perhaps the most notable problem associated with performance appraisals is raters' ability to accurately evaluate subordinates. There are a number of rater errors inherent to performance appraisals.

Rater Errors

Rater errors refer to problems that potentially occur anytime superiors rate subordinates. Errors occur for a variety of reasons, and they must be controlled if the department is to have an effective performance appraisal system. The following is a discussion of some of the most common rater errors.

Halo Effect.   The halo effect occurs when a rater evaluates a subordinate high or low on all rating dimensions because of one dimension. For example, a sergeant may believe that patrol officers should write a generous number of traffic citations. Officers who tend to write more citations receive higher ratings in all categories, while those who do not write above average numbers of tickets receive only average or below average ratings. In this example, the sergeant allows the number of citations written by officers to cloud his or her judgment about other rating dimensions.

Recency Problem.   Recency problem refers to when a recent negative or positive event unduly affects an officer's ratings. An officer may make a traffic stop that results in the seizure of several pounds of cocaine and the arrest of several mid-level drug dealers immediately prior to the end of the rating period. The sergeant doing the ratings may give this arrest undue weight and rate the officer high. It may not matter that the arrest was the only felony arrest made by the officer during the rating period, and that the officer's performance overall was less than average. Ratings should represent the average performance during the total rating period.

Rater Bias.   Rater bias refers to raters' values or prejudices distorting their ratings. People have all sorts of biases that can affect ratings: religious, race, gender, appearance, existence of a disability, prior employment history, or membership in civic clubs and organizations. Biases can help or detract from an officer's ratings, or in some cases, increase an officer's ratings.

Constant Error Problem.   Some raters are too strict, others may be too lenient, while still others tend to rate everyone in the middle. For example, a new sergeant may rate all his subordinates lower in order to show improvement in the next rating period. Constant error creates problems since all officers are eventually compared to the same overall criteria.

Unclear Standards.   Unclear standards are a problem when there is a misunderstanding about the rating dimensions or associated standards. For example, sergeants may be asked to rate their subordinates on productivity. One sergeant may define productivity one way, while another may define it differently. Varying interpretations of rating dimensions substantially affect ratings. The Behaviorally Anchored Rating Scale helps to solve this problem.

These five errors represent the most common rating errors. Raters can make a number of other mistakes. For example, raters tend to value officers who are more like themselves or dislike those who are different. This can apply to a person's appearance, background, education, hobbies, and so on. First impressions of new officers may also have an undue impact on their subsequent ratings. Finally, officers who have high-profile assignments may have an advantage over other officers because of their being perceived as better. Innumerable factors that have nothing to do with officers' performance can affect their performance appraisal ratings.

Rater Training

An effective method for controlling rater errors is rater training. Too often, supervisors are given performance appraisal forms and expected to accurately complete them. The rating process is extremely complicated and rater training is one of the better administrative mechanisms for improving ratings. In a survey of police officers, Coutts and Schneider found that many felt that raters were poorly trained, and this lack of training resulted in inadequate performance appraisals and lowered morale within the department.[28]

A training program can emphasize the standards used to evaluate officers, and it can be used to underscore the importance of making accurate ratings that distinguish good, average, and below average performers. Training can indoctrinate raters on how ratings are used and the importance of making distinctions in ratings.

Another important part of training is training raters on how to give subordinates feedback. Many superior officers fail to provide subordinates with adequate feedback on their performance. If adequate feedback is not provided, subordinates cannot be expected to improve. In the end, training is one of the most important mechanisms that a department can use to enhance the accuracy of ratings.

SEXUAL HARASSMENT

Sexual harassment is prohibited as a result of Title VII of the 1964 Civil Rights Act. **Sexual harassment** according to the Equal Employment Opportunity Commission is defined as

> … unwelcome sexual advances, requests for sexual favors, and other physical or verbal conduct of a sexual nature constitutes sexual harassment when submission to or rejection of this conduct explicitly or implicitly affects an individual's employment, unreasonably interferes with an individual's work performance, or creates an intimidating, hostile or offensive work environment.

In 1986, the U.S. Supreme Court clarified the issue of sexual harassment by specifying two distinct types of sexual harassment: (1) quid pro quo, and (2) hostile work environment.[29]

Quid pro quo sexual harassment exists when there is a tangible economic detriment as a result of a refusal to succumb to sexual advances. Economic detriment can refer to any job condition or benefit, including work schedule, promotion, overtime, assignment, or other working condition. Thus, when an employer or superior insinuates that some working condition may be affected by the refusal to submit to sex or other affections, quid pro quo sexual harassment has occurred.

Hostile work environment, on the other hand, refers to situations in which unwelcome sexual conduct has the effect of "unreasonably interfering with an individual's work performance or creating an intimidating environment."[30] The harassment must be "sufficiently severe or pervasive, so as to alter the conditions of the victim's employment and create an abusive working environment."[31] Later, the U.S. Supreme Court identified three factors that should be considered in determining whether a hostile work environment exists:[32]

1. Was the conduct physically threatening or humiliating as opposed to being just offensive?
2. Did the conduct reasonably interfere with the employee's work performance?
3. Did the conduct affect the employee's psychological well-being?

Numerous court cases illustrate that behavior that some people may see as joking or playful may be offensive and hostile to another. Actions such as commenting on one's dress or appearance, allowing pornography or lewd pictures in the workplace, continued sexual or social requests, or telling sexually suggestive jokes can contribute to the creation of a hostile workplace. For example, one study of female officers found that 74 percent reported they had received unwanted sexual attention, 71.5 percent reported suggestive remarks made about them, and 34.5 percent reported officers attempting to have a romantic or sexual relationship even after they were informed that such a relationship was unwanted.[33] Anyone in a police organization can create a hostile work environment. Numerous departments have been sued as a result of sexual harassment, and these suits often result in substantial judgments.

Departments can avoid sexual harassment by issuing policies, training officers, and ensuring that first-line supervisors properly control officers' behavior. When a department fails to do these things, it is vulnerable to a lawsuit should sexual harassment occur. More importantly, if a complaint of sexual harassment is made and the supervisor or manager fails to properly investigate the complaint, the supervisor or manager is civilly liable should there be a judgment for the complainant. Police leaders must ensure that the proper mechanisms to discourage sexual harassment are in place.

PROMOTIONS

Promotion is the process of identifying officers for leadership roles in the police department whether it is sergeants, lieutenants, captains, etc. A bad promotion decision can have long-term negative effects on a department, as poorly performing supervisors and managers can adversely affect productivity. On the other hand, highly qualified, motivated supervisors or managers can provide the leadership that a department or unit needs. Police departments must endeavor to select the best candidates for promotion.

It should be remembered that promotions are nothing more than a selection process, and as such police departments should ensure that discrimination does not occur and should strive to ensure that females and minorities are adequately represented in the supervisory and managerial ranks. Moreover, in some cases the more qualified or better officers may refuse to participate in the promotion process. They may have family duties, part-time jobs, or other activities that fit within their work schedules, and they reason that a promotion will result in a new assignment or shift that would interfere with these activities. Others enjoy the current assignment and do not wish to take a new job within the department. Regardless, police leadership must encourage all qualified officers to participate in promotional processes.

Minimum Qualifications for Promotion

Police departments generally have minimum qualifications for promotion. Years of service is generally one of these qualifications. Most departments will require an officer to have three to five years service before competing for promotion. The idea is that officers should learn the job they hold before competing for the next level. A patrol sergeant should thoroughly know patrol. A number of departments require officers to have some college education before competing for a higher rank. For example, a department may require a bachelor's degree for sergeant and lieutenant and a master's degree for positions above lieutenant. Many police departments recognize the importance of a college degree, especially for higher-ranking personnel. A third criteria used by some departments is discipline. If an officer had been disciplined within a specified time period, such as two years, he or she is not allowed to participate in the promotion process.

COMPONENTS IN PROMOTION PROCESSES

Nationally, police department use a variety of tests or procedures to promote officers. The most common procedures used are the written test, performance appraisal, and the oral interview board. Some departments will use situational tests and give points for education and training.

Written Promotional Tests

The **written promotional test** is an important part of the promotion process. It essentially measures candidates' job knowledge. Generally, police departments will post a reading list for the applicants to study. They often include the department's policies and procedures, statutory law, and police-related textbooks. For example, a written test for sergeant may include policies and procedures, the state criminal code, a textbook on criminal investigation, and a textbook dealing with police leadership. These are areas that a proficient supervisor should master. In addition to assisting in identifying promotable officers, the written test can be considered a personnel development tool as all the officers taking the test will increase their knowledge as a result of studying for the test.

Performance Appraisals

Performance appraisals are another common part of the promotion process. A good indicator of future behavior is past behavior, which makes performance appraisals an important part of the process. If officers had bad or mediocre performance appraisals in the past, it is a good indication that they will not perform satisfactorily in a higher-ranking position. As discussed above, promotability ratings should be used when using performance appraisals for promotion. Whereas a performance appraisal for a patrol officer might use criteria such as officer safety, appearance, demeanor with citizens, and so on, promotability ratings will use criteria that are more appropriate for the new rank. For example, some of the criteria for sergeants might be relations with citizens, relations with officers and superiors, writing skills—since sergeants review reports, knowledge of department programs, and so on. The performance appraisal criteria should reflect the new job.

Oral Interview Board

The oral interview board tests candidates' oral communications skills and their ability to respond to certain situations as well as their preparation to be promoted. Some of the questions that may be asked on an oral interview board include:

- What have you done to prepare yourself for promotion?
- Why do you think you would be a good sergeant, lieutenant, captain, etc.?
- How would you handle an officer who is not performing up to expectations?
- How would you deal with a situation where many of your subordinates requested vacation at the same time?

FOCUS ON: ST. LOUIS POLICE DEPARTMENT PROMOTION LAWSUITS

It is fairly commonplace for police departments to be sued as a result of promotions. However, in some cases this litigation can become very complex. In 2016, the St. Louis Police Department promoted Ronnie Robinson, an African-American male, to Lt. Colonel, the second-highest rank in the police department. Later, Major Michael Caruso, a White male, filed a race discrimination lawsuit against the department. He noted that he had more education, and time in service. He also stated that he had the highest score on the promotion examination. Later, Major Rochelle Jones, an African-American female, filed a suit over the same promotion, stating that she was discriminated against because of her gender. She alleged that she was better qualified and had more experience than Robinson.

As noted, police departments often are involved in lawsuits over promotions. This is why police departments need strict promotion criteria and testing and follow them with precision. The St. Louis case shows that problems can occur at all levels of a police department. It also demonstrates how these cases can quickly become very complicated.

Source: Based on St. Louis Post-Dispatch, "Second St. Louis Police Major sues over promotion, claims gender discrimination" http://www.stltoday.com/news/local/crime-and-courts/second-st-louis-police-major-sues-over-promotion-claims-gender/article_06f31710-047c-586f-b8f0-625fc5893b4f.html

- How would you handle a situation where your subordinates disagree with a new departmental policy?
- What actions would you take to improve the relations with the community if you were assigned to an area where the citizens are distrustful of the police?

The oral interview board can investigate a wide range of areas. It is important that critical aspects of the job are examined by the oral interview board. The board needs to investigate the officer's preparation, decision-making skills, relations with others, and knowledge and application of departmental policy.

Situational Tests

A number of police departments use situational tests as part of the promotion process. A **situational test** is where candidates for promotion are given a situation and must act out how they would deal with the situation. It might be a role play exercise where candidates for sergeant must counsel a subordinate officer, an actor, for being discourteous when dealing with citizens. Candidates for captain may be required to make a presentation to a community group about the department's policy on traffic safety. The oral interview board panel would constitute the community group and would ask follow-up questions. Sergeant candidates may be asked to review officers' reports looking for errors and incorrect grammar. A candidate for chief may be asked to review the staffing in the police department and make recommendations for improving personnel assignments. Candidates for captain may be asked to describe how they would deal with a catastrophic event such as a major fire, flood, or tornado. Such real-life situations can be informative when rating people for promotion.

Once the promotion tests have been administered, the results are combined and a ranked list is generated. When combined, some departments will give a higher weight to some of the tests. For example, some departments will weigh the written test 40 percent while the oral interview board and performance appraisal are weighted 30 percent each. Different departments have varying procedures here. Promotions are then made from the list. A police chief may promote from the top three or five candidates in some jurisdictions, while others promote consecutively from the list.

RISK MANAGEMENT

Risk management is where a police department employs attorneys or professional risk managers to evaluate police department procedures and operations to minimize liability and risk to officers while performing their police duties. Archbold, in a national study of police departments, found that about half of police departments were using risk managers to reduce their risk.[34] About half of the departments had their own risk manager, while the other half used a central government risk management office. Many departments initiated risk management after a number of lawsuits and substantial payouts to claimants. Risk management is an effort to reduce injuries and liability. It is important to note that the nature of police work exposes police officers to liability incidents every day.[35]

There are three primary areas of risk that must be monitored and controlled, workers' compensation, law enforcement liability, and police auto liability. **Workers' compensation** is initiated when a police officer is injured on the job and incurs medical expenses or lost wages. Here, the officer is compensated through the state's workers' compensation program. Cities and counties pay into the state's workers' compensation program, and when a particular city or county has a claim, the rate of payment increases. Thus, cities and police departments have a financial incentive to reduce these injuries.

Law enforcement liability is where police departments are sued for violating people's rights or unjustifiably causing injury or death to people. Lawsuits in this area cost police departments millions of dollars each year, and many of the judgments are in the millions. Some of the critical areas where law enforcement liability occur are improper arrest, deadly force, injuries and deaths associated with incarceration, prisoner transportation, illegal searches and seizures, and improper arrest tactics.

Police auto liability refers to the many lawsuits that occur as a result of police involvement in automobile accidents, especially those involving pursuits or responding to calls for service where the responding officer violates traffic codes. Nationally, police officers are involved in thousands of automobile crashes each year. Citizens involved in the crashes generally claim that the officer was negligent. These crashes often involve physical injury as well as property damage.

Risk management is not only implemented to reduce the risk of litigation; it is also implemented to protect police officers. Police work involves large numbers of hazardous situations. Moreover, police officers frequently are injured on the job. Risk management entails an examination of police activities and, where appropriate, making recommendations that reduce police officers' exposure to dangerous situations. This often involves the implementation of new procedures for officers. Police departments across the nation have large numbers of policies and procedures. They are designed to protect the public, protect police officers, and ensure that officers' actions are consistent with the law.

An important part of risk analysis is risk assessment. **Risk assessment** involves surveying the organization to determine the potential areas of liability. This is not a difficult chore since numerous lawsuits have been filed in the past, and they effectively identify risk areas. Once risk has been identified, police departments should take action to reduce risk. This also should not be difficult since the lawsuits and the actions taken by other departments can provide insights into how to remedy or reduce liability. Once corrective actions have been identified, the police executive must ensure that they are implemented and officers' behavior is consistent with the remedies.

There are three methods by which to manage risk. First is training. Police chiefs and managers must ensure that their officers are properly trained. Training curriculum can be substantially enhanced by updating it by addressing the problems that contribute to risk. Training is too often sterile where only the basics are covered. Officers should be made aware of any pitfalls that can result in risk.

Second, police departments must examine their policies and procedures to ensure that procedures when enacted on the street reduce the possibility of risk problems. Perhaps the best way to accomplish this is through police accreditation from an agency such as the Commission on Accreditation for Law Enforcement Agencies (CALEA). Regardless of how it is accomplished, a police department should review its policies periodically to ensure that the policies are up to date and that they reduce risk. Additionally, police agencies need to ensure that officers are indeed following the policies. Many liability situations occur as a result of officers not following policies or procedures.

Finally, risk can be reduced through supervision. Supervisors too frequently do not take corrective action when their subordinates fail to use proper procedures. When this occurs, bad or unacceptable behavior can become institutionalized; it becomes normal behavior. This speaks to the importance of promotions. Departments must promote officers who know the procedures and have the wherewithal to ensure they are followed.

YOU DECIDE....

You are the police chief in a small department with 60 officers. Your officers have been involved in a number of auto accidents in the past several months. Several of these accidents occurred when officers were involved in pursuits, while others occurred during normal driving. The city council is aware of the accidents, especially the high costs of replacing and repairing the damaged police vehicles, not to mention the liability costs associated with the accidents. The mayor has asked you to develop a plan that will reduce the accidents and present your plan to the city council.

Questions for Discussion

1. How would you go about studying or analyzing the problem?

2. Who would you consult with to gain more information?

3. What alternatives would you consider to reduce the number of police involved in traffic accidents?

4. Which alternatives would you implement?

Summary

This chapter explored the various processes that occur within the human resources domain. Human resources in terms of activities are fairly expansive, encompassing a variety of activities. At the lowest level, police departments recruit and hire new police officers. This is a difficult task in that many police departments are not able to hire enough new qualified officers to fill their vacant positions. Many officers are disqualified for a variety of reasons. The selection process involves a variety of steps, including written tests, physical agility tests, background investigations, polygraph examinations, medical and psychological testing, and oral boards. This extensive series of tests is designed to identify candidates who will be good police officers.

Once officers are hired, they must be trained. New police officers are trained in a basic police academy where they receive the knowledge and skills necessary to be police officers. Once they graduate from the academy they are assigned to an FTO program where they receive additional training and are evaluated on their ability to perform different police officer tasks. This is a critical stage in officer selection. Probationary officers who cannot perform at expected levels should be dismissed. Poor or mediocre police officers can cause numerous problems during their careers.

Once on the streets, officers are evaluated using a performance appraisal process. This generally is an annual process and serves to provide officers with feedback on their performance. Police departments should constantly evaluate officers, provide them with feedback, and take corrective action when necessary. If this is neglected, officers will develop habits that can cause innumerable problems for the department.

The promotion process is another critical human resources activity. Departments must identify officers who are capable of assuming leadership positions. They must be able to comprehend departmental policies and procedures and ensure their subordinates follow those procedures. When officers fail to follow procedures, they incur risk for the department. Here, police departments face risk from workers' compensation issues, law enforcement activities, and auto liability. Police departments must take steps to reduce risk. This is done through training, ensuring policies and procedures accurately reflect the operational environment, and supervision. Risk management is critical to a police organization.

Discussion Questions

1. How does affirmative action laws affect policing? Do they improve policing?
2. What are the requirements to become a police officer? Do you believe they are reasonable?
3. What tools or tests are used by police departments to select police officers? Do you believe they are reasonable? Can the system be improved?
4. What are the common errors that are made when completing a performance appraisal for subordinate officers?
5. What are the types of training that police officers receive and what are their purposes?
6. What is sexual harassment? What are the two types of sexual harassment that can occur?
7. What are the tests used in police promotions?
8. What is risk management and why is it important?
9. What are the categories of risk that police departments face?

Internet Investigations

California Commission on Peace Officer Standards and Training, "Basic Peace Officer Basic Training"
https://www.post.ca.gov/peace-officer-basic-training.aspx
Quora, "How Are the Police Promotions Given?"
https://www.quora.com/How-are-the-police-promotions-given
Law Enforcement Today, "Progressive LE Leaders Effectively Manage Departmental Risk"
http://www.lawenforcementtoday.com/progressive-le-leaders-effectively-manage-departmental-risk/

U.S. Department of State, "Sexual Harassment Policy"
https://www.state.gov/s/ocr/c14800.htm
CliffsNotes, "Affirmative Action: A Tool for Justice?"
https://www.cliffsnotes.com/study-guides/criminal-justice/police-problems/affirmative-action-a-tool-for-justice
Cheswold Police, "Police Officer Evaluation"
http://www.theiacp.org/Portals/0/documents/pdfs/Handout_PoliceOfficerEmployeeEvaluation.pdf

Officers' Rights, Discipline, and Liability: A Legal and Policy-Driven Framework

STUDENT LEARNING OUTCOMES

After reading this chapter, the student will:

■ understand the purpose and provisions of the Peace Officers Bill of rights

■ comprehend police officers' rights and limitations in areas such as freedom of speech, searches and seizures, religious practices, moonlighting, alcohol and drug use, and residency according to legislative enactments and court decisions

■ know the various forms of disciplinary action that can be taken by police leaders against officers

■ be able to discuss how the changes in (and spreading legalization of) marijuana can affect police leaders and their policies

■ know the content and potential problems for police officers under the *Brady* decision

■ understand how complaints against the police can be investigated in a fair manner

■ understand how early intervention systems may be employed by police leadership toward identifying and treating officers with personal and/or professional problems

■ be knowledgeable about how police leaders can be found liable if they are negligent in their supervision of officers

■ describe the nature and use of 42 U.S. Code Section 1983

■ be able to explain what protections against liability police have in vehicle pursuits, and the kinds of actions that can result in their being liable for damages

KEY TERMS AND CONCEPTS

- Alcohol and drug testing
- *Brady* material
- Citizen review boards
- Civil liability
- Constitutional rights (officers')
- Disposition
- Duty of care
- Early intervention systems
- Failure to protect
- Freedom of speech
- Grievance

- Marijuana conundrum
- Misuse of firearms
- Moonlighting
- Negligence
- Peace Officers Bill of Rights (POBR)
- Proximate cause
- Religious practices
- Searches and seizures
- Section 1983
- Sexual misconduct

INTRODUCTION

This chapter, in examining officer rights and discipline, is essentially a precursor to Chapter 9, where we discuss ethics and inappropriate police behaviors. These interrelated aspects of police leadership are especially delicate and important; if they are ignored or handled improperly, they can foster serious internal and external problems, increased liability, and a loss of public respect and trust.

The police, more than most segments of government, operate under the close scrutiny of the public. The media and some citizens stand ready to criticize the police when an incident goes awry. Therefore, it is also important that police leaders develop and follow sound disciplinary policies and ensure that they are properly trained to intervene in problems early. These leaders must also have a good working knowledge of departmental rules and regulations, as well as the resources available for dealing with disciplinary issues.

This chapter begins with an overview of the Peace Officers Bill of Rights and several areas in which their constitutional rights are limited under the U.S. Constitution and federal court decisions; it will be seen that, because of the unique nature of their role and responsibilities, they are held to higher standards than common citizens. We then look at the burgeoning issue of whether or not police officers should (or ever will) be allowed to ingest marijuana while off duty in states where it is legal, and the standards to which police applicants can be held with past marijuana use. Then the nature of complaints against officers is discussed, including how complaints are investigated and the kinds of outcomes and punishments that may result. Next, we examine the early intervention systems concept for identifying and helping officers who manifest problems on the job; following that is a discussion of some legal consequences of failure to properly supervise officers. Finally, the liability of police leadership is addressed in terms of their being held accountable for their subordinates' actions. The chapter includes several examples and case studies.

Note that another related area of police discipline—grievances and appeals—is discussed in Chapter 7, which concerns unions and labor relations.

PEACE OFFICERS BILL OF RIGHTS

Although they may be compelled to give up certain rights in connection with an investigation of on-duty misbehavior or illegal acts, police officers generally are afforded the same rights, privileges, and immunities outlined in the U.S. Constitution for all citizens. These rights are the basis for such legislation as the Peace Officers Bill of Rights (POBR, which is to protect police officers from undue or coercive police investigations, discussed next), labor agreements, court decisions, and civil service and departmental rules and regulations that guide an agency's disciplinary process.

Beginning in the 1990s, police officers have insisted on greater procedural safeguards to protect them against what they perceive as arbitrary infringement on their rights. These demands have been reflected in statutes enacted in many states, generally known as the "Peace Officers Bill of Rights." These statutes confer on an employee a property interest (i.e., their job is to be viewed as their property) in his or her position and mandate due process rights for peace officers who are the subject of internal investigations that could lead to disciplinary action. These statutes identify the type of information that must be provided to the accused officer, the officer's responsibility to cooperate during the investigation, the officer's rights to representation during the process, and the rules and procedures concerning the collection of certain types of evidence, especially the interrogation of the officer.

An example of a state POBR (California) is shown in the "Focus On" box.

FOCUS ON: CALIFORNIA'S "PUBLIC SAFETY OFFICERS PROCEDURAL BILL OF RIGHTS ACT"

California General Code Sec. 3300–3311 states, in part, as follows:

When any public safety officer is under investigation and subjected to interrogation by...any other member of the employing public safety department, that could lead to punitive action, the interrogation shall be conducted under the following conditions.

a. The interrogation shall be conducted at a reasonable hour, preferably at a time when the public safety officer is on duty...unless the seriousness of the investigation requires otherwise. If the interrogation does occur during off-duty time of the public safety officer being interrogated, the public safety officer shall be compensated for any off-duty time.

b. The public safety officer under investigation shall be informed prior to the interrogation of the rank, name, and command of the officer in charge of the interrogation, the interrogating officers, and all other persons to be present during the interrogation. All questions…shall be asked by and through no more than two interrogators at one time.

c. The public safety officer…shall be informed of the nature of the investigation prior to any interrogation.

d. The interrogating session shall be for a reasonable period taking into consideration gravity and complexity of the issue being investigated. The person under interrogation shall be allowed to attend to his or her own personal physical necessities.

Source: See California Government Code Section 3303–3311, https://www.insidehighered.com/sites/default/server_files/files/policeofficersbillofrights.pdf.

As noted in the statute, police officers who are under investigation are afforded certain rights. POBR statutes ensure that police officers are not subjected to coercive interrogations or questioning. Additionally, most POBRs contain language that requires the department to provide a written notice of charges; they provide that officers have a right to representation, either an attorney or a union representative; they prohibit the use of a polygraph; and they often establish procedures specifying how the information obtained in an interrogation can be used.

Although at least 17 states have enacted POBR laws, a federal version has never passed both houses of Congress.[1] Police leaders, wanting the widest possible latitude in investigating their officers' possible misconduct, as well as appropriately discipline any employee found guilty of misconduct, would prefer having the power to vigorously question suspect officers. Therefore, it is not surprising that two of their leading associations, the International Association of Chiefs of Police and the Police Executive Research Forum, have taken public stands against proposed federal POBR laws, arguing that such a law would make it harder for a department to fulfill its mission of protecting the public.[2]

Nonetheless, where such statutes exist, it is imperative that supervisors and managers become thoroughly familiar with their provisions, so that procedural due process requirements can be met, particularly in disciplinary cases when an employee's property interest might be affected. If procedural guidelines are not followed, it may result in the police department not being able to take action against an officer who has committed a crime or disciplinary infraction.

In the 1990s, police officers began insisting on greater procedural safeguards to protect them against perceived arbitrary infringement on their rights.
Source: Dmitriy Shironosov/123RF

POLICE OFFICERS' CONSTITUTIONAL RIGHTS

Over the years, the courts and legislatures have bestowed or recognized a number of rights that police officers possess. Many of these rights are constitutionally guaranteed, but others have been adopted by legislative bodies or through union negotiations. The following provides an overview of some of these rights.

Free Speech

Although the right of **freedom of speech** is one of the most fundamental of all rights of Americans, the Supreme Court indicated in *Pickering v. Board of Education* (1968:568) that "the State has interests as an employer in regulating the speech of its employees that differ significantly from those it possesses in connection with regulation of the speech of the citizenry in general." Thus, the state may impose restrictions on its employees that it would not be able to impose on the citizenry at large. These restrictions must be reasonable, however.

A police regulation may be found to be an unreasonable infringement on the free speech interests of officers if overly broad. A Chicago Police Department rule prohibiting "any activity, conversation, deliberation, or discussion which is derogatory to the Department" is a good example of one that is unreasonable, as such a rule obviously prohibits all criticism of the agency by its officers, even in private conversation.[3] Essentially, a department cannot arbitrarily regulate officers' speech. However, if officers make statements that adversely affect the department's operation, such as leaking information about an ongoing investigation, or make false statements, the courts generally will prohibit the speech.

A related area is political activity. As with free speech, governmental agencies may restrict the political behavior of their employees to prevent employees from being pressured by their superiors to support certain political candidates or engage in political activities, under threat of loss of employment or other adverse action. The federal government and many states have such statutes.

A police officer may also be protected because of his or her political affiliations. An example is a case involving the Sheriff's Department in Cook County, Illinois, where a newly elected sheriff, a Democrat, fired the chief deputy of the process division and a bailiff of the juvenile court because they were Republicans. The Supreme Court ruled that it was a violation of the employees' First Amendment rights to discharge them from non-policymaking positions solely on the basis of their political party affiliation.[4]

At the same time, police departments cannot restrict police officers' off-duty political activities. That is, they have the right to run for certain political offices as long as those offices do not create a conflict of interest or interfere with the officer's performance of duties, for example, school board. Moreover, police departments cannot restrict an officer's off-duty political activities. That is, officers are allowed to support and campaign for political candidates.

The First Amendment's reach also includes appearance. For example, the Supreme Court upheld the constitutionality of a regulation of the Suffolk County, New York, Police Department that established several grooming standards regarding hair, sideburn, and moustache length for its male officers to make officers readily recognizable to the public and to maintain the esprit de corps within the department.[5]

Searches and Seizures

The Fourth Amendment to the U.S. Constitution protects the right of the people to be secure in their persons, houses, papers, and effects against unreasonable **searches and seizures**. In an important case in 1967, the Supreme Court held that the amendment also protected individuals' reasonable expectations of privacy, not just property interests.[6]

The Fourth Amendment usually applies to police officers when they are at home or off duty in the same manner that it applies to all citizens. Because of the nature of their work, however, police officers can be compelled to cooperate with investigations of their behavior when ordinary citizens would not. Examples include searches of equipment and lockers provided by the department to the officers. The officers have no expectation of privacy that affords or merits protection.[7] Lower courts, however, have established limitations on searches of employees themselves. The rights of prison authorities to search their employees arose in a 1985 Iowa case, in which employees were forced to sign a consent form allowing such searches as a condition of hire; the court disagreed with such a broad policy, ruling that the consent form was too broad and intruded on the employee's normal reasonable expectation of privacy.[8]

Police officers may also be forced to appear in a lineup, a clear "seizure" of their person. Lineups normally require probable cause, but a federal appeals court upheld a police commissioner's ordering of 62 officers to appear in a lineup during an investigation of police brutality, holding that "the governmental interest in the particular intrusion [should be weighed] against the offense to personal dignity and integrity." Again, the court cited the nature of the work, noting that police officers do "not have the full privacy and liberty from police officials that [they] would otherwise enjoy."[9]

Self-Incrimination

The Supreme Court has also addressed questions concerning the Fifth Amendment as it applies to police officers who are under investigation. In *Garrity v. New Jersey* (1967), a police officer was ordered by the attorney general to answer questions or be discharged. The officer testified that information obtained as a result of his answers was later used to convict him of criminal charges. The U.S. Supreme Court held that the information obtained from the officer could not be used against him at his criminal trial, because the Fifth Amendment forbids the use of coerced confessions. Today, the *Garrity* rule essentially states that if an officer is compelled to provide self-incriminating information or statements, such statements cannot be used in a criminal proceeding. However, they may be used to discipline or discharge the officer as long as such interrogations are not prohibited by the state's Peace Officers Bill of Rights, other statutes, or union contract. *Garrity* requires that when police wrongdoing occurs, the department must make a decision as to pursue the matter criminally or civilly before interrogating the officer.

It is proper to fire a police officer who refuses to answer questions that are related directly to the performance of his or her duties, provided that the officer has been informed that any answers may not be used later in a criminal proceeding. Although there is some diversity of opinion among lower courts on the question of whether an officer may be compelled to submit to a polygraph examination, the majority of courts that have considered the question have held that an officer can be required to take the examination.[10]

However, there are a number of states that prohibit requiring officers to take a polygraph. For example, the California Peace Officers Bill of Rights states:

> No public safety officer shall be compelled to submit to a polygraph examination against his will. No disciplinary action or other recrimination shall be taken against a public safety officer refusing to submit to a polygraph examination, nor shall any comment be entered anywhere in the investigator's notes or anywhere else that the public safety officer refused to take a polygraph examination, nor shall any testimony or evidence be admissible at a subsequent hearing, trial, or proceeding, judicial or administrative, to the effect that the public safety officer refused to take a polygraph examination.[11]

Religious Practices

Criminal justice work often requires that personnel are available and on duty 24 hours per day, 7 days a week. Although it is not always convenient or pleasant, such shift configurations require that many criminal justice employees work weekends, nights, and holidays. It is generally assumed that one who takes such a position agrees to work such hours and abide by other conditions of the job (i.e., carrying a weapon, as in a policing position). There are occasions, however, when one's religious beliefs are in direct conflict with the requirements of the job, such as conflicts between one's work assignment and attendance at religious services or periods of religious observance. In these situations, the employee may be forced to choose between the job and his or her religious beliefs. However, departments generally must make "reasonable accommodations," which may include allowing the officer to trade shifts or take vacation time. A department does not have to make accommodations that interfere with the operation of the department. Furthermore, administrators may limit workplace proselytizing (attempts by employees to convert other employees to their religion) if it undermines or disrupts police functions; nor do administrators have to grant officers the right to refuse a lawful assignment (such was the case where a police sergeant was suspended for his unwillingness to arrest antiabortion demonstrators—he opposed abortion—and informed his superiors that he would be unable to direct his officers to arrest demonstrators actively engaged in antiabortion efforts).[12]

Title VII of the Civil Rights Act of 1964 prohibits religious discrimination in employment. Thus, Title VII requires reasonable accommodation of religious beliefs, but not to the extent that the employee has complete freedom of religious expression.[13]

Sexual Misconduct

Although we will discuss sexual misconduct more in Chapter 9, it deserves further mention here. To be blunt, criminal justice employees have ample opportunity to become engaged in affairs, incidents, trysts, dalliances, or other behavior that is clearly sexual in nature. In addition, a number of police "groupies" do in fact chase police officers and others in uniform.

FOCUS ON: NYPD ALLOWS SIKH OFFICERS TO WEAR FULL TURBANS AND GROW BEARDS

In an effort to make the NYPD as diverse as possible, NYPD Commissioner James O'Neill announced a policy change that allows Sikh officers to wear blue-colored turbans with police brass affixed to the front replacing the traditional police hat. The NYPD has 160 Sikh officers and wearing of the turban is a change in what in the past was a very strict policy. Sikh officers also have the option to wear a smaller wrap, known as a patka under the official police cap. Sikh officers may also wear a beard one inch in length in an effort

to further provide them religious accommodation. Sikh community leaders applauded the NYPD for their efforts. Reports reveal that approximately a half dozen police forces across the nation provide similar accommodations to Sikh officers.

Source: Based on David Shortell, "NYPD Changes Policy, Allows Turbans," CNN, December 29, 2016, http://www.cnn .com/2016/12/29/homepage2/nypd-sikh-officers-turbans-policy -change/.

Police sexual misconduct is often considered a hidden crime that is often unreported. Instances of sexual impropriety in police work can range from casual flirting while on the job to much worse, such as committing acts of statutory and forcible rape or sodomy.

A recent study found that about half (48 percent) of the cases of police sexual misconduct involved an officer who was employed in the South; overall, victims in the United States tended to be young, and the most serious offense charged in about a third (32.3 percent) of the cases was forcible or statutory rape. Furthermore, about one-half of these cases occurred while the officer was off duty. Taken together, these findings seem to indicate scenarios in which officers had access and opportunity to victimize a young person while under their care.[14]

Clearly, police leaders should have formal policies specifically prohibiting sex-related misconduct; broad policies that address ethical standards will not suffice because they do not specifically address situations in which police take advantage of their position and authority to become involved in sexual misconduct. Although written policies cannot alone prevent such misconduct, they will send a clear statement of the organization's priorities, goals, and commitment to confronting the problem. Training should also be provided covering such misconduct and informing officers that the agency's culture does not tolerate sexual misconduct within the ranks. Finally, police leaders should use an Early Intervention Systems (EIS, also discussed in Chapter 9) for monitoring and preventing sex-related misconduct.[15]

Residency Requirements

Many governmental agencies specify that all or certain members in their employ must live within the geographical limits of their employing jurisdiction. In other words, employees must reside within the county or city of employment. Such residency requirements have been justified by employing agencies, particularly in criminal justice, on the grounds that employees should become familiar with and be visible in the jurisdiction of employment. Additionally, they should reside and pay taxes in their employing jurisdiction. Perhaps the strongest rationale given by employing agencies is that criminal justice employees must live within certain proximity of their work in order to respond quickly in the event of an emergency. The U.S. Supreme Court has ruled that such requirements are reasonable and do not violate constitutional safeguards.[16]

Moonlighting

The courts have traditionally supported police agencies placing limitations on the amount and kinds of outside work their employees can perform.[17] Police restrictions on **moonlighting** range from a complete ban on outside employment to permission to engage in certain forms of work—work that would not result in a conflict of interest for officers. When moonlighting is allowed and regulated, the regulations generally prohibit officers from working where they may be required to use their police powers. When officers use their police powers in other jobs, it substantially increases the likelihood of **civil liability** for the department.

Misuse of Firearms

Police agencies generally have policies regulating the use of handguns and other firearms by their officers, both on and off duty. The courts have held that such regulations need only be reasonable and that the burden rests with the disciplined police officer to show that the regulation was arbitrary and unreasonable.[18] Police firearms regulations tend to address three basic issues: (1) requirements for the safeguarding of the weapon, (2) guidelines for carrying the weapon while off duty, and (3) limitations on when the weapon may be fired. [In a related vein, a relatively new legislative enactment, the Law Enforcement Officers Safety Act of 2004[19] exempts qualified police officers from state laws prohibiting the carrying of concealed weapons and allows retired officers having at least 15 years of service to carry a firearm. The act is to afford these retired officers "protection of themselves, their families and our nation's communities."]

Courts and juries are dealing more harshly with police officers who misuse their firearms. The current tendency is to "look behind" police shootings in order to determine if the officer acted negligently or the employing agency negligently trained and supervised the officer or employee. Courts have awarded damages against police officers and/or their employers for other acts involving **misuse of firearms**, such as when an officer shot a person while intoxicated and off duty in a bar;[20] an officer accidentally killed an arrestee with a shotgun while handcuffing him;[21] an unstable officer shot his wife five times and then committed suicide with an off-duty weapon the department required him to carry;[22] and an officer accidentally shot and killed an innocent bystander while pursuing another man at nighttime (the officer had received no instruction on shooting at a moving target, night shooting, or shooting in residential areas).[23] These cases illustrate the importance of training and ensuring that officers receive all required training. It also demonstrates that training curricula must be comprehensive and up to date.

Alcohol and Drug Testing in the Workplace

It is obvious, given the extant law of most jurisdictions and the nature of their work, that criminal justice employees must not be "walking time bombs," but must be able to perform their work with a "clear head," unbefuddled by alcohol or drugs.[24] Police departments often specify in their manual of policy and procedures that no alcoholic beverages will be consumed within a specified period prior to reporting for duty. Such regulations have been upheld uniformly as rational because of the hazards of the work. Enforcing such regulations will occasionally result in criminal justice employees being ordered to submit to drug or alcohol tests.

In March 1989, the U.S. Supreme Court issued a major decision on drug testing of public employees in the workplace in *National Treasury Employees Union v. Von Raab,* which upheld drug testing when there was no indication of a drug problem in the workplace and held that although only a few employees test positive, drug use is such a serious problem that the program could continue. It stated that the Customs Service had a compelling interest in having a "physically fit" employee with "unimpeachable integrity and judgment" submit to a drug test.[25] Today, police departments have policies that require police officers—perhaps even the entire agency—to submit to random drug testing. There are basically two types of policies. First, some departments require drug testing when officers transfer in or out of special units such as narcotics or SWAT. The second policy is that all officers or officers assigned to certain units are subject to random drug testing. Drug and alcohol testing may also be required as a part of a disciplinary investigation.

This section provided information on employee rights and protection. The following section examines police internal investigative processes and how police misconduct is regulated. Police disciplinary action is a complicated process that requires that departments protect accused officers' rights. However, the police must have discipline in order to provide the public with the best possible services and to avoid civil liability and public criticism.

THE MARIJUANA CONUNDRUM: TO SMOKE OR NOT TO SMOKE?

With the spread of legalized marijuana use—for both medical and recreational purposes—across the United States, a question being posed is whether or not police officers should or will be permitted to use it when off duty. This is a thorny issue, especially given that marijuana use has been one of the primary disqualifiers of police applicants for many years—some agencies in the past disqualified would-be officers for using marijuana within the past five years (it is still common for agencies to bar applicants who have used marijuana over the past three years).

How should police leaders view this matter, in general? How should agency policy be drafted? Following are some points to consider.

First, although officers might reside in a state where marijuana use is legal, marijuana remains a Schedule 1 substance under the Controlled Substances Act (which means it is determined by the Food and Drug Administration to have no medical use). Its use and possession is still a violation of federal law. Therefore, until its legal status is changed, officers would be violating federal law by its use.

With the spread of legalized marijuana use, police leaders must determine whether or not officers should or will be permitted to use it when off duty.
Source: Pe3k/Shutterstock

Another viewpoint is that, while officers could use marijuana without being in violation of their state law, they would still be subject to their agencies' conduct policies, which generally prohibit the use of illegal drugs. Therefore, if the officers' use of marijuana was discovered, they could be disciplined or terminated.[26]

Another potential hurdle is drug testing cannot distinguish between past and current use. Police officers must of course be able to prove at any time that they are not under the influence of any substance. However, today's marijuana tests do not discriminate between current and past intoxication—tests of hair, urine, blood, and saliva indicate ingestion days, weeks, even months after usage; so even if an agency allowed its officers to use cannabis recreationally while off duty, contemporary testing protocol probably still makes it difficult if not impossible to prove they were not intoxicated while on duty.[27]

In sum, police leaders probably will continue taking a hardline approach against in-service officers' use of cannabis at any time; however, agencies can always soften their requirements for applicants. Such was the case in Seattle, Washington, where the department formerly required that applicants not have used marijuana for three years. Now the rule is no use within at least one year before joining the force.[28] The option of relaxing standards of past marijuana use may soon be spreading, as recruiting pools and positions become more difficult to fill and agencies begin to realize that societal attitudes are also relaxing. As examples, the U.S. Drug Enforcement Administration bars those who have experimented with or used narcotics from becoming agents, but it can make exceptions "for applicants who admit to limited youthful and experimental use of marijuana." Furthermore, while the Federal Bureau of Investigation (FBI) bars the hiring of employees who have used marijuana in the past three years, that policy was called into question in 2014 by Director James B. Comey, who suggested that the organization might have to loosen its policy in order to attract young, computer-savvy agents who are capable of keeping up with the newest generation of cybercriminals—though he soon changed his stance.[29]

BRADY MATERIAL

Before considering the effects of *Brady v. Maryland* (1963)[30] on police officers and leadership, read the scenario presented in the accompanying "Focus On" box.

In this scenario of an officer "ducking a radio call," Jones lied to his supervisor and the IA investigators. Police officers, by virtue of their position, are—first and foremost—required to tell the truth; to do any less can be career-ending. An officer with credibility issues is unable to make cases because he or she can no longer testify effectively in court from that point forward. His or her department is required to advise the prosecutor's office of this issue—and the prosecutor is required to disclose it to the defense—in every criminal case in which

FOCUS ON: A CASE OF DUCKING THE RADIO CALL

Officer Jones is at dinner with another officer but did not notify dispatch of his status. When he is dispatched to assist an animal control unit that is struggling to pick up a large, vicious dog, he believes the call to be minor in nature, so instead he informs dispatch that he is stopping a suspicious driver (remaining at dinner break with the other officer). Dispatch sends another unit from across town to the call, and in the meantime the animal control officer, acting alone, incurs a number of severe dog bites, $10,000 in medical costs (she has medical insurance), the loss of two week's work, and potential long-term injuries. When the officer who was having dinner with Jones learns about the injured animal control officer, he notifies Jones' supervisor, who in turn contacts Jones about his lack of response. Jones continues to maintain that he saw a vehicle that needed "checking out." Largely owing to the animal control officer's injuries, the matter is referred to the department's Internal Affairs (IA) office for investigation. Upon being questioned by IA, Jones initially lies to investigators, but when presented with the other officer's statements, he finally admits that he thought the dog call was a minor problem and opted to ignore it. He is given two weeks' leave without pay, and placed on a performance review for six months.

Jones will testify during the remainder of his career. Imagine Jones and others in this position to have to endure the following type of cross-examination and/or closing argument by the defense attorney:

> Ladies and gentlemen of the jury, as you consider the testimony of Officer Jones, whom the prosecution has called as its witness, it is my duty to inform you that you are being asked to believe the testimony of an officer who will lie in his reports.

To further sully Jones' reputation, the prosecutor's office may also inform the chief of police or sheriff that they will not take any future cases in which Jones is a witness.[31]

Because of *Brady*, one large Western police agency recently discovered that more than 135 of its officers had potential *Brady* problems in a disciplinary case.[32] In this case, Brady was convicted of first-degree murder and sentenced to death. Before trial, the government failed to turn over to the defense statements made to the police wherein another party actually admitted to the murder. Brady was convicted, and appealed. The U.S. Supreme Court held that Brady was entitled to obtain those statements, and that the government's failure to provide the statements amounted to a denial of his right to due process.

Brady thus established that in a criminal case the accused has a right to any exculpatory evidence—that is, any evidence in the government's possession that is favorable to the accused and is material to either guilt or punishment.[33] Agencies are thus encouraged to review all officers' personnel files to determine if any of them has a disciplinary history that would seriously impeach his or her credibility as a witness. Any such information should also be made available to the prosecutor before such officers are allowed to testify in a criminal prosecution.[34]

In sum, the best defense against problems resulting from *Brady* is to ensure the following:

- All officers have been properly trained on their obligations and duty to disclose exculpatory material.
- The agency has a policy which requires that officers document exculpatory information and provide it to the prosecutors.
- The agency has informed IA investigators of their responsibilities via training and policy, and informed prosecutors of information which could impeach the testimony of their officers.[35]

THE NEED FOR POLICIES AND GUIDELINES

Throughout its history, policing has experienced allegations of misconduct and corruption. In the late 1800s, New York police sergeant Alexander "Clubber" Williams epitomized police brutality, as he spoke openly of using his nightstick to knock a man unconscious, batter him to pieces, or even kill him. Williams supposedly coined the term *tenderloin* when he commented, "I've had nothing but chuck steaks for a long time, and now

TABLE 6-1 Conduct Regulated by Police Departments

Failure to conform with laws	Engaging in conduct unbecoming an officer
Seeking gifts, gratuities, or bribes	Engaging in vice activities
Citizen complaints	Failure to be courteous
Failure or late to report for duty	Dereliction of duty
Incompetence	Operation of departmental vehicles in an unsafe manner
Improper use of police equipment	Dissemination of confidential information
Dishonesty	Failure to complete reports
Improper treatment of prisoners	Improper use of force
Use of alcohol or drugs on duty	Loitering in bars in uniform
Failure to obey lawful orders	Appearance
Abuse of position or police power	Failure to report being arrested in another jurisdiction
Cowardice	Insubordination

I'm going to have me a little tenderloin."[36] Williams was referring to opportunities for graft in an area of downtown New York that was the heart of vice and nightlife, often referred to as Satan's Circus. This was Williams's beat, where his reputation for brutality and corruption became legendary.[37]

Although police corruption and brutality are no longer openly tolerated, a number of events throughout history have demonstrated that the problem still exists and requires the attention of police officials. Incidents such as the shooting of unarmed men, many of whom were minorities (discussed in Chapter 9), have led many people to believe that police misbehavior today is worse than during the riotous 1960s.

Officer misconduct and violations of departmental policy are the two principal areas that involve discipline.[38] Officer misconduct includes acts that harm the public, such as corruption, harassment, brutality, and civil rights violations. Violations of policy may involve a broad range of issues, including substance abuse and insubordination or minor violations of dress and punctuality.

Police departments must have policies and procedures to guide police officer behavior. Officers must be informed of behavioral expectations, and this is accomplished through policies. As noted in Table 6-1, departments have policies regulating all manner of officer conduct; following is an example of such a policy.

FOCUS ON: PINE BLUFF, ARKANSAS POLICE DEPARTMENT OFFICER CONDUCT POLICY

The Pine Bluff, Arkansas, Police Department Policy and Procedures Manual officer conduct policy reads as follows (in abridged form):

IV. PROCEDURES

   A. GENERAL CONDUCT

      1. OBEDIENCE TO LAWS, REGULATIONS, AND ORDERS

         a. Officers shall obey the constitutional, civil and criminal laws of the city, state, and federal government.

         b. Officers shall obey all lawful orders.

         c. VIOLATIONS INCLUDE, BUT ARE NOT LIMITED TO:

            i. Committing a willful violation of constitutional civil rights that demonstrates reckless disregard.

           ii. Committing non-exempted infractions of traffic codes (e.g., driving over the speed limit, failing to observe traffic control devices, parking in unauthorized locations, failing to wear seat belts)

          iii. Inflicting punishment or mistreatment (includes both physical as well as mental) upon a prisoner or person in custody or detention or any other member of the public.

          iv. Non-exempted violations of any local, state or federal criminal or civil codes or ordinances.

    v. Refusing or failing to protect a prisoner's civil rights when such need is made known or should have been known by a competent officer.

    vi. Unprivileged publication of a false statement intending to harm the reputation of another member of this agency or any person in general (slander if done verbally and libel if put in written form).

    vii. Using excessive force to hold, affect an apprehension, arrest or detain any person.

    viii. Using prohibited devices, procedures, tactics or techniques to affect a holding, apprehension, arrest or detention of another.

2. CONDUCT UNBECOMING AN OFFICER

    a. Honesty, efficiency, and integrity are the first guidelines for a law enforcement officer's conduct. All law enforcement officers must remember that they are employed to serve the citizens of this jurisdiction. The public is entitled to courteous efficient response to requests for law enforcement services.

    b. Law enforcement officers, whether on or off duty, shall be governed by ordinary and reasonable rules of good conduct and behavior and shall not commit any act which could adversely affect the department.

    c. Officers shall not make known to any person any order or information which they have knowledge of or have received, unless it is in the performance of official duty and given to a person entitled to have the information.

    d. All officers when off duty, but in uniform, shall conduct themselves as though they were on duty.

    e. Members shall conduct themselves (on duty as well as off duty) in a manner that does not damage or have the probable expectations of damaging or bringing the public image, integrity or reputation of the Pine Bluff Police Department into discredit, disrepute or impair its efficient and effective operation.[39]

Source: Adapted from Pine Bluff Police Department Policy & Procedures Manual Policy No. 1100. Pine Bluff Police Department Used with permission. Retrieved from http://www.pbpd.org/Policies/Chapter-XI/Microsoft%20Word%20-%20POL-1100%20_ Standards%20of%20Conduct_.pdf

WHEN COMPLAINTS ARISE: NATURE AND INVESTIGATION

Internal and Civilian Investigations

There are a variety of mechanisms used by departments to investigate and process police complaints. Generally speaking, the two broad differences across departments concern whether the authority for processing the complaints is vested with the police agency itself or some form of citizen board. In the former, total responsibility of the investigation and **disposition** of complaints is vested with the department. In the latter, the citizen inclusive board (sometimes referred to as a citizen (or civilian) review board; see Figure 6-3) can either have exclusive jurisdiction over the investigation and disposition of complaints, or the board may simply review complaint investigations to ensure fairness and comprehensiveness. In some cases, the civilian body oversees the police investigation but also has authority to intervene by recommending additional investigative efforts, or reviewing the merits of the findings of the police board.

    The following section traces the complaint processing and investigative process. Regardless of the agency involved, the process is very similar across departments.

Complaint Origin

A *personnel complaint* is an allegation of misconduct or illegal behavior against an employee by anyone inside or outside the organization. *Internal complaints* arise within the organization and may involve supervisors who observe officer misconduct, officers who complain about supervisors, supervisors who complain about other supervisors or middle managers, civilian personnel who complain about officers, and so on. *External complaints* originate from sources outside the organization and usually involve the public and constitute the largest volume of complaints. The most common external complaints are citizens' complaints where individual citizens complain or charge police misconduct.

    Supervisors may receive complaints from primary, secondary, and anonymous sources. A *primary* source is the victim or a witness. A *secondary* source is a party other than the victim, such as an attorney, school counselor, or parent of a juvenile. Generally, a secondary source is an individual who learns of the misconduct from a primary source. An anonymous source is unknown, and the complaint may be delivered to the police station via a telephone call or unsigned letter.

YOU DECIDE...

Particularly in the aftermath of police shootings in Ferguson, Missouri, and other cities, it has become more commonly argued that **citizen review boards** would provide the kind of independent and transparent oversight of policing that is needed today. Today, there are more than 200 such civilian oversight entities around the country, though their powers to investigate and punish officers vary.[40] Some such boards are used to investigate disciplinary actions regarding the use of force and in-custody deaths, but also to review their police agency's budget and policies, and how police are using body-worn cameras.

However, there remains a robust debate about whether or not such boards are beneficial, and if so, which model of citizen oversight should be adopted. The fact that so few jurisdictions use such boards would indicate that police are winning this debate, arguing that the boards are often politicized and unfair to them. An example is the words of Jim Pasco, the national executive director of the Fraternal Order of Police:

> The fact of the matter is, an officer has to make a split-second decision involving life or death. And the citizen review boards tend to, by definition, be made up of civilians who have no particular experience or

insight into what went through that officer's mind... what the circumstances were.[41]

Even the establishment and power of such boards can be tricky, especially where they are independently elected officials who are not accountable to county commissioners or city council members. In addition, some states' laws protect personnel records of police officers from most public disclosure and block access to investigative records, so experts say it's critical to persuade sheriffs and other law enforcement leaders to cooperate with oversight boards.[42]

It seems the verdict is still out on whether or not local units of government are helped or hindered by having such citizen input. Because of this ongoing debate, the President's Task Force on 21st Century Policing has recommended that the federal justice department fund more research on civilian police oversight models.[43]

Questions for Discussion

1. Are citizen review boards, in your opinion, a "blessing" or a "curse." Defend your position.
2. Where they exist, how much power and authority should be granted by local ordinance to such bodies?

Every complaint, regardless of the source, must be accepted and investigated in accordance with established policies and procedures. Some complaints, however, may be disposed of without the formality of an investigation. In some cases, the accused employee's actions clearly may be within departmental policy, and a simple communication to that effect to the citizen by a supervisor would resolve the matter. Such may be the case of a citizen who is offended that officers would handcuff an elderly shoplifting suspect. Other complaints may be so trivial that further inquiry or investigation is not necessary. For example, a citizen's call to the watch commander with a general complaint that too many police officers are employed by the city is not an issue that would be handled within a disciplinary process.

Anonymous complaints are the most difficult to investigate because there is no opportunity to obtain further information or question the complainant about the allegation. Anonymous complaints are additionally troublesome for the supervisor because they negatively affect the employee's morale. Officers may view these types of complaints as unjust and frivolous and question why the department gives them any attention whatsoever. Supervisors and managers must help officers understand that complaints, regardless of their source, cannot be ignored or disregarded, and that disciplinary processes are designed to protect both the officer and organization, as well as preserve the public's trust.

Police leaders should also be aware that the most bizarre of accusations may prove true. In one western city, an anonymous complaint was received alleging that a marked city police vehicle was observed in another city 120 miles away and across state lines during the early morning hours. It was discovered that officers working in the rural outskirts of the city were making bets on how far they could travel and return during the course of a shift. Photos of officers in uniform standing next to their vehicle and the city limits sign of the city in question were discovered and used as evidence against the officers during their disciplinary hearing.

Types and Receipt

Supervisors and managers may handle complaints informally or formally. The seriousness of the allegation and preference of the complainant usually dictate whether a complaint will be investigated in a formal or informal manner. A formal complaint involves a written, signed, and/or tape-recorded statement of the allegation, and the complainant requests to be informed of the investigation's disposition.

An informal complaint is an allegation of minor misconduct made for informational purposes that can usually be resolved without the need for more formal processes. If a citizen calls the watch commander to complain about the rude behavior of a dispatcher but does not wish to make a formal complaint, the supervisor may simply discuss the incident with the dispatcher and resolve it through informal counseling as long as more serious problems are not discovered and the dispatcher does not have a history of similar complaints. However, some departments require that all complaints, no matter how minor or trivial, be handled via a formal complaint investigation process (see Figure 6-1, an example of a complaint form used to initiate a personnel investigation).

These examples are typical of the majority of complaints handled by supervisors. Few complaints involve serious acts of physical violence, excessive force, or corruption. Wagner and Decker found that the majority of complaints against officers fall under the general categories of verbal abuse, discourtesy, harassment, improper attitude, and ethnic slurs. These comprise the issues that supervisors contend with on a daily basis.[44]

The process for receiving a complaint should be clearly delineated by departmental policy and procedures. Generally, a complaint will be made at a police facility and referred to a senior officer in charge to determine its seriousness and need for immediate intervention. Complaints will usually be accepted from any person

****

Control Number_____

Date & Time Reported   Location of Interview   Interview

_____   _____   _____Verbal   _____Written   _____Taped

Type of Complaint: ____Force   ____Procedural   ____Conduct
                          ____Other (Specify)

Source of Complaint: ____In Person   ____Mail   ____Telephone
                          ____Other (Specify)

Complaint originally   ____Supervisor   ____On Duty Watch Commander   ____Chief
Received by: ____IAU   ____Other (Specify)

Notifications made: _____Division Commander   _____Chief of Police
Received by: _____On-Call Command Personnel
                          _____Watch Commander   _____Other (Specify)

Copy of formal personnel complaint given to complainant?   ____Yes ____No

****

Complainant's name: Address:
_____   _____ Zip_____
Residence Phone: Business Phone:

DOB: Race: Sex: Occupation:
_____   _____   _____   _____

****

Location of Occurrence: Date & Time of Occurrence:
_____   _____

Member(s) Involved: Member(s) Involved:
(1) _____   (2)_____
(3) _____   (4)_____

Witness(es) Involved: Witness(es) Involved:
(1) _____   (2)_____
(3) _____   (4)_____

****

(1) ____   Complainant wishes to make a formal statement and has requested an investigation into the matter with a report back to him/her on the findings and actions.

(2) ____   Complainant wishes to advise the Police Department of a problem, understand that some type of action will be taken, but does not request a report back to him/her on the findings and actions.

****

CITIZEN ADVISEMENTS

(1)   If you have not yet provided the department with a signed written statement or a tape-recorded statement, one may be required in order to pursue the investigation of this matter.

(2)   The complainant(s) and/or witness(es) may be required to take a polygraph examination in order to determine the credibility concerning the allegations made.

(3)   Should the allegations prove to be false, the complainant(s) and/or witness(es) may be liable for criminal and/or civil prosecution.

_____   _____
Signature of Complainant   Date & Time

_____
Signature of Member Receiving Complaint

FIGURE 6-1   Police Department Formal Personnel Complaint Report

who feels injured or aggrieved. Complaints may be made through a variety of means, including in person, by mail, or over the telephone. Some departments allow citizens to file complaints electronically by completing forms on the department's Internet Web page. It is possible that, as a department improves or makes reporting easier, there will be an increase in the number of complaints filed.

The Investigative Process

The investigation of complaints is a bifurcated process. Generally, all investigations and the management of complaint investigations are controlled and coordinated by an internal affairs unit (IAU). If the complaint or charge is significant, investigators from internal affairs will handle the complaint totally. If it is an informal complaint, it will be handled by a supervisor. In some cases, internal affairs will forward minor formal complaints to the unit commander for investigation. The commander will then assign the case to a supervisor who conducts the investigation. Once the investigation is completed, it is reviewed by the unit commander and internal affairs. Finally, in some cases, unit supervisors will be assigned to assist internal affairs in the investigation.

After being assigned an investigation, supervisors review all the available evidence: documents, statements, reports, and photographs. They likely will review dispatch tapes and videotapes if they exist. This initial review examines all departmental, victim, and witness information. This review provides details about the charges, circumstances around the incident, and points of contention between the officers and victims and witnesses.

Next, all the parties involved are interviewed. There is a specific order in which the interviews should be conducted: witnesses first, so that supervisors can develop questions for the complainant and the subject officer, who will be interviewed later. Witness interviews should be tape-recorded. Prior to every interview, supervisors should prepare a list of questions and then, prior to asking the questions, explain the purpose of the interview and give the witnesses an opportunity to provide a narrative statement. Then, the supervisors can follow up with specific questions and be confrontational (when the evidence or other witnesses have provided facts to the contrary) or challenging (if the witnesses' responses to confrontational questions are not believable). The goal is not to exonerate or convict the officer, but to collect factual information so that a decision can be made after all the evidence has been collected and analyzed.

After interviewing witnesses, supervisors should have a solid understanding of the case and prepare a list of questions to ask the complainant. This interview should also be tape-recorded, and the complainant should be allowed to enter a statement, give his or her side of the story, and provide independent recollection of dates, times, and descriptions. Following this, supervisors should ask specific questions regarding the incident and if the complainant has information unavailable when the complaint was filed, such as the names of witnesses.

With regard to subject officer interviews, police leaders must ensure that their supervisors know their applicable state statutes or confer with their legal advisors regarding peace officers' rights while under investigation. It must then be determined if the officer wants to have an attorney or representative present. As with other interviews, supervisors should prepare a list of specific questions beforehand and tape-record the interview. The officer should be informed of the nature of the investigation and then be allowed to provide a narrative statement about the incident. After taking the statement, supervisors should ask the officer specific questions, such as "What did you do?" "What did you say?" "Did you say _____ to the complainant?" Posing questions in this manner (instead of, say, "Do you recall …?" or "Have you ever …?") is a more effective way to obtain concrete details. If the officer's statements contradict the evidence, supervisors must ask confrontational questions in a professional manner; while this may be unpleasant, supervisors have a professional duty to determine the facts.[45]

An investigative report must then be written that contains all the relevant facts of the case. The format of this report should follow agency protocol. Generally, the investigator will summarize the charges and organize the evidence showing those pieces of evidence that support the charge and the evidence that is contradictive of the charges. Investigators may or may not provide an opinion as to the disposition of the charges. In most cases, such decisions are made at a higher level within the police organization. Investigative reports are reviewed by managers and executives and may resurface in a later **grievance** hearing or a possible civil suit. Therefore, the reports must be detailed, accurate, thorough, and unbiased.

Determination and Disposition

Once an investigation is completed, a determination as to the culpability of the accused employee is made. Each allegation should receive a separate adjudication. Following are the categories of dispositions that are commonly used:

Unfounded. The alleged act(s) did not occur.
Exonerated. The act occurred, but it is lawful, proper, justified, and/or in accordance with departmental policies, procedures, and rules and regulations.

YOU DECIDE...

Officer Sonny Brown works the transport wagon downtown for a municipal police department and has worked this assignment on evening shift for several years. He loves "hooking and booking" drunks in this tourist-based city, and takes great pride in keeping the streets safe and clean. Local business owners appreciate his efforts so much that they once honored him as the Chamber of Commerce "Officer of the Year."

You, Carol Jackson, are a recently promoted lieutenant in your county sheriff's office, and are newly assigned to oversee all jail operations on the evening shift. On your second night in this assignment, one of your sergeants approaches you about a drunk who is being booked by one Officer Brown. Apparently, the sergeant overheard the drunk complaining that Brown had injured him by kicking him off a park bench and roughly pushing him down a hill to the transport wagon. Further, the sergeant states that the drunk, after complaining of pain in his side, has been examined by medical personnel and suffered three broken ribs.

Questions for Discussion

1. How should you handle—or direct the sergeant to handle—this matter?

2. What are the sergeant's options? Responsibilities? *Your* options and responsibilities?

3. What possible policy or criminal violations did Brown commit, and what potential disciplinary or legal actions should the city police department consider?

Not sustained. There is insufficient evidence to prove or disprove the allegations made.

Misconduct not based on the complaint. Sustainable misconduct was determined but is not part of the original complaint. For example, a supervisor investigating an allegation of excessive force against an officer may find the force used was within departmental policy, but that the officer made an unlawful arrest.

Closed. An investigation may be halted if the complainant fails to cooperate or it is determined that the action does not fall within the administrative jurisdiction of the police agency.

Sustained. The act did occur and it was a violation of departmental rules and procedures. Sustained allegations include misconduct that falls within the broad outlines of the original allegation(s).

Once a determination of culpability has been made, the complainant should be notified of the department's findings (see Figure 6-2). Details of the investigation or recommended punishment will not be included in the correspondence. As Figure 6-2 shows, the complainant will normally receive only information concerning the outcome of the complaint, including a short explanation of the finding along with an invitation to call the agency if further information is needed.

Level and Nature of Action

When an investigation against an employee is sustained, the sanctions and level of discipline must be decided. Management must be careful when recommending and imposing discipline because of its impact on the overall morale of the agency's employees. If the recommended discipline is viewed by employees as too lenient, it may send the wrong message that the misconduct was insignificant. On the other hand, discipline that is viewed as too harsh may have a demoralizing effect on the officer(s) involved and other agency employees and result in allegations that the leadership is unfair. This alone can have significant impact on the esprit de corps or morale of the agency.

We have discussed the importance of having a disciplinary process that is viewed by employees as fair and consistent, meaning that similar violations receive similar punishments. It is also important that discipline is progressive and more serious sanctions are invoked when repeated violations occur. For example, a third substantiated violation of rude behavior may result in a recommendation for a one-day suspension without pay, whereas a first offense may be resolved through documented oral counseling or a letter of reprimand. Listed next are disciplinary actions commonly used by agencies in order of their severity:

Counseling. This is usually a conversation between the supervisor and employee about a specific aspect of the employee's performance or conduct; it is warranted when an employee has committed a relatively minor infraction or the nature of the offense is such that oral counseling is all that is necessary. For example, an officer who is usually punctual but arrives at briefing 10 minutes late two days in a row may require nothing more than a reminder and warning to correct the problem.

Documented Oral Counseling. This is usually the first step in a progressive disciplinary process and is intended to address relatively minor infractions. It is provided when no previous reprimands or more severe disciplinary action of the same or similar nature have occurred.

Police Department
3300 Main Street
Downtown Plaza
Anywhere, USA 99999
June 20, 2000

Mr. John Doe
2200 Main Avenue
Anywhere, U.S.A.

Re: Internal Affairs #000666-98
    Case Closure

Dear Mr. Doe:

Our investigation into your allegations against Officer Smith has been completed. It has been determined that your complaint is SUSTAINED and the appropriate disciplinary action has been taken.

Our department appreciates your bringing this matter to our attention. It is our position that when a problem is identified, it should be corrected as soon as possible. It is our goal to be responsive to the concerns expressed by citizens so as to provide more efficient and effective services.

Your information regarding this incident was helpful and of value in our efforts to attain that goal. Should you have any further questions about this matter, please contact Sergeant Jane Alexander, Internal Affairs, at 555-9999.

Sincerely,

I.M. Boss,
Lieutenant
Internal Affairs Unit

FIGURE 6-2 Citizen's Notification of Discipline Letter

Letter of Reprimand.   This is a formal written notice regarding significant misconduct, more serious performance violations, or repeated offenses. It is usually the second step in the disciplinary process and is intended to provide the employee and agency with a written record of the violation of behavior. It identifies what specific corrective action must be taken to avoid subsequent more serious disciplinary steps.

Suspension.   This is a severe disciplinary action that results in an employee being relieved of duty, often without pay. It is usually administered when an employee commits a serious violation of established rules or after a written reprimand has been given and no change in behavior or performance has resulted.

Demotion.   In this situation, an employee is placed in a position of lower responsibility and pay. It is normally used when an otherwise good employee is unable to meet the standards required for the higher position or the employee has committed a serious act requiring that he or she be removed from a position of management or supervision.

Transfer.   Many agencies use the disciplinary transfer to deal with problem officers; officers can be transferred to a different location or assignment, and this action is often seen as an effective disciplinary tool.

Termination.   This is the most severe disciplinary action that can be taken. It usually occurs when previous serious discipline has been imposed and inadequate or no improvement in behavior or performance has occurred. It may also be used when an employee commits an offense so serious that continued employment would be inappropriate.

Determining the Final Outcome

The final disposition of the internal affairs investigation is a two-pronged process. First, as noted above, there is a departmental disposition. In most jurisdictions, the chief of police is responsible for determining the final outcome. His or her decision may be based on the recommendation of the IAU or an internal hearing board. In some jurisdictions, the internal hearing board may decide on a final disposition, and the chief only reviews or ratifies it. Jurisdictions that have some form of civilian review are quite similar, although who makes the final decision varies. Some civilian review panels have the authority to make the final decision, while in other cases the civilian review panel only reviews the outcome and makes recommendations to the department.

Once a decision is made, officers often have a right to appeal their punishment to a higher authority. In essence, a police disciplinary action is a civil action, and officers often have the right to appeal their cases in court. When cases are appealed to courts, in some states the courts review the record only to determine if there was a violation of the officer's rights. Other states require that the case be heard *de novo,* whereby the court considers all the evidence and renders a decision relative to guilt and punishment. Once this process is completed, and the officer disagrees with the outcome, he or she can appeal the case to higher courts.

AVERTING PROBLEMS: THE EARLY INTERVENTION SYSTEMS

It has become a truism among police leadership that about 10 percent of their officers cause 90 percent of the problems. Indeed, some research has indicated that as little as 2 percent of all officers are responsible for 50 percent of all citizen complaints. However, there might also be times, for various reasons, when officers who are normally stellar performers act in ways that are uncharacteristically inappropriate. Nonetheless, the early identification of and intervention with employees engaging in misconduct or performance problems can be vital to preventing ongoing and repeated incidents—and possibly leading to personal injuries with citizens and lawsuits. A mechanism exists to assist police leaders in these tasks.

Early intervention systems (EIS) are a tool being adopted at an increasing rate by law enforcement agencies of all sizes and types. These systems are usually in the form of an electronic database, although some agencies find paper files are effective, and they are used to keep track of officers' problem behaviors and activities.

Certain pieces of information are collected in EIS concerning officers' behavior that will help to identify problematic behaviors early on. Some of the more common kinds of information collected by EIS are use of sick leave, the number and type of community complaints, and the number and type of use-of-force incidents.[46]

EIS therefore functions most effectively when they are used to help identify and address problems before officers get into serious trouble (e.g., before formal complaints or lawsuits arise and before an officer's well-being is compromised). The key is to view EIS as a nondisciplinary component of an agency's personnel management toolbox.

It is important to note that first-line supervisors are really the key to successful use of EIS. They are typically the first to observe potentially problematic behavior among their officers and are typically involved in the intervention process when required.

For that reason, the chief executive also has a major role within EIS, ensuring that those first-line supervisors are prepared for this major aspect of their role (i.e., be able to analyze system data—see Figure 6-3—willing to formally approach officers about personal or other problems that may be affecting their work, and following up with appropriate intervention options). In sum, the success or failure of EIS depends on the chief executive's leadership—and the knowledge that EIS are a valuable administrative tool that can enhance accountability and integrity in a law enforcement agency.[47]

LEGAL CONSIDERATIONS

Negligent failure to discipline is an area that involves both policy and supervisory liability. What are the consequences of an agency's failure to develop an adequate policy and a system to investigate and prosecute violations by officers? Is an agency required to develop a system for receiving and handling citizen complaints against an officer? Generally, case law has held that liability exists if the plaintiff is able to prove that the disciplinary process was so lacking that officers believed no consequences would result from their actions. The bases of this belief include number of citizen complaints, how discipline is handled, and the department's failure to take action in matters that needed intervention.

In *Parish v. Luckie,*[48] the plaintiff claimed that she was victim of a false arrest and rape by a member of the police department. The court found that the department had a history of ignoring and covering up complaints of physical and sexual abuse by officers. The officer in question also had a history of violent conduct. The chief would investigate only complaints against officers that were in writing and improperly applied the standard of "beyond a reasonable doubt" to determine whether or not the case was sustained.

Report Criteria: Complaints Occurred Between: 01/01/2016 AND 06/30/2017

Officer Complaints Summary Rpt #C-8   Your Agency Name Will Print Here

Number Of Complaints / Violations Alleged By Officer

The totals below represent that number of different types of Complaints / Violations alleged against each Officer, Not the number of incidents.

Officer - ID Number		Complaints	Citizen		Internal		Racial		Off Duty		Body Camera		Priority		Still Active	
Auburn, Steven	#22013	9	8	88.9%	1	11.1%	2	22.2%	2	22.2%	6	66.7%	3	33.3%	2	22.2%
Beige, Matt	#29861	8	7	87.5%	1	12.5%	2	25.0%	0	0.0%	7	87.5%	6	75.0%	0	0.0%
Black, Steve	#12647	7	7	100.0%	0	0.0%	2	28.6%	2	28.6%	4	57.1%	4	57.1%	0	0.0%
Bronze, Jennifer	#30042	3	2	66.7%	1	33.3%	1	33.3%	0	0.0%	2	66.7%	1	33.3%	0	0.0%
Brown, Alan	#22413	1	1	100.0%	0	0.0%	0	0.0%	0	0.0%	0	0.0%	0	0.0%	1	100.0%
Gold, Danny	#06744	3	2	66.7%	1	33.3%	1	33.3%	0	0.0%	2	66.7%	0	0.0%	0	0.0%
Gray, Michael	#6547	3	3	100.0%	0	0.0%	1	33.3%	0	0.0%	1	33.3%	2	66.7%	0	0.0%
Green, Tony	#22560	2	1	50.0%	1	50.0%	0	0.0%	0	0.0%	1	50.0%	0	0.0%	0	0.0%
Maroon, Patrick	#17765	5	3	60.0%	2	40.0%	2	40.0%	2	40.0%	4	80.0%	0	0.0%	0	0.0%
Orange, John	#29445	2	2	100.0%	0	0.0%	1	50.0%	0	0.0%	0	0.0%	0	0.0%	0	0.0%
Pink, John	#15484	3	3	100.0%	0	0.0%	0	0.0%	0	0.0%	2	66.7%	2	66.7%	0	0.0%
Purple, Jeff	#18032	4	3	75.0%	1	25.0%	2	50.0%	1	25.0%	1	25.0%	2	50.0%	0	0.0%
Red, Jeff	#19280	6	6	100.0%	0	0.0%	1	16.7%	0	0.0%	5	83.3%	3	50.0%	0	0.0%
Red, Mark	#18649	6	4	66.7%	2	33.3%	0	0.0%	0	0.0%	4	66.7%	3	50.0%	1	16.7%
Silver, Jon	#32663	3	3	100.0%	0	0.0%	1	33.3%	0	0.0%	0	0.0%	1	33.3%	1	33.3%
Tan, Julie	#18927	3	2	66.7%	1	33.3%	1	33.3%	0	0.0%	0	0.0%	0	0.0%	0	0.0%
Turquoise, John D.	#12345	3	2	66.7%	1	33.3%	0	0.0%	0	0.0%	1	33.3%	1	33.3%	1	33.3%
White, Ron	#00705	5	5	100.0%	0	0.0%	0	0.0%	0	0.0%	3	60.0%	2	40.0%	2	40.0%
	Totals:	76	64	84.2%	12	15.8%	17	22.4%	7	9.2%	43	56.6%	30	39.5%	8	10.5%

39	Total Number Of Incidents	13	Different Types Of Complaints
18	Different Officers Involved	76	Totals Entries (Officers *Plus* Complaint Violations Alleged)

L.E.A. Data Technologies   ADMINISTRATIVE Database   08/02/2017 12:05:49 PM   Page 1 of 1

FIGURE 6-3   Number of Complaints/Violations Alleged by Officer
Source: Number of Complaints/Violations Alleged by Officer © L.E.A. Technologies Used with permission from L.E.A. Technologies.

An example of a supervisor's failure to address problems is *Gutierrez-Rodriguez v. Cargegena.*[49] Puerto Rican drug agents came upon the plaintiff and his girlfriend in a parked car. The agents approached the vehicle in civilian clothes and with weapons drawn. The plaintiff, seeing them approaching, started his car and attempted to drive away. Without warning or notice that they were police officers, the officers began firing at the car, striking the plaintiff in the back and permanently paralyzing him. The plaintiff sued the squad, the supervisor, and the police chief in federal court under **Section 1983** (discussed below). The court found evidence of numerous complaints against the supervisor (13 separate citizen complaints filed against him in three years). The court awarded a $4.5 million judgment.

Liability may also be established in the department's past practices. In *Bordanaro v. McLeod,*[50] the court found that the agency had a widespread practice of unconstitutional warrantless entries and that the chief had knowledge or should have known that the practice was occurring. The court observed that when a large number of officers are conducting themselves in a like manner, that alone is evidence of an established practice by the department.

In *Ramos v. City of Chicago,*[51] however, the plaintiff alleged that he was beaten by police without provocation and that his beating was the result of an institutionalized practice by the Chicago Police Department, but the court did not find the city liable. The court concluded that six unrelated incidents of police brutality over a 10-year period in a police department of more than 10,000 officers failed to prove that a policy or custom existed that condoned brutality. This case is important in that it considered the size of the department and its location in its decision.

THE COST OF FAILURE: CIVIL LIABILITY

Leadership concerns behavior of both management and labor, for it is the direct responsibility of chief executive and middle managers to monitor and regulate officers' behavior and when necessary, to take disciplinary action, to ensure that negligent or illegal behavior does not recur in the future. This section explores some of the legal consequences when police supervisors fail to control officers' behavior.

What is known is that some cities have seen lawsuits against their city's police force soar. From 2010 through 2014, the 10 cities with the largest police agencies in the United States paid out over $1.4 billion in settlements and court judgments due to lawsuits against police.[52]

Indeed, in a recent three-year period, Chicago alone paid $210 million to settle 655 police misconduct lawsuits.[53]

General Types of Liability

In the years following the Civil War and in reaction to the states' inability to control the Ku Klux Klan's lawlessness, Congress enacted the Ku Klux Klan Act of 1871. This was later codified as Title 42, U.S. Code Section 1983. Its statutory language is as follows:

> Every person who, under color of any statute, ordinance, regulation, custom, or usage of any State or Territory, subjects, or causes to be subjected, any citizen of the United States or any other person within the jurisdiction thereof to the deprivation of any rights, privileges, or immunities secured by the Constitution and laws, shall be liable to the party injured in an action at law, suit in equity, or other proper proceeding for redress.

This legislation is intended to provide civil rights protection to all persons protected under the act, when a defendant acts "under color of law" (misuses power of office). It is also meant to provide an avenue to the federal courts for relief of alleged civil rights violations.

Several factors have contributed to a surge in Section 1983 actions. First, some lawyers believe that a better caliber of judges and juries can be found in the federal forum. Federal judges, who are appointed for life, can be less concerned about the political ramifications of their decisions than the locally elected judges. Furthermore, federal rules of pleading and evidence are uniform, and federal procedures of discovery are more liberal. Just as important, Section 1988 of the Civil Rights Act in 1976 allowed attorney's fees to the "prevailing party" over and above the award for compensatory and punitive damages. This provision in the law did as much to spur the use of Section 1983 as any other factor.

Leaders must be mindful that a certain level of liability is attached to the job when their subordinates fail to manage personnel correctly or when they behave improperly. They should also remember that plaintiffs generally attempt to include as many supervisors, managers, and leaders in the lawsuit as possible to enhance the probability that the award will be greater and the defendants will have the ability to pay it. This is commonly referred to as the "deep pockets" approach.

As noted, managers and supervisors may incur liability for what their subordinates do. They have direct and vicarious liability. *Direct liability* is incurred for the actions of supervisors themselves, while *vicarious* or *indirect liability* refers to when supervisors are held liable for the actions of their subordinates. For direct liability to exist the supervisor must actively participate in the act. Supervisors may incur direct liability in the following ways:[54]

1. They authorize the act. They give officers permission to do something that ultimately results in liability.
2. They are present when an act for which liability results occurs. They stand by and watch an act occur and fail to take corrective action.
3. They ratify the act. Once the act is completed, they fail to admonish or take corrective action when it comes to their attention.

One of the most commonly litigated areas of liability is **negligence**. *Simple negligence* occurs when a supervisor fails to provide the degree of care and vigilance required for a situation, while *gross negligence* is a deliberate indifference to life or property. Generally, the courts require gross negligence to hold a supervisor liable.

As a result of case law, there are currently five areas in which supervisors have been found liable as a result of negligence: (1) negligent assignment, (2) negligent failure to supervise, (3) negligent failure to direct, (4) negligent entrustment, and (5) negligent failure to investigate or discipline.[55] These areas of liability fall squarely with the supervisor and are discussed next.

Negligent assignment occurs when the supervisor assigns a task to a subordinate without first determining that the subordinate is properly trained or capable of performing the required work. Negligent assignment also occurs when a supervisor determines that an employee is not qualified for a position but fails to relieve the employee of the assignment.

An example of negligent assignment would be a supervisor who allows a subordinate to assume the duties of a police officer without completing the annual firearms training as mandated by the States Commission of Police Officers Standards and Training (POST). If the officer then inappropriately shoots a citizen, the agency (typically including the chief of police, supervisor, as well as the officer) could be liable. A second example would be an officer who has had several complaints of sexual harassment and the immediate supervisors decide to handle the matters informally rather than conduct a formal investigation required by city and department policy.

Negligent failure to supervise occurs when the supervisor fails to properly oversee subordinates' activities. The court in *Lenard v. Argento*[56] held that at a minimum a plaintiff must demonstrate that the supervisory official authorized (implicitly or explicitly), approved, or knowingly acquiesced in the illegal conduct. For example, if a supervisor knows that an officer on a number of occasions has used more force than was necessary to effect an arrest and fails to take corrective action, the supervisor can be held liable for failure to supervise in a subsequent action. Thus, anytime a supervisor becomes aware of a problem, action must be taken to rectify the problem. The courts have also examined individual cases. In *Grandstaff v. City of* Borger,[57] police officials were held liable for failing to take supervisory action after officers mistakenly opened fire and shot an innocent bystander who was attempting to help the officers. The court reasoned that the department's failure to reprimand, discipline, or fire officers constituted a failure to supervise. Supervisors' failure to act is an abdication of authority, and the courts consider this to be negligent supervision.

Negligent failure to direct occurs when supervisors fail to advise subordinates of the specific requirements and limits of the job. For example, if a police department fails to provide officers with the limits of when they can use deadly force and officers subsequently use deadly force inappropriately, the responsible supervisors can be held liable. Negligent failure to direct has specific application relative to departmental policies and procedures. If a department does not have a policy dealing with a sensitive area and officers subsequently act inappropriately, the department will be found negligent for failure to direct. Supervisors must be knowledgeable about departmental policies and be able to properly advise officers about their content.

Negligent entrustment occurs when supervisors entrust officers with equipment and facilities and fail to properly supervise the officers' care and use of the equipment, and subsequently the officers commit an act using the equipment that leads to a violation of a citizen's federally protected rights. The government in these cases must show that the officer in question was incompetent and the supervisor knew of the incompetence. A supervisor's defense in negligent entrustment is that the employee was competent to use the equipment and was properly supervised.

Supervisors must investigate complaints and work activities and take proper disciplinary actions when required. Clearly, police departments must have adequate disciplinary procedures and they must function to protect the rights of citizens. If a supervisor or department covers up or is inattentive to complaints of police misconduct, the department and supervisor are liable. Too often supervisors attempt to stall, discourage, or disregard complainants when they attempt to protest police officer actions. Such actions can ultimately lead to *negligent failure to investigate or discipline charges*.

Obviously, a department's and supervisor's defense in such cases is to establish a record of strong disciplinary procedures within the agency. This is accomplished through strong actions and documentation. Plaintiffs, on the other hand, will attempt to show that either no action or inadequate action took place. Again, EIS allow agencies to track and address in a proactive and nondisciplinary manner those behaviors that may not result in an internal affairs investigation but raise concerns about behaviors.

Next, we discuss several other potential areas of liability that are important for police leaders to ensure supervisors and managers are trained.

Other Areas of Potential Liability

PROXIMATE CAUSE   is established by asking "but for the officer's conduct, would the plaintiff have sustained the injury or damage?" If the answer to this question is no, then **proximate cause** is established, and the officer can be held liable for the damage or injury. This requirement of negligence limits liabilities, however, in situations where damage would have occurred regardless of the officer's behavior.[58] An example is where an officer is involved in a high-speed chase and the offending driver strikes an innocent third party. Generally, if the officer was not acting in a negligent fashion and did not cause the injury, there would be no liability on the officer's part.[59] However, most agency leaders have adopted very strict policies concerning police pursuits, limiting them to felony crimes or life-threatening offenders (see the "Vehicular Pursuits" section below).

Proximate cause may be found in such cases as an officer leaving the scene of an accident aware of dangerous conditions (e.g., spilled oil, smoke, vehicle debris, stray animals) without proper warning to motorists.

PERSONS IN CUSTODY AND SAFE FACILITIES   Courts generally recognize that police officers have a **duty of care** for persons in their custody. This means that police officers have a legal responsibility to take reasonable precautions to ensure the health and safety of persons in their custody—keeping detainees free from harm, rendering medical assistance when necessary, and treating detainees humanely.[60]

This general duty of care to persons in police custody seldom results in liability for self-inflicted injury or suicide because these acts are normally considered to result from the detainee's own intentional conduct, rather than from some form of police negligence.[61] For example, if a prisoner's suicide is "reasonably foreseeable," the jailer owes the prisoner a duty of care to help prevent that suicide. If the suicidal tendencies of an inmate are

YOU DECIDE...

Sgt. Gerald Jones does not understand why his subordinate officers appeal all of his disciplinary recommendations. He takes matters of discipline seriously, and it commonly takes him three to four weeks to investigate even minor matters—three to four times longer than other supervisors. Jones believes that by doing so, he shows great concern for his officers and, in fact, does not even question the officers about their behavior until the investigation is nearly complete and he has interviewed everyone involved in the matter. Jones decides to speak to his officers about the matter. He is surprised when they tell him that they do not trust him. Indeed, they fail to understand why so much time is needed for him to investigate the minor incidents. They believe that he is being secretive and is always looking for ways to find fault with their performance. Jones argues that his recommendations are consistent with those of other sergeants and

provides some examples of similar cases that were handled by various supervisors. Apparently unconvinced by Jones's argument, the next day an officer appeals one of Jones's disciplinary recommendations to you, the shift lieutenant, concerning a minor traffic accident.

Questions for Discussion

1. Based on the information presented, do you believe the officers' allegations of Sgt. Jones's unfairness is valid?

2. What requisites of sound disciplinary policy may Jones not understand that may be leading to the officers' appeals?

3. Under the circumstances, should Jones simply ignore the officers' complaints? Are their perceptions that important?

---

known, the standard of care required of the custodian is elevated. Typically, agencies have policies that require persons displaying suicidal tendencies be placed in a cell with cameras or frequent cell checks (15- or 30-minute intervals being common) by the officer responsible for the prisoner.

Another area of police liability, one that involves both persons in custody and proximate cause, is the need to provide safe facilities. Courts have even considered the design of detention facilities as a source of negligence, such as in a Detroit case where the construction of a jail's holding cell did not allow officers to observe detainee's movements, the construction of the cell doors hampered detainee supervision, there were no electronic monitoring devices for observing detainees, and there was an absence of detoxification cells required under state department of corrections rules. Therefore, following a suicide in this facility, the court concluded that these conditions constituted building defects and were the proximate cause of the decedent's death. [62]

FAILURE TO PROTECT   This form of negligence may occur if a police officer fails to protect a person from a known and foreseeable danger. These claims most often involve battered women. There are, however, other circumstances that can create a duty to protect people from crime. Informants, witnesses, and other people dependent on the police can be a source of police liability if police fail to take reasonable action to prevent victimization. The officer's conduct can place a person in peril or demonstrate deliberate indifference for their safety.

For example, one morning a California man named Penilla was on the porch of his home and became seriously ill. His neighbors called 911, and two police officers arrived first. They found him to be in grave need of medical care, canceled the request for paramedics, broke the lock and door jam on the front door of Penilla's residence, moved him inside the house, locked the door, and left. The next day, family members found Penilla dead inside the house as a result of respiratory failure. His mother sued under Section 1983, and the court found that the officers' conduct clearly placed Penilla in a more dangerous position than the one in which they found him.[63]

VEHICULAR PURSUITS

In 2007, the U.S. Supreme Court issued a major decision concerning the proper amount of force the police may use during high-speed vehicle pursuits. The fundamental question was whether or not the level of force used was proportionate to the threat of reckless and dangerous driving. The incident involved a 19-year-old Georgia youth driving at speeds up to 90 miles per hour and covering nine miles in six minutes with a deputy sheriff in pursuit. The chase ended in a violent crash that left the youth a quadriplegic; his lawyers argued that the Fourth Amendment protects against the use of such excessive force and high-speed drivers having their cars rammed by police (by intentionally stopping a fleeing vehicle in such a manner, a "seizure" occurs for Fourth Amendment purposes). Conversely, the deputy's lawyers argued that such drivers pose an escalating danger to the public and must be stopped to defuse the danger. The Court held, 8-1, that "A police officer's attempt to terminate a dangerous high-speed car chase that threatens the lives of innocent bystanders does not violate the Fourth Amendment, even when it places the fleeing motorist at risk of serious injury or death." [64]

Still, the police must act reasonably in such instances or they may be found civilly liable. Police officers are afforded no special privileges or immunities in the routine operation of their patrol; in nonemergency situations they have no immunity for their negligence or recklessness and are held to the same standard of conduct as private citizens. When responding to emergency situations, however, most jurisdictions afford the police limited immunity—some protections and privileges not given to private citizens—and are permitted to take greater risks that would amount to negligence if undertaken by citizens' vehicles. [65]

Summary

This chapter has demonstrated the importance of police leaders developing and implementing sound disciplinary policies and practices—as well as being knowledgeable of their employees' rights. Policies and training are needed for supervisors and managers to identify and respond to employee misconduct or performance problems at an early stage. Policies also ensure that discipline is administered in a consistent and equitable manner throughout the organization. Prompt, complete, and full investigations of alleged misconduct coupled with the appropriate level of discipline may minimize or even eliminate potential civil liability. The public's trust and respect are precious commodities and can be quickly lost with the disregard or improper handling of allegations of misconduct. The public expects that police agencies will make every effort to identify and correct problems and respond to citizens' complaints in a judicious manner.

Finally, police leaders must also understand that they may be found liable if failing to properly supervise their subordinates. Failure to do so may result in civil (tort) action against them. This all represents a bitter pill to swallow, but it is the price to be paid for failure; surely it is preferable for police administrators, managers, and supervisors to do all that is possible to ensure that ethical matters are first and foremost addressed (and trained for) *in-house*, rather than in the *courthouse*.

Discussion Questions

1. Delineate the rights that police officers possess, including those generally found under the Peace Officers Bill of Rights as well as areas in which they have limitations placed on their behavior and activity.
2. Review why the legalization of marijuana in several states is forcing many police leaders to modify their views and practices regarding its use.
3. Explain the *Brady* Act, and its application to police discipline.
4. Describe the various forms of disciplinary actions that may be taken against police officers.
5. Explain the basic procedure to be followed by supervisors when performing an internal affairs investigation.
6. Describe the benefits of having an early intervention systems (EIS) to identify problem officers.
7. Provide four examples of negligent supervision of police officers that have resulted in liability.
8. Explain the two types of liability that police supervisors may incur, as well as the five areas of liability.
9. Define duty of care and failure to protect, and how they apply to police supervisors and officers.
10. Explain the potential for police liability vehicle pursuits, including any protections police enjoy against liability in such pursuits; provide examples of actions in vehicle pursuits that may result in police being liable for damages.
11. Describe the nature and use of 42 U.S. Code Section 1983.

Internet Investigations

Illinois General Assembly, "Uniform Peace Officers' Disciplinary Act" http://www.ilga.gov/legislation/ilcs/ilcs3.asp?ActID=736&ChapterID=11

Las Vegas Metropolitan Police Department, Complaints Form http://www.lvmpd.com/Sections/InternalAffairs/Complaints/tabid/296/Default.aspx

National Institute of Justice, "Police Discipline: A Case for Change" https://www.ncjrs.gov/pdffiles1/nij/234052.pdf

Office of Community Oriented Policing Services, *Early Intervention Systems for Law Enforcement Agencies: A Planning and Management Guide* https://chicagopatf.org/wp-content/uploads/2016/02/EarlyInterventionSystemsLawEnforcement.pdf

The Marshall Project, "Did you know police have their own Bill of Rights?" https://www.themarshallproject.org/2015/04/27/blue-shield#.G75mTjOmS

Leadership Roles in Labor Relations: "Navigating the Waters" of Police Unionization

STUDENT LEARNING OUTCOMES

After reading this chapter, the student will:

■ understand how and why police unions were created, and some infamous related actions

■ know the extent of police membership in unions

■ understand the three collective bargaining models

■ be able to describe the roles of police management and union leaders in collective bargaining, and the kinds of issues that both can negotiate

■ be able to explain the nature and general features of union contracts

■ have knowledge of several "tips" for navigating the waters of collective bargaining

■ know how officers may engage in grievances and appeals when employee disputes arise

KEY TERMS AND CONCEPTS

- Arbitration
- Bargaining not required model
- Boston police strike
- Collective bargaining
- Contract
- Grievance
- Impasse

- Job actions
- Labor relations
- "Mandatory wear" policies
- Meet and confer model
- Negotiation
- Union

INTRODUCTION

When compared with other topics relating to law enforcement—for example, homeland security, crime in general, critical incidents, and natural disasters—the role of police unions and **labor relations** in police governance is given little attention by the public. The interaction between police labor groups and governments is almost invisible. This is unfortunate, given the weight of matters that are involved, and the fact that 14.8 million wage and salary workers in the United States belong to unions or associations—7.2 million of them employed in the public sector.[1] Indeed, where collective bargaining is found in policing, such issues as budgets, officer wellness, privatization of services, civilianization, recruitment, health care, and pension benefits must be resolved, to name a few.

It will be seen that the police labor movement has a long and sometimes sordid and painful history, with officers at times taking drastic measures to express displeasure with their work environment. Some of those measures include **job actions** such as work stoppages (strikes and "blue flu"), engaging in work slowdowns and speedups (reducing revenues and issuing fewer or more citations, respectively), issuing a vote of no confidence (to voice displeasure with management), and engaging in picketing and holding sit-ins. Certainly, some of their tactics have left the community left to wonder who is there to "serve and protect."

This chapter explores several aspects of police unionization and labor relations. First, we briefly consider the history of police unions, and then explore the affiliations and operation of police in unions today. Next is a review of several models of collective bargaining, and following that is a look at the roles of both police and union leaders in negotiations of labor **contracts**, to include the vast array of issues that can be negotiated. Next, we look at the process for addressing grievances and appeals by officers who feel aggrieved in terms of the contract's provisions, and conclude the chapter with some tips for police leaders who must "navigate the waters" of unionism. Several case studies (in the form of "Focus On" and "You Decide" boxes) are included as well, inviting the reader to assume different roles in collective bargaining. (Note that collective bargaining also involves *negotiation* and *communication*, as discussed in Chapter 5.)

A BRIEF HISTORY OF POLICE UNIONS

Origins

Police employee groups started forming as early as the Civil War. These early groups were fraternal organizations, rather than unions, and even today, much of the collective bargaining that occurs in police departments is managed by these fraternal organizations (discussed below). These fraternal organizations primarily were concerned with employee health and welfare, to include death benefits and welfare insurance for their members. Police officers did not actively unionize until the passage of civil service reform, which gave them some degree of job protection.

The late 1800s and early 1900s, however, were a time of social unrest, political strife, and labor violence. After witnessing the economic gains made by trade unions, firefighters, and other public workers, the American Federation of Labor (AFL) began receiving requests for charters from local police benevolent associations who were clamoring to join organized labor. The unionization of the police caused a firestorm of protest, as police executives did not want their officers forming unions and alliances with political, labor, and social activists; trade unions were viewed as a threat to the national security. A number of police groups attempted to affiliate with the early AFL; by September 1917, there were 37 charters with a membership of over 4,000 police officers, mostly in small and medium-sized cities.[2]

The Boston Police Strike

Whenever the history of police unions is discussed, the infamous **Boston police strike** of 1919 will be at the center of the conversation due to its loss of life, destruction, and public attention. A number of conditions precipitated the strike:

> The morale of Boston policemen prior to the strike was low because of distressingly inadequate working conditions, among which were vermin-infested station houses, wages too low for the post-World War I inflationary period, working hours ranging between seventy-three to ninety hours per week, a requirement that officers pay for their uniforms, and the use of favoritism in assigning officers to the best positions.[3]

Yet, the primary cause of the strike rested with Police Commissioner E.V. Curtis's refusal to recognize the **union**. He had prohibited officers from joining the union and had filed charges against several officials of the union. Eventually, three-fourths of the Boston police force would strike.[4]

The strike lasted four days, after which "the Commonwealth dismissed the strikers and destroyed the union," with 1,100 striking police officers losing their jobs.[5] Seven lives were lost and hundreds of people were injured as a result of rioting, and immense property damage was suffered before the state's National Guard restored order.

President Woodrow Wilson severely condemned the police and the strike:

> A strike of policemen of a great city, leaving that city at the mercy of an army of thugs, is a crime against civilization. The obligation of a policeman is as sacred and direct as the obligation of a soldier. He is a public servant…and he has no right to prefer any private advantage to public safety.[6]

Governor Calvin Coolidge also condemned the strike, making his now-famous declaration that "There is no right to strike against the public safety by anybody, anywhere, anytime."[7]

However tragic the strike was for the city, it did result in significant gains for Boston police. Salaries were increased significantly, officers were no longer required to purchase their uniforms, and a pension system

Governor Coolidge inspects troops he brought to Boston to quell the police strike in January 1919.
Source: Keystone/Hulton Archive/Getty Images

was created. It was also a defining moment for the fledgling police labor movement, causing distrust and hatred of the police and solidifying politicians' and the public's positions against police unions and organizations.

POLICE UNIONS TODAY

As indicated above, unions are a formidable force in contemporary policing—particularly in the Northeast, Midwest, and Western states—and they tend to play a greater role in larger departments. Unions retain lobbyists who work in the political system to advance union causes and actively support (through endorsements and funding) their preferred political candidates; indeed, some larger departments even have a member of leadership staff (such as a deputy chief of operations) assigned to work with the union leaders.

Once unions are recognized in a jurisdiction, the relationship between the department and the governmental entity is codified in a contract or memorandum of understanding. The contract specifies the rights and privileges of its employees and places restrictions on the political entity and police administrators. In effect, the contract has the force of law. The contract can only be changed via renegotiations, which occur generally on a multi-year cycle as agreed upon by the union and police management.

There are two major police associations in the United States: the Fraternal Order of Police (FOP), the oldest, founded in 1915 in Pittsburgh, reporting a membership of over 300,000, with lodges in all 50 states; and the National Association of Police Organizations (NAPO), essentially an association of independent bargaining units which works cooperatively on national legislation affecting their membership, with a membership of 220,000 in 4000 local associations.[8]

In addition to these organizations, there are a number of AFL-CIO affiliated unions with substantial police membership. The most prominent of these is the International Union of Police Associations, which reports a membership of 100,000; the International Brotherhood of Police Officers has about 10,000; there are other smaller groupings of police officers within larger communication and government employees associations, but no reliable membership figures are available.[9]

Figure 7-1 shows the status of **collective bargaining** agreements in police agencies of all sizes. As noted in the table, more than one-third (35 percent) of all agencies have an active collective bargaining agreement in force; furthermore, 62 percent of agencies in cities with more than 250,000 population have such an agreement.

Collective bargaining also has been shown to have an impact on officers' salaries. According to a survey by the federal Bureau of Justice Statistics, starting salaries for officers are about 19 percent higher in departments with a collective bargaining agreement for sworn personnel as compared to departments without such an agreement.[10]

Member organizations such as the Peace Officers Research Association of California (see the "Focus On" box) can provide individual officers and associations an advantage when using their professional services. This is especially true for smaller agencies whose associations may not have skilled members to properly negotiate the complexities of labor contract negotiations.

Population served	Total	Active	Expired	No agreement
All sizes	100%	35%	33%	32%
1,000,000 or more	100%	71	21	7
500,000–999,999	100%	53	37	10
250,000–499,999	100%	61	15	24
190,000–249,999	100%	56	22	22
50,000–99,999	100%	58	20	22
25,000–49,999	100%	55	23	22
10,000–24,999	100%	56	25	19
2,500–9,999	100%	42	26	32
2,499 or fewer	100%	12	46	42

FIGURE 7-1 Status of collective bargaining agreements
Figure taken from p. 15, Appendix Table 3, *Local Police Departments, 2013,* Bureau of Justice Statistics, https://www.bjs.gov/content/pub/pdf/lpd13ppp.pdf
Note: Detail may not sum to total because of rounding.
Source: Bureau of Justice Statistics, Law Enforcement Management and Administrative Statistics (LEMAS) Survey, 2013.

FOCUS ON: PEACE OFFICERS RESEARCH ASSOCIATION OF CALIFORNIA

The Peace Officers Research Association of California (PORAC) represents 69,000 state and local public safety members and more than 920 associations—by far the largest organization representing public safety officers in the nation. PORAC prides itself on representing the interests of "rank-and-file" peace officers. PORAC provides individual officers and associations a number of professional services, including legal defense, labor contract negotiations, and insurance and medical benefits.[11]

MODELS OF COLLECTIVE BARGAINING

For a police agency to become involved in the collective bargaining process, doing so must first be authorized under state law. Thus, police collective bargaining occurs on a state-by-state basis. Today, 36 states have some form of collective bargaining rights for police officers.[12] According to DeLord,[13] police unions not having the right to collectively bargain are restricted to "collective begging" with the elected officials. When public employers can dictate the terms of employment and discipline at will, executives are more likely to be heavy-handed and avoid mediating disputes with the union. Therefore, having collective bargaining does provide for periodic interaction between both sides.

Three Models

Because collective bargaining varies from state to state depending on their respective statutes, there is a great deal of variation as to how police departments engage in collective bargaining. That is, each state places certain requirements on police and governmental labor negotiations.

In all cases, the governmental entity and the union are required to bargain in good faith.

Nonetheless, at times the two sides arrive at an **impasse** or are unable to agree on an issue. In such cases three general models exist to attempt to resolve the deadlock: (1) the binding arbitration model, (2) the meet and confer model, and (3) bargaining not required model.[14]

In states that allow **binding arbitration**, both sides submit the issue and their positions in writing to a "neutral" third party or arbitrator who then decides the outcome, with the decision conforming to state laws and labor standards. This occurs after the two sides cannot come to agreement and an impasse has occurred. The arbitrator hears the case and makes a decision, acting in place of a trial before a judge or jury. Given that role, the arbitrator must be unbiased and attempt to pursue an outcome that is fair and reasonable to all parties. When selecting an arbitrator, however, both sides may examine the potential arbitrators' records to see how they have ruled in previous negotiations; unions will not want an arbitrator who is perceived to have favored management in the past, and vice versa.

The **meet and confer** model is similar to the binding arbitration model. Here, again, police officers are allowed to form and join a union or collective bargaining entity and negotiate with management. However, management is only legally obligated to meet and confer with the employee group. There is no mechanism to resolve impasses on issues. When there is an impasse, the employer can unilaterally implement its best offer to the employees. Basically, officers must accept what the government offers. Management must do two things: first, management must meet with the union in a timely manner; second, management must negotiate with union representatives and attempt to agree on matters of concern to the union. Although management should negotiate in good faith, management does not have an obligation or often the motivation to accept the union's proposals. At best, this model results in officers being able to convey their concerns to management, and management providing officers with information about the department's positions and operation. This sharing of information may allow the two sides to come to a better understanding about the disputed issues.

There are 12 states that have the **bargaining not required model**. In these states, collective bargaining has not been authorized by the state, or such labor practices have been deemed unconstitutional. The complete absence of any form of bargaining can result in a lack of communication between police leaders and rank-and-file officers; that, in turn, can prevent police leaders from being aware of officers' problems and concerns. So the **negotiation** process can have an impact on officer morale. If a department does not have formal collective bargaining, it should at least have some mechanism to poll officers to identify issues.

ROLES OF UNION LEADERS AND MANAGEMENT: STRIVING FOR COLLABORATION AND COOPERATION

To state the obvious, there are inherent conflicts between police management and labor with regard to bargaining issues, as both sides must advocate for their constituencies. However, this has begun to change, as there are certain "articles of faith" that might be borne in mind by both sides.

First, while employee associations must advocate for their membership, it is best that they recognize that they—like management—are to look out for officers' wellness and safety while protecting and serving the community. And while both unions and management must maintain a certain level of strain in their advocacy roles, they must not personalize the conflict and must attempt to maintain a cooperative, productive relationship. In sum, it is best if both strive to minimize or eliminate rancor.

Police union leaders are elected and typically want to remain in office. However, they must not view their role as antagonistic, where negotiating is a zero-sum game where the union only wins if management loses. There are any number of examples of cooperation and collaboration where zero-sum was not in play. One is when officers in Brookline, Massachusetts, were asked to receive extra training and work additional hours to provide security at the Boston Marathon following the horrific 2013 bombings there; the union agreed, recognizing how important those efforts were to protect public safety. Another example would be **"mandatory wear" policies**, which includes body armor and seat belts. As discussed in Chapter 11, many police officers take issue with such policies for a variety of reasons, so several police labor leaders and management have worked to change the culture in their organizations regarding such policies; they have learned that an essential starting point is soliciting officers' views, as such policies have a direct impact on officers' daily lives and well-being.

Regarding seat belts, in the Prince George's County program discussed in Chapter 11, in the aftermath of several fatal car crashes involving officers, labor and management leaders supported mandatory seat belt policies and the "Arrive Alive" campaign; both sides also jointly filmed a video emphasizing seat belt safety.[15]

With respect to body armor, Houston and Fort Worth, Texas, union leaders and management involved officers in deciding which types of vests to purchase and thus gained support for that mandatory wear policy. Responding to officer concerns that wearing body armor was too uncomfortable in these warm environments, labor and management worked together to select a cooler exterior vest option.[16]

Another example of labor–management collaboration is in Philadelphia, where both sides partnered to address the significant toll that stress, dangerous working conditions, and traumatic incidents can take on officer wellness. A posttraumatic stress disorder (PTSD) program was created wherein a joint letter was sent to officers

YOU DECIDE...

Your city has a population of about 100,000, with an ethnic composition of 52 percent Anglo, 38 percent African-American, and 10 percent Latino. The police force, while composed of 200 sworn officers, has only about 20 percent women and minority officers. The city's central business district has deteriorated since the opening of a new shopping mall on the outskirts of the city, and the chief of police is receiving pressure from the mayor and governing board to bring down crime in the central business district—where the largest concentration of minorities and lower-income residents in the city resides.

The agency received a state justice grant to implement a bicycle patrol unit in the central business district (to be composed of one sergeant and five patrol officers). The police association, representing all patrol officers and sergeants, pointed out to the chief that the bargaining agreement has a seniority bidding clause for all shifts and certain designated job assignments. However, because the agreement does not include a bike unit, the city attorney issues an opinion saying that the chief of police can select all six bike officers without regard to the collective bargaining agreement.

The chief is under pressure from the city manager, mayor, and council to see that women and minority officers are given preference for these new assignments. He knows that if he follows the collective bargaining agreement only the most senior officers and sergeants—all older white males—have a chance of getting the bike assignments.

The chief disseminates an intradepartmental memo stating that all officers can apply for the new bike patrol unit, and that he will ultimately make the selection without giving consideration to their seniority. Several senior officers and sergeants immediately file a grievance alleging that the chief has violated the agreement's seniority-bidding provisions. Next, several female and minority officers approach the association president (a patrol officer) to say the association betrayed them by not upholding their right to obtain these high-profile assignments; they also argue that women and minority bike officers are badly needed in the downtown core.

If the dispute heightens, however, the chief knows his job might be in jeopardy; conversely, the association president could be removed from that position if he is seen as allowing the chief of police to violate the work agreement—while also facing a divided membership if the police bargaining unit is perceived as fighting only for its older white male members.

Questions:

1. What are the issues presented here?
2. Who are the key stakeholders in the situation?

3. What might be some options for you, as the police chief, in response to this crisis? As the union president?

Source: M. Polzin and R. G. DeLord, *Police Labor-Management Relations (Vol. II): A Guide for Implementing Change, Making Reforms, and Handling Crises for Managers and Union Leaders* (Washington, D.C.: U.S. Department of Justice, Office of Community Oriented Policing Services, 2006), pp. 58–50.

that included information about available assistance programs. Labor and management in Philadelphia also supported such mandatory wear seat-belt policies after losing a number of officers.[17]

What separates the police union from police leaders is the realm of politics: the union has the ability to endorse and financially support a political candidate and work in his or her campaign. What impact does this political involvement have? Any proposed change or reform can become a political contest. In addition to contributions of money to candidates, the union can seek to influence the general public and voting through press conferences, direct mail, billboards, radio, and television. Police unions have therefore become major factors in the court of public opinion, because they can deal directly with the elected officials, the media, and the public—bypassing the chief executive.[18]

NEGOTIATING CONTRACT PROVISIONS

Issues for Negotiation

The two primary issues for police management and labor collective bargaining groups are (1) pursuit of better pay, benefits, and working conditions, and (2) broad political issues. In terms of pay, benefits, and working conditions, these groups are constantly lobbying for their membership. They scrutinize their pay relative to other police departments and the pay rates of the public sector in their jurisdiction. They look for differences to point out when requesting raises.

Negotiating for better pay is not a simple matter. For example, beginning salaries may be increased to attract more officers, but the salaries for veteran officers may not be raised or only moderately raised by the government. The opposite is also true—salary is not the only pay issue. Police departments often have specialist positions such as detective, accident investigator, K-9 handler, SWAT officer, gang unit, field training officer, and so forth. These specialists often receive some form of pay differential or extra salary. Thus, the amount of this differential often becomes an issue when the union and government are engaged in collective bargaining.

With regard to working conditions, unions constantly strive to have more control over police deployment and operations, while police leaders desire to maintain a large measure of control and discretion over those areas. Police employee organizations often bargain for shift assignment, criteria for transfers to specialized units, equipment, and promotion systems and eligibility. Another sticky area concerns seniority, which unions often emphasize over ability or experience. From management's standpoint, if seniority was the sole or primary criterion for transferring officers to the detective unit, the unit may become staffed with personnel who are not as adept in investigations.

In summary, there is a wealth of issues that police leaders and unions attempt to influence. If one side cannot make gains in one area, it will use the issue to make demands in other areas.

Two Sides at the Table

As noted earlier, labor negotiations typically involve a dialogue between labor and management that is intended to develop a written agreement that will bind both parties concerning such issues as working conditions, salaries, and benefits. Negotiations at times are also used to prevent or to resolve disputes concerning such issues.

Management normally prefers a narrow scope of negotiations because it means less shared power, while the union may opt for the widest possible scope. The number of negotiating sessions may run from one to several dozen, lasting from a few minutes to many hours, depending on how close or far apart union and management are when they begin to meet.

Figure 7-2 depicts a typical configuration of the union and management bargaining teams. Positions shown in the broken-line boxes typically serve in a support role and may or may not actually be important in the bargaining. Management's labor relations manager (lead negotiator) is often an attorney assigned to the human resources department, reporting to the city manager or assistant city manager and representing the city in grievances and arbitration matters; management's chief negotiator may also be the director of labor relations or human resources director for the unit of government involved or a professional labor relations specialist. Similarly, the union's chief negotiator normally is not a member of the organization involved; rather, he or she will be a specialist who is brought in to represent the union's position and to provide greater experience, expertise, objectivity, and autonomy. The union's chief negotiator may be accompanied by some people who have conducted surveys on wages and benefits, trends in the consumer price index, and so on.

Note that in the minds of many chief executives, the agency administrator should *not* appear at the bargaining table; it is difficult for the chief executive to represent management one day and then return to work among the employees the next. Rather, management is represented by a key member of the command staff having the executive's confidence.

The issues, and the way in which they are presented, will impact how the negotiations will go. In the initial session, the chief negotiator for each party will make an opening statement. Management's representative will often go first, touching on general themes such as the need for patience and the obligation to bargain in good faith. The union's negotiator will generally follow, outlining what the union seeks to achieve under the terms of the new contract. Ground rules for the bargaining may then be reviewed, modified, or developed. The attention then shifts to the terms of the contract that the union is proposing.

Both sides need to understand what it is they are attempting to accomplish. Ultimately, unless a total impasse is reached, agreement will be obtained on the terms of a new contract. The union's membership will vote on the contract as a whole (see a sample contract in the "Focus On" box). If approved by the membership, the contract then goes before the necessary government officials and bodies for approval.[19]

From a civilian point of view, it might seem that most issues on which police and union leaders bargain are relatively straightforward, a "no-brainer." Everyone wants their police officers to be proficient in all aspects of their work—as well as fair and constitutional while doing so.

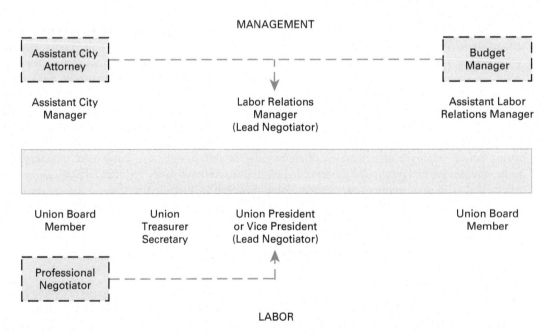

FIGURE 7-2 Union and management Collective Bargaining Teams
Source: Union and management Collective Bargaining Teams, Union and Management Bargaining Teams by Jerry Hoover. Reno Police Department. Used by permission from Jerry Hoover.

FOCUS ON: A SAMPLE POLICE UNION CONTRACT—AND AN ASSIGNMENT

Following are excerpts from portions of an actual contract between an eastern U.S. city and its police department. Shown are most of the major topics that are contained in the contract as well as a brief description of each. The actual contract has been heavily edited for brevity, and redacted as to its actual location.

Preamble

This Contract is entered into by and between the CITY OF _____ and the (union name), to maintain and promote a harmonious relationship between the City and the police employees.

Article 1—Recognition

The City hereby recognizes (union name) as the exclusive representative of the bargaining unit, consisting of Police Officers, Sergeants, Lieutenants, and Captains within the Police Department.

Article 2—Holidays

Each full-time employee of the _____ Police Department shall be entitled to receive annually the following 12 legal holidays [they are listed].

Article 3—Workweek

The workweek for regular officers, supervisors, and command staff shall be 40 hours, consisting of 8 hours per day, 5 consecutive days, with 2 consecutive days off per week.

Article 4—Overtime

All full-time employees (except those attending the recruit academy) shall be paid time and one-half for all hours exceeding 8 hours per day and/or 40 hours per week.

Article 5—Vacations

Each employee with less than 6 years of service shall be allowed 2 calendar weeks paid vacation; each employee with at least 6 years of service but less than 16 years shall be allowed three 3 weeks of paid vacation; each employee with more than 16 years shall be allowed 4 weeks paid vacation.

Article 7—Sick Leave

Each employee shall be allowed 1 day of sick leave with pay for each month of regular full-time service; unused sick leave may be accumulated to 150 days.

Article 10—Insurance

The City shall provide and pay for the following insurance for all employees covered by this Contract [included are life insurance and workers' compensation contributions]

Article 11—Seniority

Advancement in rank, work assignments, shift bid assignments, and vacation scheduling shall be made with consideration given to officer seniority.

Article 14—Salaries

Per contract effective date, each employee shall receive a general wage increase (per appendix A) (the attachment describes pay increases for each rank as well as detective stand-by pay, shift differential -officers receive added salary per month if working evening and midnight shifts - as well as an educational bonus for receipt of a college degree in a related discipline).

Article 17—Strikes

The Union and the employees expressly agree that there will be no strikes, slowdowns, work stoppages, mass absenteeism, or mass resignations.

Article 18—Grievance Procedure

[The entire process—consisting of three steps—is provided for addressing disputes.]

Article 21—Management Rights

The Union recognizes the City's rights, power, and authority to: manage its operations; determine the size of the workforce; hire, promote, transfer, or lay off employees; discipline, suspend, or discharge permanent employees for cause; introduce new methods of operations and facilities and technological changes; and to determine the type and size of equipment to be used.

Article 23—Probationary Period

The probationary period for a regular, full-time police officer is one year after the employee's graduation date from the recruit academy.

Article 24—Examinations

The City may require any police employee to undergo a physical, psychiatric, and/or psychological examination (by a licensed professional) should the need be indicated; the City will pay for such examination(s).

Article 25—Substance Abuse Policy

[A lengthy section describes the Employee Assistance Program, provisions concerning the use of drugs and alcohol, and random drug and/or alcohol testing.]

YOU DECIDE...

A new police department contract provision requires that all patrol officers must pass a firearms qualification or be terminated. The contract provides that if an officer fails to qualify on the first two attempts, he or she must enter a 30-day remedial firearms training program during which time they also surrender their firearms and work inside on desk assignments. Then, if the officer fails to demonstrate firearms proficiency on the range within 30 days after remedial training, termination may result. Officers must score a minimum of 240 points out of 300 (80 percent) in order to carry a firearm on duty.

The officers' union argues strenuously that the policy change is not justified and unnecessarily drives its members toward termination. The union initially presented a counteroffer that would extend the 30-day remedial training period to 90 days; however, management "refused to even look at it." The union argues that no police department in the state has such a rule—which, it believes, could force a number of officers to lose not only their careers but also their homes, health insurance, and other personal possessions. It also claims that there simply are no sufficient shooting ranges for officers to use.

Questions for discussion

1. Whose viewpoint do you agree with, and why?

2. Is the firearms proficiency scoring too strict? Too lenient?

3. Are there any viable options for preparing the officers to pass the test, or modifying the contract's provision?[20]

ADDRESSING CONFLICT: GRIEVANCES AND APPEALS

In unionized departments, there is generally a provision in the contract that outlines how **grievances** are handled. All police departments should have a formalized grievance procedure to adjudicate grievances, allowing for problems to be aired and rectified with minimum negative impact on the department and its morale. Such procedures establish a fair and expeditious process for handling employee disputes that are not disciplinary in nature; they may involve a broad range of issues, including those shown above in the box.

The simplest and preferred method for settling officers' grievances is through informal discussion. The employee explains his or her grievance to the immediate supervisor, allowing him or her to vent any frustrations as well as explain the problem. Most complaints can be handled in this manner, thus reducing the number of grievances. Those complaints that cannot be dealt with informally are usually handled through a more formal grievance process, as described next.

The process for formally handling grievances will vary among agencies and may involve several levels of action. Following is an example of how a grievance might proceed:

Level I: A grievance is submitted in writing to the unit commander after the officer's informal discussions with the supervisor have failed to resolve the issue. The commander will be given a specified number of days to respond to the employee's grievance. If the employee is dissatisfied with the outcome, the grievance moves to the next level.

Level II: At this level, the grievance proceeds to the chief of police, who will be given a specified timeframe to render a decision. In some departments, grievances may go directly to the police chief without first being examined by the unit commander.

Level III: If the employee is not satisfied with the chief's decision, the grievance may proceed to the city or county manager, who will usually meet with the employee and/or representatives from the bargaining association, if the department is unionized, and attempt to resolve the matter. In a nonunion police agency, the city manager's decision is typically the final outcome; some jurisdictions allow the grievance outcome to be appealed to the city council.

Level IV: In unionized police departments, if the grievance is still not resolved, either party may request that the matter be submitted as an **appeal** to arbitration (discussed above). The arbitrator's decision can generally be appealed to a state court.

IN SUM: "NAVIGATING THE WATERS" OF UNIONIZATION

It should now be clear that collective bargaining is an essential part of police leadership. City and county governing boards expect their police leaders to represent their interests well; conversely, there is an expectation by labor that the union will be a strong advocate for its membership and their positions. However, when their relationship becomes antagonistic, everyone suffers; the challenge is to keep that conflict within a healthy range.

Given that, four principles of collective bargaining—communication, cooperation, trust, and respect—are of utmost importance. As a general rule, police leaders who actively engage the union in discussions will accomplish far more than those who employ hostile isolation. Therefore, it is generally best for the following actions to occur:[21]

- Management should avoid entering every contract negotiation fighting to gain control over discipline and working conditions; nor should the union seek only higher pay and benefits. Rather, they should develop a shared vision of community safety—and then realize that the methods used to gain that vision are negotiable.

- Police leaders should avoid rushing to judgment. If an employee is, say, being investigated for an alleged brutality complaint caught on video, both sides should be patient and let the criminal and internal affairs investigators complete their jobs. The media may press for an immediate response from both. There is no requirement that either party respond to questions quickly; sometimes a "no comment until all the facts are in" statement will suffice and is most appropriate.

- Police leaders should recognize the pressures that exist during a crisis or controversy. During a high-profile incident, there may be pressure from union members to take certain public positions that may appear confrontational to management, or vice versa. Although some statements or actions are required as a part of the role each has to play, communication, cooperation, respect, and trust become valuable to avoiding unnecessary conflicts.

- Leadership should not attempt to defend the indefensible: Assume that a police lieutenant is caught driving under the influence and the chief deems that a minor suspension is appropriate. Or, an employee is arrested for driving under the influence and the union defends his actions as a result of "job stress." In such instances, union and management must be aware that the public might see such "discipline" as too lenient and preferential.

- Leadership should remember that elected officials do not like to make waves, and all battles are won and lost in the court of public opinion. Much of what happens in a police agency is open to the public, and any conflict between management and the union during a crisis or controversy will be played out in the media. Information leaks occur during high-profile incidents, and management and unions need to realize that all of their words and actions will be brought to light. Efforts by management and the union to resolve conflicts before they escalate will go a long way toward preventing a public collision.

- Avoid making an end run. When police leadership goes around the union to communicate with or to encourage the rank and file to support or oppose an issue, a union backlash is sure to come. The union has a role to play, and its leadership was elected to speak for the members on labor-related issues. The same holds true for the union when it decides to make an end run to the city or county manager or to elected officials.

YOU DECIDE...

A new police union contract is being negotiated in your city, where a group of activists have launched a "Keep Police Accountable" movement. In the aftermath of several recent and questionable police shootings, this faction is actively campaigning to make the police more transparent.

However, an impasse has been reached in negotiating following proposals put forth by the police union: (1) officers may not be interrogated within 48 hours after being involved in an incident (during which time officers may also review all body camera footage as well as consult a free attorney), (2) information on past officer misconduct cannot be recorded or retained in his or her personnel file, (3) any misconduct complaints that are received more than 180 days after an alleged incident will not be considered, and (4) the local civilian review board may not recommend disciplinary action against officers for misconduct.

Due to the impasse, you—a professional arbitrator—are retained to resolve the issues. What will be your recommendations concerning each of these four issues, and why?

Summary

This chapter has left no doubt that police collective bargaining and the labor movement have had a profound impact on all levels and aspects. At times, the police desire to be represented has resulted in a fractured history. Police strikes in the early 1900s took a heavy toll and resulted in a long-term prohibition of and public enmity toward police unions. Indeed, it would take several decades before the states would even allow police officers to bargain collectively. Still today, with policing having more than seven million union members, there remains room for police and union leaders' perspectives to be marked by strain and division, and for the public to look askance at the positions of each. However, a number of examples were provided here where today's police and union leaders are working very successfully in an atmosphere of collaboration and cooperation for the public good.

We also examined three collective bargaining models, ranging from no collective bargaining to binding arbitration. Some states have opted to disallow police and other public employees to be engaged in collective bargaining. In those states, there is the possibility of a lack of communication between police leaders and rank-and-file officers that, in turn, can prevent police leaders being aware of officers' problems and concerns.

The grievance procedure process was also examined, as well as some general "tips" provided for police leaders in navigating the waters of unionization.

It is clear that, as with the topic of police civil liability (discussed in Chapter 6), it is far better to learn about collective bargaining, negotiation, and union contracts "in-house," rather than having to learn about them by virtue of grievances and even lawsuits in the courthouse. The public deserves and can have no less.

Discussion Questions

1. How and why did police unions evolve?
2. What was the Boston police strike; how did it affect the police labor movement?
3. To what extent is collective bargaining authorized in the United States?
4. What are some of most prominent police unions in the United States?
5. Relations between both police management and union leaders are optimal in what way?
6. What are the three models of collective bargaining?
7. What types of provisions are generally found in a police labor contract?
8. What is a grievance, and how does the system that police leaders use for dealing with one when it arises function?

Internet Investigations

Federal Mediation and Conciliation Service
   https://www.fmcs.gov/services/resolving-labor
   -management-disputes/collective-bargaining-mediation/
Fraternal Order of Police
   https://www.fop.net/Faq.aspx

National Association of Police Organizations
   http://www.napo.org/
Police Contracts Database
   http://www.checkthepolice.org/database/

CHAPTER 8

Financial Administration: "Doing More with Less" Since the Great Recession

STUDENT LEARNING OUTCOMES

After reading this chapter, the student will be able to:

- review generally how the Great Recession affected police leaders and their budgets and operations
- explain several measures police leaders might undertake to stretch resources and enhance budgets, including workload analysis, agency surveys, grant writing, civilianization, and mobilizing stakeholders
- define and relate strategic planning to the budgeting process
- define a budget
- explain the budget cycle's four steps
- distinguish among the three different budget formats and know the advantages and disadvantages of each

KEY TERMS AND CONCEPTS

- Audit
- Budget
- Budget approval
- Budget cycle
- Budget execution
- Budget formulation
- Expenditures
- Fiscal year
- Great Recession

- Line-item budget
- Mobilizing stakeholders
- Performance budget
- Planning–programming–budgeting system (PPBS)
- Program budget
- Strategic planning
- Workload analysis
- Zero-based budget (ZBB)

INTRODUCTION

Providing local (city and county) police services is an expensive undertaking; in fact, the cost of deploying one sworn police officer is $131,000; personnel costs, including salaries and benefits, are typically 80 percent to 90 percent of a department's operating **expenditures**.[1] Therefore, the importance of police leaders understanding all facets of financial administration cannot be overstated.

Money is the key to nearly everything police agencies do; indeed, the police chief executive and staff will likely be judged on how well they compete with other governmental entities in obtaining funds necessary for meeting the agency's mission and goals—and how successful they were in defending their budgets against cuts. Money is the fuel that powers the organization. As Frederick Mosher observed, "Not least among the qualifications of an administrator is one's ability as a tactician and gladiator in the budget process."[2]

The **Great Recession**, beginning in 2008 and lasting about 18 months, impacted police agencies of all sizes and forced police leaders to devote the bulk of their time trying to identify where budgets and functions could be cut—and where doing so would cause the least damage. The resulting "do more with less" mentality fomented at that time has tentacles that reach out to today's agencies, creating a "new normal" for today's police leaders. This chapter discusses some of the recession's lingering vestiges.

In addition to being a political document, as noted above, the agency budget is also a *planning* document (both are discussed more below). **Strategic planning** also became a much more integral aspect of the police leader's job since the recession. Indeed, if unlimited funds were available, planning would not be needed. The aforementioned financial crisis also had a profound effect on the ability of police agencies to plan strategically for staffing and other needs. As a result, today's agencies must view planning as more important than ever for determining staffing needs and in getting the resources to meet these needs.

Although this chapter is not intended to prepare the reader to be a fiscal analyst or an expert on the more intricate aspects of financial administration, it will provide a foundation for and insight concerning some of its basic methods and issues. Therefore, to begin, we look at general areas where the police leader must develop fiscal acumen—to include a workload analysis and several means by which one may enhance the agency budget (e.g., grants, civilianization), we consider the need for mobilizing stakeholders and strategic planning.

Next, we focus on the heart of the chapter: budgeting. Included are discussions of budget definitions and uses; key elements of the budget process (formulation, approval, execution, and audit); and several budget formats. The chapter concludes with a summary, key terms and concepts, discussion questions, and internet resources. Five exhibits and a real-world problem provide further insight into the police leader's fiscal duties.

Budgeting and financial administration in general are a main part of the police leader's duties.
Source: Win McNamee/Getty Images News/Getty Images

FIRST THINGS FIRST: ENHANCING BUDGETS AND FINANCIAL STEWARDSHIP

Possessing insight into the world of fiscal affairs requires more than merely knowing how to plan for and spend monies. Therefore, next we discuss some peripheral but nevertheless important matters that will bear heavily on the task of budgeting, discussed later.

Knowing What the Job Entails—and What the Competition is Doing

To have financial insight and confidence, police leaders must first know what the job entails in order to provide optimal service to the community and meeting overall agency demands. Toward that end, a **workload analysis** should be completed at least every three years to ensure the department has adequate staff to address the needs of the community and allow for strategic planning. (It is noteworthy that many agencies strive to achieve a "recommended officers per 1,000 population" or a "national standard" for staffing; however, this standard generally is not useful for determining staffing needs.)[3] Furthermore, some agencies use their jurisdiction's crime rate, as published by the Federal Bureau of Investigation's *Uniform Crime Reports*, to compare their productivity, efficiency, and so on with those of other agencies. Again, doing so is inadvisable, as many variables within a community affect crime. Probably, the best use of UCR data is for an agency to compare itself from year to year. Note, too, that calls for service (CFS) are used instead of crime rates as workload indicators. Typically, only a small percent of a police department's CFS are crime-related in nature; much more common are CFS for order-maintenance duties. Therefore, it is far better for a police leader to divide officers' time into calls for service, administrative duties, and community policing and problem-solving (see Exhibits 8-1 and 8-2) and use these statistics rather than the crime rate to justify staffing requests.[4]

EXHIBIT 8-1 An Organized Approach to Budget Cutting in Corpus Christi[6]

When the Great Recession made the prospect of significant budget cuts a reality in Corpus Christi, Texas, a new police chief in the agency of 450 sworn personnel established 30 "reorganization and efficiency teams" composed of members of the agency and community. Believing that patrol should remain a priority, the CCPD began by transferring 41 employees from other assignments to patrol, eliminating many specialized units and emphasizing community policing. Officers distributed surveys door to door, asking citizens to list their concerns. Problem-solving teams were developed and a workload analysis was performed (resulting in personnel being assigned at times and at places where they were most needed); overtime was eliminated (saving a half million

The annual budget allows agencies to establish a work program for the coming fiscal year, manage and control resources, properly align costs and services, provide effective and efficient use of resources, and indicate mission priorities, goals, and objectives.

Source: Diego Grandi/Shutterstock

dollars over three years) by moving personnel from desk jobs to the streets. Emphasis was placed on tracking repeat offenders, and the use of reserve officers (primarily using retired officers) was boosted. Volunteers (most of whom were retired officers or military personnel) began logging 500 hours per month, including working at school crossings (which previously cost about $700,000 per year for paid guards). Responses to minor traffic accidents were reduced, and leased buildings and facilities were consolidated (saving $250,000). Meanwhile, overall crime was down 15 percent (with robberies declining 20 percent, drive-by shootings, 50 percent).

Although such an analysis can be very complicated—examining, beat assignments, shift configurations, the nature and numbers of officers dispatched to CFS, the average service and travel time for CFS, discretionary patrol time, and so on)—there are a number of resources available to assist in this endeavor.[5]

Once the staffing levels have been identified, the department should compare its salary and benefits package to other agencies in the surrounding area. For most employees today, money alone is not a motivator; however, the absence of money can be a de-motivator (note that in a related vein, we discuss collective bargaining in Chapter 7). Employees soon learn how their salaries and benefits stand in comparison with other nearby agencies; thus, it is important for the agency to keep pace with the pay schedule in its labor market lest their employees leave for what they perceive as greener pastures. A simple telephone survey can be conducted of agencies in the area. Comparisons should be made of positions with similar job responsibilities, not rank, because ranks differ from one agency to another—that is, a shift commander may be sergeant in one department and a lieutenant in another. Such surveys should include the base rate of pay, insurance, and other benefits for each community by position. Also, take into account shift configuration (e.g., eight-, ten-, or twelve-hour work schedules) and any perks such as take-home vehicles, recruitment bonuses, educational incentives, and shift differential pay.[7]

Strategies for Enhancing the Bottom Line: Growth, Grants, and Civilianization

Following are several suggestions for enhancing and stretching the budget. Although these measures will not be successful in all jurisdictions and at all times, police leaders should be sensitive to their potential to be "winning strategies."

Population Growth

First is *population growth*, which often occurs when middle-class persons move into a city's existing area or into newly annexed areas. While middle-class residents do not typically experience high crime rates, these citizens are normally well informed, concerned about their safety and police services, and thus demand greater police services. In addition, annexation (the incorporation of new territory into the domain of a city, country, or state) will sometimes bring growth to police staffing.[8]

Grants

Many police leaders have developed expertise in augmenting their operating budgets with different types of grants. Indeed, many times expensive capital improvement budget items—upgraded communications technology included the more powerful 800 MHz radios, dispatching systems, mobile data terminals, and laptops

---

EXHIBIT 8-2 Expanding and Annexing in Mesa, Arizona[9]

A quarter century ago, the city of Mesa, Ariz., was a quiet suburb of Phoenix with a large number of winter residents and an estimated population of 165,000. Recently, Mesa's population grew to 465,000, and so did the amount of land annexed for residential and commercial development. As a result, the Mesa Police Department found itself servicing twice the territory it covered just a quarter century earlier.

Along with this growth in population and area, Mesa increased its police expenditures; in fact, the budget increased more than 10 times over that span of time, which not only exceeded the rate of population growth but also far outpaced inflation, growing by an average of 8 percent each year during this period.

A major reason for this budget increase was the city's expansion of its police force, which grew from 643 sworn officers to 855, or 33 percent. Another reason is that per-unit labor costs for both sworn officers and civilian employees became much more expensive than they were 10 years earlier. Higher salaries and the escalating price of benefits for sworn officers were reasons for the increase in personnel costs in Mesa, where the cost of police pensions alone rose by as much as 33 percent in one year.

for police vehicles—are obtained via grant funding. Capital budgets also included expenditures for buildings, vehicles, and property. Generally, the more expensive items are funded by bonds, and the less expensive items by grants, general funds, or asset-forfeiture funds. Police departments can access a variety of external funding sources, including state and federal grants, foundations, and business groups.[10]

There are caveats with receiving "free money" from grants, however, and police leaders should heed the adage "beware of feds bearing gifts." The major problem is simply that, if local officials accept federal funding—particularly for hiring additional police officers—they also promise to retain these officers and keep current staffing levels after the federal contributions expire. However, some agencies simply fail to plan adequately for the phaseout of federal assistance; then, after what is typically three years of grant funding, the department can find itself struggling to locate the funds to do so.

A beginner's step-by-step guide for writing competitive grants is available at: http://www.policegrantshelp .com/grants101/.[11]

Civilianization

There has been a long-standing debate about civilianization in policing, which entails reducing the number of sworn officers and hiring civilians to perform many police duties (note, however, that agencies do typically hire civilians in nonenforcement positions such as crime analysis, crime prevention, and dispatching).

This concept has at times been fiercely resisted by many unions, chiefs, and mayors, all of whom prefer to expand the ranks of sworn personnel.

Since they are not required to undergo the same comprehensive training as uniformed police, however, civilian employees can replace sworn officers in many tasks while ultimately commanding a lower salary (as well as few, if any, fringe benefits). In addition, civilianization can allow citizens to become more knowledgeable about their police and familiar with problems affecting the community.[12]

EXHIBIT 8-3 Using Volunteers to Great Advantage

In 2014, the Houston Police Department considered adding nonsworn employees to operations and command positions. Usually occupied by uniformed officers, 443 positions were identified as potential candidates for civilianization, including roles in narcotics and technical surveillance divisions. Then, in 2015, the Denver Sheriff Department placed civilians in charge of mailroom functions, technology management, the Vehicle Impound Facility, and the Juvenile Work Program. The Corpus Christi, Texas, Police Department benefits from civilianization in its Criminal Investigation and Animal Control divisions.

In all of these examples, civilian personnel were assigned solely to positions that avoid interference in investigations or other police matters.[13]

Other Pointers: Capitalizing on Sensational Incidents

The occurrence of major crime events can bring about a loud call for more police resources. The reporting of mass killings, murder of a police officer, random shootings at schools, increased gang violence and so on certainly carry an emotional element and can be a powerful rationale for making budget requests. Even when the crime rate is decreasing, violent crimes may fuel citizens' and politicians' fears.

Regarding the mobilizing of stakeholders, police leaders should never forget that there exists a natural constituency of neighborhood groups, civic organizations, and business groups that are concerned about crime. In addition, the creation of community policing and problem-solving has greatly expanded police departments' ties to the community.[14] Citizens and citizen groups often ally themselves with the police and lobby for more police resources.

Finally, many people have difficulty understanding the concept of and need for *strategic planning* (discussed briefly in Chapter 1) as it relates to finances and the future. So, take, for example, a high school senior who is pondering where to attend a college or university. Some preliminary questions to ponder would include: what are my aptitudes and interests? What kinds of careers fit those aptitudes and interests? How do I achieve that goal? And to achieve that goal, can I afford to go to an out-of-state school? Are scholarships available to me? Will I have to work part- or full-time while in school? Can I get family help? Will I be able to afford (or even need) a car while in school? How will I pay for books, tuition, housing, and other living expenses? This is an example of how individuals strategically plan.

This is strategic planning for the short and long term. This exercise is not unlike that of a police executive who wishes to have some better plan of taking the agency where it needs to go. Strategic planning thus means seeing both the big picture and its operational implications. As Heracleous observed, the purpose of strategic thinking is to discover novel, imaginative strategies "that can rewrite the rules of the competitive game and to envision potential futures significantly different from the present."[15]

Strategic thinking is, therefore, compatible with strategic planning. Both are required in any thoughtful strategy-making process and strategy formulation.[16] Strategic planning is also a leadership tool and a process; it shapes and guides what an organization is, what it does, and why it does it, with a focus on the future.[17]

Excellent examples of strategic planning abound; for example, see the strategic plan of the U.S. Department of Justice for 2014–2018 at: https://www.justice.gov/sites/default/files/jmd/legacy/2014/02/28/doj-fy-2014-2018-strategic-plan.pdf.[18]

EXHIBIT 8-4 Using Smart Policing and Force Multipliers: The Case of Camden, New Jersey[19]

The City of Camden, New Jersey, was struggling for survival even before the Great Recession. In addition to being the nation's poorest city (36 percent of residents living in poverty), its violent crime rate was more than five times that of the nation. Drug and gang crimes abounded, and 40 percent of its violent crimes were committed by youths. Many veteran as well as new officers were laid off or demoted, while others saw their salaries cut, and the agency's budget was cut by 25 percent. The police chief began seeking ways to restructure the department so as to use a smart policing strategy with remaining officers, and the first move was to eliminate or reduce specialized units and move administrative and investigative personnel to the streets. Technologies were introduced to move to a "smarter" approach that would be a force multiplier. A real-time tactical operations center was created and a gunshot location system was implemented in the city's high-incident areas. Automated license-plate readers were used to detect stolen vehicles and vehicles associated with criminals.

Yet, despite their best efforts, the severe budget cuts and loss of personnel resulted in rising crime rates. With fewer officers on the streets, criminals became more brazen, while citizen fear of crime, city homicides, and calls for service (CFS) escalated. Eventually, the city felt compelled to begin discussing a plan for consolidating its force with county agencies—a change that would save the city $14 million per year. A plan was devised whereby nearly 300 city officers would be laid off, but about half of them could be hired into the new agency through an application process. The city and county did indeed consolidate in 2013.

The key lesson to be learned from the Camden experience as other jurisdictions attempt to develop proactive responses to crime is that technology is not a substitute for police officers being deployed on the streets.

THE BUDGET

In this section, we focus on budgeting, to include its elements, types (with several examples provided), formulation, and execution. Included is a brief explanation of the role of auditing.

A Working Definition

The word **budget** is derived from the old French word *bougette*, meaning a small leather bag or wallet. Initially, it referred to the leather bag in which the Chancellor of the Exchequer carried documents stating the government's needs and resources given to the English Parliament.[20] Later, it came to mean the documents themselves. More recently, budget has been defined as a plan stated in financial terms, an estimate of future expenditures, a policy statement, the translation of financial resources into human purposes, and a contract between those who appropriate the funds and those who spend them.[21] To some extent, all of these definitions are valid.

In addition, the budget is a management tool and a comprehensive plan, expressed in financial terms, by which a program is operated for a given period. It includes (1) the services, activities, and projects comprising the program, (2) the resultant expenditure requirements, and (3) the resources available for their support.[22]

It is also "a plan or schedule adjusting expenses during a certain period to the estimated income for that period."[23] Lester Bittel added:

> A budget is, literally, a financial standard for a particular operation, activity, program, or department. Its data are presented in numerical form, mainly in dollars—to be spent for a particular purpose—over a specified period of time. Budgets are derived from planning goals and forecasts.[24]

Although these descriptions are certainly apt, one writer warns that budgets can involve an inherently irrational process: "Budgets are based on little more than the past and some guesses."[25] Police leaders sometimes base a new budget on previous budgets and neglect considering the future to any degree. Any new operations or programs must be paid for and therefore included in a budget.

As noted above, financial management of governmental agencies is clearly political. Anything the government does entails the expenditure of public funds.[26] Thus, the most important political statement that any unit of government makes in a given year is its budget. Essentially, the budget causes administrators to follow the gambler's adage and "put their money where their mouth is."[27] When demands placed on government increase while funds are stable or decline, the competition for funds is keener than usual, forcing justice agencies to make the best case for their budgets. The heads of all departments, if they are doing their jobs well, are also vying for appropriations. Special-interest groups, the media, politicians, and the public, with their own views and priorities, often engage in arm twisting during the budgeting process.

Key Elements: Budget Cycle, Formulation, Approval, Execution

Administrators must think in terms of a budget cycle—simply put, how long a budget lasts, which is a time frame that can vary from agency to agency. In government (and, therefore, all public criminal justice agencies) the budget cycle is typically set on a fiscal-year basis. Some states have a biennial budget cycle; their legislatures, such as those in Kentucky and Nevada, budget for a two-year period. Normally, however, the **fiscal year** is a 12-month period that may coincide with a calendar year or, more commonly, will run from July 1 through June 30 of the following year. The federal government's fiscal year is October 1 through September 30. The budget cycle is important because it drives the development of the budget and determines when new monies become available.

The budget cycle consists of four sequential steps, repeated every year at about the same point in time: (1) budget formulation, (2) budget approval, (3) budget execution, and (4) budget audit.

Budget Formulation

Depending on the size and complexity of the organization and the financial condition of the jurisdiction, budget formulation—which involves the preparation of a budget so as to be able to allocate funds in accordance with agency priorities, plans, and programs, and to deliver necessary services—can be a relatively simple or an exceedingly difficult task; in either case, it is likely to be the most complicated stage of the budgeting process. The administrator must anticipate all types of expenditures—that is, payment for goods or services, to settle a financial obligation indicated by an invoice, contract, or other such document—and predict expenses related to major incidents or events that might arise. Certain assumptions based on the previous year's budget can be made, but they are not necessarily accurate. One observer noted that "every expense you budget should be fully supported with the proper and most logical assumptions you can develop. Avoid simply estimating, which is the least supportable form of budgeting."[28] As noted earlier, financial administration is heavily grounded in planning. As a criminal justice administrator, discussing budget formulation, stated:

> The most important ingredient for any budgeting process is planning. Administrators should approach the budget process from the planning standpoint of "How can I best reconcile the [criminal justice] needs of the community with the ability of my jurisdiction to finance them, and then relate those plans in a convincing manner to my governing body for proper financing and execution of programs?" After all, as budget review occurs, the document is taken apart and scrutinized piece by piece or line by line. This fragmentation approach contributes significantly to our inability to defend interrelated programs in an overall budget package.[29]

To illustrate, let us assume that a police department budget is being prepared in a city having a manager form of government. Long before a criminal justice agency (or any other unit of local government) begins to prepare its annual budget, the city manager and/or the staff of the city have made revenue forecasts, considered how much (if any) of the current operating budget will be carried over into the next fiscal year, analyzed how the

TABLE 8-1 Budget Preparation Calendar for a Large Police Department

What Should Be Done	By Whom	On This Date
Issue budget instructions and applicable forms	City administrator	November 1
Prepare and issue budget message, with instructions and applicable forms, to unit commanders	Chief of police	November 15
Develop unit budgets with appropriate justification and forward recommended budgets to planning and research unit	Unit commanders	February 1
Review unit budget	Planning and research staff with unit commanders	March 1
Consolidate unit budgets for presentation to chief of police	Planning and research unit	March 15
Review consolidated recommended budget	Chief of police, planning and research staff, and unit commanders	March 30
Obtain department approval of budget	Chief of police	April 15
Forward recommended budget to city administrator	Chief of police	April 20
Review recommended budget by administration	City administrator and chief of police	April 30
Approve revised budget	City administrator	May 5
Forward budget document to city council	City administrator	May 10
Review budget	Budget officer of city council	May 20
Present to council	City administrator and chief of police	June 1
Report back to city administrator	City council	June 5
Review and resubmit to city council	City administrator and chief of police	June 10
Take final action on police budget	City council	June 20

Source: U.S. Department of Justice, National Advisory Commission on Criminal Justice Standards and Goals, *Police* (Washington, DC: U.S. Government Printing Office, 1973), p. 137.

population of the jurisdiction will grow or shift (affecting demand for public services), and examined other priorities for the coming year. The city manager may also appear before the governing body to obtain information about its fiscal priorities, spending levels, pay raises, new positions, programs, and so on. The city manager may then send department heads a memorandum outlining the general fiscal guidelines to be followed in preparing their budgets. It is a fiscal point from which to plan the departments' budgets.

On receipt of the city's guidelines for preparing its budget, the heads of functional areas, such as the chief of police, have a planning and research unit (assuming a city large enough to have this level of specialization) prepare an internal budget calendar and an internal fiscal policy memorandum. (Table 8-1 shows an internal budget calendar for a large municipal police department.) This memo may include input from unions and lower supervisory personnel. Each bureau is then given the responsibility for preparing its individual budget request.

In small police agencies with little or no functional specialization, the chief may prepare the budget alone or with input from other officers or the city finance officer. In some small agencies, chiefs and sheriffs may not even see their budget or assist in its preparation. Because of tradition, politics, or even laziness, the administrator may have abdicated control over the budget. This puts the agency in a precarious position indeed; it will have difficulty engaging in long-term planning and spending money productively for personnel and programs when the executive has to get prior approval from the governing body to buy items such as office supplies.

The police department planning and research unit then reviews the bureau's budget request for compliance with the budgeting instructions and the chief's and city manager's priorities. Eventually, a consolidated budget is developed for the entire police department and submitted to the chief, who may meet with the planning and research unit and bureau commanders to discuss it. Personalities, politics, priorities, personal agendas, and other issues may need to be addressed; the chief may have to mediate disagreements concerning these matters, sometimes rewarding the loyal and sometimes reducing allotments to the disloyal, which can be a dangerous political game.[30] Requests for programs, equipment, travel expenses, personnel, or anything else in the draft budget may be deleted, reduced, or enhanced. The budget is then presented to the city manager. At this point, the chief executive's reputation as a budget framer becomes a factor. If the chief is known to pad the budget heavily, the city manager is far more likely to cut the department's request than if the chief is known to be reasonable in making budget requests, engages in innovative planning, and has a flexible approach to budget negotiations. Regardless, the chief must be able to justify all requested expenditures in the budget.

The city or county manager consolidates the police budget request with those from other department heads and then meets with them individually to discuss their requests further. The manager then directs the city finance officer to make any necessary additions or cuts and then to prepare a budget proposal for presentation to the governing body. The general steps in budget development are shown in Exhibit 8-5.

EXHIBIT 8-5 Steps in Budget Development: The California Highway Patrol

Following is a description of how the $1.96 billion budget for the California Highway Patrol (CHP) is typically developed. According to the budget section, "It is an all-year and year-on-year process" that begins at the level of the 8 divisions and 103 area offices/dispatch centers, where budget requests originate. The requests are dealt with one of three ways: (1) funded within the department's base budget, (2) disapproved, or (3) carried forward for review by CHP personnel.

At the division level, managers review the area requests, make needed adjustments, and submit a consolidated request to the budget section at headquarters. This section passes input from the field to individual section management staff (e.g., planning and analysis, personnel, training, and communications) for review. Budget section staff meet with individual section management staff. Within two or three months, the budget section identifies proposals for new funding that have department-wide impact and passes them on to the executive level.

The commissioner and aides review the figures along with those from other state departments and agree on a budget to submit to the governor. The governor submits this budget to the legislature, which acts on it and returns it to the governor for signature.

Source: Excerpt from Hal Rubin, "Working Out a Budget," *Law and Order.* Copyright © 1989 by Hendon Publishing Company.

Budget Approval

With the city/county manager's proposed budget request in hand, the governing board begins its deliberations on the budget. The manager may appear before the board to answer questions concerning the budget; individual department heads also may be asked to appear. Suggestions for getting monies approved and appropriated include the following:

1. Have a carefully justified budget.
2. Anticipate the environment of the budget hearing by reading news reports and understanding the priorities of the council members. Know what types of questions elected officials are likely to ask.
3. Determine which "public" will be at the police/sheriff's department's budget hearing and prepare accordingly. Public issues change from time to time; citizens who were outraged over one issue in a given year might be incensed by another issue the next.
4. Make good use of graphics in the form of pie charts and histograms; short case studies of successes are normal and add to the impact of graphics.
5. Rehearse and critique the presentation many times.
6. Be a political realist.[31]

After everyone scheduled has spoken, the city council or county commission directs the manager to make further cuts in the budget or to reinstate funds or programs cut earlier, and so on. The budget is then approved. It is fair to say that at this stage, budgeting is largely a legislative function that requires some legal action, as a special ordinance or resolution approving the budget is passed each year by the governing board.

The columns in Table 8-2 indicate the budget amount requested by a chief of police, the amount recommended by the city manager, and the amount finally approved by the city council.

Budget Execution

The third stage of the process, budget execution, has several objectives: (1) to carry out the organization's budgeted objectives for the fiscal year in an orderly manner, (2) to ensure that the department undertakes no financial obligations or commitments other than those funded by the city council, and (3) to provide a periodic accounting of the administrator's stewardship over the department's funds.[32]

TABLE 8-2 Police Operating Budget ($) in a Community of 100,000 Population

Description	FY 2017–2018 Expenses	FY 2017–2018 Expenses	FY 2018–2019 Police Request	City Manager	City Council
Salaries/wages					
Regular salaries	28,315,764	28,392,639	32,221,148	32,221,148	32,221,148
Overtime	1,976,165	1,564,421	1,902,875	1,902,875	1,422,875
Severance pay	456,712	452,465	454,936	0	0
Holiday pay	790,952	1,182,158	1,396,958	1,396,958	1,396,958
Callback pay	1,205,947	1,326,534	1,476,925	1,395,241	1,395,241
Subtotals	32,745,540	32,918,217	36,916,222	36,916,222	36,436,222
Employee benefits					
Retirement	6,345,566	6,485,888	8,069,521	8,069,521	8,069,521
Group insurance	2,256,663	2,467,406	2,752,718	2,752,718	2,752,718
Life insurance	86,797	106,164	234,590	234,396	234,396
Disability insurance	1,452,885	1,588,686	2,346,909	2,346,038	2,024,398
Uniform allowance	376,079	386,827	392,750	392,750	392,750
Medicare	154,730	160,868	200,058	198,739	198,739
Long-term disability	22,583	42,974	96,517	96,517	96,517
Subtotals	10,695,303	11,238,813	14,093,063	14,090,679	13,769,039
Services and supplies					
Office supplies	124,357	98,292	102,485	102,485	102,485
Operating supplies	454,563	296,569	540,661	540,661	540,661
Repair/maintenance	496,922	390,941	466,118	466,118	466,118
Small tools	98,508	1,576	24,175	24,175	24,175
Professional services	674,263	580,359	668,765	668,765	668,765
Communications	574,757	446,200	784,906	784,906	784,906
Services and supplies					
Public utilities	222,935	232,773	242,008	242,008	242,008
Rentals	162,840	192,294	226,071	226,071	226,071
Vehicle rentals	1,668,416	2,193,926	2,363,278	2,363,278	2,169,278
Extradition	40,955	44,411	40,000	40,000	40,000
Other travel	8,649	10,123	46,500	46,500	46,500
Advertising	4,662	4,570	8,100	8,100	8,100
Insurance	656,360	1,190,257	1,884,921	1,884,921	1,884,921
Books/manuals	32,285	24,813	24,404	24,404	24,404
Employee training	94,029	60,851	0	0	0
Aircraft expenses	0	0	30,000	30,000	30,000
Special inventory	22,527	26,465	30,000	30,000	30,000
Other services and supplies	2,386,201	2,039,651	2,386,201	2,386,201	2,386,201
Subtotals	7,723,229	7,834,071	9,868,593	9,868,593	9,868,593
Capital outlay					
Machinery and equipment	1,144,301	204,964	0	0	0
Totals	52,308,373	52,196,065	60,877,878	60,875,494	60,073,854

Supervision of the budget execution phase is an executive function that requires some type of fiscal control system, usually directed by the city or county manager. Most cities and counties utilize sophisticated automated finance software programs to manage their jurisdiction's budget, with the various departmental finance personnel using the program to manage the agency's budget and produce reports. Periodic reports on accounts are an important element of budget control; they serve to reduce the likelihood of overspending by identifying areas in which deficits are likely to occur as a result of change in gasoline prices, extensive overtime, natural disasters, and unplanned emergencies (such as riots). A periodic budget status report tells the administrator what percentage of the total budget has been expended to date (Table 8-3).

TABLE 8-3   A Police Department's Budget Status Report ($)

Line Item	Amount Budgeted	Expenses to Date	Amount Encumbered	Balance to Date	Percentage Used
Salaries	16,221,148	8,427,062.00	0	7,794,086.00	52.0
Professional services	334,765	187,219.61	8,014.22	139,531.17	58.3
Office supplies	51,485	16,942.22	3,476.19	31,066.59	39.7
Repair/maintenance	49,317	20,962.53	1,111.13	27,243.34	44.8
Communications	392,906	212,099.11	1,560.03	179,246.86	54.4
Utilities	121,008	50,006.15	10,952.42	60,049.43	51.4
Vehicle rentals	1,169,278	492,616.22	103,066.19	573,595.59	51.9
Travel	23,500	6,119.22	2,044.63	15,336.15	34.7
Extraditions	20,000	12,042.19	262.22	7,695.59	61.5
Printing/binding	36,765	15,114.14	2,662.67	18,988.19	48.4
Books/manuals	12,404	5,444.11	614.11	6,345.78	48.8
Training/education	35,695	19,661.54	119.14	15,914.32	55.4
Aircraft expenses	15,000	8,112.15	579.22	6,308.63	57.9
Special investigations	15,000	6,115.75	960.50	7,922.75	47.2
Machinery	1,000	275.27	27.50	697.23	30.3
Advertising	4,100	1,119.17	142.50	2,838.33	30.8

Prudent administrators normally attempt to manage the budget conservatively for the first eight or nine months of the budget year, holding the line on spending until most fiscal crises have been averted. Because unplanned incidents and natural disasters can wreak havoc with any budget, this conservatism is normally the best course. Then the administrator can plan the most efficient way to allocate funds if emergency funds have not been spent.

The Audit

The word *audit* means "to verify something independently."[33] The basic rationale for an **audit** of a budget—which is an objective examination of the financial statements of an organization, either by its employees or by an outside firm—was described by the controller general of the United States as follows:

> Governments and agencies entrusted with public resources and the authority for applying them have a responsibility to render a full accounting of their activities. This accountability is inherent in the governmental process and is not always specifically identified by legislative provision. This governmental accountability should identify not only the object for which the public resources have been devoted but also the manner and effect of their application.[34]

After the close of each budget year, the year's expenditures are audited to ensure that the agency spent its funds properly. Budget audits are designed to investigate three broad areas of accountability: financial accountability (focusing on proper fiscal operations and reports of the justice agency), management accountability (determining whether funds were utilized efficiently and economically), and program accountability (determining whether the unit of government's goals and objectives were accomplished).[35]

Financial audits determine whether funds were spent legally, the budgeted amount was exceeded, and the financial process proceeded in a legal manner. For example, auditors investigate whether funds transferred between accounts were authorized, grant funds were used properly, computations were made accurately, disbursements were documented, financial transactions followed established procedures, and established competitive bidding procedures were employed.[36] Police administrators should welcome auditors' help to identify weaknesses and deficiencies and correct them.

Budget Formats

The three types of budgets primarily in use today are the line-item budget (or object-of-expenditure budget), the performance budget, and the program (or results or outcomes) budget. Two additional types, the **planning–programming–budgeting system (PPBS)** and the **zero-based budget (ZBB)**, are also discussed in the literature but are used to a lesser extent.

Line-item budget is a budget format that breaks down its components into major categories, such as personnel, equipment, contractual services, commodities, and capital outlay items.

The Line-Item Budget

Line-item budgeting (or *item budgeting*) is the most commonly used budget format. It is the basic system on which all other systems rely because it affords control. It is so named because it breaks down the budget into the major categories commonly used in government (e.g., personnel, equipment, contractual services, commodities, and capital outlay items); every amount of money requested, recommended, appropriated, and expended is associated with a particular item or class of items.[37] In addition, large budget categories are broken down into smaller line-item budgets (in a police department, examples include patrol, investigation, communications, and jail function). The line-item format fosters budgetary control because no item escapes scrutiny.[38] Table 8-3, shown above, demonstrates a line-item budget for police. Each demonstrates the range of activities and funding needs of each agency.

The line-item budget has several strengths and weaknesses. Its strengths include ease of control, development, comprehension (especially by elected and other executive branch officials), and administration. Weaknesses are its neglect of long-range planning and its limited ability to evaluate performance. Furthermore, the line-item budget tends to maintain the status quo; ongoing programs are seldom challenged. Line-item budgets are based on history: this year's allocation is based on last year's. Although that allows an inexperienced manager to prepare a budget more easily, it often precludes the reform-minded chief's careful deliberation and planning for the future.

The line-item budget provides ease of control because it clearly indicates the amount budgeted for each item, the amount expended as of a specific date, and the amount still available at that date (see, e.g., Table 8-3).

You Be the: Police Chief/Sheriff

Your city of 650,000 people and nearly 7,000 employees is in dire financial straits, with no end in sight unless bold actions are taken. The city council has held several public hearings to consider alternative courses of action to get out of the fiscal doldrums, but most such meetings result in very little agreement on how to resolve the problems.

Look at the following options that have been proposed and debated, and *determine the pros and cons and possible ramifications of each*, as well as the numbers of citizens who would be positively or negatively affected if implemented:

1. Whether to lease 150 traffic speed cameras in school zones, which could generate $29 million in the first year alone.
2. Whether to terminate 350 city employees—about 5 percent of the total—from the city's payroll for a savings of about $25 million; or, alternatively, lay off 100 employees and offer voluntary buyouts for 300 employees for a total cost of $14 million; or simply let them leave or retire on their own terms, which would save $15 million.
3. Whether to restore a 4.6 percent pay cut taken from city employees two years ago, which would cost about $20 million.
4. Whether to eliminate vacant, nonpublic-safety positions ($2.6 million savings), reduce the materials and supplies budgets for all city divisions ($3.3 million savings), and reduce some healthcare expenses ($3.4 million).
5. Whether to raise property tax rates for all citizens.
6. Whether, as suggested by one council member, to discontinue other non-state mandated responsibilities, such as eliminating the police department and turn over those duties to the county sheriff's office.[39]

The Performance Budget

The key characteristic of a performance budget is that it relates the volume of work to be done to the amount of money spent.[40] It is input–output oriented, and it increases the responsibility and accountability of the manager for output as opposed to input.[41] This format specifies an organization's activities, using a format similar to that of the line-item budget. It normally measures activities that are easily quantified, such as the number of traffic citations issued, crimes solved, property recovered, cases heard in the courtroom, and caseloads of probation officers. These activities are then compared with those of the unit that performs at the highest level. The ranking according to activity attempts to allocate funds fairly. Following is an example from a police department: The commander of the traffic accident investigation unit requests an additional three investigators (due to the

TABLE 8-4   **Example of a Police Performance Budget**

Category		Amount
Units/activities		
Administration (chief)	Subtotal	$
Strategic planning		$
Normative planning		$
Policies and procedures (formulation, etc.)		$
Patrol	Subtotal	$
Calls for service		$
Citizen contacts		$
Special details, etc.		$
Criminal investigation	Subtotal	$
Suspect apprehension		$
Recovery of stolen property		$
Transportation of fugitives, etc.		$
Traffic services	Subtotal	$
Accident investigation		$
Issuance of citations		$
Public safety speeches, etc.		$
Juvenile services	Subtotal	$
Locate runaways/missing juveniles		$
Arrest of offenders		$
Referrals and liaison, etc.		$
Research and development	Subtotal	$
Perform crime analysis		$
Prepare annual budget		$
Prepare annual reports, etc.		$

increase in major and fatal crashes over the past three years), which the chief approves. Later, the chief might compare the unit's output and costs to these measures before the three investigators were added to determine how this change affected productivity.[42] An example of a police performance budget is provided in Table 8-4.

Advantages of the performance budget include a consideration of outputs, the establishment of the costs of various police agency efforts, improved evaluation of programs and managers, an emphasis on efficiency, increased availability of information for decision making, and the enhancement of budget justification and explanation.[43] The performance budget works best for an assembly line or other organization where work is easily quantifiable, such as paving streets. Its disadvantages include its expense to develop, implement, and operate because of the extensive use of cost accounting techniques and the need for additional staff (Figure 8-1 illustrates the elements used to determine the cost of providing police services); the controversy surrounding attempts to determine appropriate workload and unit cost measures (in policing, although many functions are quantifiable, such reduction of duties to numbers often translates into quotas, which are anathema to many people); its emphasis on efficiency rather than effectiveness; and the failure to lend itself to long-range planning.[44]

Determining which functions in policing are more important (and should receive more financial support) is difficult; therefore, in terms of police agency budgets, the selection of meaningful work units is difficult and sometimes irrational. How can a police agency measure its successes? How can it count what does not happen?

The Program Budget

The best-known type of budget for monitoring the activities of an organization is the program budget, developed by the RAND Corporation for the U.S. Department of Defense. This format examines cost units as units of activity rather than as units and subunits within the organization. This budget becomes a planning tool; it demands justification for expenditures for new programs and for deleting old ones that have not met their objectives.

Police agencies probably have greater opportunities for creating new community-based programs than do the courts or corrections agencies. Some of these include crime prevention and investigation, drug abuse

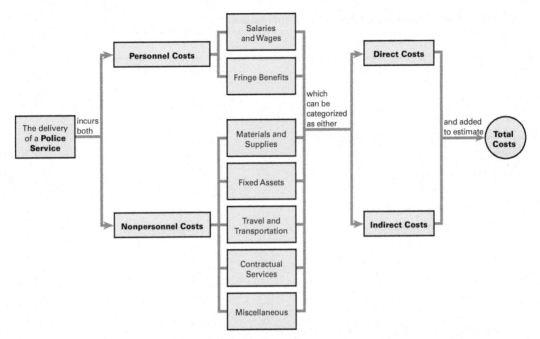

FIGURE 8-1 Elements in the Total Costs for Police Services
Source: U.S. Department of Justice, National Institute of Justice, Measuring the Costs of Police Services (Washington, DC: 1982), p. 20.

education, home security, selective enforcement (e.g., drunk driving) programs, and career development for personnel. Each of these endeavors requires instructional materials or special equipment, all of which must be budgeted. For example, traffic crash investigations (TCI) may be a cost area. The program budget emphasizes output measures. Outputs for TCI include the number of accidents handled and enforcement measures taken (such as citations issued, driving under the influence of alcohol and/or drugs (DUI) and other types of arrests made, and public safety speeches given). If the budget for these programs were divided by the units of output, the administrator could determine the relative cost for each unit of output or productivity. The cost of TCI, however, entails more than just the TCI unit; patrol and other support units also engage in this program.

Thus, the program budget is an extremely difficult form to execute and administer because it requires tracking the time of all personnel by activity as well as figuring in the cost of all support services and supplies. For this reason, police agencies rarely use the program budget.[45] Some advantages of the program budget, however, include its emphasis on the social utility of programs conducted by the agency; its clear relationship between policy objectives and expenditures; its ability to provide justification for and explanation of the budget; its establishment of a high degree of accountability; and its format and the wide involvement in formulating objectives, which lead employees at all levels of the organization to understand more thoroughly the importance of their roles and actions.[46]

An example of a police program budget is presented in Table 8-5.

PPBS and ZBB Formats

General Motors used the PPBS as early as in 1924,[47] and the RAND Corporation contributed to its development in a series of studies dating from 1949.[48] By the mid-1950s, several states were using it, and Secretary Robert McNamara introduced PPBS into the Defense Department in the mid-1960s.[49] By 1971, a survey revealed, however, that only 28 percent of the cities and 21 percent of the counties contacted had implemented PPBS or significant elements of it,[50] and in 1971 the federal government announced that it was discontinuing its use.

PPBS is a decision-making tool that links the program under consideration to the ways and means of facilitating the program. It is thus "a long-term planning tool, better informing decision makers of the future implications of their actions, and is typically most useful in capital projects."[51] PPBS treats the three basic budget processes—planning, management, and control—as coequals. It was predicated on the primacy of planning.[52] This future orientation transformed budgeting from an annual ritual into a "formulation of future goals and policies."[53] The PPBS budget featured a program structure, ZBB, the use of cost-budget analysis to distinguish among alternatives, and a budgetary horizon, often five years.[54]

TABLE 8-5 **Example of a Police Program Budget**

Program Area		Amount
Crime prevention	Subtotal	$
Salaries and benefits		$
Operating expenses		$
Capital outlay		$
Miscellaneous		$
Traffic crash investigation	Subtotal	$
Salaries and benefits		$
Operating expenses		$
Capital outlay		$
Miscellaneous		$
Traffic crash prevention	Subtotal	$
Salaries and benefits		$
Operating expenses		$
Capital outlay		$
Miscellaneous		$
Criminal investigation	Subtotal	$
Salaries and benefits		$
Operating expenses		$
Capital outlay		$
Miscellaneous		$
Juvenile delinquency prevention	Subtotal	$
Salaries and benefits		$
Operating expenses		$
Capital outlay		$
Miscellaneous		$
Special investigations	Subtotal	$
Salaries and benefits		$
Operating expenses		$
Capital outlay		$
Miscellaneous, Etc.		$

Associated with PPBS, the zero-based planning and budgeting process requires managers to justify their entire budget request in detail rather than simply to refer to budget amounts established in previous years.[55] That is, each year, all budgets begin at zero and must justify any funding. Following Peter Phyrr's use of ZBB at Texas Instruments, Governor Jimmy Carter adopted it in Georgia in the early 1970s and then as president implemented it in the federal government for fiscal year 1979. An analysis of this experience at the Department of Agriculture indicates that although its use saved $200,000 in the department's budget, it costs at least 180,000 labor hours of effort to develop.[56]

It is important to note that few organizations have budgets that are purely in one format or another; therefore, it is not unusual to find that because of time, tradition, and personal preferences, a combination of several formats is used.

Summary

This chapter focused on a very important area of police leadership: financial administration, primarily budgeting; included were its elements, cycles, and formats. Emphases were also placed on means by which police leaders may stretch their resources and enhance budgets. It is clear that leaders must develop skill and acumen regarding these matters, particularly in budget formulation and execution.

Discussion Questions

1. What are some of the kinds of factors of policing a workload analysis would consider?

2. How might a regional police agency survey be accomplished, and what is its purpose?
3. In what way can grants and use of civilians be used to stretch resources and enhance budgets?
4. What is strategic planning, and how does it relate to financial administration?
5. What is a budget? How is it used?
6. What is a budget cycle? What is its importance in budgeting?
7. What is involved in formulating a budget? In its approval and execution?
8. List four budget formats that have been used in the past. Which type is used most frequently? What are its component parts as well as advantages?

Internet Investigations

Budgeting in Small Police Agencies—Best Practices Guide
   http://www.theiacp.org/portals/0/pdfs/BP-Budgeting.pdf
FBI Budget Request for FY2017
   https://www.fbi.gov/news/testimony/fbi-budget
   -request-for-fiscal-year-2017

U.S. Department of Justice Strategic Plan, 2014–2018
   https://www.justice.gov/sites/default/files/jmd/legacy/
   2014/02/28/doj-fy-2014-2018-strategic-plan.pdf
PoliceGrantsHelp.com
   http://www.policegrantshelp.com/grants101/

Managing the Work of Police

CHAPTER 9

Ethics and Accountability: Building a Culture of Integrity and Trust

STUDENT LEARNING OUTCOMES

After reading this chapter, the student will:

- have a basic understanding of absolute and relative ethics, and their relationship to policing
- be able to explain what is meant by *noble cause corruption*
- know how police leaders might create a culture of integrity, by inculcating such concepts as constitutional policing, legitimacy, and procedural justice
- know the kinds of improper or illegal officer behaviors that supervisors and managers must address
- define and provide distinctions between acceptable and deviant lying by police
- know the definition of bias-based policing, why it can be so problematic in policing, and what police leadership can do to address it
- be able to define proximate cause and failure to protect
- know the meaning of gratuities, and reasons for and against their receipt by officers

KEY TERMS AND CONCEPTS

- Absolute ethics
- Accepted lying
- Bias-based policing
- Constitutional policing
- Deontological ethics
- Deviant lying
- Duty of care
- Dynamic Resistance Response Model (DRRM)
- Entrapment
- Ethics
- Excessive force

- Gratuities
- Knapp Commission
- Legitimacy
- Negligence
- Noble cause corruption
- Oath of Honor
- Procedural justice
- Relative ethics
- Slippery slope
- Use of force

INTRODUCTION

Few chapters in this textbook are as important or grave in their content as this one. This chapter concerns concepts that all police leaders must know: instilling a culture of ethical behavior and integrity and minimizing or eliminating serious police transgressions and other violations of public trust. These leaders, being responsible for the manner in which their subordinates wield their power and authority, are heavily implicated in these areas. The responsibility for ensuring that subordinates act correctly relative to their position in an acceptable and effective manner lies squarely at their door. Police officers must conduct themselves in a professional and ethical manner.

First, we frame the question of ethics by discussing ethics generally, including its philosophical underpinnings and types; then we move to the matter of ethical problems specific to police leadership and management, including the police codes of ethics and conduct. Next is an important aspect of ethics and accountability in today's police environment: creating a culture of integrity; here we include discussions of constitutional policing, legitimacy, and procedural justice. Following that is a review of inappropriate police behaviors as they relate to ethical conduct; included here are sections on lying and deception, gratuities and corruption, use of force, sexual relations, and bias-based policing. The chapter also includes a number of exhibits and case studies that present ethical issues dilemmas.

ETHICS, GENERALLY

Philosophical Foundations

The term *ethics* is rooted in the ancient Greek idea of character. **Ethics** involves doing what is right or correct and is generally used to refer to how people should behave in a professional capacity. Many people would argue, however, that there should be no difference between one's professional and personal lives. Ethical rules of conduct essentially should transcend everything a person does.

A central problem with understanding ethics is that there is always the question as to "whose ethics?" or "which right?" This becomes evident with controversies such as the death penalty, abortion, use of deadly force, or gun control. How individuals view a particular controversy largely depends on their values, character, or ethics. Both sides on controversies such as these believe they are morally right.

Another area for examination is **deontological ethics**, which does not consider consequences but instead examines one's duty to act. The word *deontology* comes from two Greek roots, *deos* meaning duty and *logos* meaning study. Thus, deontology means "the study of duty." When police officers observe a violation of law, they have a duty to act. Officers frequently use this as an excuse when they issue traffic citations that, on their face, have little utility and do not produce a beneficial result for society as a whole. When an officer writes a traffic citation for a prohibited left turn at two o'clock in the morning when no traffic is around, the officer is fulfilling a departmental duty to enforce the law. From a utilitarian standpoint (which judges an action by its consequences), however, little if any good was served. Here, duty trumped good consequences.

Immanuel Kant, an eighteenth-century philosopher, expanded the ethics of duty by including the idea of "good will." People's actions must be guided by good intent. In the previous example, the officer who wrote the traffic citation for an improper left turn would be acting unethically if the ticket was a response to a quota or to some irrelevant cause. On the other hand, if the citation was issued because the officer truly believed that it would result in some good, he or she would have been performing an ethical action. Some people have expanded this argument even further. Kania[1] argued that police officers should be allowed to freely accept gratuities because such actions would constitute the building blocks of positive social relationships between the police and the public. In this case, duty is used to justify what under normal circumstances would be considered to be unethical. Conversely, if the officers take the gratuity for self-gratification rather than to form positive community relationships, then the action would be considered unethical by many people.

Absolute and Relative Ethics

Ethics usually involves standards of fair and honest conduct, and what we call the conscience, the ability to recognize right from wrong, and actions that are good and proper. There are absolute ethics and relative ethics. **Absolute ethics** issues have only two sides; something is either good or bad, black or white. The original interest in police ethics focused on unethical behaviors such as bribery, extortion, excessive force, and perjury, which were always considered wrong. Other contemporary examples would be that police officers, it is universally agreed, should not be selling drugs or pocketing protection money.

Exhibit 9-1 is an actual case that came to light when one of the authors was performing a study of a Midwestern police department.

EXHIBIT 9-1 When Police Managers Themselves Become Corrupt: A Case Study

While performing a comprehensive study of a Midwestern police agency, to include interviews of many officers, a consultant learns that the night shift captain continually hounds his officers to make more DUI arrests. When they do so, officers must transport the arrestee 15 miles to the regional jail. Due to the need to perform the required tests and paperwork, the officer must thus leave his or her beat unprotected for 2–3 hours. Later, it is discovered that the night shift captain, knowing which beats are without an officer and using burglary tools, has been committing burglaries of retail businesses while officers are away and busy with their DUI arrests. He is arrested, convicted, and sentenced to prison.

Issues of **relative ethics** are more complicated and can have a multitude of sides with varying shades of gray. Here, the problem lies with the fact that allegations of corruption can mean different things to different people. If a community appears to accept relative ethics, especially in police dealings with, say, gang members or drug traffickers, it may send the wrong message to the police: that there are few boundaries placed on police behavior, and that, at times, "anything goes" in their fight against crime. As Kleinig[2] pointed out, giving false testimony to ensure that a public menace is "put away" or the illegal wiretapping of an organized crime figure's telephone might sometimes be viewed as "necessary" and "justified," though wrong.

When relative ethics are given life and practiced in overt fashion by the police, it is known as **noble cause corruption**—what Thomas Martinelli[3] defined as "corruption committed in the name of good ends, corruption that happens when police officers care too much about their work." This viewpoint is also known as the "principle of double effect." It holds that when an act is committed to achieve a good end (such as an illegal search) and an inevitable but intended effect is negative (the person who is searched eventually goes to prison), then the act might still be justified.

Officers might "bend the rules," such as not reading a drunk person his rights or performing a field sobriety test; planting evidence; issuing "sewer" tickets (i.e., writing a person a ticket but not giving it to him, resulting in a warrant issued for failure to appear in court); "testilying" (e.g., lying in court about the defendant's actions); or "using the magic pencil," where police officers write up an incident in a way that criminalizes a suspect. A powerful tool for punishment, noble cause corruption carries with it a different way of thinking about the police relationship with the law; officers operate on a standard that places personal morality above the law. They become legislators *of* the law, and act as if they *are* the law.[4]

Given the huge amounts of money with which today's officers might be bribed to protect buildings and residences where drug dealers live and work, police leaders must be ever vigilant to protect against corruption.
Source: njgphoto/Getty Images

YOU DECIDE: EVIDENCE—AND A POSSIBLE CAREER—LOST

Late one night, Officer Nichols is involved in a massive, drug bust of several residences, during which time she absentmindedly placed a bag of drugs on the hood of her car. Approximately an hour later when leaving another call, she remembered that she had forgotten to mark and secure the bag of drugs from the previous call. She immediately returned to the scene and discovered the bag of drugs had apparently slid off the car hood and landed in a bush on the side of the road. In her report, she does not mention this disregard of evidentiary procedures. Later, at the preliminary hearing at which time the defense counsel asks Nichols if she ever left this piece of evidence unattended (and thus breaking the chain of custody), she testifies that she did not (she is quite certain that no one saw her leave the bag unattended, and knows that if she admits to her inattention to the evidence, the guilty party will go free).

1. Assume that someone did in fact make a videotape of the bag being left unattended and posted it on YouTube. What, if any, actions may be taken against Nichols by the courts as a result of her testimony in trial? What impact may her having lied have on the case after the fact?

2. How should Nichols' department respond to this revelation and what potential discipline may be imposed? Could/should she later be charged with perjury?

CHALLENGES FOR POLICE LEADERS

Obviously the kinds of ends-justifies-means, noble cause behaviors that are mentioned above often involve arrogance on the part of the police and ignore the basic constitutional guidelines their occupation demands. Middle managers would be naïve to assume that their subordinates will always tell the truth and follow the law. For their part, when red flags surface, police leaders and managers must look deep for reasons behind this sudden turn of events, and make reasonable inquiries into the cause.[5] They must not fail to act, lest noble cause corruption be reinforced and entrenched; their inability to make the tough decisions that relate to subordinate misconduct can be catastrophic.

We further discuss the police executives' and managers' roles later in this chapter.

YOU DECIDE: GETTING THE JOB DONE? OR, A TOXIC ORGANIZATION

Gothamville is a Midwestern city with a high crime rate and poor relations between the police and the public. The new reform mayor and police chief campaigned on a platform of cleaning up crime in the streets and ineffectiveness of government. They launched a commission to investigate what was termed a "litany of problems" within the police department. The investigation found that officers routinely lied about the probable cause for their arrests and searches, falsified search warrant applications, and basically violated rules of collecting and preserving evidence. They were also known to protect each other under a "shroud of secrecy" and to commit perjury in front of grand juries and at trials. These problems were found to be systemic throughout the agency; however, greed and corruption were not the motivating factors behind officers giving perjured testimony. Officers believed that their false testimony and other such activities were the only means by which they could put persons they believed guilty behind bars. Worse yet, the study also found that prosecutors routinely tolerated or at least tacitly approved of such conduct. The study also found that many police officers did not consider giving false testimony to be a form of corruption, which they believed implies personal profit. Instead, they viewed testifying as just another way to "get the job done."

Questions for discussion:

1. Do you believe that the officers' means of lying about the basis for their arrests and searches justified the end result of making arrests?

2. What about the prosecutors' tolerance of the officers' unethical behavior? To what ethical standards should the prosecutor's office be held?

3. As a police manager, when these kinds of behaviors come to light, what punishment, if any, do you think is warranted for the persons involved?

4. What actions, if any, could a manager take to oversee officers' activities to prevent and detect such behaviors?

On my honor, I will never

betray my badge, my integrity,

my character or the public trust.

I will always have the courage to hold

myself and others accountable for our actions.

I will always uphold the constitution, my

community, and the agency I serve.

FIGURE 9-1   Law Enforcement Oath of Honor
Source: "Law Enforcement Oath of Honor," in The International Association of Chiefs of Police. Used with permission.

Codes of Ethics and Conduct

One of the primary purposes of ethics is to guide police decision making. Over the past decades, several types of codes of ethics and honor have been written to provide general guidelines for officer behavior.

As an example, the Law Enforcement Oath of Honor is shown in Figure 9-1. This oath concisely incorporates value statements and provides the underpinnings of police professionalism. Note also that state statutes and departmental policy govern police behavior.

When in doubt, police officers should consider the ethical consequences of their actions or potential actions to evaluate how they should act or proceed. It is impossible for a police department to formulate procedures that address every possible situation an officer may encounter. Therefore, other behavioral guidelines must be in place to assist officers when making operational decisions.

CREATING A CULTURE OF INTEGRITY

A Threshold Question: Are We "Guardians" or "Soldiers"?

The contemporary chasm between police and minorities, and many people in society at large, often revolves around how the police are now too often being seen as "soldiers" or "warriors." Certainly, the recent killings by police of young African-American men and others have caused many people to ask whether or not there exists within the police culture a "warrior mindset." Given that, it is time for police executives to consider the sort of image they project to the public and to minority communities in particular. The 21st Century Task Force stated:

> Law enforcement culture should embrace a guardian mindset to build public trust and legitimacy. Toward that end, police and sheriffs' departments should adopt procedural justice [discussed below] as the guiding principle for internal and external policies and practices to guide their interactions with the citizens they serve.[6]

There is a significant distinction between the two roles; former Shoreline, Washington, Police Chief Susan Rahr questioned this distinction:

> Why are we training police officers like soldiers? Although police officers wear uniforms and carry weapons, the similarity ends there. The missions and rules of engagement are completely different. The soldier's mission is that of a warrior: to conquer. The rules of engagement are decided before the battle. The police officer's mission is that of a guardian: to protect. The rules of engagement evolve as the incident unfolds. Soldiers must follow orders. Police officers must make independent decisions. Soldiers come into communities as an outside, occupying force. Guardians are members of the community, protecting from within.[7]

"In Boston, we don't train our recruits to be a military force. I want my officers to come out as problem-solvers, not an occupying force," thus stated Boston Police Commissioner William Evans. And, as Kansas City, Missouri, Chief Terry Zeigler put it, "For a long time, the police academy has been based on a military boot camp type of philosophy. That is missing the point. Policing is mostly about manners and courtesy."[8]

Taking on a warrior's mentality is only good with incidents like active shooter situations where officer survival is paramount. According to Camden County (New Jersey) Police Chief Scott Thomson, "It's a question of the 'crime-fighter' versus the 'community-builder' mentality. We need to have a cultural shift in policing to the latter to regain the trust and legitimacy that has been recently lost." Use of force is discussed more thoroughly below.

Related Concepts: Constitutional Policing and Legitimacy

As noted above, several race-related events from 2014 to present have led to a careful review of police practices and calls for reform. At the heart of this issue are questions of race relations, compelling many police leaders to look at their agency's culture in a new light. Protests and riots have centered on the experiences of minority communities with police and questions of disparate treatment, particularly with respect to the use of deadly force.

Police chief executives are now becoming much more heavily involved in what is termed constitutional policing—a cornerstone of community policing and problem-solving efforts. When a police agency develops policies and practices that advance the constitutional goals of protecting citizens' rights and provides equal protection under the law, then, as New Haven (Connecticut) Police Chief Dean Esserman put it, "The Constitution is our boss. We are not warriors, we are guardians. The [police] oath is to the Constitution."[9]

Constitutional policing, then, forms the foundation of policing, especially community policing. Police agencies cannot form positive and productive relationships with the citizens they serve if those communities do not trust the police or if the communities do not believe that the police see their mission as protecting civil rights as well as public safety. Too often, concerns with constitutional aspects of policing occur only after the fact—when police officials, community members, and the courts look at an officer's actions to determine whether or not laws, ordinances, or agency policies were violated. Now, there is a growing recognition among police leaders that constitutional policing should be on the minds of all agency members on an everyday basis.

A related concept is that of police **legitimacy**: the extent to which the community believes that police actions are appropriate, proper, and just, and its willingness to recognize police authority. If the police have a high level of perceived legitimacy, community members tend to be more willing to cooperate with the police and to accept the outcome of their interactions with the police. Public confidence involves the belief that the police are honest, are trying to do their jobs well, and are striving to protect the community against crime and violence. Moreover, legitimacy reflects the willingness of residents to defer to the law and to police authority, that is, their sense of obligation and responsibility to accept police authority. Finally, legitimacy involves the belief that police actions are morally justified and appropriate to the circumstances.[10]

Clearly, this relationship with the citizenry is what Sir Robert Peel had in mind when he made his oft-quoted statement that "The police are the public, and the public are the police."

Procedural Justice

Procedural justice and police legitimacy were discussed briefly in Chapter 1; here we elaborate on those discussions, as they both relate to the creation of a culture of integrity.

Adopting procedural justice as the guiding principle for policies and practices can be the underpinning of a change in culture, and should also contribute to building trust and confidence in the community. Succinctly put, procedural justice revolves around four central principles: (1) treating people with dignity and respect, (2) giving individuals "voice" during encounters, (3) being neutral and transparent in decision making, and (4) conveying trustworthy motives.[11]

Put another way, a federal publication espoused the four pillars of procedural justice, which help to think of the pillars as tools that, when used, build mutual respect and trust between officers and the community members they serve. They are as follows:

1. The first pillar is the *perception of fairness to all*. Note that this is not just about outcomes. In determining whether their treatment by police officers was fair, citizens will consider the process by which the officer's decision was made as much as the outcome of a decision. Often, the outcome of an interaction is less important than the interaction itself—whether respectful treatment was experienced by the parties involved. If, say, a person deems he or she was treated fairly and with respect in receiving a traffic ticket, he or she is much less likely to lodge a complaint against the officer. Officer demeanor plays a key role in the interaction.

2. The second pillar of procedural justice concerns *voice*. All people want to be heard and feel as though they have a measure of control over their fate; this helps them to feel that their opinions matter and that someone is listening to their side of the story and giving some consideration to their concerns.

3. The third pillar of procedural justice, *transparency and openness of process*, means that the processes by which decisions are made do not rely upon secrecy or deception. Here, key decisions are made out in the open as much as possible as opposed to behind closed doors. No one likes to feel that the outcome of a police interaction is being decided upon merely by another person's whim; when officers are as transparent as possible, community members are more likely to accept the outcome, even if unfavorable.

4. The fourth pillar of procedural justice, *impartiality and unbiased decision making*, means decisions are made based on relevant evidence or data rather than on personal opinion, speculation, or guesswork. Americans have a strong sense of fairness (certainly more so in our social media–connected world); people want the facts. When people take the extra few minutes to make apparent to others the data used to make decisions, understanding and acceptance are generally the outcome.[12]

It is therefore imperative that each organization develop, publicize, convey, and practice its values and mission statements, such as those shown in Exhibit 9-2 for the U.S. Department of Homeland Security (DHS). This exhibit, in effect, brings together constitutional policing, legitimacy, and procedural justice.

EXHIBIT 9-2   Mission and Values Statements, U.S. Department of Homeland Security

Recently the Secretary of the federal Department of Homeland Security, Jeh Johnson, set out to develop new mission and values statements for the Department that would encompass the views of the agency's 226,000 personnel. Nearly 3,000 DHS employees answered his call for ideas for the new statement, and they provided many thoughtful answers. The three words most often invoked in the employees' submissions were "honor," "integrity," and "safeguard." These words are therefore contained in the statement. The word "values" was included to reference, among other things, our missions to preserve and promote this Nation's immigrant heritage and humanitarian spirit, as well as the freedoms and civil liberties we must balance and preserve in the pursuit of our security mission. Johnson wanted to limit the statement to one sentence. Furthermore, in the development of this statement, Johnson consulted all three of his predecessors in DHS. Johnson added that "My hope is that our people will see it as the capstone of our Unity of Effort initiative, and our unifying mission statement for now and long after I am Secretary of Homeland Security." Following is the result of that effort—and it should be noted that, as is preferred by many law enforcement practitioners, the statement is concise yet meaningful:

> *With honor and integrity, we will safeguard the American people, our homeland, and our values.*

This new mission statement was added to the Department's existing core values, which are:

Integrity

"Service Before Self"—Each of us serves something far greater than ourselves. To our nation, we represent the President and the Congress. To the world, seeking to visit or do business with us, we are often the first Americans they meet. We will faithfully execute the duties and responsibilities entrusted to us, and we will maintain the highest ethical and professional standards.

Vigilance

"Guarding America"—We will relentlessly identify and deter threats that pose a danger to the safety of the American people. As a Department, we will be constantly on guard against threats, hazards, or dangers that threaten our values and our way of life.

Respect

"Honoring Our Partners"—We will value highly the relationships we build with our customers, partners, and stakeholders. We will honor concepts such as liberty and democracy, for which America stands[13].

YOU DECIDE: FAIR, PROCEDURAL POLICING—OR NOT?

For the following scenario, respond to the questions posed at the end in the context of the above discussions of procedural justice (while also, ideally, applying the above information concerning the "warrior vs. guardian" concept and constitutional policing).

A police officer gave a woman a ticket for making an illegal turn. When the woman protested that there was no sign prohibiting the turn, the officer pointed to one that was bent out of shape, leaning over and hardly visible from the road. Furious and feeling the officer hadn't listened to her, the woman decided to appeal the ticket by going to court. The day of her hearing arrived, and she could hardly wait to speak her piece. However, when she began to tell her side of the story the judge stopped her and summarily ruled in her favor, dismissing the case.

How did the woman feel? Vindicated? Victorious? Satisfied?[14] How would the officer feel? Was justice served in this case?

INAPPROPRIATE POLICE BEHAVIORS

Most of the efforts to control police behavior are rooted in statutes and departmental policies and procedures. These written directives stipulate inappropriate behavior and, in some cases, the behavior or actions that are expected in specific situations. However, not every situation can be accounted for and therefore officers are often required to make decisions in situations where there are no clear guidelines or that allow for discretionary decision making. In such instances, officers must also use their common sense and sense of fairness and ethics. Some observers have referred to illegal police behavior as a "**slippery slope**": officers tread on solid or legal grounds but at some point slip beyond the acceptable into illegal or unacceptable behavior. These slippery slopes serve as a point of analysis for the behaviors addressed in this section, which discusses areas in which officers can get into trouble: (1) lying and deception, (2) acceptance of gratuities and corruption, (3) improper use of force, (4) verbal and psychological abuse, (5) violations of civil rights, and (6) improper sexual relationships.

Officer Lying and Deception

Police officers lie or deceive for different purposes and under varying circumstances. In some cases, their misrepresentations are accepted and considered to be an integral part of a criminal investigation, while in other cases they are not accepted and are viewed as violations of law. Barker and Carter[15] examined police lying and perjury and developed a taxonomy that centered on accepted lying and deviant lying. **Accepted lying** includes police activities to apprehend or entrap suspects. This type of lying is generally considered to be trickery. **Deviant lying**, on the other hand, refers to occasions when officers commit perjury to convict suspects or are deceptive about some activity that is illegal or unacceptable to the department or public in general.

Accepted Lying. Deception has long been used by the police to ensnare violators and suspects. For many years, it was the principal method used by detectives (particularly undercover agents) and police officers to secure confessions and convictions.[16] It is allowed by the law, and to a great extent, it is accepted by the public.

The courts have long accepted deception as an investigative tool. In *Illinois v. Perkins*,[17] the U.S. Supreme Court ruled that police undercover agents who are posing as inmates are not required to administer the *Miranda* warning to incarcerated inmates when investigating crimes. The Court essentially separated trickery from coercion. Coercion is strictly prohibited, but trickery by police officers is unquestionably acceptable. Lying, although acceptable by the courts and the public in certain circumstances, does result in an ethical dilemma. It is a dirty means to accomplish a good end; the police use deception to gain the truth relative to some event.

Another problem with deception is **entrapment**. Entrapment occurs when the idea of a crime begins with the police rather than the suspect, and the police facilitate the commission of a criminal act. The courts examine the offender's predisposition to commit the crime. If no predisposition exists, then the police have engaged in entrapment. Should police undercover officers be allowed to give drugs to suspects so that the suspects can be apprehended for possession? Should suspects be encouraged by undercover police officers to burglarize a business so that the suspects can be arrested?

Deviant Lying. In their taxonomy of police lying, Barker and Carter[18] identified two types of deviant lying: lying that serves legitimate purposes and lying that conceals or promotes crimes or illegitimate ends.

Lying that serves legitimate goals occurs when officers lie to secure a conviction, obtain a search warrant, or conceal police omissions during an investigation. Lying becomes an effective, routine way to sidestep legal impediments. When left unabated by police supervisors, managers, and administrators, lying can become organizationally accepted as an effective means to nullify legal entanglements and other obstacles that stand in the way of convictions. Examples include officers misrepresenting the fact that they used the services of confidential informants to secure search warrants, concealing that an interrogator went too far and coerced a confession, or perjuring themselves to gain a conviction.

Lying to conceal or promote police criminality is, without a doubt, a very egregious form of police deception. Examples of this form of lying range from officers' lying to conceal their using excessive force when arresting a suspect to obscuring the commission of a criminal act. Barker and Carter[19] and Skolnick[20] reported that the practice is commonplace in some departments. They reasoned that the police culture approves and, in some cases, promotes it.

Deception and lying must be dealt with. First, supervisors must fully understand what is acceptable and what is not acceptable behavior; a line must be drawn. Second, this information must be communicated to officers on a regular basis. Third, supervisors must inquire into and actively supervise officers' cases. If supervisors inquire into and investigate the extent of deception and lying by individual officers, officers are less likely to engage in unacceptable deception. Finally, when problems are identified, supervisors must take immediate disciplinary action. If supervisors promote deception by failing to respond to it, they are only worsening the problem.

Accepting Gratuities

Gratuities are commonly accepted by police officers as a part of their job. Restaurants and convenience stores frequently give officers free or half-price food and drinks, while a number of other businesses routinely give officers discounts for services or merchandize. Many police officers and their superiors accept these gratuities as a part of the job, while other agency leaders "draw the short line," meaning they have policies prohibiting such gifts and discounts; this is the argument that "the only clean item of value is your paycheck."

There are two basic arguments *against* police acceptance of gratuities. First is the slippery slope argument, discussed earlier, which proposes that gratuities are the first step in police corruption. Once gratuities are received, police officers' ethics are subverted and officers are open to additional breaches of their integrity. Also, officers who accept minor gifts or gratuities are then obligated to provide the donors with some special service or accommodation. Second, some propose that receiving a gratuity is wrong since officers are receiving rewards for services that, as a result of their employment, they are obligated to provide.

Kania[21] attempted to categorically justify police officers' acceptance of gratuities. He argued that shopkeepers and restaurant owners often feel an indebtedness toward the police, and gratuities provide an avenue of repayment. He also maintained that the acceptance of gratuities does not necessarily lead to the solicitation of additional gratuities and gifts or corruption. Officers are able to differentiate what is appropriate and develop their own ethical standards and adhere to them.

Notwithstanding Kania's arguments, history and studies have taught police leaders that accepting of gratuities can lead to grave problems of corruption in law enforcement. Perhaps the most notorious and disgraceful example can be found in the 1972 **Knapp Commission** *Report on Police Corruption* in New York City.[22] The commission found that a large number of officers were not only accepting gratuities but that the active solicitation of gratuities and gifts was institutionalized within the department. If the gifts and gratuities were not forthcoming, the police often issued summonses or otherwise harassed the shopkeeper or business owner. The commission characterized a majority of the officers as "grass-eaters," who freely accepted gratuities and sometimes solicited minor payments and gifts; others were described as "meat-eaters," who spent a significant portion of the workday aggressively seeking out situations that could be exploited for financial gain. These officers were corrupt and were involved in thefts, drugs, gambling, prostitution, and other criminal activities.

Once a police agency decides on implementing a gratuities policy, it should ensure that all officers are familiar with the policy; and certainly all leaders must fully enforce it and aggressively investigate any evidence or indication that officers may be violating the department's policies.

Improper Use of Authority and Force

As noted earlier, citizens bestow a substantial amount of authority on police officers. A central problem in police supervision occurs when officers improperly use this authority. Improper use of authority can range from being disrespectful to the inappropriate use of deadly force. To this end, Carter[23] has attempted to provide a typology of abuse of authority by police officers. His categories include (1) physical abuse and excessive force, (2) verbal and psychological abuse, and (3) legal abuse and violations of civil rights.

YOU DECIDE:

Following is an actual situation that occurred in a small (30,000 population) university town in the Midwest. Assume that after occurring in essentially the same manner on several occasions, you, as shift commander, are informed of the situation.

Night shift officers in the city have virtually no place to go eat after midnight. Indeed, there is only one restaurant open in the city. Typically, as officers are about to leave the restaurant, at about 1 A.M., a slightly intoxicated local gentleman—well known in the area as he owns and operates a late-night club—comes in and offers to pay for their meals. This individual's business is also known in the area for operating illegal gambling devices on the premises as well as other criminal activities. When the officers decline his offer, he then loudly broadcasts to all patrons his intention to follow through and gives the wait staff the money to pay for their meal.

As the shift lieutenant, how would you address these situations? What is needed to prevent their occurring in the future? What are the potential negative consequences of allowing this to occur?

PHYSICAL ABUSE AND EXCESSIVE FORCE Physical abuse and **excessive force** can occur when the police use either deadly or non deadly force. The use of excessive physical force often results in substantial public scrutiny. Indeed, such instances of improper use of police authority and excessive force have received national attention. Perhaps, one of the best examples involved Rodney King in 1991, who was brutalized by several members of the Los Angeles Police Department. Local incidents may not receive national media coverage and result in widespread rioting like this one did, but they oftentimes have the same dramatic, chilling effects in a community.

Regardless of the type of force used, it must be used by police officers in a legally accepted manner. Police officers are allowed to use only that force necessary to effect an arrest. Thus, the amount of force that a police officer uses is dependent on the amount of resistance demonstrated by the person being arrested. This concept is taught to police officers in training academies. Figure 9-2 provides a good means of visualizing what is the proper use of force in a given situation.

A MODERN APPROACH TO DETERMINING THE PROPER USE OF FORCE How much force is reasonable for a police officer to use against a suspect? An enormous amount of thought was invested in responding to that question over the past 30 years, leading to the development of various force continuums. Drawn in the shape

Allegations of excessive force by police can quickly lead to community outrage, demonstrations, and even violence, while often putting a national spotlight on the allegations.
Source: Bilgin Sasmaz/Anadolu Agency/Getty Images

of a staircase, ladder, wheel, or in some other fashion, these traditional use of force continuums attempted to determine which type of force (usually ranging from mere presence to verbal commands, empty-hand control holds, personal weapons, less-lethal weapons, carotid restraint, and deadly force) an officer could use in response to a suspect's behavior.

Even when agency policies accompanied the continuum (as they always should), such continuums have always been confusing to most police officers. "How far and when do I 'climb the next rung' of the ladder" sort of confusion could and did exist. Such continuums also fail to properly represent the dynamic encounter between the officer and a resistant suspect and to take into account the wide array of tools that are available to officers today; it is too difficult for a department to dictate by a continuum in what situations, say, a baton or pepper spray or Taser or other less-lethal weapons should be used.

Instead, many agencies now have policies requiring their officers to be "objectively reasonable" in their use of force; an example of the language defining what is objectively reasonable is as follows:

> In determining the necessity for force and the appropriate level of force, officers shall evaluate each situation in light of the known circumstances, including, but not limited to, the seriousness of the crime, the level of threat or resistance presented by the subject, and the danger to the community.

A new approach to determining proper use of force has recently been developed by two special agents of the Federal Bureau of Investigation and asserts to "more accurately reflect the intent of the law and the changing expectations of society" and provides officers with "simple, clear, unambiguous, and consistent guidelines in the use of force."[24]

Known as the **Dynamic Resistance Response Model (DRRM)**, this approach combines a use of force continuum with an application of four broad categories of suspects. *Dynamic* indicates that the model is fluid, and *resistance* demonstrates that the suspect controls the interaction. In this view, a major failing of past continuums has been that the emphasis is on the officer and the amount of force used. DRRM instead emphasizes that the suspect's level of resistance determines the officer's response. The model also delineates suspects into one of four categories (see Figure 9-2).

As shown in Figure 9-2, if a passively resistant suspect fails to follow commands and perhaps attempts to move away from the officer or escape, appropriate responses include using a firm grip, control holds, and pressure points to gain compliance. An aggressively resistant suspect—one who is taking offensive action by

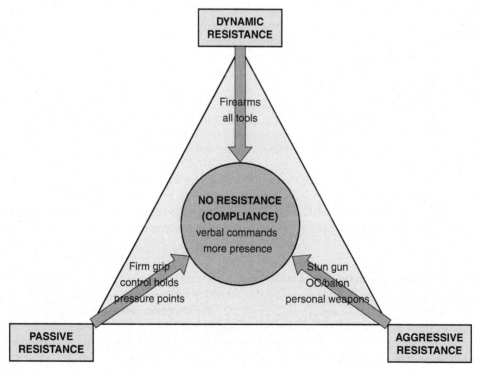

FIGURE 9.2 Dynamic Resistance Response Model
Source: FBI Law Enforcement Bulletin, Sept. 2007

attempting to push, throw, strike, tackle, or physically harm the officer—on the other hand, would call for such responses as the use of personal weapons (hands, fists, feet), batons, pepper spray, and a stun gun. Finally, because a deadly resistant suspect can seriously injure or kill the officer or another person, the officer is justified in using force, including deadly force, as is *objectively reasonable* to overcome the offender.

In the DRRM, a suspect's lack of resistance (compliance) is in the center of the triangle, which is emphasized as the goal of every encounter. If a suspect's resistance level places him on one of the three corners of the triangle, the officer's response is intended to move the suspect's behavior to the center of the triangle and compliance. The sole purpose of the application of force is to gain compliance.

DEADLY FORCE Deadly force is an extension of excessive physical force. Deadly force, however, is more problematic because of its outcome and the fact that it generally leads to considerable scrutiny by the public and authorities; and it can result in disorder and possibly rioting by citizens.

When a police officer deliberately kills someone, a determination is made as to whether or not the homicide was justified to prevent imminent death or serious bodily injury to the officer or another person. James Fyfe[25] opined that officers used the split-second syndrome to justify shootings, especially when bad shootings occur. The split-second syndrome essentially implies that officers must make deadly force decisions in a matter of a precious few seconds. Fyfe noted that the syndrome makes three assumptions. First, no two shootings are alike; therefore, it is virtually impossible to establish principles that can be used to diagnose potential shooting situations. Second, because of the stress and time limitations, it should be expected that police officers will make errors. The circumstances, stress, and time limitations should justify police actions, and any criticism of police officers is unwarranted, especially by non police personnel who do not understand police procedures or do not have an appreciation of the problems encountered by officers. Third, any evaluation of police decision making should be based on the perceived exigencies. If a citizen has or is perceived to have committed an act justifying deadly force, it is a key factor in justifying the shooting.

Fyfe further asserted that adherence to the split-second syndrome can lead to unnecessary violence. In many shooting instances, police officers have the time to analyze the situation and make reactive decisions. Police officers can avoid split-second decision situations by taking actions before the situation escalates. When there are fight calls or calls involving weapons, officers should deploy tactics or obtain assistance that reduces the need for deadly force.

Police supervisors have the primary responsibility for ensuring that officers respond to various calls correctly. Supervisors should counsel officers when they become lax and make sure they use proper procedures when approaching a suspect or answering a call. If officers follow procedures, the need to make split-second decisions about using deadly force will diminish.

Incidents that also involve minority group members will often heighten the tension and lead to charges of racism against the entire police agency; one columnist offered that "it is the police culture, more than race, that is at the crux of the problem … a mentality of brutality." In response to excessive use of force by police, one organization, Human Rights Watch, stated in a report:

> Police abuse remains one of the most serious and divisive human rights violations in the United States. The excessive use of force by police officers, including unjustified shootings, severe beatings, fatal chokings, and rough treatment, persists because overwhelming barriers to accountability make it possible for officers who commit human rights violations to escape due punishment and often to repeat their offenses.[26]

Human Rights Watch also noted in the report that officers who repeatedly commit human rights violations tend to be a small minority, but that they are protected, routinely, by the silence of their fellow officers and by flawed systems of reporting, oversight, and accountability; by the scarcity of meaningful information about trends in abuse; by lack of data regarding the police departments' response to those incidents; and by their plans or actions to prevent brutality.

VERBAL AND PSYCHOLOGICAL ABUSE Police officers sometimes abuse citizens by berating or belittling them. They antagonize citizens knowing that as police officers they are wrapped in the shroud of authority, and that citizens must take the abuse. One of the most common methods used by police officers to verbally abuse citizens is profanity. Unfortunately, profanity has become a part of the police culture and many officers' everyday speech. When profanity is used liberally in the work setting, it increases the likelihood that it will be used inappropriately.

Profane language tends to polarize a situation. A citizen will either passively submit or respond aggressively, in either case causing the citizen to distrust and dislike the police. When police officers use profanity, especially in an aggressive, personal manner, the focus shifts from the problem to the officer's language; and when it is used, profanity can easily create greater physical risks to the officer. Furthermore, even if the officer intended to resolve the situation, it may no longer be possible because of the harm caused by the language. And, because it can incite situations, profanity also increases the potential for liability (see Chapter 6) and citizens' complaints; therefore, it also heightens the possibility of the officer facing administrative action.

For all these reasons, the use of profanity by the police toward citizens is not justified, wise, or advised. Supervisors should discourage its use and review every instance in which an officer used profanity with a citizen.

LEGAL ABUSE AND VIOLATIONS OF CIVIL RIGHTS   Legal abuse and civil rights violations concern police actions that violate a citizen's constitutional or statutory rights. This abuse usually involves false arrest, false imprisonment, and harassment. For example, a police officer may knowingly make an unlawful search, charge the suspect with a crime, and then lie about the nature of the search. Another example occurs when police officers hassle a criminal to gain information or hassle a business owner to obtain some monetary gain.

Supervisors and managers play a key role in preventing legal abuse and violations of citizens' civil rights. Supervisors frequently back up officers when responding to calls and observe situations that lead to an arrest. They should ensure that officers' decisions to arrest are based on probable cause, not some lesser standard. They should also review arrest reports and question officers when arrests are not observed to ensure that the arrests meet the probable cause standard.

This is critical since research has long indicated that officers frequently base their decisions to arrest on factors such as a suspect's demeanor, [27] socioeconomic status,[28] race,[29] age,[30] relationship between the suspect and victim,[31] and the preference of the complainant.[32] When police officers allow such factors to substitute for probable cause, they are abusing their authority. Officers should provide the same level of services to all citizens, and they should use consistent decision-making criteria when making an arrest that excludes race, gender, or social standing.

Improper Sexual Relations

Although no accurate data exist, it seems that a significant number of officers engage in improper sexual relationships. While studying deviance in a southern city, Barker[33] found that the officers believed that about one-third of the department engaged in improper sexual relationships while on duty. This in itself is problematic, because officers who participate in this activity are not only showing poor judgment, they may also be compromising their ability to objectively enforce the law. Although many of the liaisons could be deemed romantic encounters, some of them may very well be associated with illicit activities.

Sapp[34] noted that because of their authority, police officers have a number of opportunities to sexually harass citizens. They have the authority to stop and talk with citizens, and in many cases, they can limit their freedom. They also perform work activities while unsupervised and in relative isolation. Although the majority of police officers may never sexually harass other citizens, a significant number do.

Because sexually related improprieties can and do occur, police supervisors and managers must be vigilant of such inappropriate behaviors, seven types of which have been identified:[35]

1. *Nonsexual Contacts that Are Sexually Motivated.* An officer will stop another citizen without legal justification to obtain information or get a closer look at the citizen.
2. *Voyeuristic Contacts.* Police officers attempt to observe partially clad or nude citizens. They observe apartment buildings or college dormitories. In other cases, they roust citizens parked on lovers' lanes.
3. *Contacts with Crime Victims.* Crime victims generally are emotionally distraught or upset and particularly vulnerable to sexual overtures from officers. In these instances, officers may make several return visits and calls with the intention of seducing the victim.
4. *Contacts with Offenders.* In these cases, officers may conduct body searches, frisks, and patdown searches. In some cases, officers may demand sexual favors. Offenders' complaints of sexual harassment will not be investigated by a department without corroborating evidence, which seldom exists.
5. *Contacts with Juvenile Offenders.* In some cases, officers have exhibited some of the same behaviors with juveniles that they have with adults, such as patdowns, frisks, and sexual favors. There have also been cases in which officers assigned as juvenile or school liaison officers have taken advantage of their assignment to seduce juveniles.
6. *Sexual Shakedowns.* Police officers demand sexual services from prostitutes, homosexuals, and others engaged in criminal activity as a form of protection.
7. *Citizen-Initiated Sexual Contacts.* Some citizens are attracted to police officers and attempt to seduce them. They may be attracted to the uniform, authority, or the prospect of a "safe" sexual encounter. In other cases, the citizen may be lonely or may want a "break" when caught violating the law.

Again, supervisors and managers must closely scrutinize subordinates' activities to prevent or reduce the incidence of sexual misconduct. If they fail to investigate or pursue allegations of sexual misconduct, in essence they are condoning it. This only leads to additional and possibly more outrageous conduct on the part of some of the officers. Supervisors may not be able to completely eliminate such behavior, but through thoughtful supervision, they can minimize it.

A "Hot Button" Issue: Bias-Based Policing

An ongoing issue in which police find themselves open to criticism and even disciplinary action involves bias-based policing. This issue has driven a deep wedge between the police and minorities, many of whom claim to be victims of this practice. Indeed, a New Jersey state police superintendent was fired by that state's governor for statements concerning racial profiling that were perceived as racially insensitive.

Many people remain convinced that the justice system unfairly draws minorities into its web, and that police methods are at the forefront of this practice. Bias-based policing—also known as racial profiling or "driving while black or brown" (DWBB)—occurs when a police officer acts on a personal bias and stops a vehicle simply because the driver is of a certain race.

Anecdotal evidence of bias-based policing has been accumulating for years, and now many people and groups (such as the American Civil Liberties Union) believe that all "pretext" traffic stops are wrong, because the chance that racism and racial profiling will creep into such stops is high.

For their part, many police executives defend such tactics as an effective way to focus their limited resources on likely lawbreakers; they argue that profiling is based not on *prejudice* but on *probabilities*—the statistical reality that young minority men are disproportionately likely to commit crimes. As explained by Bernard Parks, an African American and former police chief of Los Angeles:

> We have an issue of violent crime against jewelry salespeople. The predominant suspects are Colombians. We don't find Mexican-Americans, or blacks, or other immigrants. It's a collection of several hundred Colombians who commit this crime. If you see six in a car in front of the Jewelry Mart, and they're waiting and watching people with briefcases, should we play the percentages and follow them? It's common sense.[36]

Still, it is difficult for the police to combat the public's perception that traffic stops of minorities simply on the basis of race are widespread and prejudicial in nature.

The best defense for the police may be summarized in two words: *collect data*. Collecting traffic stop data helps chiefs and commanders determine whether officers are stopping or searching a disproportionate number of minorities and enables them to act on this information in a timely fashion. In 1999, Connecticut was the first state to require all its municipal police agencies and the state police to collect race data for every police-initiated traffic stop;[37] by mid-2001, at least 34 states either had enacted laws that included data collection or were considering data-collection legislation. It is anticipated that eventually all states will require the tracking of race data for all contacts. Technology is available to the police, including mobile data computers and wireless handheld devices, for this purpose.

The International Association of Chiefs of Police has issued a comprehensive policy statement on biased policing and data collection. The association "believes that any form of police action that is based solely on the race, gender, ethnicity, age, or socioeconomic level of an individual is both unethical and illegal," but that data-collection programs "must ensure that data is being collected and analyzed in an impartial and methodologically sound fashion."[38]

YOU DECIDE: REDNECK CAUSES ESCALATION TO BLACK AND BLUE

Officer Burns is known to have difficulty in relating to and dealing with persons of color and others who are socially different from himself. Burns admits to his sergeant that he grew up in a prejudiced home environment and that he has little sympathy or understanding for people "who cause all the damn trouble." The officer received sensitiv- ity and diversity training at the academy but took off days when annual refresher training was taught in-service; the department did not keep records of officers' atten- dance at such training sessions. The supervisor fails to understand the weight of the problem and has very little patience with Burns. So, believing it will correct the matter, the supervisor decides to assign Burns to a minority section of town so he will improve his ability to relate to diverse groups. Within a week, Burns responds to a disturbance at a housing project where residents are partying noisily and a fight is in progress. Burns immediately becomes upset, yelling at the residents to quiet down; they fail to respond, so Burns draws his baton and begins poking residents and ordering them to comply with his directions. The crowd immediately turns against Burns, who then has to call for backup assistance. After the other officers arrive, a fight ensues between residents and officers, and several officers and residents are injured and numerous arrests are made. The following day the neighborhood council meets with the mayor, demanding that Burns be fired and threatening a lawsuit.

Questions for Discussion

1. Is there any liability or negligence present in this situation? If so, what kind?
2. How could/should the agency's leaders have dealt with Burns' lack of sensitivity in a more constructive manner?

Summary

This chapter has examined police behavior from ethical, legal, and constitutional standpoints. We defined the philosophical underpinnings and types of ethics, some related challenges for police leaders, and how a nationally espoused code of conduct attempts to guide good behavior. Following was a broad approach to creating a culture of integrity, including, first and foremost, whether or not police officers are to serve as "guardians" or as "warriors," and the related concepts of constitutional policing and legitimacy, and affording procedural justice. Then we identified the kinds of specific activities that can be problematic for officers, supervisors, managers, and organizations (e.g., lying, accepting gratuities, improper use of authority and force, and biased policing). We also considered how supervisors might be found liable for the inappropriate acts and deeds of their subordinates.

Ethics forms the foundation for police officer behavior. Leaders must ensure that officers understand ethics and the role ethics plays in their profession, and that their boundaries are not violated.

Discussion Questions

1. Define ethics and provide examples of what is meant by relative as well as absolute ethics (including noble cause corruption).
2. Describe some of the challenges of police leaders in guiding ethical behavior and preventing and addressing related problems.
3. Review how an agency might go about creating a "culture of integrity," including constitutional policing, legitimacy, and acting in accordance with dictates of procedural justice.
4. Define and provide distinctions between acceptable and deviant lying by police.
5. Explain what constitutes improper use of force by the police.
6. Describe police use of force as set forth in the Dynamic Resistance Response Model (DRRM), including its application to four broad categories of suspects.
7. Define gratuities and give common reasons for and against their receipt by officers.
8. Provide a thorough explanation of bias-based policing.

Internet Investigations

FBI Law Enforcement Bulletin, "Police Corruption: An Analytical Look into Police Ethics"
   https://leb.fbi.gov/2011/may/police-corruption-an-analytical-look-into-police-ethics
International Association of Chiefs of Police, "Ethics Toolkit"
   http://www.iacp.org/ethics

Institute for Criminal Justice Education, "Reducing Law Enforcement Liability: Reviewing the High Risk Critical Areas"
   http://www.icje.org/articles/ReducingLaw EnforcementLiability.pdf
Office of Community Oriented Policing Services, "Ethics and Integrity"
   https://cops.usdoj.gov/Default.asp?Item=2469

CHAPTER 10

Community Policing and Problem Solving: Addressing Crime and Disorder

STUDENT LEARNING OUTCOMES

After reading this chapter, the student will:

■ be able to describe some problems and clear confusion regarding the use of jargon and some definitions used in policing

■ know the extent to which community policing and problem solving has spread across the nation, and the importance of training and education for the concept

■ be able to explain how organizational culture, field operations, and external relations influence the problem-oriented policing approach

■ know the key roles of all ranks of sworn personnel in operationalizing and maintaining community policing and problem solving

■ have knowledge of several related concepts, including CompStat, smart policing, intelligence-led policing, and predictive policing

■ understand why evaluation of problem solving efforts is of critical importance

■ know why police leaders must keep their focus on community policing and problem solving when addressing homeland security, cybercrime, and in the application of science

KEY TERMS AND CONCEPTS

- Assessment
- Chief executive
- Community (problem-oriented) policing
- CompStat
- External relations
- Field operations
- First-line supervisor
- Impact evaluation

- Intelligence-led policing
- Middle manager
- Organizational culture
- Predictive policing
- Problem-solving
- Smart policing
- Surveys

INTRODUCTION

This chapter, like many before it in this book, makes obvious that a completely different skill set is required of today's police leaders than in the past. First, the former kinds of indicators of police productivity that mattered and were counted —calls for service handled, arrests made, response times, even miles driven per shift—have far less if any importance in today's policing milieu. Even if 9/11 had not happened (which placed another complete set of challenges in front of police leaders), they must brave constricting budgets; recruiting, hiring, and retaining quality personnel; and coping with a national view that police at times use inappropriate (and lethal) force, among other problems.

In the face of all these challenges, the public now expects police officers to be much less reactive and highly proactive in accomplishing long-term problem solving with regard to crime and disorder in their neighborhoods. In doing so, police leaders must also learn methods of gathering and analyzing data, and putting it to use in deploying resources to the best possible purpose. Added to that is the understanding that "Oh, and by the way, and you will also master smart, CompStat, intelligence-led, and predictive policing." And, for good measure, we will throw in such crime prevention strategies as situational policing, problem-oriented policing, crime prevention through environmental design (CPTED), rational choice and routine activity theories, and general knowledge of crime places.

Does all of this demand too much of today's police leaders? It might seem that the bar is set too high for any mortal being. No doubt many aspiring or actual leaders believe that is the case. At minimum, then, this set of methods and cognitive demands points out, perhaps more than ever, the value of training, mentoring, formal education (e.g., police institutes, postsecondary education), and the benefit of experience—if there is any hope that the person "wearing the gold badge" will have any chance of success.

We assume that, because it has been in existence and practice since the late 1980s and now has a vast body of related literature, the reader possesses a fundamental knowledge of the **community policing and problem-solving** strategy—to include the SARA problem-solving process and such related concepts as those mentioned above. We simply cannot cover all of that in this chapter in great detail, nor do we believe it is necessary to do so. Rather, we take a more advanced approach that focuses on roles and responsibilities of leaders and managers.

First, we briefly discuss what we see as erroneous terms, jargon, and definitions now in use in the policing field, and then briefly review the extent that community policing and problem solving is now in use in the nation; we also touch on a critical, *sine qua non* appendage to that strategy—recruit training and formal education. Next is a discussion of the key roles of police chief executives, middle managers, first-line supervisors, and patrol officers in this practice, and then we touch on several related strategies: **CompStat**, **smart policing**, **intelligence-led policing** (ILP), and **predictive policing**. After looking at the problem with measuring the results of police initiatives and responses, we then consider the role of community policing and problem solving in homeland security, cybercrime, and science. Several case studies ("Focus On" and "You Decide" boxes) are included to encourage the reader to become engaged in problem-solving efforts.

FIRST THINGS FIRST: BE JUDICIOUS WITH THE JARGON

As French philosopher Voltaire wrote, "If you wish to converse with me, define your terms." That is an excellent vantage point from which to begin our discussion.

Today, some police leaders express the view that the current era of policing is ÍLP or predictive policing. Still others say we are in an information era, or that "we're not doing community policing now, we're doing CompStat" (discussed below). We believe that the general use—and at times misuse— of words such as "era" and police use of language and clichés is problematic and creates more harm and confusion than it prevents.

Policing is indeed in an information "age" but not in an information "era." The three primary eras of policing (political, reform, and community) have not changed; therefore, the time has come to seriously question this use of clichés and tendency to label things anew.

This is not a minor issue for the field. Indeed, one of the long-standing, major criticisms of policing has been its tendency to quickly and, to some, blithely put new labels on different strategies and tactics (which have sometimes been caustically termed as policing's "flavor of the month") and to use labels that are not altogether accurate. As an example of this drift into "era-speak," a member of the command staff, Los Angeles Police Department, once described predictive policing as follows:

> The LAPD has assumed a leadership role in translating these successes into the next era of policing: predictive policing. By developing, refining, and successfully executing on the predictive-policing model, the LAPD is leveraging the promise of advanced analytics in the prevention of and response to crime.[1]

With what we believe is a high degree of irony, a mere two months before the aforementioned comments were published, an assistant U.S. Attorney General stated at a predictive-policing conference:

I think our first order of business is to define what we mean by "predictive policing." We've become so accustomed to labels in law enforcement. Is predictive policing just another label for another policing model? Or is it a larger concept—something that incorporates many policing paradigms?[2]

It is time for police leaders to be much more wary in terms of describing its role and functions.

In sum, we believe that problem solving, ILP, smart policing, and predictive policing are not separate and distinct management tools and strategies. Rather, they are all management tools for *analyzing crime* (under the SARA problem-solving process, discussed below) and will advance the evolution of problem-oriented policing to better address twenty-first-century challenges of crime and disorder.[3] As stated by one police chief, "When I came to my department, I tried to stay away from buzz words. I put it simply—the focus is on good police work."[4] And as an academic described it, "By 2022 chiefs may be able to answer accurately the all-important question, 'What business are you in?'"[5]

EXTENT AND PREPARATION

All Across the Land...

The community policing and problem-solving strategy has been spreading. According to a survey by the federal Bureau of Justice Statistics (BJS),[6] police agencies with a community policing component now employ about 88 percent of all local police officers. Tables 10-1 and 10-2 demonstrate the entrenched nature of community policing and problem solving in local police agencies. The former shows the percentage (by size of population served) of agencies having a mission statement with a community policing component as well as those having problem-solving partnerships or agreement with other local organizations (e.g., mental health, homeless, school). The latter shows the extent of agency community-policing policies regarding geographic assignments of officers, officers who are actively encouraged to be engaged in problem-solving projects, and whether or not officers' problem-solving efforts are included as part of their annual performance evaluation.

A close examination of survey data reveals that

- about 7 in 10 local police departments (including about 9 in 10 departments serving a population of 25,000 or more) have a mission statement that includes a community policing component;
- a majority of agencies serving 50,000 or more residents actively encourage patrol officer involvement in problem-solving projects;
- most departments serving 25,000 or more residents, including more than 90 percent of those serving a population of 100,000 or more, used geographic beat assignments for patrol officers;
- most departments serving 100,000 or more residents included such projects in the performance evaluation of officers;
- about half of all local police officers are employed by a department that actively encourages officers' involvement in problem-solving projects.[7]

Indeed, during the past decade, the BJS survey found significant increases in the percentage of departments with a community policing component in all population categories.

TABLE 10-1   Community-oriented policies (mission statement and projects)

Population served	Mission statement with community policing component	Problem-solving partnership or agreement with local organization
All sizes	68%	32%
1,000,000 or more	86	86
500,000–999,999	97	59
250,000–499,999	91	67
100,000–249,999	87	61
50,000–99,999	91	59
25,000–49,999	87	52
10,000–24,999	81	41
2,500–9,999	74	29
2,499 or fewer	50	21

Source: Local Police Departments, 2013: Personnel, Policies, and Practices by Brian A. Reaves Table 8, p. 8, BJS, Local Police Departments, May 2015, https://www.bjs.gov/content/pub/pdf/lpd13ppp.pdf

TABLE 10-2   Community-oriented policies (geographical assignments, etc.)

Population served	Geographic assignments for patrol officers	Patrol officer involvement in problem-solving projects	
		Actively encouraged	Included in performance evaluation
All sizes	44%	33%	30%
1,000,000 or more	100	57	36
500,000–999,999	90	71	54
250,000–499,999	93	73	64
100,000–249,999	93	74	57
50,000–99,999	83	62	49
25,000–49,999	64	49	42
10,000–24,999	49	43	38
2,500–9,999	32	32	30
2,499 or fewer	40	21	21

Source: Local Police Departments, 2013: Personnel, Policies, and Practices by Brian A. Reaves Table 9, p. 9, of BJS, Local Police Departments, May 2015, https://www.bjs.gov/content/pub/pdf/lpd13ppp.pdf.

To help the reader to first get into a problem-oriented policing mindset, the "You Decide" box presents a problem for consideration.

Sine Qua Non: Academy Preparation

The expanding application of community policing and problem solving also makes clear that, in addition to police leaders possessing a thorough understanding of this strategy, they must also ensure that the essential of this practice is conveyed to their officers (see the Seattle, Washington, example in the "Focus On" box). Today, training for this strategy must first take into account the milieu in which the police function.

As noted in Chapter 9, there is now a push for the police to become more like "guardians," as opposed to "soldiers." Certainly, what police are taught, and how, must be reflective of that emphasis.

Obviously, the preparation for and proliferation of the problem-solving strategy begins in the recruit academies; indeed, nearly all (97 percent) academies (which train 98 percent of recruits) provide training in this practice, with an average of more than 40 hours of instruction per recruit. A majority of those departments serving 10,000 or more residents are training all new recruits for eight hours or more in community policing skills

YOU DECIDE: PROBLEMS IN THE PARK

Paxton Park holds tremendous significance for the predominately older African American and Hispanic residents of the city's Hillsborough District. Built during the late 1960s, since then the park has increasingly deteriorated and become a haven for drug dealers and gang members. Today, few residents dare use the park. Nearby residents frequently report all manner of suspicious activities there, including persons who are under the influence harassing children and homes abutting the park used as crash pads for drug users. In most instances, the police response is to send a police unit by the park to disperse the drug dealers. Few arrests are ever made. On infrequent occasions the countywide consolidated narcotics unit and the department's special weapons and tactics unit launch an enforcement program; while this approach usually involves a large number of arrests, it also generates complaints of

excessive force and racism by offenders and residents alike. The department has also initiated a narcotics tip line for residents, but few calls have been made since it was installed six months ago. You, a shift lieutenant, assign Sgt. Marie Brewer to a district that includes the park. Brewer has recently attended a problem-oriented policing seminar and believes that the drug and other problems at the park could be handled in a different manner than in the past. You then call a shift meeting to discuss how they might approach the problem.

Questions for Discussion

1. What responses might be considered by the shift (be sure to include all organizations that could help)?

2. How would you have Sgt. Brewer evaluate their successes?

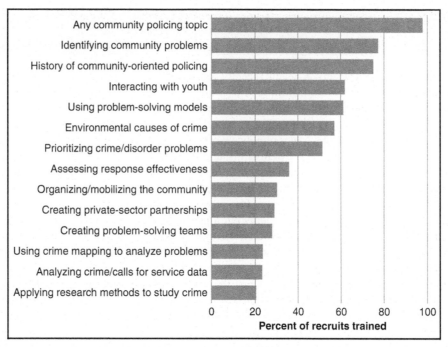

TABLE 10-3   Community policing topics in basic training programs in state and local law enforcement training academies

Source: State and Local Law Enforcement State and Local Law Enforcement Training Academies 2013 by Brian A. Reaves Fig. 7, p. 7, Bureau of Justice Statistics July 2016, p. 7, https://www.bjs.gov/content/pub/pdf/slleta13.pdf.

such as problem solving and developing community partnerships. Training topics in academies include how to identify community problems (77 percent), the history of community policing (75 percent), interacting with youth (62 percent), using problem-solving models (61 percent), environmental causes of crime (57 percent), and prioritizing crime and disorder problems (51 percent).[8] Table 10-3 shows the complete listing of related topics now offered in recruit academies.

Interacting with youth is an important component of police academy training in the problem solving strategy.

Source: Courtesy of Federal Bureau of Investigation, USA

FOCUS ON: TRAINING FOR COMMUNITY POLICING AND PROBLEM SOLVING: THE SEATTLE APPROACH

A police training academy in Seattle recently broke with many years of tradition, shifting away from a military model and instead having a goal of training "guardians" of communities. The class of 29 recruits was still taught the basics of police work—interviewing, report writing, use of firearms, and so on—but the instructions also included an increased emphasis on expressing empathy, adhering to constitutional requirements, and treating citizens with respect and dignity. The entire academy put a premium on verbal skills and de-escalation techniques, as well as using communication and behavioral psychology as a tool to gain control and compliance; the underlying assumption was that the best control tactic is to get voluntary compliance.[9]

Sue Rahr, a former county sheriff who administers the state training commission that oversees the academy, wanted the training to be grounded in the Constitution and developed the overall theme of the guardian model.[10] Rahr found support in Plato's book The Republic, where he describes guardians of the state who are gentle with citizens but fierce with enemies, excel at judging what is true and best, and responsible for the management of society. Plato proposed the establishment of an additional class of citizens, the guardians who were philosophical and responsible for management of the society itself. Such special people would be specially tested and trained for determining whether they were qualified to do so.[11] This training and training sessions included recruits spending time candidly sharing their personal stories, or oral biographies, while embracing the guardian concept. The class chose "Guardians of the Gate" and "We the People" as its mottos—even having T-shirts made with those inscriptions.[12]

OTHER CONSIDERATIONS FOR IMPLEMENTATION AND PRESERVATION

In addition to training, the organizational culture, field operations, and external relations are also important for the successful implementation of community policing and problem solving. We briefly examine those three elements next.[13]

1. **Organizational Culture:** Human resources will always be the "heart and soul" of organizational culture. For employees, it answers the question, "What's in it for me?" Any major change in an organization requires that a review of all human resources is conducted. Community engagement and problem solving require new skills, knowledge, and abilities for everyone in the organization. Therefore, areas such as recruiting, selection, training, performance evaluations, promotions, and honors and awards should be reviewed to ensure they promote and support the organization's transition to community policing and problem solving. Agencies must also work closely with the various labor organizations, which will be concerned with any proposed changes in shifts, beats, criteria for selection, promotion, and discipline. It is wise to include labor representatives in the planning and implementation process from the beginning.

2. **Field Operations:** The primary concern with field operations is to structure the delivery of patrol services to assist officers in dealing with the root causes of persistent community problems. The first issue raised here is whether a specialist versus generalist approach will be used. It has not been uncommon for agencies to begin implementation with an experimental district composed of a team of specially trained officers. The experience of many agencies, however, suggests that department-wide implementation should occur as quickly as possible. This will eliminate the common criticism that problem-solving officers do not do "real police work" and receive special privileges. If allowed to fester, this attitude can quickly impair any implementation efforts. A decentralized approach to field operations involves assigning officers for a minimum of one year to a beat and shift to learn more about a neighborhood's problems.[14]

3. **External Relations:** Collaborative responses to neighborhood crime and disorder are essential to the success of this strategy, requiring new relationships and the sharing of information and resources among the police and citizens, local governmental agencies, service providers, and businesses. Police must educate and inform their external partners about police resources and neighborhood problems using surveys, newsletters, community meetings, and public service announcements. Press releases about collaborative problem-solving efforts should be sent to the media and news conferences held to discuss major crime reduction efforts. Citizen police academies—which allow citizens an opportunity to examine the work and culture of policing—are also an excellent way to bridge with the community.

A citizens academy participant learns the tools and techniques of recovering latent print evidence.
Source: Courtesy of Federal Bureau of Investigation, USA

Citizen **surveys** can also be used to provide information to patrol officers, evaluate program effectiveness, and prioritize crime and disorder problems. The mood of the public should be a vital consideration when the police make public policy decisions. Done scientifically, however, surveys are very labor-intensive and expensive. Therefore, consideration should be given to using volunteers (such as college and university students) for the phone contacts and perhaps a university research center for data analysis. Persons who are about to conduct community surveys will find a very valuable resource in a joint publication by the federal Bureau of Justice Statistics and the Office of Community Oriented Policing Services: *Conducting Community Surveys: A Practical Guide for Law Enforcement* Agencies, at: https://www.bjs.gov/content/pub/pdf/ccspglea.pdf; it explains the use of surveys by police agencies and includes survey development, administration, and interpretation of results.

ROLES OF PERSONNEL OF ALL RANKS

In addition to training, implementing, and putting the problem-solving approach into practice and sustaining this strategy, obviously, such a transition brings new roles and challenges for police practitioners of all ranks. Next, we discuss some of those key roles.

First, Beware the "Toxic" Leader

A dynamic that might occur in any of the following rank levels is that of toxic leadership, which can spell the demise of any agency's community policing efforts, where the key to success lies in the relationship between the patrol officers and the neighborhoods they serve. As Karl Bickel put it, "Toxic leaders that poison the workplace environment demoralize personnel, create disincentives, produce unnecessary stress, stifle creativity, decrease risk taking, and promote themselves on the backs of the rank and file, while they present an obstacle to organizational transformation and the institutionalization of community policing."[15]

Such leaders (i.e., middle managers and first-line supervisors) may be arrogant and possess a perfectionist attitude, lack in self-confidence, be shallow and condescending toward subordinates, engage in bullying, and cause rifts among staff members; such attitudes in a community policing organization may well kill all efforts to establish and maintain problem solving and its many related facets (e.g., training, evaluation, reward system, community meetings) that accompany that effort. Such leaders can also severely impair employee morale and job satisfaction on the part of enthusiastic officers who enjoy the challenges of problem solving and the long-term benefits it affords. This, in turn, can ultimately lead to a more toxic organizational culture, described above. Therefore, if an agency displays symptoms of toxic leadership—low morale, disgruntled employees, high rates of sick leave use and turnover, citizen complaints, and so on—the problem must be dealt with sooner than later (in order to avoid the "rotten apple spoiling the barrel" dynamic). Demotions, transfers, even terminations (where legitimately documented and provided in applicable personnel regulations) may be in order.[16]

Chief Executives

Of course, the police **chief executive** is ultimately responsible for all of the facets of this philosophy and practice, from implementation to training to evaluation. Given that, what is needed is chief executives who are willing to do things that have not been done before, or as one writer put it, "risk takers and boat rockers within a culture where daily exposure to life-or-death situations makes officers natural conservators of the status quo."[17] These are chief executives who become committed to getting the police and neighborhoods to work together to attack the roots of crime. For them, "Standing still is not only insufficient … it is going backwards."[18]

Therefore, a police executive must be a viable change agent. In any hierarchy the person at the top is responsible for setting both the policy and tone of the organization. Within a police agency, the chief or sheriff has the ultimate power to make change, particularly one as substantive as community policing. The chief executive must be both visible and credible and must create a climate conducive to change. Under this philosophy, chief executives must focus on the vision, values, mission, and long-term goals of policing in order to create an organizational environment that enables officers, government officials, and community members to work together. By building consensus, they can establish programs, develop timelines, and set priorities. They should honor the good work done in the past but exhibit a sense of urgency about implementing change while involving people from the community and the department in all stages of the transition. The chief executive's roles and responsibilities include the following:

- Articulating a clear vision to the organization
- Understanding and accepting the depth of change and time required to implement the methods and practices
- Assembling a management team that is committed to translating the new vision into action
- Being committed to removing bureaucratic obstacles whenever possible

Many police organizations boast talented and creative chief executives who, when participating in the change process, will assist in effecting change that is beneficial and lasting. James Q. Wilson put it this way:

> The police profession today is the intellectual leadership of the criminal justice profession in the United States. The police are in the lead. They're showing the world how things might better be done.[19]

Middle Managers

Middle managers also play a crucial role in this philosophy. The emphasis on problem solving necessitates that middle managers draw on their familiarity with the bureaucracy to secure, maintain, and use authority to empower subordinates, helping officers to actively and creatively confront and resolve issues, sometimes using unconventional approaches on a trial-and-error basis.

There are many significant contributions middle managers can make to the changing culture of the agency to embrace and sustain it. First, they must build on the strengths of their subordinates, capitalizing on their training and competence.[20] They do so by treating people as individuals and creating talented teams. They must "cheerlead," encouraging supervisors and patrol officers to actually solve the problems they are confronting.[21] It is also imperative that middle managers *not* believe they are serving the chief executive's best interests by preserving the status quo. The middle managers are the gatekeepers and must develop the system, resources, and support mechanisms to ensure that the officers, detectives, and supervisors can perform to achieve the best results. Their supervisors and officers cannot perform without the necessary equipment, resources, and reinforcement.[22]

Middle managers, like their subordinates, must also be allowed the freedom to make mistakes—and good middle managers protect their subordinates from organizational and political recrimination and scapegoating when things go wrong. Put another way, middle managers cannot stand idly by while their people are led to the guillotine, and they must protect their officers from the political effects of legitimate failure.[23] They must not allow their problem-solving officers to revert to traditional methods. They must be diplomats and facilitators, using a lot more persuading and negotiating (toward win-win solutions) than they did under the traditional "my way or the highway" management style.[24]

The roles and responsibilities of middle managers during the changeover include the following:

- Assuming responsibility for strategic planning
- Eliminating red tape and bottlenecks that impede the work of officers and supervisors
- Conducting regular meetings with subordinates to discuss plans, activities, and results

The position of middle managers in a community policing environment was well described by Kelling and Bratton:

> The idea that mid-managers are spoilers, that they thwart project or strategic innovation, has some basis in fact. Mid-managers improperly directed can significantly impede innovation. Yet, ample evidence exists that when a clear vision of the business of the organization is put forward, when mid-managers are included in planning, when their legitimate self-interests are acknowledged, and when they are properly trained, mid-managers can be the leading edge of innovation and creativity.[25]

First-Line Supervisors

Perhaps the most challenging element of police leaders who must lead the change in agency culture lies in bringing into the fold (and sustaining) the attitudes and practices of **first-line supervisors**. The primary contact for street officers with their organization is through their sergeant, so the quality of an officer's daily life is often dependent on his or her immediate supervisor.

There is perhaps inherent reluctance on the part of first-line supervisors to avoid change. Herman Goldstein put it this way:

> Changing the operating philosophy of rank-and-file officers is easier than altering a first-line supervisor's perspective of his or her job, because the work of a sergeant is greatly simplified by the traditional form of policing. The more routinized the work, the easier it is for the sergeant to check. The more emphasis placed on rank and the symbols of position, the easier it is for the sergeant to rely on authority—rather than intellect and personal skills—to carry out [his or her] duties…. [S]ergeants are usually appalled by descriptions of the freedom and independence suggested in problem oriented policing for rank-and-file officers. The concept can be very threatening to them. This … can create an enormous block to implementation.[26]

Obviously, it is absolutely essential that supervisors are convinced that this approach makes good sense in today's environment.

The Patrol Officer

The shift to community policing and problem solving centers on those singular individuals who comprise the "backbone" of policing: the patrol officers. The most powerful resources an organization possesses are thinking, creative, and innovative police officers who, when supported by information, the community, training (in problem identification, analysis, and response), and internal support systems that reward and motivate them, are capable of providing long-term solutions to problems.

A major departure of this strategy from the conventional style of policing lies with the view that the line officer is given much more discretion and decision-making ability and is trusted with a much broader array of responsibilities. As indicated above, however, the shift to a problem-oriented policing perspective centers on the supervisors, who should encourage officers to take the initiative in identifying and responding to beat problems. Their officers are more challenged and have opportunities to follow through on individual cases and analyze and solve problems, which will give them greater job satisfaction. Using patrol officers in this manner also allows the agency to provide sufficient challenges not only for the better-educated officers but also for those officers who remain street-level functionaries throughout their careers.

One of the debates often heard with respect to this strategy is whether officers have enough time to engage in problem-solving activities. Officers have been known to complain that "We're too busy for community policing and problem solving," that they are going from call to call and have little time for looking at neighborhood problems and disorder. To such statements, we would argue that police leaders don't have time *not* to change to a problem-oriented policing strategy. William Geller and Guy Swanger put it thusly: "The classic problem here is being too busy bailing out the boat to fix the hole in the hull."[27] And as Price Pritchett and Ron Pound observed, police leaders should focus on determining how to "Ditch those duties that don't count much, even if you can do them magnificently well."[28]

The need for available time presents a leadership challenge that begins with *managing calls for service,* which often requires comprehensive workload analysis, call prioritization, alternative call handling, and differential response methods.

OTHER RELATED STRATEGIES FOR THE LEADER'S MENTAL ARSENAL

Today's police leaders must also be knowledgeable about several relatively new and popular approaches for addressing crime and disorder, all of which are related to the analysis function of community policing and problem solving: CompStat, smart policing, ILP, and predictive policing. Next, we briefly discuss each (there now exists a vast and growing body of literature concerning each; to begin, see the Internet Investigations section at the end of the chapter).

YOU DECIDE: THE HORRENDOUS HIGHWAY HANGOUT

The Burger Barn is the most popular fast-food restaurant in town and it is open 24 hours a day. It is located in the middle sector of town where two highways intersect; this is a busy four-lane commercial area that is adjacent to a low-income residential area consisting of mobile homes, apartment complexes, and small single-family homes. Sgt. Maas advises you, his shift lieutenant, that there has been a tremendous increase in calls for service at the location. Upon checking computer-aided dispatch records, you discover that calls for service (CFS) to the Burger Barn had increased to nearly 90 per month. Further analysis reveals that the majority of CFS occurs during the late night/early morning hours, peaking between 1:00 a.m. and 3:00 a.m. The CFS mostly involve large crowds of juveniles, fights, noise disturbances, shots fired, and traffic congestion and accidents. A few police officers have even been injured while attempting to break up fights. The restaurant's manager has attempted to limit access to the building during the peak hours, allowing only

five juveniles inside at any one time. This approach has resulted in long lines forming outside and has increased the number of disturbances and fights. Employees are frequently harassed by angry customers waiting for service in the building. Many of the juveniles are cruising and driving carelessly, paying little attention to the traffic signals and contributing significantly to congestion, which is creating a backup on the adjoining highway, generating a letter of complaint from the state highway patrol to the police chief.

Questions for Discussion

1. How would you have Sgt. Maas and other personnel thoroughly *analyze* the problem?

2. What *responses* may be considered (be sure to include all organizations that could help)?

3. How would you attempt to empirically *evaluate* their successes?

CompStat

CompStat—discussed in more length in Chapter 12 in terms of its practical application—has actually been applied as a crime management tool in many agencies and in some form since 1994, when it was developed by the New York City Police Department. Its emphasis on examining data for directing police resources has been very successful, leading it to be described as "revolutionizing law enforcement management and practice,"[29] while others have termed it as "perhaps the single most important organizational/administrative innovation in policing during the latter half of the 20th century."[30] CompStat requires police commanders to generate frequent crime activity reports, so officers begin proactively thinking about ways to deal with crime in terms of suppression, intervention, and prevention. Commanders must explain at CompStat meetings what tactics they have employed to address crime patterns, what resources they have and need, and with whom they have collaborated.[31]

Smart Policing

A much more recent concept to be developed, an offshoot of CompStat, is smart policing, which emphasizes the use of data and analytics as well as improved crime analysis, performance measurement, and evaluation research. In June 2009, the federal Bureau of Justice Assistance (BJA) began soliciting grant proposals for "smart policing" initiatives (SPI), seeking proposals that would identify or confirm effective crime-reduction techniques that other agencies could replicate.[32] Perhaps the most important element of SPI was to be research partnerships, which BJA emphasized in the call for proposals, with police and academics working together to test solutions that were informed by crime science theories and assessed with sound evaluation. Since BJA made its first 10 SPI awards to police agencies in 2009, to date, grants have been awarded to dozens of local law enforcement agencies conducting SPI projects. Findings thus far suggest that smart policing programs can significantly reduce violent crime (Philadelphia); creative use of crime analytics and crime analysis resources, coupled with targeted problem-solving approaches, can also reduce violent crime in historically violent police districts (Los Angeles); and problem-solving teams can prevent violence in stubborn chronic hot spots (Boston) and reduce service calls and property crime at troubled high-traffic convenience stores (Glendale, Arizona).

Intelligence-led policing

Intelligence-led policing originated in Great Britain, where police believed that a relatively small number of people were responsible for a comparatively large percentage of crimes; they believed that officers could reduce crime more effectively by focusing on the most prevalent offenses occurring in their jurisdiction.[33] Intelligence is information; furthermore, "information plus analysis equals intelligence," and without analysis, there is no intelligence. Intelligence is what is produced after the collected data were evaluated and analyzed by a trained intelligence professional.[34] Crime analysts keep their fingers on the pulse of crime in the jurisdiction: which crime trends are up, which ones are down, where the hot spots are, what type of property is being stolen, and so on. Intelligence analysts, on the other hand, are likely to be more aware of the specific *people* responsible for crime in the jurisdiction—who they are, where they live, what they do, who they associate with, and so on. Integrating these two functions—crime analysis and intelligence analysis—is essential for obtaining a comprehensive grasp of the crime picture. *Crime analysis* allows police to understand the "who, what, when, and where," while *intelligence analysis* provides an understanding of the "who"—the crime networks and individuals.[35]

Predictive Policing

The term predictive policing is another relatively new law enforcement concept that "integrates approaches such as cutting-edge crime analysis, crime-fighting technology, intelligence-led policing, and more to inform forward thinking crime prevention strategies and tactics."[36] The police have always known, for example, that robberies surge near check-cashing businesses, that crime spikes on hot days and plummets during the rain, that residential burglaries often occur on Sunday mornings (while people are attending church services), and that Super Bowl Sunday is usually the slowest crime day of the year.[37] But officers' minds can store and remember only so much data. So when the police monitor crime data and query a computer system for historical and real-time patterns, they can predict, more systematically, over a bigger area, and across shifts and time spans, where crimes are likely to occur. More important, the crime analysis software does not forget details, get sick, take vacation, or transfer to a different precinct. So if commercial robberies were high in, say, March 2016, their software will predict another spike in March 2017, and the police can then look at the types of businesses that were hit, their locations, and time of day. The system can even analyze a robber's modus operandi—what was said, type of weapon used, and so on.[38]

A LEADERSHIP CONUNDRUM: THE CHALLENGES OF MEASURING RESULTS

Although the four-part SARA problem-solving process should be well known to readers of this textbook by now, there is one aspect of that process that commands further examination: **assessment**, which is the final stage and where officers evaluate the effectiveness of their responses and use the results to revise their responses, collect more data, or even redefine the problem. For some if not most problems, assessment is simple: making before/after comparisons of crimes and calls for service to see if the responses worked and the problems diminished, or if a problem resurfaced later, and so on. At a higher level, assessments can include measures such as environmental crime prevention surveys and neighborhood fear reduction surveys.

The Police Leader's Challenge: Impact Evaluation

What is most challenging for police leaders, however, concerns the value of only performing an assessment of the responses versus accomplishing a full-blown evaluation. The problem is that an assessment does not provide a complete measure of whether the problem-oriented policing initiatives made a difference. For that to be determined, an **impact evaluation** of the initiative is required. Assessments and evaluations are thus different from, but complementary to, one another. Assessments—which can also be termed outcome evaluations—ask the following kinds of baseline questions: Did the response occur as planned, and did all the response components work? Did the response result in fewer calls for service to the area? More arrests?

On a higher cognitive plane, however, an evaluation asks: if the problem declined, did the *response* cause the decline?

The accompanying "Focus On" box demonstrates some of the challenges involved with assessments vis-à-vis evaluations and further explains the differences between the two approaches.

Another aspect of and use for measurement—police productivity—is discussed in Chapter 12.

HOMELAND SECURITY AND SCIENCE: GIVING EACH DUE CONSIDERATION

Following we briefly discuss several ancillary, related concepts that will bear on community policing and problem solving in the future. Note that a much more complete discussion of homeland security is provided in Chapter 13.

Keeping the Focus on Community Policing

Community policing is believed to provide quality police service for the long term. Still, some police officers may resist—and continue to oppose—the transition to community policing and problem solving if they view it as "soft" on crime or not "real" policing for today's needs.

Many agencies and their government leaders—and some police academies —have placed more emphasis on tactics and equipment in recent years, especially since homeland security became an important operational imperative

FOCUS ON: ASSESSING WHAT "WORKS"

1. Assume that the police have recently observed a spike in evening ATM robberies located on the exterior of banks in a particular part of the city. They increase patrols so as to be more visible in the area, employ stakeouts, and add more detectives to work the cases. Within a month, reports of robberies near these ATMs plummet, and of course the police believe their efforts were responsible for the virtual elimination of the problem. But can they be certain of their reasoning? What if a private security firm offered a free month's worth of patrolling to the banks if they contracted their services, several of the affected banks installed outside cameras, and the person responsible for most of these robberies decided to change to residential burglaries as a more lucrative and less dangerous way to "earn a living?" Therefore, it is not known whether enhanced police efforts were responsible for the improved situation at ATMs or some other causal factor might have intervened. The differences between assessment and evaluation are thus considerable and obvious.[39]

2. Assume that after performing a careful analysis, problem-solving officers determine that in order to curb a street prostitution problem they will heighten patrols in the area, change several streets to one-way—thus creating several dead-end streets to thwart cruising "johns," and work with courts and social services so that convicted prostitutes receive probation and assistance to gain the necessary skills for legitimate employment. An assessment under SARA could, for example, determine whether the crackdown occurred, and if so, how many arrests police made; whether the street patterns were altered as planned; and how many prostitutes received job skills assistance.[40]

Note, however, that a SARA assessment does not answer the question, "What happened to the problem?" Here is where an impact evaluation would come into play for determining if the implemented initiative caused the decline. Assume that during the analysis stage of SARA, an evaluation team conducted a census of prostitutes operating in the target area, and asked the traffic engineering department to install traffic counters on the major thoroughfare and critical side streets to measure traffic flow and to determine how customers move through the area. The evaluation team also made covert video recordings of the target area to document how prostitutes interact with potential customers. Then, after the response was implemented, the team repeated these measures to see if the problem declined. As a result of these measures, they discovered that instead of the 23 prostitutes counted in the first census, only 8 could be found—a significant reduction. They also found a slight decline in traffic on the major thoroughfare on the weekends, but not at other times; however, there was a statistically significant decline in side-street traffic on Saturday nights. New covert video recordings show that prostitutes in the area have changed how they approach vehicles. In short, the team now has evidence that the problem has declined after response implementation.[41]

for many police departments. As noted by Chief Betsy Hard of the Bloomfield, Connecticut, Police Department, "Academies are emphasizing the edicts the profession is receiving—homeland security and intelligence—not problem solving or community policing."[42] Similarly, Chief Theron Bowman of the Arlington, Texas, Police Department stated that "One of my greatest challenges is ensuring that community policing moves forward. It is who we are and what we do. It isn't who other departments are yet. As police officers and experts on the community policing philosophy, we need to take a leadership role and show other departments what the community orientation is all about."[43]

Obviously, consistent, progressive leadership will be necessary in the future to advance and spread community policing. All agency leaders must communicate to employees that community policing is not a short-lived program or an appendage to the agency but rather a philosophical approach to delivering police services in a democracy. Furthermore, given that patrol officers work directly with the public, agencies must stress to new officers—throughout recruitment, academy training, and in their daily service—that the agency adheres to the community policing philosophy. Even during the recruitment process, agency personnel should seek to adopt screening processes that select persons who have a service orientation and will be committed to community policing. Agency leaders must also ensure that policies and procedures are congruent with the problem-oriented policing philosophy, that officers are evaluated in a community policing context and receive commendations for their successes, and that officers who serve as role models and leaders to others in the agency are promoted and rewarded.

What Role for Local Police in Homeland Security?

In the view of many police administrators, the emphasis on homeland security often resulted in reduced community policing funding and efforts. Some observers believe that soon after 9/11 community policing was in effect kicked to the curb, as large portions of police budgets were allocated to homeland security efforts. Still, the proactive principles of community policing and problem solving, and its emphasis on developing good relationships with the community, have not been lost on homeland security. Therefore, many police experts agree that community policing and homeland security are complementary, not mutually exclusive—that it does not have to be an either/or proposition.

Certain elements of community policing are compatible and, perhaps, should coexist with antiterrorism efforts. The first among these elements is the strategic requirement for geographic focus. Community policing requires police officers have a permanent beat to become familiar with community members, identify problems, and find solutions to these problems. Antiterrorism activities also require familiarity with the territory. This will enable police officers to detect suspicious movements of goods and people. Hence, geographic assignment may still be a valuable component for both community policing and antiterrorism policing. In fact, geographic focus is considered necessary to develop the other components of community policing and antiterrorism policing, that is, community partnerships.[44]

The second main component of community policing that may be compatible with antiterrorism is problem solving. Several terrorism scholars have pointed out that the underlying causes of terrorism should be addressed. The skills that are developed under a community policing model such as problem solving could be useful for antiterrorism policing. For instance, the problem-solving model SARA could still be used to analyze the events surrounding terrorism phenomena. Ordinary events or crime could be analyzed to unravel these events' connections to the preparations for a terrorist attack or planning. In particular, skills in crime analysis, crime mapping, crime prevention through environmental design, and other crime prevention strategies that have been learned in community policing could become the intervention and analytical models for antiterrorism policing.

One of the problem solving infrastructures that emerged with antiterrorism policing is the use of Intelligence Centers or Fusion Centers. Through the collaborative efforts of local, state, and federal agents, these centers gather, analyze, and share intelligence information for the prevention and control of terrorism and other crimes. Evidence shows that problem solving seems to be embraced in both the community policing and the homeland security policing eras. The third component of community policing that may be compatible with antiterrorism policing is community participation. Policing could take advantage of the community members' inputs to intelligence information. Such participation could only emerge when trust between the community and the police exists. Community information is important in gathering information about terrorist plots and detecting terrorists.[45]

Cybercrime and Community Policing

Cybercrime involves an array of electronic devices, and is generally the electronic manipulation of data through the addition or deletion of files and/or a theft of information. Specific offenses include identity theft, cyber stalking via social network sites or email, child pornography, cyber bullying, embezzlement, theft, and various forms of fraud.

Cybercrime is the fastest-growing type of criminal activity in the world. Indeed, the likelihood of suffering from a violent, person-to-person crime in the physical world is now lower than being the victim of a virtual crime. Why face a bevy of bank cameras and security officers at a robbery, when cybercrimes are much more profitable and less risky?

Cybercriminals are no longer amateurs who play with computers just to see "what happens." Expert hackers have become suppliers of sensitive information, computer programs and packages, and other tools that end users need to carry out criminal enterprises. Online criminals even shop for batches of stolen credit card numbers and other identifying information, bank account numbers and passcodes, and skimming devices.[46]

Problem-oriented policing must address cybercrime differently, as the problem often exists in both electronic and physical communities. However, the SARA problem-solving process can be used to address this type of crime. First, police scan and determine the local problems, using crime report data, citizen interviews, and personal observations. Next, they conduct an analysis, determining the causes of cybercrime, what other crimes have derived from cybercrime victimization, the most basic forms of victimization, and the available resources for addressing cybercrime. Then, police develop a variety of responses, considering what other communities have done to remedy the cybercrime problem, the kinds of interventions that might work, and the sources of data that will be gathered. Finally, they assess their responses: was the intervention plan implemented correctly? Were the listed goals obtained? Have new challenges arisen and, if so, how can they be addressed?[47]

Police should also request assistance from community agencies to help them address the problem of cybercrime. For example, are local banks informing their customers of the risks related to online banking? Are computer repair stores offering customer vulnerability assessments to determine if an individual's computer is infected or at risk?[48]

Applying Science to Policing

The police have accomplished much in the last few decades, to include developing new strategies of crime control and prevention, introducing problem-oriented policing, hot spot policing, CompStat, smart policing, predictive and intelligence-led policing, crime mapping, and other strategic innovations. New technologies have included major advancements in automatic fingerprinting systems and DNA testing. The police have begun to break down the walls separating them from academia, often enlisting the help of researchers.

Given that, however, policing experts such as David Weisburd and Peter Neyroud[49] believe there is still a fundamental disconnect between science and policing. By "science" they mean the broad array of methods and technologies, to include advances not only as mentioned above in forensics but also in social science, which often has been neglected by the police. In short, there needs to be greater use of scientific models of inquiry such as problem-oriented policing. They argue that despite these advances, science has yet to move center stage.

For example, most police practices are not systematically evaluated, and we still know too little about what works and under what conditions in policing due to lack of impact evaluation. Often, the introduction of research leaps from a "bright idea" of police practitioners or researchers rather than through systematic development of knowledge about practice. Then, police leaders try to diffuse the idea more widely in their agencies, and across agencies, without adequately having researched what the real effect was. In turn, police science is often ignored even when the evidence is unambiguous. Take, for example, the continued application of boot camps and other programs that have been shown to be ineffective but continue to be supported and implemented by police agencies.[50]

How can policing be moved to include science to a central place? First, science must become a natural and organic part of the police mission, both because it can help them to define practices and programs that have promise and because it can allow them to assess such innovations in terms of how well they work, and at what cost.[51]

Summary

As stated by one source, community-oriented policing became "a mantra for police chiefs and mayors in cities big and small across the country."[52] As was seen in Tables 10-1–10-3, the community policing and problem-solving approach to addressing crime and disorder has spread rapidly and is being covered widely in recruit training across the nation. This chapter examined this strategy and the important roles of police leadership within it. As stated in the introduction, those leaders must ensure, by whatever means, that they have the knowledge to confront and deal with the vast array of challenges that face them.

Discussion Questions

1. Which "era" is policing now in? How would you defend your response?

2. To what extent is community policing and problem solving now practiced in local police agencies in the United States, and to what extent is related training provided?

3. What purposes are served by police leaders looking at organizational culture, field operations, and external relations under this strategy?

4. How would you describe the roles of the chief executive, middle manager, first-line supervisor, and patrol officer in the practice of this approach?

5. What are meant by CompStat, smart policing, intelligence-led policing, and predictive policing?

6. What problems exist with assessment vis-à-vis impact evaluation, and how is the latter performed?

7. Why must police leaders keep their focus on community policing and problem solving when addressing homeland security and cybercrime, and in the application of science?

Internet Investigations

Bureau of Justice Assistance, *CompStat: Its Origins, Evolution, and Future in Law Enforcement Agencies*
http://www.policeforum.org/assets/docs/Free_Online _Documents/Compstat/compstat%20-%20its%20 origins%20evolution%20and%20future%20in%20 law%20enforcement%20agencies%202013.pdf

Bureau of Justice Assistance, *Reducing Crime Through Intelligence-Led Policing*
https://www.ncirc.gov/documents/public/reducing _crime_through_ilp.pdf

Center for Problem-Oriented Policing, "Situational Crime Prevention"
http://www.popcenter.org/about/?p=situational

Center for Problem-Oriented Policing, "The Key Elements of POP"
http://www.popcenter.org/about/?p=elements

National Institute of Justice, "Overview of Predictive Policing"
http://www.nij.gov/topics/law-enforcement/strategies/ predictive-policing/Pages/welcome.aspx

Office of Community Oriented Policing Services, "Problem Solving"
https://cops.usdoj.gov/Default.asp?Item=2558

CHAPTER 11

Officer Wellness, Safety, and Stress: Identifying and Managing Harms

STUDENT LEARNING OUTCOMES

After reading this chapter, the student will understand:

- some of the dangers and hazards that arise as police officers perform their duties
- the meaning of officer wellness, and the steps for developing an agency wellness campaign
- how police agency culture must often be changed to accommodate a wellness program
- how training, policies, and technologies relate to police leadership and officer wellness
- arguments for state and local agencies having formal Occupational Safety and Health Administration health regulations
- what programs several cities have developed to address problems relating to officer safety and wellness
- how an employee assistance program functions
- the nature and causes of stress in policing, how officers can reduce their stress levels, and the responsibility of police leaders in this endeavor

KEY TERMS AND CONCEPTS

- Employee assistance program
- Occupational hazards (of policing)
- Occupational Safety and Health Administration (OSHA)
- Proactive/reactive approaches to wellness
- Stress (recognition and management)
- Training, policy, technology (roles of in police wellness)
- Wellness and safety plan

INTRODUCTION

There is a side of policing, and its leadership, that we would prefer not to discuss: the harms that are done to officers by virtue of the hazards of their work. Indeed, for more than a century people have written about the hazards of policing. In 1879, Sir William Gilbert observed that "When constabulary duty's to be done, the policeman's lot is not a happy one."[1] Furthermore, William A. Westley, who performed one of the first sociological studies of police subculture, observed that "The policeman's world is spawned of degradation, corruption and insecurity. He walks alone, a pedestrian in Hell."[2] Finally, we might also borrow a line from Shakespeare's play "King Henry IV" (1597), in which he wrote, "Uneasy lies the head that wears the crown." With a little variation, the same might also be said for today's police officer: "Uneasy lies the head that wears the badge."

The job of policing has never been easy, but the danger and frustration that have always accompanied the work of policing seem to be at higher levels today than ever before, as they daily confront heavily armed, arrogant, and often mentally disturbed offenders. Furthermore, as will be seen later, exacerbating this situation is the fact that even their own organizations and policies and practices generate tremendous levels of stress for officers.

In addition, the recent Great Recession translated into safety and wellness issues for the police, as budget cuts often resulted in layoffs, furloughs, hiring freezes, retirement incentives, as well as reduction or elimination of police training and health prevention programs. Such cutbacks also resulted in larger patrol areas to cover, declines in the number of available backup officers, and increased stress levels.

Therefore, police leaders must be concerned with the health and well-being of their employees, ensuring that employees are mentally and physically prepared for the challenges of the workplace. Protecting our police officers—the agency's greatest investment—is a moral and practical imperative. This obligation is one that requires a holistic approach—and often a change in agency culture. That is the subject of this chapter.

The chapter begins with a review of the hazards of policing as an occupation, including the mortality rate of and attacks on its officers and the debilitating physical and mental effects of the work. Then we discuss how a police agency might go about developing a formal wellness and safety program, including addressing the need for change in agency culture. Included are the key roles of agency leaders, **training, policy, and technologies** in this endeavor. Next, we briefly review the advantages to be realized if state and local law enforcement agencies have formal occupational safety and health regulations, and following that is a look at what a number of federal agencies and task forces are doing and recommending in fomenting officer wellness. Finally, we examine the primary types of stressors that are typically found in police work, and how to manage the stress that is inflicted on officers. Included are a number of case studies of successful agency wellness efforts, and problems for readers to consider.

OCCUPATIONAL HAZARDS OF POLICING: THE ISSUES

Although it is now a *statistically* safer time in which to serve in policing than the decade of the 1970s, when 1,114 officers were feloniously killed[3]—as compared with 541 officers murdered during the 2000s[4]—as noted above, because of the proliferation of gang members, drug-affected and mentally challenged citizens, and all manner of well-armed criminals, policing has never been more dangerous or had more **occupational hazards** than it does today. On average, one law enforcement officer is killed in the line of duty somewhere in the United States every 61 hours.[5] Indeed, the occupational fatality rate for law enforcement is three to five times greater than the national average for the working population.[6]

Furthermore, in recent years our nation has observed a shocking increase in felonious assaults on officers. Over the past decade, there has been an average of 58,930 assaults a year on officers, resulting in 15,404 injuries. Each loss of a police officer also results in long-term negative ramifications for the family and agency survivors.[7]

In addition, the mere fact of performing their duties places officers at particularly high risk for early deaths, heart attacks, and other health-related problems. Aside from the most obvious and well-known risks that arise, that is, assaults by suspects and other assailants, police officers also face elevated risks from vehicle crashes, accidental injuries resulting from foot pursuits and other common police activities, exposure to hazardous substances and communicable diseases, stress and fatigue, poor nutrition, and a variety of other physical and mental health risks.[8]

The mental well-being of officers is also an important consideration, especially when one suffers from posttraumatic stress disorder (PTSD) or severe depression, which can lead to suicide. PTSD can be triggered by experiencing traumatic events, such as crime scenes or exceptionally heinous acts, and can affect returning military veterans who experienced combat trauma.[9]

Given these occupational risks, there is a need for holistic programs that promote health, wellness, and safety among police officers, focusing on all of these issues and addressing cardiovascular fitness, chronic

The National Law Enforcement Officers Memorial Fund, Washington, DC
Source: National Law Enforcement Officers Memorial Fund

disease prevention, alcohol and drug use and abuse, nutrition, weight management, exercise and conditioning, injury prevention, safe driving, stress management, and resilience to trauma.[10]

TRANSITIONING FROM WARTIME SOLDIER TO PEACETIME COP: PROS AND CONS

Police agencies have always appreciated—if not outright preferred—bringing military veterans into their ranks. Such individuals have respect for the chain of command, understand rank structures, know how to wear a uniform, and possess mental and physical discipline as well as skills that most nonmilitary personnel simply do not possess. Furthermore, veterans' preference has been given to job applicants for decades, particularly in the federal government. As a result, while just 6 percent of the population at large has served in the military, 19 percent of police officers are veterans.

Now, however, as policing is generally trying to transform itself from a "soldier" to a "guardian" mindset (discussed in Chapter 9), research by the Marshall Project indicates that this preference for military veterans is generating serious problems. First, with one in five police officers literally coming home as warriors—returning from Afghanistan, Iraq, or other assignments—data show that today's veterans are quicker to resort to force in policing situations. Such studies have also found that veterans who work as police are more vulnerable to self-destructive behavior (e.g., alcohol and drug abuse, PTSD, suicidal tendencies).[11]

This is not a recently recognized problem. In 2009, the U.S. Department of Justice and the International Association of Chiefs of Police jointly published a guide for police agencies concerning the recruitment of military veterans, warning that "Sustained operations under combat circumstances may cause returning officers to mistakenly blur the lines between military combat situations and civilian crime situations, resulting in inappropriate decisions and actions — particularly in the use of less lethal or lethal force."[12] However, most law enforcement agencies do little or no mental health screening for officers who have returned from military deployment, and they provide little to nothing in the way of treatment.

There are legal impediments to officers' obtaining such treatment. For instance, the federal Uniformed Services Employment and Reemployment Rights Act prohibits agencies from requiring blanket mental health evaluations. Also, because of the Americans with Disabilities Act, police departments are unable to reject a job candidate for having a PTSD diagnosis.

As a result, the only point at which most of the nation's law enforcement officers are given a mental health analysis is during the initial hiring process, and the rigor of the screening varies widely.

In short, the extent to which a safety net exists for veterans who become officers and are struggling or demonstrate mental health issues is generally minimal to completely absent. The dilemma is made more acute by the fact that, while police leaders should be able to remove unstable police officers from the street before they hurt someone or themselves, officers often do not feel they can ask for help without jeopardizing their careers or looking weak in the eyes of peers. Still, early intervention is key; waiting for someone to harm a citizen or self-destruct should not be an option.[13]

A WELLNESS AND SAFETY PLAN AND CHANGE OF AGENCY CULTURE

Proactive and Reactive Approaches

Police leaders must recognize that accountability to their officers is the number one factor in providing the best safety and wellness practices. Leaders are responsible, for example, to see that constant equipment compliance checks, proper weapons deployment, and policy and procedure enforcement are performed in order to minimize officer injuries and fatalities. Such ongoing monitoring and the enforcing of compliance will set the tone for meeting high standards, expectations, and practices for ensuring officer safety. Following is a description of how to develop a well-rounded program of officer wellness.

First, however, it should be noted that developing a wellness and safety program can be approached either proactively or reactively. When an organization acts proactively, it anticipates issues and attempts to ward off problems; a **proactive** campaign can also encourage employees to use existing services, such as the Philadelphia Police Department does with its health and wellness programs (both proactive approaches are described in the accompanying "Focus On" box). When an agency is **reactive**, it develops campaigns, policies, and training programs to address a problem or issue that has emerged, such as when there has been a surge in officer injuries resulting from preventable traffic crashes.[14]

Leadership and Management

Given that leadership and management are the cornerstones to ensuring officer safety, health, and wellness, the first step is for organizational leaders to "walk the walk"—maintain their *own* health and fitness, thus setting the example for all. Management should also ensure that officers are provided the best safety policies and procedures, opportunities to train and workout (see the "Focus On" box), and resources to make safety a priority for the organization.

Given that law enforcement is, and will always be, very labor-intensive, it is important that police leaders develop and maintain employee wellness programs.

Source: NicoElNino/Shutterstock

FOCUS ON: PROACTIVE APPROACHES TO WELLNESS CAMPAIGNS: PHOENIX AND PHILADELPHIA

Bouts of oppressive heat can create a host of issues: dehydration, heatstroke, fatigue, cramps, and rash. Given their location in a desert climate, Phoenix, Arizona, police officers are especially vulnerable to these threats. The police department launched its "Beat the Heat" campaign to educate officers on the risks of heat-related injury and ways to mitigate those risks. The department produced a "Beat the Heat" training video for officers (see https://www.youtube.com/watch?v=ywgd8Gs9KI4). Furthermore, during major incidents, the agency's Safety Unit ensured adequate hydration was available for responding officers. Overall, the campaign ran for one year, during which the department saw no reports of heat-related injuries.

The Philadelphia Police Department launched several initiatives designed to proactively address ailments adversely affecting police personnel and their families. This holistic approach to health and wellness seeks to reduce the number of members who are impacted by serious ailments or are unavailable to work while managing health problems within their family. Each health and wellness pro-

gram is disseminated through the police department's intranet, bulletins, and a general message is read at roll calls for three consecutive days. A suicide prevention course is conducted to help officers and supervisors recognize the signs of suicidal peers and educate them on available resources and appropriate actions. Psychologists provide confidential mental health services in areas such as marriage counseling, parenting, bullying, and other job-related or personal stresses. A drug and alcohol awareness program, seminars to support families with children with autism and special needs, and a health fair provide employees and family members with eye care, cardiovascular, pulmonary, blood pressure, cholesterol, and cancer tests are available to officers. Employees can receive fitness and nutrition counseling, and a nutritionist meets with officers to adjust dietary habits in coordination with a fitness plan.

J. Hill, S. Whitcomb, P. Patterson, D. W. Stephens, and B. Hill, *Making Officer Safety and Wellness Priority One: A Guide to Educational Campaigns* (Washington, DC: Office of Community Oriented Policing Services, 2014), pp. 15–16.

FOCUS ON: CITY OF BOCA RATON'S ON-DUTY TRAINING FACILITY

The Police Department of the City of Boca Raton, Florida (BRPD), developed an on-duty exercise program, written directly into policy, as a part of a broader emphasis on health and wellness. Two exercise rooms are provided and maintained by the department and the city, and qualified instructors are available to assist in developing individualized exercise routines. Officers are permitted to exercise while on duty within specified guidelines; specifically:

- officers working 10- or 12-hour shifts can exercise during their meal period provided they have supervisor approval
- officers working eight-hour shifts can exercise on duty for a maximum of three hours per week.
- officers who wish to go jogging may use

approved outdoor routes, but they must notify dispatch of their location while exercising and be available for immediate duty.

The BRPD found that by implementing these kinds of programs within smaller units (e.g., a squad), they realized broader participation, generated subtle peer pressure to participate, created a supportive environment and friendly competition among officers, and promoted a group culture of fitness and health throughout the agency. Recruitment and retention were also positively impacted (the exercise program was advertised as a job "perk," and the people attracted to the agency were more fitness-minded).

Adapted from Kuhns, et al., *Health, Safety, and Wellness Program: Case Studies in Law Enforcement*, pp. 7–8.

Developing a wellness campaign—fostering a safe working environment, protecting the safety of officers, and supporting health and wellness priorities—actually resembles a problem-oriented policing effort (such as that described in Chapter 10), using the following steps:[15]

1. Identify and analyze issues: first, assess the agency's health and wellness problems and what must be done to reduce them. Also, consider the existing culture: does there appear to be any incentives or concern with employee health and fitness? In addition, certain types of data can be examined: agency trends with regard to employee sickness, car crashes, alcohol-related offenses, suicide, lost days due to illness, or declines in officer fitness. Finally, employees themselves can be asked to indicate any wellness-related concerns and suggested improvements; surveys and focus groups can also be employed. Doing so will inform the leaders while also involve officers in the problem-solving process.

2. Establish goals and objectives: a goal is general (e.g., "Decreasing the Numbers of Employees Getting Injured on On-duty Car Crashes"), while objectives are the means of reaching the goal (e.g., using training, posters, shift briefings on such things as use of safety belts, not exceeding speed limits, being more attentive to safe driving, and so on). Note, however, that some wellness goals may involve increases in agency budgets (e.g., increasing the numbers of officers who obtain a yearly physical exam); funding is discussed more below.

3. Develop strategies: with goals and objectives in mind, a strategy can be crafted for putting the plan into action. This moves the program to the blueprint phase, and must include how the program will be communicated, funded, implemented, and so on.

4. Consider key messages, branding, and design: assigning a name to the campaign will define why it exists. It should involve a visual identity, including a logo and a name so the initiative will stand out and gain employee interest, buy-in, and participation. See the "Focus On" box.

5. Identify a budget and resources: as noted above, additional funding may be required for certain fitness campaigns; however, police agencies can be very resourceful (e.g., many have obtained private funds for purchasing body armor, police dogs). Agencies might develop partnerships with various community and professional organizations as well as seek grants; public health organizations, physicians' organizations, and insurance providers may be approached as well.

6. Establish evaluations and measurements: finally, the agency must try to avoid the "We did these things, and believe they worked, but we're not sure" kind of program evaluation—especially where the tax dollars are concerned. The department should attempt to show—with empirical data—that its fitness program achieved its goals. Such an assessment may not be within the purview of in-house employees, so assistance might be sought from someone (e.g., university faculty) who is specially trained in evaluation research.

FOCUS ON: DEVELOPING A MESSAGE: "ARRIVE ALIVE" IN MARYLAND

In Prince George's County Maryland, fatal automobile accidents involving officers became one of the top three causes of officer fatalities. Therefore, police leaders were compelled to consider what efforts might be taken to help reduce such fatalities. The agency determined that many factors played a role in collisions: distractions in the patrol vehicle, excessive speed, and officers not wearing their seatbelts. Although policy required officers to wear their seatbelts while their vehicle was in motion, many officers believed seatbelts would make it more difficult for them to respond effectively to ambushes or other situations, as well as making access to their sidearm more difficult.

Simply ordering officers to wear their seatbelts was not seen as an effective solution, so police executives sought a way to change officers' viewpoints. The result was a safety initiative called "Arrive Alive," which involved showing a video to each officer in the department (featuring graphic footage of department crashes, along with heartfelt testimonials from eight survivors of officers killed in crashes); parking a demolished cruiser near the gas pumps where officers fill up their gas tanks that displayed safety messages (to buckle up, slow down, pay attention, and arrive alive); and issuing a weekly driver-safety message over the radio.

Adapted from Kuhns, et al., *Health, Safety, and Wellness Program: Case Studies in Law Enforcement*, pp. 13–16.

NEED FOR TRAINING, POLICY, TECHNOLOGY

Ongoing training is important to ensure that officers understand the contributing risk factors that can lead to an injury or death. First is training in the balancing of risks; for instance, they should understand the need to assess the potential hazards involved in foot pursuits: possibly being alone and without backup, and possibly chasing someone who may be armed, is in better physical condition, and while in unfamiliar areas. In sum, officer training should emphasize that sometimes the safety risks may not be worth pursuing a fleeing suspect.

Tactical training is also important, as it enables officers to keep their skills honed for emergency driving, handling violent encounters, and operating less-lethal and lethal weapons. Best practices can be demonstrated through classroom learning, range driving, use of firearms and driving simulators, and computer-based situations and scenarios. Such training is crucial in safeguarding officers' lives. It must also be borne in mind, however, that attention to safety and risk management also applies to training, which itself can be hazardous and even fatal, such as the case where a SWAT hostage rescue exercise on a commuter train resulted in one of the role players, a reserve officer, being killed with a supposedly unloaded firearm.[16]

For their part, police leaders should review tactical, pursuit, driving, and other related policies and procedures to ensure they are up to date for risk factor mitigation (e.g., high-speed vehicle pursuit policies should cover the types of pursuits permitted, who will supervise them, maneuvering/evasive driving, and mandatory training to ensure the implementation of best practices). And, given that officers do not always read updates of policies and procedures, agencies should post and ensure the reading of such materials, and discuss them at roll call.

An additional benefit from training is prevention of injuries. An example is Contra Costa County, California, which found an increasing number of injuries resulting in officer downtime and increasing workers compensation costs due to sprains and strains. They implemented a training program to address injuries caused by lifting, pushing, pulling, twisting, bending, and stooping, as well as proper techniques for stepping over barriers to avoid tripping hazards. The overall cost of police injuries after implementation of the training program was reduced from $3.5 million per year to $1 million per year over a two-year period.[17]

Another training and policy consideration for enhancing safety involves the use of technologies, including wearing effective safety gear (e.g., body armor) and maintaining appropriate types of weaponry. First, there are countless stories of body armor having saved officers' lives. As stated in a federal publication, 99.4 percent of officers now wear body armor when on duty.[18]

Regarding agencies' weaponry, it is important that police arsenals are able to compete with the criminal element. With criminals commonly using assault weapons, an officer showing up at a gunfight with a handgun will only jeopardize the safety of his or her own life. Due to the proliferation of assault weapons on the street, more and more agencies are adding high-powered assault rifles to their arsenals. Equipping officers with state-of-the-art weaponry can help to reduce risk of injury or death.[19] Task force operations, whether local, regional, or federal, are established to address high-incident-based criminal activity, often involving drugs and weapons. Officers on task forces who serve arrest warrants are particularly at risk, so agencies must understand those risks and determine what can be learned from these tactical operations.[20]

Finally, another critical area for consideration is court security. As anyone who watches national news knows, each year officers and deputies are assaulted and even killed by offenders while working in court. Understanding the vulnerabilities in court security and prisoner transportation is critical to ensure their safety; training and policies should also address defensive tactics, terroristic and/or bomb threats, high-risk trials, and attacks in the courtrooms.[21]

WHY NO OSHA UNITS IN POLICING?

Given that police officers routinely face the kinds of health and safety threats described above, one would think that occupational health and safety would be a routine focus of the field—as is common in the United Kingdom and Canada. Such is not the case in the United States. Moreover, we do not know how many officers are affected each year by such job-related threats. Therefore, the field could significantly benefit from adopting a standardized and comprehensive approach to occupational health and safety.[22]

The **Occupational Safety and Health Administration (OSHA)** exists to provide health regulations for all private-sector and federal government employees. By law, each federal law enforcement agency must provide safe and healthful places and conditions of employment; acquire, maintain, and require the use of safety equipment; and keep records of and report all occupational accidents and illnesses.[23]

However, the act does not apply to state and local law enforcement agencies. Therefore, less than half of U.S. states mandate that their law enforcement agencies meet even basic occupational health and safety program components such as maintaining a safe and healthful work environment and tracking/reporting workplace accidents or injuries. While some police agencies, such as those mentioned above, have initiated health fairs, wellness checks, and physical fitness programs, the majority of such agencies do not.[24]

Focusing on occupational health and safety is "smart business." Personnel are a department's most valuable resource, and officers who are healthy are less likely to suffer injuries at work, more likely to return to duty quickly after injury, and have higher job satisfaction. Such programs can also reduce medical and mental health visits, and ultimately reduce the annual amounts spent on medical visits by employees. Such programs can also reduce legal liability, because physically fit officers may use less forceful tactics when faced with a situation that has potential for excessive force. For example, the court in *Parker v. District of Columbia*[25] found the police agency to be liable for an officer using excessive force due to the officer's poor physical fitness. Occupational safety programs can also improve police–community relationships, because healthy officers may also be less likely to be the subject of complaints by demonstrating fewer inappropriate, stress-related behaviors involving excessive force and helping officers to work with the community in a more positive manner.[26]

WHAT FEDERAL AGENCIES AND TASK FORCES ARE DOING

Following are descriptions of efforts being taken at the federal level for enhancing police officer safety and wellness:

- The safety of our nation's officers is a top priority for the U.S. Department of Justice. In 2011, the Attorney General released the Officer Safety Toolkit to share resources with federal, state, local, and tribal law enforcement leaders. The program, called VALOR, has trained more than 22,000 officers in health and wellness techniques, as well as dealing with all types of threats (see www.valorforblue.org).

- Also in 2011, the Officer Safety and Wellness Group (OSW; see www.cops.usdoj.gov/Default.asp?Item=2603) was formed, following an eight-year period in which officer killings increased by 53 percent over the previous eight-year period. A partnership between the federal Office of Community Oriented Policing Services and the Bureau of Justice Assistance, OSW focuses on reducing officer deaths and addressing officer wellness issues, providing a number of tools and resources toward encouraging adoption of a culture of safety and wellness in police agencies. Topics discussed include officer deaths and injuries from gunfire, psychological health and suicide, leadership, creating a culture of wellness, motor vehicle operations, and reducing officer deaths and injuries.[27]

- Finally, the President's 21st Century Police Task Force[28] devoted an entire "pillar" in its final report to officer safety and wellness. The task force noted that a large proportion of officer injuries and deaths involve poor physical health due to poor nutrition, lack of exercise, sleep deprivation, substance abuse, and motor vehicle accidents. It stated that "Supervisors would not allow an officer to go on patrol with a deficiently maintained vehicle, an un-serviced duty weapon, or a malfunctioning radio—but pay little attention to the maintenance of what is all officers' most valuable resource: their brains."[29] The task force felt strongly that a nationwide repository for officer injuries is "desperately needed,"[30] and that the culture of law enforcement needs to be transformed: "Support for wellness and safety should permeate all practices and be expressed through changes in procedures, requirements, attitudes, and behaviors... encouraging officers to seek help without concern about negative consequences. The 'bulletproof cop' does not exist. The officers who protect us must also be protected. Their wellness and safety are crucial for them, their colleagues, and their agencies, as well as the well-being of the communities they serve."[31]

WHAT CITIES ARE DOING: SELECTED CASE STUDIES

Following are five brief descriptions of agency approaches to health and wellness—programs often being initiated due to demonstrated wellness and safety problems in their organizations:

- Fort Worth Police Alcohol Awareness
    After seeing an increase in the number of officers having problems with and being arrested for alcohol-related offenses, the Fort Worth, Texas, Police Department found that a culture of hard drinking coupled with a reluctance to seek help exacerbated the issue. In response, a mandatory alcohol awareness training program was initiated for all ranks, emphasizing the seriousness of the problem, educating officers about

the dangers of alcohol and abuse, fostering an environment in which officers are encouraged to seek help when needed, and deemphasizing the culture of hard drinking. Presentations featuring discussions on alcohol awareness and stress management were made available to all officers, and an outside mental health agency was hired to provide a confidential, in-house peer support program, eliminating the fear of reprisal. The agency realized a decline in both stress-related incidents and alcohol-related offenses.[32]

- Columbus Police Work to Prevent Injury

    Columbus, Ohio, police saw a substantial rise in injury reports resulting in thousands of lost and restricted workdays. Thinking many such injuries were preventable, a system called Non-Punitive Close Call Reporting was implemented in which officers share their mistakes in a group setting to prevent similar or more serious mishaps and to decrease officer injuries by increasing cooperative learning, heightening safety awareness, and preventing both new and repeated close calls. The nonpunitive nature of the program is paramount, and the agency also developed spreadsheet-based documentation and a reporting mechanism as a means to analyze results. Close call discussions occur at least once a week during roll-call meetings, and the program is being expanded to include more shifts and officers. Preliminary results suggest injury rates either remained steady or slightly decreased.[33]

- Las Vegas Police Focus on Substance Abuse and Suicide Prevention

    The Las Vegas, Nevada, Metropolitan Police Department wanted to reduce incidents of substance abuse and suicide among officers, and began emphasizing intervention and prevention. The Maintenance of Values and Ethics (MOVE) program mandates intervention for both the employee and command staff when instances of substance abuse are identified. An **employee assistance program** provides access to suicide intervention programs, and a unit intervenes in the case of misconduct related to substance abuse. The agency has seen a reduction in the number of employees arrested for substance-related reasons and that significant interventions have been made for suicidal employees.[34]

- Sacramento Police Focus on Health and Wellness

    During a four-year period, workers compensation claims for the Sacramento, California, Police Department averaged $2.1 million per year for sworn employees. To reduce these expenditures and the number of on-duty injuries, the agency contracted for a professional to give officers nutritional advice; provide customizable workout plans; and inform officers about exercise safety, healthy living, and creative ways to remain active. Later, an on-duty workout program was established, with two weekly, hour-long workout sessions available to on-duty employees. Over the next two years, the number of employees participating in the program increased, and a corresponding 59 percent decrease in workers compensation claims was achieved.[35]

- Reno Police Department and Resiliency

    The Reno, Nevada, Police Department initiated a pilot program that included 15 volunteer officers who were given advanced lipid screening (blood tests to screen for levels of blood cholesterol and triglycerides, indicating an elevated risk of stroke). The officers entered a program that included nutritional advice, exercise, counseling, lab-directed health coaching, and pharmacology. Then they were reevaluated, with the insulin-resistant officers having significantly reduced their risk factors. Given this success, a department-wide wellness or "resiliency" policy was enacted that includes nutrition, exercise, mental awareness, and sleep counseling. An annual wellness fair/clinic for officers and their families is provided as well as a defense course that uses jiu-jitsu training, in which officers learn techniques for separating themselves from offenders so they can use other nonlethal tools necessary for control (thus reducing injuries to both officers and suspects during altercations).[36]

RECOGNIZING AND MANAGING STRESS

As shown above, the work environment of policing often has very adverse effects on officers. In addition to the physical and mental conditions described above, police work generates stress, defined as a force that is external in nature and that causes both physical and emotional strain upon the body.[37] In other words, stressors are situations or occurrences outside of ourselves that we allow to turn inward and cause problems.

No human being can exist in a continuous state of stress. The body strives to maintain its normal state, homeostasis, and to adapt to the alarm, but it can actually develop a disease in the process. Thus, it is extremely important for police leaders to recognize stress and its impact on their officers as well as their productivity.[38]

Stress can come from one of four general categories: (1) organizational and administrative practices, (2) the criminal justice system, (3) the public, and (4) stress intrinsic to police work itself. Next, we briefly discuss each.

The Police Organization Itself

A primary source of stress is the police organization itself. One survey of police officers found that organizationally based problems were the most stressful problems for police officers.[39] Police departments typically are bureaucratic, authoritarian organizations. As Zhao et al.[40] note, the "dark side of bureaucracy" creates a substantial amount of stress for officers. Police agencies are unique in their operation and consequently place a number of restrictions on how police officers conduct their activities.

The Criminal Justice System

The criminal justice system can be a source of stress when officers have difficulty interacting with other components of the system or complying with the decisions made and actions taken by other criminal justice agencies. For example, judges might openly display hostile attitudes toward the police, or prosecutors fail to show proper respect to officers, arbitrarily dismissing cases, having them appear in court during regularly scheduled days off, and advocating rulings restricting police procedures.[41] The courts—and their rulings—can have the most direct impact on police officers and probably are the greatest source of stress from the criminal justice system. Another example occurs when parole officers and probation officers do an inadequate job of supervising parolees, which results in their being involved in an inordinate amount of crime.

The Public

Most citizens recognize that the police perform an important function in our society; however, given the current chasm between the police and citizens in many communities, there are numerous individuals and groups that view the police with great disdain. Furthermore, routine police work involves arresting citizens, issuing citations, and ordering citizens to change their behavior when, for example, they intervene in domestic violence or disorder situations. Often, to resolve problems, they make half of the participants happy, but must make the other half unhappy.

Stressors Intrinsic to Police Work Itself

As noted earlier, police work is fraught with situations that pose physical danger to officers. Anytime officers confront a felon, especially if drugs are involved, there is the potential for physical violence. Domestic violence, felonies in progress, and fight calls often require officers to physically confront suspects. Even noncrime-related tasks bring high levels of stress, such as delivering death messages to citizens, visiting injured officers who are in the hospital, and so on. It would seem that the nature of police work, since it includes dealing with dangerous police activities and dangerous people, would be the most stressful part of the occupation.

Police work, by its very nature, is fraught with stress and danger.
Source: Courtesy of Federal Bureau of Investigation, USA

YOU DECIDE...

Hill City is a relatively small community of about 80,000 people, whose police department has developed an aggressive Repeat Offender Program (ROP). Its eight hand-picked and specially trained officers engage in forced entries into apartments and houses, serving search warrants on the "worst of the worst" wanted felons. Their work is dangerous and physical, thus all of ROP's officers are in top physical condition. The supervisor overseeing the ROP team, Sgt. Lyle, was a drill instructor in the military prior to joining the force. He has developed an impressive training regimen for the ROP officers. They usually work out on their own time at least once a week, have high *esprit de corps*, and pride themselves on never losing a suspect or a physical confrontation. They often go out partying together to "blow off steam." They generally consider themselves to be elite and "head and shoulders above the rest."

One day, while the team was attempting to serve a robbery warrant at a local motel, the suspect escaped through a rear window and led three ROP officers on a foot pursuit. After running extremely hard for about six blocks, the officers became exhausted and were unable to maintain their chase. The following week, the same suspect robbed a fast-food establishment, and during his escape he killed a clerk and seriously wounded a police officer.

Irate because the ROP team failed to catch the suspect earlier, many of the agency's patrol officers begin criticizing the ROP team—whose members they consider to be unjustifiably exalted *prima donnas*. One patrol officer even comments to a newspaper reporter that the entire team should be disciplined and that ROP should be disbanded. In one instance, a fight nearly ensued between two officers.

The situation has now reached a boiling point, causing nearly all officers to take one side or another, fomenting a lot of intra-agency stress and turmoil and resulting in officers requesting sick leave and vacation time at levels never seen before.

Sensing that the agency is being torn apart both from within and without, you, the administrative captain, ask your four lieutenants for input to deal with the public and the press, reduce internal strife, and determine if any procedural or training issues require the department's attention. You further inform the lieutenants to solicit input from the six supervisors concerning means of reducing or ending the high level of hostility among their patrol officers.

Questions for Discussion

1. Should Sgt. Lyle shoulder any responsibility for the suspect situation and its aftermath (dissension within the department)? What kinds of inquiries might you make to determine whether or not this is the case?

2. Given that this seems to have become an agency-wide stress problem, what might your lieutenants recommend?

3. Should the ROP team be disbanded or continued under different supervision, training, and methods of operation?

Keys to Controlling Stress

Stress is a part of living; indeed, the only way to be completely stress-free is to die—and most of us do not wish to be that comfortable. Given that stress is a part of living, appropriately recognizing and coping with its effects is a paramount concern.

Certainly, the kinds of holistic wellness programs discussed above can help to reduce stress. Police agencies need a comprehensive wellness program to assist officers in coping with stress, but if that fails or is absent, an employee assistance program (EAP) should be available to help officers to cope with substance abuse, psychological, or family problems. Counseling for officers to gain the ability to overcome such problems can be contracted by the governmental unit with an outside psychological services agency; or, if out-of-pocket expenses are to be paid at some point by the officer, often a sliding scale fee basis can be arranged based on the officer's income.

In short, it is imperative that officers learn to manage their stress before it causes deep physical and/or emotional harm. One means for doing so is to view the mind as a "mental bucket," with people and events continually "ladling water from out of the bucket." Officers must therefore strive to keep their mental bucket "full"—through hobbies or activities that provide daily relaxation. Exercise, proper nutrition, and positive lifestyle choices (such as not smoking and moderation with alcohol) are also essential for good health.

Summary

This chapter has generally addressed the hazards of police work and how officers may be assisted in achieving wellness and safety, while managing their resulting stress levels. This is a critical area of police leadership, as agencies must formally plan for meeting the wellness needs of their human resources just as they plan for the purchase of capital equipment or for operations. When human resources are neglected, the results may be realized in officers losing their lives, work time, productivity, and public confidence. Too often, police departments neglect or take their personnel for granted, even though people are a department's most important asset.

Leaders also play a key role in recognizing and managing employee stress. They must ensure that supervisors constantly evaluate their subordinates, make judgments about their stress and wellness levels, and, when necessary, encourage officers to seek help. Managers must also provide guidance and support to the supervisors, ensuring that departmental resources are available to combat problems obviating wellness, and that professional assistance is provided to officers whose work has become debilitated as a result of personal or occupational problems. First-line supervisors can work with officers to reduce stress, but managers are the ones who must supply the resources and tools to accomplish the mission.

Discussion Questions

1. What do the data tell us about the hazards of policing as an occupation?

2. How would you define officer wellness?

3. What are the steps for developing an agency wellness campaign?

4. How must police agency culture militate against, and often be changed in order to accommodate, a wellness program?

5. How do police training, policies, and technologies relate to leadership and officer wellness?

6. What are the arguments for state and local agencies having formal Occupational Safety and Health Administration health regulations?

7. How and why have some police agencies developed programs to address problems relating to officer safety and wellness?

8. What are the primary causes of stress in policing? How officers can reduce their stress levels? What are some of the responsibilities of police leaders in assisting supervisors and officers managing their stress levels?

9. How does an employee assistance program function?

Internet Investigations

A Guide to Occupational Health and Safety for Law Enforcement Executives
    www.bja.gov/publications/perf_le_occhealth.pdf
BJA Fact Sheet, Officer Safety Initiatives
    https://www.bja.gov/Publications/OfficerSafety FS.pdf

BJA VALOR Officer Safety Initiative
    https://www.valorforblue.org/Home/About
In Harm's Way: Law Enforcement Suicide Prevention
    http://policesuicide.spcollege.edu
BJA Public Safety Officers' Benefits Program
    http://www.psob.gov

CHAPTER 12

Police Productivity: Improving Performance

STUDENT LEARNING OUTCOMES

After reading this chapter, the student will:

- understand the meaning and importance of police productivity and the elements contained within productivity
- be able to describe the types of planning that occur in a police department
- know the importance of using citizen surveys
- know how CompStat works and how it can benefit a police department
- be knowledgeable of how call management and differential police response affect police patrol operations
- be able to explain the different types of patrol modes and where they are most appropriately used
- be able to describe the implications of the Kansas City patrol study
- know how directed patrol works
- understand when saturation patrols or crackdowns should be used
- be able to describe when stop and frisk is appropriately used
- know how tactical units can be used
- be able to differentiate the preliminary and follow-up investigations
- comprehend how enforcement, education, and engineering are used in the traffic function

KEY TERMS AND CONCEPTS

- Accountability
- Automobile patrol
- Aviation patrol
- Bicycle patrols
- Call management
- Circadian rhythm
- Citizen surveys
- CompStat
- Computer-aided dispatch
- Delayed response
- Directed patrol
- D-runs
- Effectiveness
- Efficiency
- Equity
- Follow-up investigation
- Foot patrol
- Horse patrol
- Kansas City patrol study
- Marine patrol
- Operational control
- Place-based treatment
- Preliminary investigation
- Productivity
- Quotas
- Routine preventive patrol
- Saturation patrols/crackdowns
- Shift rotation
- Strategic plan
- Strategic planning
- Tactical units
- Tactical planning
- Workload

INTRODUCTION

There are several differences between government agencies, including the police, and the private sector. One important difference is that private corporations are evaluated based on their profits and the cost of their stock. If a corporation's profits increase and the value of its stock increases, the corporation is considered successful. Police departments do not make a profit, nor do they have stock. However, it is important to evaluate their effectiveness and hold them accountable for the quality of services provided to their constituents. It can be perplexing as we must consider the productivity and effectiveness of individual officers, as discussed Chapter 5, as well as the productivity of individual units and the department as a whole. Moreover, what criteria should be used in such evaluations?

PRODUCTIVITY MEASUREMENT

What Is Productivity?

Productivity measurement is important because managers and supervisors must make judgments about the relative success of their subordinates and operational units. This generally entails comparing their productivity to some standard. In some cases, officers are compared to one another using averages; in other instances, they are compared to some universal departmental or unit standard. The latter method is inherently superior to the former for two reasons. First, if averages are used, half of the officers, regardless of productivity, will always be below the average. Second, the use of averages means that the work group, rather than leaders and managers, is setting productivity levels. This often occurs with traffic enforcement officers who have work group–established quotas that are lower than the number of citations that can be easily written in a given shift. Regardless of the method used, productivity measures must be established to hold officers, units, and the department accountable.

A host of potential measures exist. Nearly every activity a police officer performs can be measured; this infers that every police unit can be evaluated in terms of performance. It is critical to focus on the correct or informative measures, because officers pattern their behavior and activities using prescribed performance standards and expectations. For example, if a patrol sergeant emphasizes traffic citations or field interviews, officers will tend to write more tickets and possibly neglect other activities. The New York City Police Department emphasized field interrogations for a period of time resulting in massive numbers of these activities by officers.[1] On the other hand, if a sergeant or commander fails to comment about or investigate officers' performance at domestic violence calls, officers may develop the attitude that such calls are unimportant and feel free to deal with them less judiciously. Productivity measurement is important in molding police officer behavior and contributes heavily to overall departmental effectiveness.

Productivity theoretically refers to how well the police provide services to citizens. It is the relationship between the resources used by a police department and the amount or level of services provided.[2] Schermerhorn notes that productivity is a "summary measure of the quantity of work performance, with resource utilization considered."[3] These definitions point to four general concerns when attempting to measure productivity: efficiency, effectiveness, equity, and accountability. We briefly discuss each concern.

Efficiency refers to the accomplishment of a given task with a minimum expenditure of resources. Constituents want to minimize costs while maximizing outputs (desired outcomes such as services, arrests, or stolen property recovered by the police). The various strategies to accomplish a given task must be considered and the ones that not only achieve desired objectives but also do so at the lowest cost should be implemented. For example, should detectives or patrol officers be assigned to teams? How many patrol units should be dispatched to calls? Can the department take some citizen reports by telephone? Do all crimes need to be investigated? Such questions affect a department's efficiency.

The calculation of efficiency measures is no easy task; costs of activities are generally computed by examining the number of personnel, amount of equipment and staff support, and the amount of noncapital supplies (such as gasoline, paper, and electricity consumed by the program). The cost of outputs, on the other hand, is either difficult or impossible to compute. For example, how can we determine how many accidents or deaths were prevented by setting up a drunk-driving check lane? Nonetheless, the police should strive to increase organizational efficiency.

Gaines, Famega, and Bichler provide an example of efficiency. They conducted a study of police responses to burglar alarms and found that in Fontana, California, the department received 8,529 alarms in one year. Of this total, only 22 (.02 percent) were actually burglaries or some other crime, and only one arrest was made as a result of responding to all the alarm calls.[4] It was estimated that average response consumed 16.77 minutes of time per officer, with two officers being dispatched to each call. The average hourly wage of officers was $53.75. Thus, the alarm calls cost the department $256,603 for the year; however, this cost included only patrol officer salaries, and the actual costs are considerably higher if overhead costs such as dispatching, administration, and so forth are considered. Obviously, if the department could reduce its burglar alarm calls, it would result in substantial savings in fiscal and personnel resources.

Managers maximize efficiency through program planning, while supervisors can increase efficiency through proper assignment and supervision. The commander of the criminal investigation unit must examine the volume of reported crimes and then decide how to allocate detectives. These decisions require the commander to ensure that functions or units within the detective division are staffed at the proper level. Too many detectives in an area will result in wasted personnel. On the other hand, too few detectives result in a lowered clearance rate. Once allocation decisions are made, supervisors must ensure that detectives handle cases properly and expediently.

Effectiveness refers to how well the task is performed, regardless of cost, as a result of program activities: Were program goals met? The calculation of measures of effectiveness requires the identification of goals and goal achievement strategies. If objectives were not completely met, how close did the program come to doing so? For example, a police supervisor might decide to implement a problem-solving initiative in an area with low-income housing that had high numbers of calls for service (CFS) during the past six months. A goal might be set to reduce the number of CFS by 25 percent in the next two months. Strategies to achieve this objective might include increased patrol, increased citizen contacts, crime prevention activities, neighborhood cleanups, and problem solving. If officers are given an assignment or dispatched to a call, did they satisfactorily resolve the situation? If officers must repeatedly return to family disturbance calls, it may indicate that they are taking inappropriate measures on the first occasion. Supervisors must use follow-up calls and activities to ensure that officers make every effort possible to adequately manage situations.

Equity refers to the quality of police services delivered to various groups in the community.[5] All citizens' problems should receive the same level of concern. This is accomplished through operational planning. Equity in police services frequently becomes a political focal point. Citizens are concerned with the number of patrol units in their area, the probability of being victimized, and the response time of the police. If police services in their area are perceived to be consistent with those of other areas, citizens are more likely to have a positive image of the police. To a large extent, equity is at the root of police legitimacy and procedural justice problems. For years, the police did little in many minority neighborhoods. Minorities often received fewer or inferior services and viewed this as an inequitable situation.[6] As a result of community policing and problem solving, the police today are attacking crime, drug, and disorder problems in many minority communities. The end result is that more minorities are being stopped and questioned by the police more frequently. This can result in a perception of inequity since minorities are stopped at higher rates than nonminority citizens. On the other hand, if the police continue to allow greater levels of lawlessness in some areas relative to others, equity becomes an issue.

Finally, **accountability** refers to whether resources are used for proper purposes and infers that the police as public servants should provide services that meet public concerns and needs.[7] Moore advises that citizens have a right to demand that their police departments be accountable.[8] Police officers too often see their role as that of "crime fighters" and want to subjugate other responsibilities. Research indicates, however, that the public consistently requests the police to be more involved in peacekeeping and service activities than in law enforcement activities.[9] Police leaders must ensure that officers understand their role in society and meet these citizen expectations.

Traditional Views Relative to Police Productivity

Police leadership historically has been more concerned with efficiency than effectiveness, equity, or accountability. Police managers and supervisors concentrated on the number of activities generated by officers or units (outputs). Such measures include number of citations issued, number of arrests, percentage of cases cleared by arrest, amount of drugs confiscated, number of citizen complaints about police services and conduct, conviction rates, amount of stolen property recovered, and so on. These conventional measures, some of which are collected by most agencies for the FBI's Uniform Crime Reports (UCR), have been used as the primary source of officer and department performance criteria; increases or decreases in these areas have been used to measure productivity. However, they do not indicate that the department, unit, or officers are achieving specified goals and objectives. Police officers may write large numbers of traffic citations, but if they are written at locations where there are few accidents or for violations other than those that contribute to accidents at specific locations, the officers' efforts will not contribute to the objective of reducing the number of traffic accidents. In the same vein, if patrol officers fail to patrol in high-crime areas, patrolling will not have a maximum affect.

This does not mean that managers and supervisors should not monitor traditional measures of productivity. Research indicates that officers vary in their outputs. For example, Walsh examined the arrests for one precinct in New York City and found varying rates of felony arrests across patrol officers. He found that 63 officers did not make a felony arrest during the year; 59 officers had 1 to 8 arrests; 19 officers had 9 to 20 felony arrests; and 15 officers had 25 to 69 felony arrests.[10] These data indicate that some officers were exerting more effort, especially in the area of felony investigations, than other officers. Walsh's data demonstrates the importance of productivity monitoring. Every critical area of police work can be examined similarly. However, activity monitoring does not equate to evaluating the department's response to community problems.

Spelman compared traditional police productivity measures to bean counting.[11] Police managers or supervisors too often focus on the number of activities, rather than what the activities are supposed to accomplish. For example, if the number of arrests increases from one year to the next, does this mean that the department is doing better? Police activities should be directed toward some problem or goal. The police are productive when they solve some problem or accomplish a desired goal. (Note how commanders are now being evaluated in New York City Police Department, as an outgrowth of the city's CompStat strategy, discussed later.)

WHAT IS A PRODUCTIVE POLICE DEPARTMENT TODAY?

A productive police department is engaged in a number of processes that provide a variety of services to its constituents. Obviously, effectiveness, efficiency, equity, and accountability are guiding principles when delivering these services. However, how should a department focus on and interact with a community? The National Institute of Justice identified six attributes of a healthy police department, with *healthy* being operationalized as maximally serving the community.[12]

First, a department knows what it wants to accomplish. It has articulated goals and objectives. This is usually accomplished in a strategic plan as discussed in Chapter 1. This means that the department has scanned the community and identified specific problems and has taken action to deal with them. Police departments must be proactive, especially at the operational level. This equates to the implementation of a variety of strategies and tactics.

Second, a healthy or productive department knows its citizens. What do citizens, citizen groups, and neighborhoods desire from their police? Police departments should serve the legitimate interests of the citizens they serve. This entails understanding citizens' needs and perceptions at the lowest level. Each neighborhood may have its own unique problems, and citizens expect the police to address them. This means that policing is tailored to meet these demands and expectations.

Third, a police department should know its business. That is, it constantly monitors activities to determine if services are increasing, and if so, which services are increasing and where they are allocated. This means examining calls for service, arrests, traffic accidents, crimes, and other activities or services provided by the police. When these indices are monitored by time and geography, a department can better understand current levels of service and future trends.

Fourth, a department must understand the demands of the business. Police departments have limited resources, personnel, and budgets. These resources also include others in the community that provide a support function for police services, such as other agencies and partnerships. A department must understand where and the activities for which these resources are expended. The department must ensure that it maintains the budget so that goals and objectives can be met. It also allows managers to anticipate budgetary needs as service levels increase.

Fifth, a good department knows its people. Police managers and supervisors must know what motivates their subordinates, and develop reward structures that maintain high levels of motivation. Managers and supervisors must ensure that officers are prepared for their job assignments. They must determine whether officers have the correct training and the personality or ability to work in a particular assignment. For example, a highly productive patrol officer may not necessarily be a good investigator. Interests and personality often determine the assignments for which an officer is best suited.

Finally, a productive police department provides its constituents with feedback on police activities and what is occurring in the jurisdiction. If police officials expect citizens to cooperate and provide information and support to the department, they must meet with these groups and explain what the department is doing about their problems. Managers and supervisors should meet with officials from those agencies that work with the department on police-related activities. Most importantly, police managers and supervisors should provide feedback to their subordinates regarding the job that is being done and those goals and objectives that are important.

The above sections described some of the principles that identify a productive police department. The following section examines how productivity has been measured. Traditional methods largely have been inaccurate and represent a more bureaucratic perspective about productivity. Later sections will examine more current methods that attempt to incorporate contemporary principles regarding productivity.

IMPROVING POLICE PRODUCTIVITY THROUGH PLANNING AND PROBLEM SOLVING

Police departments must constantly strive to improve productivity by looking for better ways of providing services to citizens and monitoring expenses. At the same time, departments must be able to better identify problems. Four important innovations have contributed to improved productivity: planning, problem solving, citizen surveys, and CompStat. These innovations are addressed in this section.

If a police agency is to be effective in its productivity, a large percentage of its officers' activities must relate to solving some community problem, reducing crime and disorder, or helping citizens. Police departments have attempted to accomplish this objective through **strategic planning**, discussed briefly in Chapter 1, which is an administrative process that drives agency vision, mission, and goals; it may also be defined as "a systematic, and continuous process of analyzing internal and external conditions in order to make more accurate decisions that effectively deal with problems and issues."[13] Planning, roughly stated, is deciding what the police agency should be doing; it is the linking of current activities to future conditions. It is decision making regarding operational activities based on anticipated contingencies.[14] Planning results in goals and objectives for the department and individual units within the department. Once goals and objectives are identified, activities must be implemented to accomplish them. Activities can be in the form of programs, strategies, and tactics.

As shown in Figure 12-1, top-level administrators monitor and evaluate the environment or community and identify the department's mission and police department goals. This process results in tone and direction for the department. Here, strategies and responsibilities are assigned to individual units in the department. Mid-level managers or unit commanders then break these goals down into unit-level objectives and develop programs to accomplish the objectives. Finally, supervisors are charged with ensuring that officers perform according to operational plans and achieve the desired objectives. They ensure that work is conducted as envisioned. The planning process becomes the link between internal measures or productivity and external needs.

Referring back to the Tucson Police Department's goal of reduce, solve, and prevent crime as discussed in Chapter 1, the department identified three objectives:

1. Establish effective enforcement initiatives
2. Enhance investigative initiatives
3. Engage the community in joint problem-solving and crime prevention activities[15]

Finally, to complete the strategic planning process, each objective is assigned programs and action plans. They consist of statements that describe in more precise language about what is to be accomplished. Each program or action plan is also assigned to a specific unit or commander and given a time line for accomplishment. The action items for the objective Establish Effective Enforcement Initiatives include:

1. Research and implement methods to reduce violent crime
2. Conduct educational outreach campaign
3. Implement the data-driven approaches to crime and traffic safety
4. Develop and implement crime prevention strategies based on targeted operational planning and other data-driven approaches
5. Establish a unit dedicated to metal theft

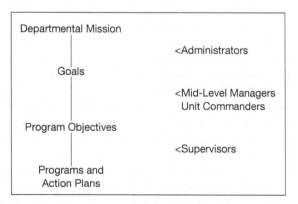

FIGURE 12-1 The Planning Process

6. Modernize and enhance the capability of the division crime response units, expand to two squads per division, each with 8–10 unmarked vehicles, surveillance and recording equipment
7. Establish/renew the crime prevention unit
8. Research and develop a plan to work with victims to reduce repeat victimization
9. Establish a unit dedicated to graffiti
10. Establish a vice unit [16]

Today, many police departments use a detailed strategic planning process where goals are identified and programs or tactics are matched to the goals. The **strategic plan** has a number of advantages. First, it results in leaders identifying priorities or goals. This helps to ensure that the department and individual units remain focused on priorities. Second, it results in **tactical planning** where the police administrative staff consider various operational tactics and select the most promising ones to apply to specific problems. Third, it results in operational control. **Operational control** is where supervisors guide subordinates to ensure that their activities are consistent with tactics or programs to ensure success.

Another similar organizational form that enhances police productivity is community policing. Essentially, community policing focuses on concerns in the community. Problem solving is the primary tactic used in this strategy, with the police department attempting to identify a problem and then developing a plan to solve it. As problems are identified, they are included in the planning process. Each problem is handled differently, depending on the nature of the problem, and the police department works with other units of government or private agencies in deploying workable solutions.

The evaluative criteria employed in the traditional policing model, such as crime rates, clearance rates, and response times, are problematic since they do not advise if the problem is alleviated. Under a community policing philosophy, the department must gauge its success by examining the impact of programs or tactics on the problems themselves; did the program eliminate or reduce the problem irrespective of how arrests were made, calls answered, or some other measure of outputs? A manager may increase patrols in a high-crime area, but if the level of crime is not affected, it is a waste of personnel and new tactics must be enacted.

CITIZEN SURVEYS

Another important method of identifying problems and focusing police efforts is citizen surveys, which add a measure of accountability to police services.[17] Police departments should be responsive to citizen needs and expectations. One method of identifying these needs is **citizen surveys** (discussed briefly in Chapter 10). The use of a citizen survey is a method of collecting information that is of concern to the police from its citizens. They can assist a police leader in identifying problems and resulting programs or action plans. Citizen surveys can provide a great deal of information:

1. Perceptions of crime problems
2. Perceptions of disorder in the area
3. Fear of crime
4. Citizen satisfaction with police services and performance
5. Citizen satisfaction with other related governmental services

As noted, citizen surveys serve a variety of purposes. Figure 12-2 shows the results of a national study of how police departments used survey data.

Figure 12-2 shows that police departments use citizen surveys for a variety of purposes that range from accountability to gathering information about citizen's needs. Primarily, they use them to evaluate the department officers and programs. However, these surveys are also used to identify problems, assign officers, and to provide information to patrol officers. They are helpful in identifying goals for inclusion in the department's strategic plan.

Surveys can be stratified to meet the department's informational needs. For example, the department can perform business or residential surveys. People residing in apartment complexes, especially high-crime complexes, can be surveyed. Finally, information can be collected by neighborhood or area, allowing the police to identify and concentrate on neighborhood problems.

Wells, Horney, and Maguire investigated the utility of citizen feedback on police officers. Unfortunately, they found that feedback has had little effect on officers' performance, attitudes, or activities.[18] The research demonstrates that police managers and supervisors must make a more concerted effort to ensure that survey results and other citizen feedback are incorporated in officers' activities. Managers can accomplish this through enhanced supervision and the incorporation of citizen feedback into policies and directives.

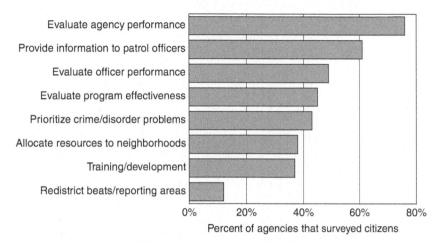

FIGURE 12-2 Uses of citizen survey information by local police departments
Source: M. Hickman and B. Reaves. *Local Police Departments, 2003* (Washington, DC: Office of Justice Programs, 2006): 22.

YOU DECIDE...

You recently were hired as the chief of police. You came from a police department in another state and are unfamiliar with the city's problems. The police department has received a great deal of criticism from the city council because the crime rates have been increasing. The local newspaper has been critical of the department because of a number of excessive force complaints and lawsuits against the city. It is evident that the police department has a number of problems in terms of community relations. You understand that you and the department are in a difficult situation. Consequently, you decide to take the community's temperature by administering a citizen survey in the community. You believe that this will give you insights into the underlying problems that must be addressed.

Questions for Discussion

1. Would you try to survey citizens from all areas of the city or only certain areas? If you only survey certain areas, which areas would you survey?

2. Since you are not familiar with the city, who would you consult with to ensure that you were measuring the correct or important problems in the city?

3. What areas do you think you would attempt to address in your survey?

COMPSTAT AND CRME ANALYSIS

The New York City Police Department (NYPD) pioneered CompStat in the mid-1990s. **CompStat** (also discussed briefly in Chapter 10) is a computerized tool for tracking the most serious crimes and mapping them to determine patterns and trends through crime analysis, and to hold commanders accountable for reducing crime in their areas. CompStat has become a business management tool, being adopted by departments throughout the country. Four principles govern CompStat: timely and accurate intelligence, effective tactics, rapid deployment, and relentless follow-up and assessment, as shown in Figure 12-3. The assessments contain information gathered and mapped electronically; several maps can be overlapped to form layers of statistical information that can be projected onto video screens. A dense pattern of dots, or hot spots, on a map suggests a spree of criminal activity and means someone is going to be held accountable for the causes and solutions.

In essence, CompStat brings accountability to policing.[19] By examining crime maps, managers can identify problems with some level of specificity. Once problems are identified, managers can devise strategies and tactics to counteract them. Because CompStat is a continuous process, it allows managers and supervisors to have a "real-time" view of crime problems. It allows for continuous and instantaneous planning.

The map contained in Figure 12-4 shows the burglaries for a portion of Fontana, California. Some areas have larger numbers of burglaries than other areas. Patrol commanders can use the map to assign officers and deploy different police strategies. A variety of maps can be generated. For example, burglaries for one week, one month, or six months or more can be mapped. Maps showing a variety of crimes can be mapped. For example, a unit commander may be interested in FBI Part I crimes or all violent crimes in an area. The maps serve to (1) assist in devising strategies, (2) focus attention and police resources, and (3) hold commanders and their units accountable for their operations. CompStat has been a significant innovation in law enforcement.

COMPSTAT Process: Crime Control Strategy (Courtesy of the FBI LEB, April 2004)

Crime Reduction Principles

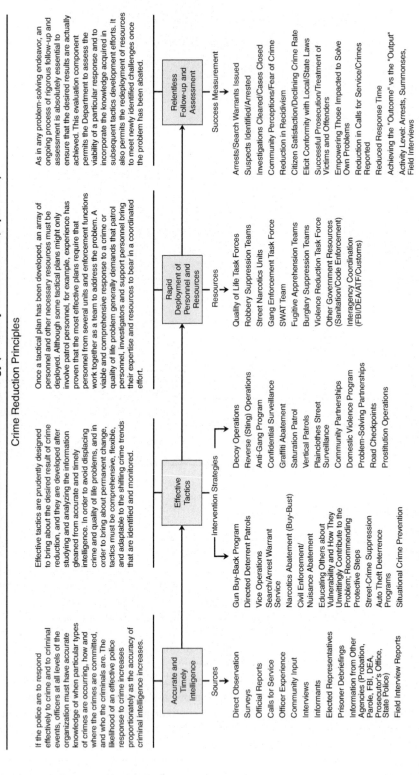

FIGURE 12-3 CompStat Process: Crime Control Strategy
Source: Jon M. Shane, "CompStat Design," "FBI Law Enforcement Bulletin (May 2004): 12–21.

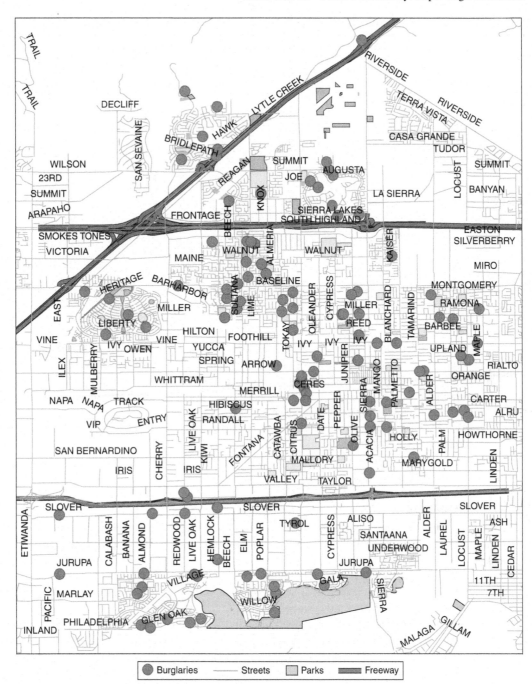

FIGURE 12-4   Crime Map of Fontana, California
Source: Crime map of Fontana. Reproduced with permission from Cite of Fontana

CompStat is partly responsible for contributing to significant improvements in the way many departments control crime and conduct daily business. The core management theories of CompStat, "directing and controlling," have been demonstrated to be effective means for controlling crime. But the CompStat process also has an inherent opportunity for developing leaders, instilling in people a sense of willingness to accomplish the goals of the organization using initiative and innovation.

It is imperative that police leaders and managers understand the basics of this approach—especially given that, unfortunately, today it seems that CompStat is often oversimplified. Many believe that CompStat refers to aggressive or data-driven policing, where police commanders are frequently grilled about crimes in their areas of responsibility—and they are even castigated, transferred, or demoted if they fail to affect crime in their respective command areas. This is the modality originally developed by the New York City Police Department. Police captains, using crime maps, would meet periodically and explain to upper echelon commanders why crime problems had not been eliminated or reduced in their command areas. This results in a greater emphasis

TABLE 12-1 Analytic Computerized Functions in Police Departments by Size of Department

Population served	Percent of departments using computers for—				
	Intelligence gathering	Crime analysis	Analysis of community problems	Crime mapping	Hotspot Identification
All sizes	40%	38%	28%	27%	13%
1,000,000 or more	85%	100%	77%	100%	92%
500,000–999,999	90	100	81	100	100
250,000–499,999	93	100	80	100	80
100,000–249,999	82	96	75	94	66
50,000–99,999	72	88	70	82	56
25,000–49,999	63	69	52	60	31
10,000–24,999	49	53	43	41	19
2,500–9,999	42	37	27	23	9
Under 2,500	26	21	14	11	5

Source: B. Reaves. *Local Police Departments, 2007* (Washington, DC: Bureau of Justice Statistics, 2010): 22.

on law enforcement. Bond and Braga advise that this management system is more likely to generate reactive police responses as opposed to proactive or crime prevention responses.[20] CompStat is also counterproductive in improving community relationships as officers must concentrate on crime problems.[21]

Although originally CompStat was designed to hold police commanders accountable for problems in their respective areas, today, CompStat is more of a general term encompassing a number of crime analysis functions. Table 12-1 shows the degree to which police departments are using CompStat-like programming.

Although some departments may still use CompStat solely for the purpose of holding commanders accountable, CompStat has expanded in some departments to include a variety of other computerized functions under the rubric of crime analysis, as shown in Table 12-1.

Crime Analysis

Crime analysis generates weekly crime activity reports for unit commanders, especially patrol commanders. Crime data are readily available, offering up-to-date information that is then compared at citywide, patrol, and precinct levels. The role of commanders has changed under crime analysis: they stop simply responding to crime, and begin proactively thinking about ways to deal with it in terms of suppression, intervention, and prevention. Commanders consider what tactics they can deploy to address crime patterns, what resources they have and need, and with whom they can collaborate.

Over time, crime analysis has evolved to include other data: census demographics, arrest and summons activity, average response time, domestic violence incidents, unfounded radio runs, personnel absences, and even citizen complaints and charges of officer misconduct. Many scholars and practitioners believe that crime analysis has played a prominent role in the significant crime reductions seen across the nation.

FOCUS ON: ST. LOUIS DIRECTED PATROL AND SELF-INITIATED ENFORCEMENT IN HOT SPOTS

The St. Louis Police Department was experiencing a substantial firearm violence and robberies in several areas in the city. The department's crime analysis unit identified the hot spots where the violence was occurring. The department decided to implement directed patrols in these areas. Officers who were assigned to perform directed patrols were instructed to drive slowly though the hot spot areas and to engage in self-initiated contacts such as arrests, pedestrian checks, occupied vehicle checks, unoccupied vehicle checks, foot patrols, and problem solving. Essentially, patrol and citizen contacts were enhanced. The patrols were deployed from 3:00 p.m. until 7:00 a.m. when the most firearms-related crimes occurred. The self-initiated activities resulted in a reduction in the number of firearm assault rates. The self-initiated activities, however, did not affect the robbery rate. The increased patrols did not have an impact on crime.

The St. Louis experience demonstrates that reducing crime is a complex matter. Some strategies are effective for some crimes, but not others. It also shows that police departments often must deploy a variety of activities with each focusing on a different set of crimes to be effective. It also demonstrates that police departments must evaluate their strategies and tactics to ensure that they work. Police departments too often implement tactics and assume they work when in fact they do not.

Source: Based on National Institute of Justice, "Program Profile: Directed Patrol and Self-Initiated Enforcement in Hot Spots (St. Louis, Missouri" https://www.crimesolutions.gov /ProgramDetails.aspx?ID=482.

OPERATONAL PRODUCTIVITY

The previous sections examined productivity in general. The following sections focus on police operations in terms of refining tactics and operations to be more effective and efficient. The key to enhanced productivity can be found in a department's operational units. Operational units contain the largest number of officers and are responsible for the majority of police activities. Improvements in police operations can substantially increase productivity.

Resource Allocation

Governments authorize police departments a number of police officers. For example, the San Francisco Police Department has 2,313 police officers.[22] This will change over time as the city council authorizes additional officers, and during negative economic times, the city council may freeze hiring for budgetary reasons. Larger police departments seldom have their authorized strength because of officer turnover, retirements, resignations, or terminations. They constantly hire and train officers.

Police leaders have limited resources. It appears that San Francisco has a large number of police officers, but the department is responsible for a city of approximately 850,000. Most police departments have a limited number of officers relative to the population they serve. Police chiefs and their management staff must allocate officers to the various units within the department. This is a complicated process since unit commanders are constantly clamoring for additional officers.

Allocation decisions should be based on workload. **Workload** is the amount of activities and time spent on those activities. Patrol officers answer numerous calls for service; detectives investigate criminal cases; and training staff provide training to a number of officers. Additionally, all officers have administrative duties such as paperwork, appearing in court, and meetings. Large and medium-sized police departments have computerized systems that identify the amount of time each activity consumes. For example, departments can determine the average amount of time spent on answering calls for service, investigating crimes such as homicide, sexual assault, and burglaries or investigating traffic crashes. A department then can multiply the number of activities and the time for each activity to calculate the number of officers assigned to each unit. This is not absolute, but it provides the best estimate of how to allocate officers. Workload should be continuously monitored to ensure that officers are allocated to enhance efficiency and effectiveness.

Patrol Operations

Large jurisdictions develop their patrol operations into precincts or districts and patrol beats. Figure 12-5 shows a map of the Phoenix Police Department's Mountain View Precinct. The Mountain View Precinct is one of seven precincts in Phoenix. The precinct is also divided into three squads consisting of 17 patrol beats. In constructing the beat maps, the police department attempted to have an equal amount of workload in each of the 17 beats.

Call Management and Prioritizing Police Calls for Service

Call management is a process for screening and prioritizing calls for service (CFS). Today most police agencies have **computer-aided dispatch (CAD)** systems that are capable of prioritizing calls by their importance when received by the department. Obviously, more dangerous and in-progress calls such as robberies and assaults would receive the highest priority and an immediate response from patrol units, while a general request for information may bring a delayed response. Police departments have clearly established dispatch protocols that determine the priority of call responses, such as the following:

- *Priority 1:* Danger to life and/or property is imminent, or a crime of a serious nature is in progress. Examples include an armed robbery in progress, a shooting with the suspect on the scene, a major accident, and so on.

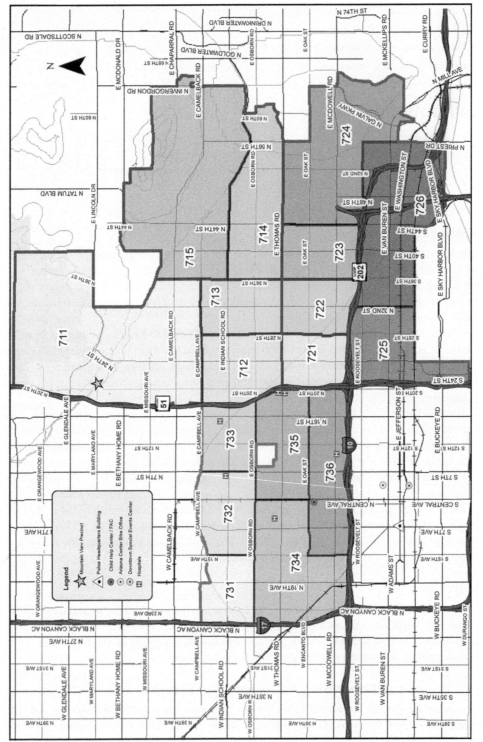

FIGURE 12-5 Beat Configuration for the Phoenix Police Department's Mountain View Precinct

Source: Mountain View Precinct; used with permission from Phoenix Police Department.

- *Priority 2:* Threat to a person or property is possible or a breach of the peace is occurring. Examples include a loud argument or verbal disturbance, an unruly shoplifter in the custody of store security, loud music or party, and so on.

- *Priority 3:* No threat to life or to property exists, and a delay in response would not cause undue inconvenience to the citizen. Examples include theft of property that occurred days ago, a request for a house watch, a dead animal in the road, and so on.

Oftentimes, the volume of CFS will exceed the number of personnel who are available to respond. In this case, police agencies are forced to hold the calls and delay their response. Policies generally will guide the amount of time in which a call may be delayed. For example, Priority 1 calls may require an immediate response in all cases, Priority 2 calls can be held for 15 minutes, and Priority 3 can be held for 30 minutes. When a pending call cannot be assigned to an officer within the established time limit, it is usually the responsibility of the dispatcher to notify a field supervisor or watch commander. The supervisor may need to direct communications to relieve an officer from a nonessential activity, such as a less serious call, or to hold the call for the next available officer. Police managers should monitor CFS and ensure that the priority system is working. If CFS become backlogged during certain times or days, the patrol commander should consider reallocating officers to ensure that high-priority calls are not being neglected for an appreciable amount of time.

As noted, police departments receive a large volume and variety of CFS. The Sacramento Police Department, a medium-sized agency with 639 sworn officers, received about 400,000 calls in 2015, and about 230,000 required an officer to respond. The top five types of calls received by the department were:[23]

1. Incomplete call (where the caller hung up or did not respond)
2. Disturbance call (a fight or argument)
3. All units broadcast (information provided to all officers)
4. Welfare check (officer dispatched to check on a sick or injured person)
5. Suspicious person or circumstances (citizen reporting something suspicious)

Calls for service, although a driving force in police patrol, is not the only activity to which officers must attend. For example, Sacramento police officers responded to 231,592 CFS in 2015. Additionally, the officers initiated 115,697 calls. That is, while patrolling they intervened in 115,697 incidents that required a police presence.[24] Officers while on patrol often see situations that they investigate. When allocating patrol officers, managers must ensure that officers have an adequate amount of patrol time where they can observe activities on their beats.

Differential Police Response

A number of alternatives are available to reduce officer workload and increase productivity, producing more time for officers to perform other activities. They have been developed and tested by the National Institute of Justice, and they include telephone report units, delayed mobile response (stacking calls, setting appointments),

---

FOCUS ON: 911 CALLS AND PRIORITIZATION

Handling CFS is a major responsibility of police departments. When people call the police, even for the most trivial matter, they expect the police to respond. Some cities have more difficulties than others when responding to CFS. One report from Detroit during the city's bankruptcy found that in one case where a citizen called the police to report a burglary, it took officers four hours to respond. A study of the city's response times showed that their response time to nonemergency calls was 56 minutes. However, mystifying was that the response time to emergency calls was 58 minutes. This demonstrated that the department was having patrol allocation problems or call prioritization problems. A number of departments do much better. New York will respond to a nonemergency call in 22 minutes and about half that time for emergency calls. Dallas had a response time of 22 minutes for nonemergency calls and less than nine minutes for emergency calls.

There is a variety of problems that can affect response time, including poor patrol allocation, shortages of officers, ineffective call prioritization system, a lack of field supervision and leadership, and so on. Police leaders and patrol managers should constantly monitor response times for problems and develop solutions to these problems.

Source: Based on The Economist (12/10/15) http://www.economist .com/blogs/democracyinamerica/2015/12/police-response-times.

walk-in reports, and use of non-sworn personnel in lieu of patrol officers (such as civilian evidence technicians, animal control officers, community service specialists). Each is discussed briefly next.

TELEPHONE REPORTING

One of the most effective call alternative strategies for relieving officer workload is the telephone report unit (TRU). Reports are handled over the telephone rather than by a patrol officer dispatched to the scene. TRUs provide several advantages for police agencies and the public. For example, a Priority 3 call (discussed earlier) can take 45 to 60 minutes for an officer to respond to, while a telephone report can be handled in 10 to 15 minutes and at the convenience of the caller. A telephone reporting unit may handle as much as 25 to 50 percent of an agency's non-investigative reports. This accounts for a considerable amount of the workload and frees officers in the field to engage more in community problem solving.

Evaluations of this approach have consistently shown it to be efficient and without a loss in citizen satisfaction. In addition to the volume of work that can be handled by TRUs, experience has shown that they save enormous amounts of time with respect to completion of a report, and also save money on vehicle maintenance costs. They also afford sworn officers more time for self-initiated activities and arrests.[25]

DELAYED RESPONSE

Delayed response means that the presence of a police officer is required at the scene, but the incident is sufficiently minor in nature that a rapid dispatch is not necessary. Such instances include "cold" larcenies and burglaries, unoccupied suspicious vehicle calls, and vandalism calls. The trend today is to develop formal delayed-response strategies that specify the types of calls that can be delayed, and for how long. Factors to be considered are the seriousness of the call, presence or absence of injuries, and amount of damage. Most departments' policies state a maximum delay time, such as 30 or 45 minutes, after which the closest available unit is assigned to the call.[26]

Although the delayed response does not directly reduce officer workload, it does help make the existing workload more manageable. It increases the likelihood that officers will receive calls in their area of assignment, resulting in fewer cross-beat dispatches, and prevents officers from being interrupted while on another assignment (such as community policing activities).

The call taker must inform the citizen that an officer will not arrive immediately; studies have found that once the call taker informs the citizen of the expected police arrival time, citizen satisfaction is not adversely affected by the delay.[27] Citizens understand that police officers must answer more important calls first.

WALK-IN/MAIL-IN/WEB REPORTING

Many police agencies also have instituted programs that encourage citizens to come to the nearest police facility at their convenience to file a report. The recent trend by police agencies to decentralize patrol operations through various community policing initiatives has resulted in an increase in neighborhood police mini-stations. These provide an excellent and convenient place for citizens to complete walk-in reports or to pick up or deliver reporting packages.

Most recently, agencies are utilizing their Web sites to allow Internet reporting of certain crimes. This is convenient to large numbers of citizens since Internet services are now in many homes and businesses. If a department uses Internet reporting, it should ensure that the electronic reporting form is understandable and easy for citizens to complete.

USE OF NON-SWORN PERSONNEL

The use of volunteer and non-sworn personnel to handle non-emergency CFS has gained considerable popularity over the years. Many agencies utilize volunteers who have been trained in citizen police academies, reserve police academies, and senior volunteer programs to handle some of the workload traditionally handled by uniformed officers. This may include parking control, directing traffic, taking minor offense reports, providing information to the public, and so on.

Another concept used by many police agencies to reduce officer workload is the Community Service Officer (CSO) program, using non-sworn personnel in the field and to respond to CFS, thus eliminating the requirement for an officer's presence. A CSO may engage in traffic accident investigations, take vandalism reports, perform parking enforcement, conduct basic crime scene investigations and collect evidence, dust for fingerprints, and perform other related duties. In some agencies, CSOs also staff mini-stations to handle telephone and mail-in reporting requests, again eliminating the need for an officer at these locations.

The civilianization of police agencies is another area that should be explored. It makes little sense to assign a fully trained and qualified police officer to administrative or support duties when those responsibilities can be better handled by non-sworn personnel. Some of the areas being civilianized in police agencies include dispatching, research and planning, crime analysis, finance, parking enforcement, custody, technical/computer support, and animal control.

Police departments are using a variety of these differential police responses. For example, Sacramento police officers in 2015 took 39,239 reports at the scene, while taking another 20,007 online. The department received another 8,138 reports by phone or where citizens filed the reports at a police station.[28] Thus, about 42 percent of the reports were taken through a differential response procedure. Police leaders and managers should carefully review how their departments and units respond to CFS and maximize differential response procedures. These procedures can free up officers for other assignments.

PATROL UNITS

Patrol is the backbone of a police department. Patrol officers respond to CFS, and the patrol function is the most visible aspect of any police department. Patrol essentially is the face of the department. A department's patrol unit contains the largest number of officers, with between 55 and 95 percent of all sworn officers with smaller departments having a larger percentage of officers assigned to patrol. Patrol officers routinely have a number of objectives, including:

- Answer CFS
- Enforce laws
- Maintain order
- Assist citizens
- Apprehend offenders
- Investigate crimes
- Coordinate with other police units

Police officer on patrol
Source: Michael Matthews/Alamy Stock Photo

PATROL SHIFTS

Police departments, except for the smallest, are responsible for providing 24-hour coverage, resulting in departments deploying shifts of officers over time (specialization by geography). The most common patrol shifts are:

- 5 X 8 hour shifts
- 4 X 10 hour shifts
- 3 X 12 hour shifts

The most common is where officers work 5 days a week for 8 hours each day, followed by 12-hour shifts and then 10-hour shifts.[29] Historically, the eight-hour shift dominated shift design. Departments began to implement 10-hour shifts in the 1980s. The 10-hour shift provided several advantages. First, it allowed for overlapping shifts so departments could deploy more officers during peak crime and CFS periods. Second, departments had time to conduct roll calls without paying overtime. Eight-hour shifts did not allow time for roll call except for overtime. Third, it allowed departments to establish short training programs that did not require officers to lose a shift or require overtime payment. A number of police unions helped to institute 12-hour shifts through collective bargaining. Officers saw three-day work weeks as a desirable benefit.

Research of the length of shifts showed that officers working 10-hour shifts got more sleep as compared to officers working the other two types of shifts. Officers working 12-hour shifts experienced more sleepiness and lower levels of alertness. Officers working eight-hour shifts worked more overtime. Since the productivity associated with each shift was about the same, it appears that the four 10-hour shifts likely have the greatest advantages for the department and officers.[30]

Shift rotation is another factor when designing patrol shifts. However, most departments use permanent shifts (72 percent).[31] Departments that rotate shifts do so periodically, for example, every two weeks, monthly, or quarterly. This allows officers to be off duty at different times. A problem with rotating shifts is that it interrupts officers' circadian rhythm. The **circadian rhythm** is the body's biological clock, and when interrupted can cause stress, tiredness, and a lack of alertness. When officers rotate shifts, it likely takes several days for officers' circadian rhythm to adjust. When departments rotate shifts, they should do so infrequently so that officers do not have to adjust and readjust frequently.

METHODS OF PATROL

Police departments have a variety of methods by which to patrol, including automobile, bicycle, horse, marine, and aviation patrol. **Automobile patrol** is the most common form of patrol. It is efficient as it allows officers to cover larger geographical areas and respond more quickly to CFS. It also allows officers to carry more equipment that may be needed when responding to a call, such as weapons and report forms. Many departments have mobile computer terminals in their cars, allowing officers immediate access to a variety of data. The random nature of patrolling may also prevent some crimes, and it allows officers to observe situations that require police intervention.

Bicycle patrols became popular in the 1980s as a way of implementing community policing; police officers could more easily meet and interact with citizens. Bicycle patrols are more expensive than automobile patrols since they cover less geographical area, and consequently they became less popular. However, a number of cities have retained bicycle patrols, especially in areas that are heavily populated with pedestrians, especially tourists. For example, a city may use bicycles in a popular historical area or a tourist destination. Bicycles allow for increased interaction with people, at the same time allowing for increased mobility. They help to reduce crime and serve to enhance public relations.

Many of our larger cities are adjacent to rivers and lakes requiring some form of marine patrols. **Marine patrols** are used to reduce crime on waterfronts, especially smuggling. Large amounts of drugs are smuggled into our cities by water. Marine patrols also enforce marine safety laws to enhance public safety. They are also used sometimes to search for missing persons or drowning victims. Marine patrols are fairly expensive and police managers should limit their use. Police managers should match the number of marine patrols with the department's needs.

A number of departments use horse patrols. **Horse patrols** are especially effective in large rugged areas such as parks. They are an effective public relations tool and many citizens take photos with the horses, and officers often allow children to sit on the horse with them. However, horse patrols are expensive in terms of purchasing, stabling, caring, and transporting them. Horse patrols should only be used when there is a significant need.

Mounted police officers can serve a number of functions.
Source: Marmaduke St. John/Alamy Stock Photo

Aviation patrol is the use of fixed-wing aircraft, helicopters, or drones to perform police tasks. They perform a number of functions. Many jurisdictions use them when searching for suspects or vehicles. Air patrols can assist in locating them. A number of jurisdictions use aviation patrols to search for lost people. Hikers sometimes get lost, especially in rugged mountainous areas, and aircraft can search large geographical areas. Maintaining a fleet of airplanes or helicopters can cost in the millions of dollars, which make them prohibitive for many departments. A number of departments are utilizing drones in place of aircraft. Drones are relatively inexpensive and easy to operate. Citizens in some jurisdictions have complained when departments began to deploy drones for fear of violating privacy and spying on citizens. However, in reality, drones are no more intrusive as aircraft.

A number of departments utilize **foot patrols**, where officers walk a beat. Foot patrols were the primary mode of patrolling before the widespread use of automobile patrols. Foot patrols again became popular as a method to communicate with citizens, and it was seen as a vital part of community policing. In 1978, the Flint, Michigan, Police Department implemented foot patrols as did the Newark, New Jersey, Police Department a few years later. Foot patrols in Flint and Newark did not have an impact on crime, but they did increase citizens' perceptions of safety.[32] Familiarity with neighborhood police officers made citizens feel better about crime and the police.

Today, a number of departments deploy foot patrols in business districts and areas frequented by tourists. They provide feelings of safety, prevent crimes, and serve a public relations function. Several departments have used foot patrols to counter crime and disorder in certain high-crime areas, including New York City,[33] Newark,[34] and Philadelphia.[35] In all three cases, the departments used place-based treatments. **Place-based treatments** are where a department identifies a high-crime area and deploys strategies to deal with the specific crime problem in the area. Foot patrols were the primary treatments in the three cities, and crime was reduced in all three cities. In some cases, drug trafficking and related violence was the target, while in other cases violent crime was the target of the intervention. In some cases, foot patrols are supplemented with automobile patrols, gang unit officers, or detectives. There is a body of research demonstrating that police managers must identify crime problems and think outside the box and fashion nontraditional responses to them. Options are discussed in more detail in the following section.

PATROL STRATEGIES

This section describes several patrol strategies that are available to police commanders. Given that police departments often face high-crime areas and hot spots of crime, commanders need to consider alternative patrol arrangements to affect crime and disorder. It is important to match patrol responses with the problems at hand.

Routine Preventive Patrol

The primary mode of patrol is routine preventive patrol. **Routine preventive patrol** is where patrol officers are assigned to geographical beats across the department's jurisdiction, and they patrol randomly in the beat areas. Historically, police managers believed that routine preventive patrol was the most effective way to prevent crime. Would-be offenders would see the police and be deterred from committing a crime, and if they were not deterred, patrol officers were in a position to observe the crime and make an arrest.

From 1972 through 1973, researchers investigated the impact of patrol in the **Kansas City patrol study**. The researchers increased patrol in some areas, kept it the same in other areas, and removed it altogether (except for emergencies) in some areas. In areas where patrols were removed, officers from other areas were dispatched to answer CFS. The researchers found that crime did not substantially change in the three experimental areas. They concluded that routine preventive patrols were not effective in dealing with crime or citizens' perceptions of crime.[36] The researchers did not advocate that patrol be eliminated. They saw patrol as a way to disperse officers so that they could respond more rapidly to CFS. In other words, police managers needed to consider other more productive strategies to supplement routine preventive patrol when dealing with crime problems.

Directed Patrol

Directed patrol is placing additional officers in areas where there are concentrations of crime or disorder. These hot spots can be analyzed to determine the nature of the offenses and possibly the cause. Additional officers can then be assigned or directed to those specific areas. Sherman and Weisburd researched directed patrols and found that increasing officers in high-crime areas could reduce crime.[37] Research has shown that directed patrols can have an impact on specific offenses or crime problems, drug-dealing locations,[38] crack houses,[39] armed robberies,[40] and violent crime.[41] This research demonstrates that police departments can use additional officers to affect crime problems in specific locations.

A variation on directed patrol is directed patrol runs or D-runs. **D-runs** are where officers are assigned to a specific location for a specified period of time.[42] For example, an officer could be assigned to go to a specific intersection and remain there during a time period when there generally is a high volume of traffic crashes. The officer's presence likely will reduce the incidence of accidents. D-runs can be used to deter crime. For example, if an area experiences a high volume of street crimes during a period of time, officers can be dispatched to the area during the crime times. D-runs are effective in problem areas when the problems occur at specific times.

Saturation Patrols or Crackdowns

Saturation patrols or **crackdowns** are where large numbers of police officers are temporarily assigned to a high-crime area. Here, police officers observe for violations and make arrests. In some cases, especially high-crime and disorder areas, the police make as many arrests as possible to gain control over the area. The additional police officers and the arrests have a deterrent effect on crime and disorder in the area.[43] For example, the police in Indianapolis used high-volume traffic stops, enforcement, and field interviews in drug market areas to reduce drug trafficking and crime. The increased enforcement resulted in a decrease in auto thefts and burglaries.[44] Similarly, the Houston Police Department flooded the seven highest crime areas with 655 officers and used zero-tolerance policing, high-visibility patrol, and problem solving to attack crime problems. Their efforts resulted in a reduction in Part I crimes.[45]

Saturation patrol and crackdowns have their problems. Scott analyzed a number of them and found that they had only a short-term effect.[46] They are difficult to sustain since they require large numbers of officers. However, Sherman noted that saturation patrols and crackdowns are an effective way of bringing order to an area that is plagued by crime and disorder. He advised that intermittent crackdowns in a high-crime area can sustain reductions in crime and disorder.[47] Thus, saturation patrols and crackdowns are viable police tactics in high-crime areas, especially when specific problems are the focal point.

Stop and Frisk

The U.S. Supreme Court gave the police the authority to stop and frisk suspicious persons in *Terry v. Ohio*.[48] Essentially, when a police officer questions a suspicious person, the officer has the right to pat that person down for weapons if the officer has a reasonable suspicion that the person might be armed with a weapon. The Court determined that police officers should have the ability to protect themselves when confronting suspects.

The New York City Police Department took stop and frisk further. In 2003, the department conducted 160,851, such activities, and by 2010, the number had grown to about 600,000.[49] Police officers were encouraged to conduct many stops and frisks, and many of them appeared to be indiscriminate. It is not clear if the department had a quota system in place. Minorities were overrepresented in the stops, which led to claims of racial profiling.

Regardless, Weisburd and his colleagues examined crime in New York City and found that crime had declined during the period of increased stops and frisks even though the number of police officers had also declined. They could not attribute the decline to the stops and frisks since other factors may have contributed to the crime declines. Nonetheless, stop and frisk may be a viable tool to affect crime rates.

This section has described a number of strategies that police departments can use to affect crime and disorder. What is important is that police managers must analyze their crime problems and deploy strategies that more effectively reduce crime and disorder.

SPECIALIZED TACTICAL UNITS

Many larger departments have specialized tactical units that are assigned to patrol. These units are not to be confused with special weapons and tactics units (SWAT). SWAT teams respond to special situations such as hostage, barricaded persons, dangerous crimes in progress, and the service of warrants for criminals with a history of violence. **Specialized tactical units** are designed to provide additional resources that can be used to attack specific crime or disorder problems or hot spots of activity. They are also designed to provide patrol commanders with a measure of flexibility. They can be deployed in a variety of ways, undercover, saturation patrols, foot patrols, stakeouts, and so on. Their methods can be molded to fit the needs of the situation.

Larger and middle-sized police departments use crime analysis to identify crime problems and trends. These units can identify areas with entrenched or emerging crime problems. Patrol commanders often deploy officers across beats and, consequently, often do not have the resources to concentrate on these types of problems. A specialized tactical unit provides patrol commanders with flexibility—they can assign officers in this unit or squad to address these problems. For example, if the department receives several reports of drunkenness, fights, and disorders in an area or at a particular location, the commander can deploy officers from a specialized tactical unit to deal with the problem. In this case, officers would saturate the area and make a number of arrests. This could occur repeatedly until the problem is abated. Sometimes specialized tactical officers attempt to arrest repeat offenders. Departments can identify those offenders who committed greater numbers of crimes, and specialized tactical officers have the time and flexibility to attempt to find and arrest them. A specialized patrol unit or squad becomes a supplemental force that can be used for problem solving or other community policing activities. Commanders can constantly review crime statistics and identify new targets for the unit.

CRIMINAL INVESTIGATION UNITS

Nationally, 10–15 percent of a department's sworn personnel are assigned to a detective unit. In larger departments, investigations are the responsibility of detectives who are assigned full-time to this role. In smaller agencies, patrol officers are responsible for conducting investigations due to the limited number of employees and workload of the department. Some departments divide responsibility for investigations between patrol and detective units whereby patrol units investigate minor offenses or, in some cases, the majority of all offenses.

The investigative workload in our nation's largest cities requires specialization within the detective unit. The most common detective specializations are "crimes against property" units and "crimes against persons" units. Even more specialization frequently occurs within these two broadly defined units; for example, common units found in crimes against persons units include homicide, sex crimes, domestic

---

YOU DECIDE...

You have been promoted to captain and placed in charge of the 8:00 p.m. until 4:00 a.m. patrol watch. You are in charge of all patrol activities for the city. You have 60 officers in your command, including 12 that are assigned to a tactical squad. You have reviewed the patrol beats and found that they are designed so that each beat contains about the same amount of workload. There has been a rash of homicides in the two gang areas in the city, and violent crime has been increasing in several other areas as well. The chief has asked that you use your tactical squad to tamp down the crime problems.

Questions for Discussion

1. How would you go about identifying the areas or hot spots of crime that need addressing?

2. Would you attempt to enlist the service of any other units in the department or personnel from other city departments? If so, who would you attempt to work with and what would you want them to do?

3. Would you make any changes to your patrol officer allocation and distribution?

4. How would you deploy your tactical squad?

Law Enforcement Resource Center
Intelligence Unit
LERC Assistant Division Commander
    Crime Gun Intelligence Group
    Perpetrator Information Center
    Real Time Crime Center
Violent Crimes Division
Homicide Unit
    Homicide Squads
    Assault Squad
Robbery Unit
    Robbery Section
    Economic Crimes Section
    Generalist Squad
Special Victims Unit
    Crimes Against Children Section
    Domestic Violence Section
    Missing Person/Cold Case Section
    Sex Crimes Section
Violent Crimes Enforcement Division
Violent Crimes Investigative Unit
    Violent Crimes Intelligence Section
    Gang Squad
    Illegal Firearms Squad
    Violent Crimes Investigative Squad
Violent Crimes Enforcement Unit
    Violent Crimes Enforcement Squad
    Fugitive Apprehension Section
    Federal Grant (Byrne Grant)
Narcotics & Vice Division
High Intensity Drug Trafficking Area/Investigative Support Center
Drug Enforcement Unit
    Drug Enforcement Unit—Interdiction
    Drug Enforcement Unit—Undercover Squad
    Career Criminal Squad
    Drug Enforcement Unit—Metro Meth Section
    Administrative Enforcement Squad
Street Crimes Unit
    Undercover Squad
    Tactical Enforcement Squad
    Vice Section
    Cyber Crimes
    Administrative Enforcement Squad

FIGURE 12-6 Organization of the Kansas City Police Department's Investigations Bureau

violence, and crimes against children. Burglary, robbery, and auto theft are common crimes against property units. Figure 12-6 provides a listing of the organization of the Kansas City Police Department's (KCPD) Investigations Bureau.[50]

The KCPD has four primary investigative divisions, and each division contains several units and there are squads within each of the units. The department has about 1,400 officers and a substantial investigative workload. Upon examining the KCPD's investigative organization, the department has a large number of units that have specific responsibilities. When deciding to create a unit two factors have to be considered. First, is there a volume of criminal activity that justifies the unit? If not, the function should be folded into another unit. Second, do detectives clear an adequate number of cases to justify the personnel or the unit? These units need to be productive.

Regardless of agency size or organizational structure, part of the criminal investigation responsibility will always be assumed by patrol. In some cases, patrol officers will make an arrest at the scene, and if they do not, the case is forwarded to detectives for a follow-up investigation. Their activities are particularly critical during the initial or preliminary investigation of a crime and provide a basis for the follow-up investigation.

Preliminary Investigation

In terms of the **preliminary investigation**, the first officers responding to crimes will be patrol officers. These officers immediately establish control of the scene and detain any suspects who remained on the scene. They, as part of the preliminary investigation, complete several tasks including:

- Determine if additional assistance will be necessary and may request assistance from detectives, arson investigators, the coroner, or evidence technicians.
- Summon medical assistance render first aid to any injured parties.
- Control access to the area to prevent the destruction of evidence.

The order in which these activities are performed will vary and should be prioritized on the basis of danger to the officer or others present at the scene followed by taking the steps necessary to prevent the loss of evidence. Once the scene has been secured, the officers will interview victims and witnesses.

The preliminary investigation is crucial to the successful solution and prosecution of a crime. In fact, patrol officers make the majority of the felony arrests for any given police department. Mistakes made during the preliminary investigation can almost never be rectified, particularly those dealing with the collection of physical evidence. Once patrol officers complete the preliminary investigation, they prepare a report documenting their actions and the evidence and information that were collected. It is important that managers review the preliminary investigative reports to ensure that all steps were followed and documented. Patrol officers too often provide abbreviated information. Reviews can provide officers training and ensure quality.

At the conclusion of the preliminary investigation, a decision must be made whether to assign the case for a follow-up investigation. When detectives are assigned cases, they are one of three types: (1) *walk-throughs*, when the suspect has been identified and apprehended; (2) *where-are-theys*, when the suspect has been identified but officers have been unable to make an apprehension; and (3) *whodunits*, when the preliminary investigation did not result in identification of the perpetrator.[51] The type of case will dictate the amount of effort exerted by the detective and the types of investigative actions taken. Walk-throughs and where-are-theys will receive considerably more attention than whodunits.

Follow-Up Investigation

The **follow-up investigation** will be initiated when the case is turned over to the detective unit. If a suspect has already been arrested, the detective's primary responsibility is to process the materials and evidence gathered so the prosecutor can file charges and present the case in court. In some cases, the detective will further investigate in an effort to develop a stronger case.

Homicide detective processing case information
Source: Mikael Karlsson/Alamy Stock Photo

Obviously, the most difficult cases are those in which the investigator must identify the suspect. Investigators sometimes retrace the steps already completed to ensure that no evidence was missed. An attempt will be made to locate additional witnesses by contacting everyone in the area where the crime occurred. *Modus operandi* files (files that describe how known suspects commit specific crimes) can be examined to learn if any similar crimes have been reported in the past. Informants can be interviewed in the hope that they will be able to provide information about the crime. Attempts will be made to trace stolen property or vehicles involved in the crime.

It is important to understand how cases are solved and the interplay among detectives, evidence, and investigative activities. The RAND Corporation examined the investigative practices in 153 large police departments. The researchers found that detectives did not generally solve cases by hard work, inspiration, or science but instead focused on and solved easy cases. Only about 3 percent of solved cases were solved by detectives exerting extraordinary investigative effort.[52] Subsequent examinations of how evidence affects case outcomes have substantiated these findings with only a few exceptions, such as when cases are solved as a result of specific suspect information provided by victims and witnesses. Other information has little impact on whether a case is solved.[53]

Eck attempted to refine our understanding of the investigative process and identified three categories of cases facing investigators: (1) weak cases that cannot be solved regardless of investigative effort (unsolvable cases), (2) cases with moderate levels of evidence that can be solved with considerable investigative effort (solvable cases), and (3) cases with strong evidence that can be solved with minimum effort (already solved cases).[54] Eck found that cases within the "already solved" category did not require additional investigative effort or time, and the "unsolvable cases" should not be investigated because it would be a wasted effort. Eck concluded that detectives should be assigned the "solvable cases." Such cases have the potential to be solved with additional effort. Investigative supervisors and managers must ensure that effective case screening techniques are used so that investigations can result in the maximum number of cases cleared.

Criminal investigations are processes beginning with the early stages of the preliminary investigation and concluding with the results of the follow-up. Police department operations commanders must ensure that patrol officers and detectives follow protocols. This means that they should periodically review case files to determine if proper procedures were followed at the preliminary investigation as well as the follow-up. It is critically important that detectives fully investigate solvable cases. It is also important to review the quality of reports since they document the investigation and are used in court proceedings.

TRAFFIC UNITS

Large and medium-sized police departments have traffic units. The primary purposes of these units are to reduce and investigate traffic crashes and to expedite the flow of vehicular and pedestrian traffic. This is accomplished through enforcement, education, and engineering.

Officer using a laser gun to catch speeders
Source: Peter Casolino/Alamy Stock Photo

ENFORCEMENT

Traffic enforcement can have a positive impact on traffic crashes. For example, DeAngelo and Hansen examined traffic crashes in Oregon after the state reduced the Oregon State Police by 35 percent as a result of budget cuts and found that it resulted in a dramatic reduction in the number of citations issued and increased crashes and injuries and fatalities.[55] Other studies have shown that DUI enforcement can deter DUI behavior and safer driving behavior by nondrinking drivers.[56] There is research showing that increasing enforcement has a greater impact in reducing traffic violations as opposed to the fines or sanctions.[57]

Traffic unit commanders must design strategies to enhance enforcement and visibility as they reduce traffic violations and traffic crashes. DUI should receive the highest priority in terms of enforcement since this offense results in large number of deaths and injuries each year. Traffic units typically use sobriety checkpoints, and saturation patrols to apprehend drivers who are under the influence. Major studies in Missouri and Ohio show that saturation patrols are more effective than sobriety check points in that more arrests are made and they likely have more of a deterrence effect.[58] Some departments publicize their sobriety check points and saturation patrols. This has a deterrent effect on DUI, and for the most part, does not affect the number of impaired drivers that are apprehended.

Traffic officers patrol and write citations when they observe violations. Traffic unit managers should attempt to guide officers to write citations for the offenses that cause crashes at the locations where crashes tend to occur. Traffic officers have a tendency to write citations where they can easily write large numbers of citations, which may not be where large numbers of crashes occur. Traffic commanders can also schedule traffic check points at locations where large numbers of accidents occur to write citations for seatbelt violations, registration violations, and driver's license violations. This can have a deterrent effect. As noted above, traffic enforcement reduces traffic violations and crashes.

Since traffic officers write large numbers of citations, many come to believe that they have quotas, and some departments may have **quotas**. However, most departments do not. Quotas are a public relations problem if citizens learn that a department has one. Generally, traffic officers write the number of citations that is fairly consistent with other traffic officers. Traffic officers often have a quota that is established by the work group, not managers. Nonetheless, traffic unit managers must guide traffic officers in terms of where citations need to be issued to affect traffic crashes and other problems.

EDUCATION

Police departments are involved in educating the public. Education is an effective way to reduce bad driving behavior and reducing traffic crashes. Officers can conduct education programs in schools focusing on speeding, use of cell phones while driving, defensive driving, and DUI. These programs are especially helpful for newly licensed drivers. A number of states require drivers who have accumulated a number of points on their driver's license to attend education programs. Departments have implemented bicycle safety and pedestrian safety programs for school children. Traffic unit managers should tailor these programs for the traffic problems that exist in their community.

ENGINEERING

Traffic unit commanders should geographically analyze traffic crashes to identify concentrations of crashes. When there is a concentration, there generally is a cause. Making changes to traffic signage, installing stoplights or lighting, or changing traffic flow patterns can reduce accidents. For example, the police identified a large number of crashes at an intersection in Redlands, California. Upon analysis of the crashes and the intersection, it was determined that a curve in the approach to the intersection prevented drivers from seeing a red-light at the intersection until the last minute, resulting in vehicles running the red-light and crashes. The police department had the time for the caution light increased and the number of crashes was reduced. Simple solutions often can reduce crashes.

Summary

This chapter addresses productivity. First, it examines the general principles that should be considered to improve a police department's overall productivity. Second, it examines patrol, criminal investigation, and traffic enforcement, three of the primary divisions in any police department, to identify how productivity can be achieved. In terms of overall productivity, we identify the measures of productivity. Police leaders should instill these measures in their overall goals and integrate them in their operational procedures. We discuss CompStat and crime analysis in terms of guiding police operations. It is important to match operational strategies with crime and disorder problems confronting the department. Police departments must constantly evaluate problems and alter operations to ensure that the department remains abreast with changing conditions.

Patrol, criminal investigation, and traffic managers too often become complacent and continue operations as usual. This is easy to do given these units' typical workload. Also, the commanders of these units often become bogged down in the everyday minutia that is associated with command. However, they must continuously examine their units' operations and productivity to determine if adjustments need to be made.

Discussion Questions

1. Measuring police productivity is important. How would you measure efficiency, effectiveness, equity, and accountability?

2. What are strategic planning, tactical planning, and operational control and who is responsible for each?

3. If you were constructing a citizens' survey, what questions would you include in the survey?

4. What is CompStat?

5. What are the various mechanisms associated with a differential police response?

6. What are different patrol modes and when are they most appropriate?

7. Does routine preventive patrol prevent crime?

8. What are saturation patrols or crackdowns and when are they appropriate?

9. What is stop and frisk? When should it be used?

10. What are the elements of a preliminary investigation? What is a follow-up investigation?

11. How can enforcement, education, and engineering improve traffic conditions?

Internet Investigations

The PricewaterhouseCoopers Endowment for the Business of Government. "Accountability: The New York City Police Department's CompStat Model"
  http://www.businessofgovernment.org/sites/default/files/CompStat.pdf

Harvard Kennedy School, "Measuring Performance in a Modern Police Organization"
  https://www.ncjrs.gov/pdffiles1/nij/248476.pdf

Quora, "What Are Reasonable Metrics for the Productivity of the Police?"

  https://www.quora.com/What-are-reasonable-metrics-for-the-productivity-of-the-police

Police Patrol, "Departments: Best Practices for Operational Plans
  http://www.policemag.com/channel/patrol/articles/2012/01/operations-plans.aspx

Center for Problem-Oriented Policing, "The Benefits and Consequences of Police Crackdowns"
  http://www.popcenter.org/responses/police_crackdowns/

CHAPTER 13

Managing Homeland Security and Critical Events

STUDENT LEARNING OUTCOMES

After reading this chapter, the student will:

■ know the definition of terrorism

■ know the primary international groups that are involved in terrorism

■ be able to discuss the various right-wing and environmental terrorist groups operating in the United States

■ understand the process by which Americans become radicalized

■ be knowledgeable about the types of weapons of mass destruction and conventional armaments

■ know the various agencies housed in the Department of Homeland Security

■ be able to describe the National Infrastructure Protection Plan

■ understand what constitutes national critical infrastructure

■ know how a fusion center functions

■ be able to discuss how public education is an important homeland security program for police departments

■ know why it is important for police departments to develop relationships with private security agencies

■ describe how the National Incident Management System operates and its components

KEY TERMS AND CONCEPTS

- Alfred P. Murrah Federal Building
- Al Shabaab
- Al Qaeda
- Animal Liberation Front
- Arizona Patriots
- Biological WMDs
- Boko Haram
- Chemical WMDs
- Command
- Conventional weapons
- Critical infrastructure assets
- Customs and Border Protection
- Cyber infrastructure
- Earth First
- Earth Liberation Front
- Federal Emergency Management Agency
- Finance/Administration

- Fusion centers
- Hamas
- Hezbollah
- Homeland security
- Human assets
- Immigration and Customs Enforcement
- Incident command center
- Incident command system
- Intelligence-led policing
- Islamic State of Iraq and the Levant (ISIS)
- Jabhat al-Nusra
- Ku Klux Klan
- Layered response
- Liaison officer
- Logistics section
- Lone wolf
- National Incident Management System
- National Infrastructure Protection Plan

- Nuclear WMDs
- Oklahoma Constitutional Militia
- Operations section
- Patriot Council
- Physical infrastructure
- Planning section
- Private security
- Public information officer
- Radicalization
- Safety officer
- Secret Service
- Southern Poverty Law Center
- Terrorism
- Transportation Security Administration
- Unified command
- U.S. Citizenship and Immigration
- U.S. Coast Guard
- Weapons of mass destruction

INTRODUCTION

In an era of terrorism and homeland security, the popular police slogan "to protect and to serve" takes on a new meaning. When a disaster or terrorist attack occurs, even though federal agencies play a major role in mediating their effects, local police and other public safety personnel are the first to respond and must care for the injured, control the situation, and minimize the damage that occurred. Local police agencies have a monumental task when there is a catastrophic event. The importance of a police presence during national emergencies was demonstrated in New Orleans in the wake of Hurricane Katrina and in New York City and Washington, DC, after the 9/11 attacks; and in both situations, the police were overwhelmed. We must recognize the importance of local police agencies not only in terms of responding to such events but also that police agencies are on the front line in terms of preventing terrorist attacks in our communities.

This chapter examines police leadership and management in the context of homeland security. There are two important security aspects addressed in this chapter. First, we broadly examine homeland security as it relates to local police agencies and roles of individual officers as threat assessors and first responders. We begin with an overview of homeland security, including a description of the terrorist threat. We examine important topics, including the federal Department of Homeland Security (DHS) and its role in protecting our national infrastructure and the responsibilities of local police agencies in terms of threat assessment, identifying primary targets in our critical infrastructure, partnering with the private sector, ensuring officer safety, and as first responders to acts of terrorism.

Second, we examine the response to major incidents, including terrorist attacks and natural and man-made disasters. Since these events are often large and complex in scale, it requires that responding agencies have precision and coordination in their responses. The DHS has developed the National Response Framework and the National Incident Management System in order to have a uniform and coordinated response to critical events. These procedures outline a layered response to events whereby the federal, state, and local agencies work together when responding to any type of disaster, including terrorist attacks.

THE TERRORIST THREAT

Today, we live in a dangerous world in which war, famine, and politics are causing substantial discontent on every continent. Much of this anger is directed toward the United States. There is a litany of reasons ranging from our support for Israel to the perceived ill-treatment of citizens of other countries by American multinational corporations to our wars in Afghanistan and Iraq. Terrorists see the United States as a means to rally support and hatred. They regularly burn American flags and pictures of American presidents. They are able to keep the political waters boiling with their rhetoric, which in turn results in an increasing number of people who hate America and who are potential terrorists.

Terrorists pose a threat to all countries. Many if not all countries have been attacked by terrorists, including the United States. **Terrorism** is defined in Title 22 of the U.S. Code, Section 2656f(d) as "premeditated,

Ground zero following the 9/11 attacks in New York city. *Courtesy of Federal Bureau of Investigation, USA*

politically motivated violence perpetrated against noncombatant targets by subnational groups or clandestine agents, usually intended to influence an audience." Today, the bulk of these acts are perpetrated by Islamic extremists who attack western ideas or who desire to institute Islamic states or caliphates. They routinely attack civilians in an effort to create fear and affect governments.

There are a number of groups that desire to carry out attacks—attacks that embolden and strengthen these groups—on the United States. Some of the most prominent groups are mentioned here. **Hamas**, which is housed in Palestine and at the center of the Israeli-Palestinian conflict, gets its support from Kuwait, Iran, and Saudi Arabia. It routinely attacks civilian Israeli targets. **Hezbollah** is located in Lebanon and receives financial and logistic support from Syria and Iran. In 2006, Hezbollah battled the Israeli army to a standstill. In the past, Hezbollah has attacked American targets oversees and it is conceivable that it will stage attacks in the United States in the future.[1]

The most known and feared group today is the **Islamic State of Iraq and the Levant (ISIS)**, which declared a caliphate in an effort to convert the Muslim world to its jihadist view. ISIS has controlled large swaths of land in Syria and Iraq. Iraqi and American forces are in the process of retaking control of ISIS territory. American forces concentrated on destroying Al Qaeda after the 9/11 attacks decimating its leadership, including killing Osama bin Laden. Nonetheless, **Al Qaeda** remains a significant force. It has decentralized with Al Qaeda affiliates in several countries, including Al Qaeda central in Pakistan and Afghanistan, Al Qaeda in the Arabian Peninsula located primarily in Yemen, and Al Qaeda in the Islamic Maghreb located primarily in Libya. Another group that recently declared its independence from Al Qaeda is the **Jabhat al-Nusra**, which is located in Syria. Al-Nusra is one of the most dangerous groups in that it has continuously increased its power and control, and although concentrating its efforts in Syria, once its power is consolidated, it likely will engage in international terrorism.[2]

Two other groups located in Africa present a danger to the United States. **Boko Haram**, which is located in Nigeria, attacks Christians, security and police forces, schools, politicians, and Muslims who are perceived as collaborators. In 2015, the group kidnapped 276 school girls. It has launched attacks in Cameroon, Chad, Niger, and Nigeria.[3] **Al-Shabaab**, located in Somalia, is loosely affiliated with Al Qaeda. It has been involved in bombings and suicide attacks, with the most notable occurring in 2013 when the group attacked the Westgate mall in Nairobi killing 67 people. In 2015, the group attacked a university in Garissa, Kenya, killing 150, mainly Christian students.[4] These two groups although focusing on Africa routinely attack western interests and have had a devastating impact on the region.

When thinking about terrorism and attacks on the United States, we too often think only of foreign or Middle Eastern groups. However, the United States has a number of groups that have waged attacks on American soil. These groups are primarily right-wing hate groups. Right-wing extremist groups are located throughout the United States and include a number of militias, Christian-based groups, and the Ku Klux Klan; in 2016, the Southern Poverty Law Center estimated that there were 917 active hate groups in the United States.[5]

The best-known example of right-wing terrorism in the United States is the 1995 bombing of the **Alfred P. Murrah Federal Building** in Oklahoma City. The bombing was carried out by Timothy McVeigh and Terry Nichols, members of a right-wing group. They discharged 5,000 pounds of explosives that resulted in 168 deaths and demolished the building. Members of the **Arizona Patriots** were convicted of plotting to bomb the Simon Wiesenthal Center. They raised money by committing a series of robberies. Members of the **Patriot Council** plotted to use ricin, a poisonous biological agent, to attack government installations and officials. Members of this group were the first to be charged under the Biological Weapons Anti-Terrorism Act. Members of the **Oklahoma Constitutional Militia** were arrested and convicted for planning attacks on gay and lesbian bars, abortion clinics, and the offices of the **Southern Poverty Law Center**. The **Ku Klux Klan** has a long history of terrorist acts against African-Americans, Jews, and Catholics. Best known for cross burnings, its members have been implicated in bombings and other related activities. Again, there are numerous right-wing organizations in America that profess hatred for the government, taxation, minorities, and religious groups.

A number of extremist groups are engaged in environmental and animal rights terrorist activities. According to White, the **Earth Liberation Front (ELF)** formed in 1992 in the United Kingdom and quickly migrated to the United States. Today, it is composed of a number of radicals from **Earth First**, the **Animal Liberation Front (ALF)**, and other environmentalists who are opposed to the destruction of our environment.[6] ELF does not stage attacks on people, but has been involved in a number of attacks on property. Their aim is to cause as much economic

Dzhokhar Tsarnaev (white hat) and Tamerlan Tsarnaev (black hat), the individuals responsible for the Boston Marathon bombings, shortly before the attacks on April 15, 2013. Courtesy Federal Bureau of Investigation.
Source: Dorset Media Service/FBI/ Alamy Stock Photo

damage to those who destroy the environment. Martin notes that members have destroyed a forest station in Oregon, poisoned Mars candy bars, destroyed a livestock research laboratory at the University of California at Davis, spiked trees in logging areas, liberated minks in Wisconsin, and committed arson at a Vail, Colorado, ski resort. Additionally, animal rights support groups have attacked numerous individuals, universities, and private entities involved in animal research.[7] These incidents demonstrate that police departments must pay attention to environmental and animal rights groups as well as other terrorist organizations.

LONE WOLF TERRORISTS: AMERICA'S NEW THREAT

The groups discussed above pose a threat to American cities, but the immediate threat comes from homegrown lone wolf terrorists or small cells. A **lone wolf** is defined as "a person who acts on his or her own without order from—or connections to—an organization."[8] In 2015, there were 79 terrorist plots interdicted in the United States, and in 2016, there were 43.[9] Most of these cases were lone wolf.

Generally, when lone wolf terrorists are discussed, people envision radical jihadi terrorists. However, we have seen a variety of lone wolf terrorists in terms of philosophy, politics, and mental stability in the United States. Adam Lanza killed 20 children at a Sandy Hook elementary school; he was mentally unstable. Ted Kaczynski committed 16 bombings over a 17-year period; his rationale was he was attacking technology. Dylann Roof killed eight people at a Charleston, South Carolina, church; he hoped to start a race war. We tend to refer to these types of attacks as mass murders, not terrorist attacks. However, they do promote the fear of terrorism. Hamm and Spaaj have studied mass murderers and terrorists and found that although there are differences, there are many similarities.[10]

Nonetheless, there have been a number of Islamic radicals who have perpetrated attacks in the United States. In the Orlando nightclub shooting American-born Omar Mateen killed 39 people and wounded dozens of others; Mateen called the police during the shooting and declared his allegiance to ISIS. Muhammad Youssef Abdulazeez opened fire at the Chattanooga Navy Reserve center, killing four marines; the Federal Bureau of Investigation (FBI) reported that he was inspired by foreign terrorist propaganda. Nidal Malik Hasan killed 13 soldiers at Fort Leavenworth, Kansas; Hasan had been in contact with Anwar al-Awlaki, a cleric who fomented Jihadist extremism. Syed Farook and Tashfeen Malik killed 14 people and injured 22 others in an attack on a social services agency in San Bernardino, California; it was believed they were radicalized by ISIS propaganda.

FOCUS ON: CHATTANOOGA TERRORIST ATTACK

On July 16, 2015, Muhammad Youssef Abdulazeez attacked military recruiting centers in Chattanooga, Tennessee, killing four marines. Abdulazeez first drove by the center and opened fire. He then went back to the center and opened fire and continued firing, shooting 30 to 45 rounds. James Comey, Director of the FBI, stated that the shooting was motivated by terrorist propaganda. Abdulazeez ultimately was killed by responding police officers.

This incident demonstrates the randomness of lone wolf shootings. They essentially can occur anywhere. Police departments must be able to respond at a moment's notice. Lone wolf shootings require that police departments have response plans in place.

Source: Based on Fausset, Richard et al. "Gunman Kills 4 Marines at Military Site in Chattanooga," New York Times, July 16, 2015.

In sum, a terrorist attack can come from a number of directions involving a variety of actors. This makes the jobs of police leaders more complex in that they must be aware of numerous groups' activities in their jurisdictions. It means that police officials must be prepared for a variety of contingencies; they must engage in homeland security planning.

Radicalization: The Greatest Threat to America

Radicalization is the greatest threat to the United States.[11] There have been a number of Americans who have gone to the Middle East to engage in jihadi wars. There have been several thousand would-be jihadists (jihad terrorism is discussed below) who have similarly traveled from Europe; since they are Europeans, they can easily travel to the United States. Such actions demonstrate that they have the psychological or political background to engage in terrorist acts in the United States and Europe. Many of these individuals were radicalized before going to the Middle East, while others likely were radicalized while there.

Essentially, the radicalization process is where someone accepts an extremist belief system, generally jihadist, and consequently has the wherewithal to support or carry out violence to effect changes in society. Jihadists have as their primary goals to bring down the United States and to establish a caliphate in the Middle East. Mirahmadi has identified five risk factors that contribute to radicalization.[12] First is ideology, beliefs, and values—a view that western society is a threat to Islam. Second, political grievances are created as a result of human rights abuses and a lack of civil liberties and rights in their home countries. Third, economic factors including a lack of employment, deprivation, and financial incentives for joining a radicalized group. Fourth, sociological factors are alienation, acculturation problems, marginalization, and discrimination. Finally, there are psychological factors such as mental illness and posttraumatic stress disorder. Thus, there is a combination of factors that lead to radicalization.

Radicalization is a process. Horgan notes that it generally starts when people become frustrated with their lives.[13] The above risk factors contribute to this frustration, demonstrating that there are numerous ways for someone to begin the radicalization process. Generally, the radicalization process consists of four phases: (1) pre-radicalization, (2) indoctrination and increased group bonding, (3) conversion and identification, and (4) acts of terrorism or planned attacks.[14] Pre-radicalization is where the subject becomes disenchanted or frustrated. The indoctrination and increased group bonding phase is where the subject becomes increasingly exposed to radical information. This may occur when the subject begins to concentrate on radical material on the Internet, associates with a radical group of friends, or attends a mosque that has a radical imam. This phase essentially involves inculturalization, where radical ideas are integrated into the subject's belief system. Phase three, conversion and identification, is where the subject joins or accepts the ideas of the radical movement. He or she becomes a total believer. Finally, the subject becomes so radicalized that he or she plans or perpetrates terrorist acts.

Europe has had a more substantial problem with radicalized terrorists as compared to the United States. Muslims who have come to America have had an easier time integrating in our society as compared to France, Great Britain, and other European countries. Nonetheless, there have been several cases where people have become radicalized and committed terrorist acts—the San Bernardino shootings, the Chattanooga navy reserve center, and the Orlando nightclub shooting, to name a few.

The radicalization process is addressed through prevention, intervention, and rehabilitation.[15] Prevention consists of addressing the root causes of radicalization by implementing programs that better integrate disenfranchised communities into larger society, such as the Montgomery County, Maryland, program discussed below. The object is to provide the individual hope. Intervention serves to disengage the potentially radicalized individual through mental health services and religious counseling. It attempts to provide other mechanisms for self-expression. Intervention attempts to move the radicalized individual to accept conventional societal norms.

Finally, rehabilitation focuses on working with individuals who have been arrested, but desire to reform. This can be accomplished through counseling and other integration programing. There is a real need for rehabilitation in our nations' prisons and jails.

There have been efforts to prevent radicalization. A program in Montgomery County, Maryland, BRAVE, involved a network consisting of a number of stakeholders, including the faith community leaders, public officials, law enforcement, educators, and social service providers.[16] The goal of the network is to construct a cohesive community network committed to public safety and to serve as an early warning network of trusted adults. It is a cross-cultural endeavor designed to develop better understanding among the various groups in the county. It provides individuals with an opportunity to bond with conventional citizens and institutions. After three years of operation, the network had over 3,000 participants. The program is being adopted in Denver and Prince George County, Maryland. Law enforcement can play an important role in these types of programs using a community policing model.

A primary tool used by radical extremists to recruit members is social media. Stern advises that the United States has not done enough to counter the extremist information on social media.[17] Although the federal government is sponsoring efforts to provide counter messaging, local communities can also engage in such messaging. Police leaders can work with local clubs, mosques, and so on to develop local social media outlets. They can serve as an alternative to the radicalized information found on social media. This can include chat rooms, community information that would be of interest to young people, and information about social groups in the area.

Police managers should attempt to identify potential programs or populations within their jurisdiction and proactively implement prevention mechanisms. This is best accomplished by working with individuals and groups within the community.

THE ULTIMATE THREAT: WEAPONS OF MASS DESTRUCTION

In terms of homeland security, the greatest threat is **weapons of mass destruction (WMD)**.[18] A WMD is any explosive, incendiary, poison gas, chemical, biological, or nuclear device that can have substantial widespread devastation.[19] WMDs can be biological, chemical, or nuclear (discussed below). WMDs have the potential capacity to cause large numbers of deaths and injuries and destruction, especially in heavily populated areas. For example, exploding a small nuclear devise in a city such as Chicago, New York, or Los Angeles could inflict substantial destruction. Moreover, it would have residual effects. It would overload the police and other first responders and hospitals. It would substantially affect the economy, having an impact on thousands of persons who were not directly affected by the explosion. It would cripple a city, resulting in numerous problems that could potentially last for years or decades. To some extent, the primary purpose of using WMDs is not the initial death and injuries but the residual effects that possibly could be more destructive to a country than the initial impact.

Nuclear Weapons of Mass Destruction

Of all the weapons of mass destruction, nuclear devices raise the most concern (witness the angst and fear caused in mid-2017 when North Korea threatened a nuclear strike against Guam). Even a small nuclear weapon detonated in one of our large cities would result in catastrophic destruction and large numbers of casualties. Moreover, the presence of nuclear materials—radiation—would result in long-term problems for the country.

Nuclear weapons of mass destruction can be used in at least three different ways: (1) a dirty bomb, (2) attacks on nuclear power plants, and (3) diversion of nuclear material or weapons. Dirty bombs use conventional explosive materials but are wrapped or contain some type of radioactive material. The conventional explosion causes the radioactive materials to be dispersed, resulting in contamination.

There have been previous attempts to use a dirty bomb. In 1996, Islamic rebels from Chechnya planted such a device in a park in Moscow. Although not detonated, it contained dynamite and Cesium 137, a by-product of nuclear fission. In 2002, Abdullah Al Muhajir, also known as Jose Padilla, was arrested by federal authorities for plotting to construct and detonate a dirty bomb in the United States. There is evidence that terrorists see a dirty bomb as a plausible weapon that could inflict substantial damage.

Crashing a large aircraft or by using large amounts of explosives at a nuclear power plant could have the same effects as a dirty bomb, except the effects would be of a larger magnitude. Such an explosion could cause the reactor core to melt down (such as occurred at Chernobyl) or spent fuel waste to be spread across a large geographical area. The effects could be devastating, and the clean-up could take decades. As discussed above, if terrorists acquired a nuclear weapon detonated in the United States, it would have devastating effects on America.

Biological Weapons of Mass Destruction

Biological weapons of mass destruction can be bacteria, viruses, or biological toxins. Because there are numerous contagions that pose a real health threat to large numbers of people, biological terrorism is a genuine threat to the United States. Diseases such as smallpox and anthrax could infect large numbers of people over a large geographical area. There is a great deal of speculation that terrorist groups possess or are attempting to possess biological weapons. There was substantial publicity and public fear in 2001 when someone mailed anthrax to several locations in the United States causing five deaths. In dealing with biological terrorism, containment and prevention are of the utmost importance.

Mere possession of an agent does not make it a weapon. The agent must be "weaponized"; that is, the would-be terrorist must develop or possess a mechanism that can disperse or disseminate the agent within a target area. Obtaining and weaponizing a biological agent is extremely difficult and dangerous for the terrorists. Police administrators should remain in contact with hospital and other medical personnel to monitor if any patients with biological agents have been identified.

Chemical Weapons of Mass Destruction

Used historically, chemical warfare was a primary weapon in World War I, in the Iraqi-Iranian War, and the Syrian government has used chemical weapons to attack its civilian population. The use of chemical weapons in World War I caused one million casualties. Thus, chemical weapons are not new, and countries continue to develop new, more deadly compounds that pose a greater risk to the United States.

Chemical weapons of mass destruction have different levels of toxicity and lethality, and there is a variety of chemicals that can be used as a WMD. Some of the chemicals that may be used are insecticides, which have a low level of toxicity, but are readily available. On the other hand, weapons grade chemicals are potentially dangerous. Chemicals such as mustard gas, sarin, and VX are extremely lethal. As with biological weapons, the effectiveness of a chemical threat is to a large extent based on the delivery system. Many experts believe that chemical weapons cannot produce the same level of casualties as nuclear or biological weapons. Large quantities of the chemical would have to be effectively released to have a significant impact. Local police agencies must work closely with federal and state homeland security officials in order to maintain a level of readiness. They should also monitor the sales of chemicals that could be used to make a chemical weapon.

Conventional Weapons

Radiological, biological, and chemical weapons present the greatest danger from a terrorist attack, but the terrorist attacks in the United States have been conducted using **conventional weapons**. Airplanes were used in the 9/11 attacks, where a limited number of bombings have occurred; firearms have been used in the overwhelming

Dynamite hidden by Eric Rudolph, who was convicted on bombings of abortion clinics, and recovered by the FBI. *Courtesy of Federal Bureau of Investigation, USA*

majority of attacks; and there have been a few incidents where knives or other bladed instruments were used. Another trend in terrorist attacks has been the use of vehicles. Terrorists used vehicles to kill pedestrians in Nice, France, London, and Stockholm. Firearms are the most commonly used weapon since these weapons are easily obtainable in the United States.[20] Moreover, firearms are problematic since many states allow for carrying a concealed weapon or allow people to carry firearms openly. Here, police administrators should attempt to strictly enforce all federal, state, and local gun statutes and ordinances.

DEPARTMENT OF HOMELAND SECURITY

Homeland security is a governmental effort to protect national **critical infrastructure assets**. According to the DHS, there are three primary categories of critical infrastructure: (1) human, (2) physical, and (3) cyber.[21] **Human assets** refer to the large numbers of people who congregate because of living situations, working conditions, or social events and who need to be protected. Homeland security efforts focus on protecting groups of people to prevent a large number of casualties. Thus, numbers of people drive protection decisions. Although people can be the targets of terrorist attacks, infrastructure is also important. **Physical infrastructure** refers to transportation (air, rail, waterway, and roadway infrastructure); manufacturing facilities, especially petrochemical facilities; large employers; and nuclear facilities, such as reactors, storage devices, and materials being transported regionally or nationally. In essence, an attack on a physical infrastructure facility may not result in a large number of deaths, but it could have a significant economic impact in the region or country. Finally, **cyber infrastructure** refers to information networks used to transfer vast amounts of information and to coordinate business, industry, banking, and to a large degree, people's daily lives. It also refers to keeping information secure from those who would access and steal it for illegal or illegitimate uses.

Homeland security, although initially envisioned to respond to terrorist attacks, became much broader, addressing a range of hazards. This was primarily the result of the Federal Emergency Management Agency (FEMA) being included in the DHS. Figure 13-1 demonstrates the different and varied threats to critical infrastructure. America has had relatively few terrorist attacks on its critical infrastructure, but other threats have had numerous impacts. Regardless, making individual infrastructures more resilient for terrorist attacks will to some extent increase their protection from other threats such as natural disasters. We therefore must be diligent in identifying and taking measures to increase security and resilience.

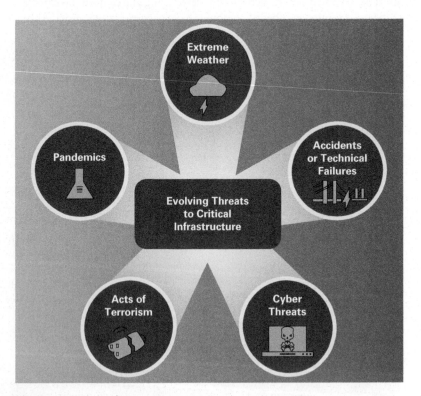

FIGURE 13-1 Threats to Critical Infrastructure
Source: DHS (2013). NIPP 2013 *Partnering for Critical Infrastructure Security and Resilience*. Washington, D.C.: DHS, p. 8.

Organization and Responsibilities

Although **homeland security** encompasses all levels of government, the federal government is primarily responsible for the security of the homeland. This responsibility lies primarily with the DHS. The DHS is one of the largest departments in the federal government; the DHS currently has approximately 200,000 employees. It was formed to better coordinate the numerous agencies that can play a role in case of a terrorist attack on the United States. Additionally, it has a number of corollary responsibilities. First, FEMA and other agencies within the Department respond to natural and man-made disasters as well as terrorist attacks. The DHS also coordinates with other agencies to prevent and minimize terrorist attacks. Figure 13-2 shows the DHS's organizational chart.

The DHS has a number of support agencies as well as enforcement agencies. The support agencies include

- Science and Technology
- National Protection and Programs
- Health Affairs
- Partnership and Engagement
- Intelligence and Analysis
- Operations Coordination

These agencies provide support and research to enhance homeland security. They work with other federal agencies as well as with state and local agencies to develop more effective homeland security responses.

In addition to the support agencies, the DHS has several enforcement agencies and support agencies that provide direct support when an event occurs. They include:

- U.S. Customs and Border Protection (CBP)
- U.S. Citizenship and Immigration
- U.S. Coast Guard
- Federal Emergency Management Agency (FEMA)
- U.S. Immigration and Customs Enforcement (ICE)
- U.S. Secret Service
- Transportation Security Administration (TSA)

Most of these agencies are involved in providing direct federal law enforcement. **Customs and Border Protection** guard our nation's borders. The **Coast Guard** is responsible for our ports and waterways. **Immigration and Customs Enforcement** is charged with apprehending illegal immigrants and investigating homeland security crimes within the United States. The **Secret Service** provides executive protection and investigates identity fraud and money laundering. The **Transportation Security Administration** provides security at our nation's airports. However, the **U.S. Citizenship and Immigration** is involved in handling illegal immigrates once they have been detained. The **Federal Emergency Management Agency** is responsible for providing support at events such as terrorist attacks and natural and man-made disasters.

Police administrators must maintain good working relationships with these agencies as they represent the primary defense in homeland security. Local and state agencies are the first responders to any events, but federal agencies help prevent and mitigate the effects of any disasters or attacks. There is a **layered response** where local agencies are the first to respond to an event. If it cannot be properly handled by local agencies, state agencies are called upon to assist. If the event overwhelms state resources, then federal assistance is requested.

The Department's primary responsibility is prevention. That is, the DHS is seen as the agency that will coordinate all efforts to prevent attacks on the United States. As such, the DHS devised the National Infrastructure Protection Plan to provide prevention guidance.

The National Infrastructure Protection Plan

In 2002, the DHS published the **National Infrastructure Protection Plan (NIPP)**. This document has served as the guideline for organizing homeland security in the United States. The plan is designed to provide coordination among the numerous federal, state, and local agencies in protecting the nation's critical infrastructure and key resources. Essentially, the plan enumerates a homeland security process.[22]

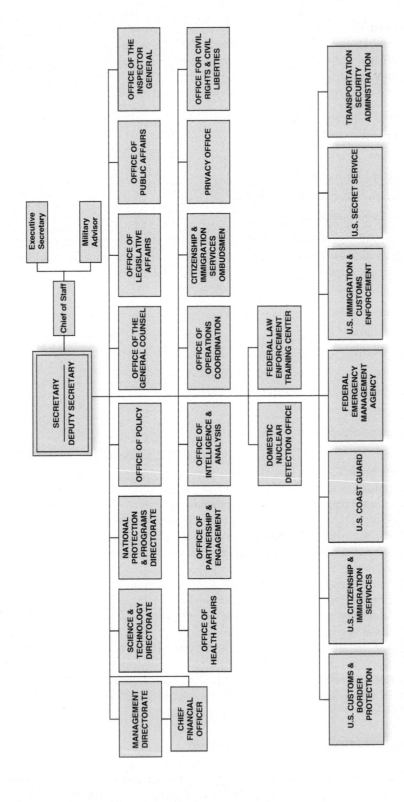

FIGURE 13-2 Organization for the U.S. Department of Homeland Security

Source: Department of Homeland Security, *Organizational Chart,* https://www.dhs.gov/sites/default/files/publications/Department%20Org%20 Chart_2.pdf Accessed April 5, 2017.

TSA officials inspect an Amtrack train. Courtesy of TSA.
Source: Department of Homeland Security official photo

YOU DECIDE...

As noted in this chapter, terrorist attacks would be directed at critical infrastructure assets. There are all sorts of such potential targets in any given city. Police departments should be in the process of identifying these assets. Once identified, the department should be considering responses should a terrorist attack or other significant events occur. You have been appointed to the department's Homeland Security Unit. Captain John Patrick, the unit commander, has directed you to identify potential targets in the city. No such efforts preceded this request, so you must begin anew.

Questions for Discussion

1. What types or categories of critical infrastructure should concern you?

2. What criteria should you use when deciding? For example, the list very likely will include a gasoline storage facility, but should gasoline service stations be included as well?

3. Is there anyone in the community that you could consult to advise you when decision making?

4. Will local politics come into play when developing this list, especially if someone's business is not included?

5. What should the department do once this list is compiled?

The NIPP requires local police departments to identify the critical infrastructure assets in their jurisdiction be they human, physical, or cyber. Figure 13-3 shows the various types of critical assets as identified by the DHS. Every jurisdiction will have a number of these assets. They should be identified. Next, the level of protection each asset has in place should be assessed. This can be physical security such as fences, alarms, and security personnel. Then the level of risk should be determined; what is the level of danger if the asset is compromised. Police officials should work with other government and business and corporate officials to improve security. Finally, police managers must ensure that their departments have response plans in place that coordinate with other emergency response agencies.

HOMELAND SECURITY AT THE LOCAL LEVEL

Homeland security today represents a major operational area for state and local governments. If there is a terrorist attack or major disaster, state and local officials are first to respond. During this initial response, they must control the situation and mitigate the damage as much as possible. It may take days or even weeks for the necessary federal assets to arrive on the scene. This places a substantial burden on local and state resources, which are limited and often inadequate, especially if a major disaster occurs.

> - Chemical sector
> - Commercial facilities sector
> - Communications sector
> - Critical manufacturing sector
> - Dams sector
> - Defense industrial base sector
> - Emergency services sector
> - Energy sector
> - Financial services sector
> - Food and agriculture sector
> - Government facilities sector
> - Healthcare and public health sector
> - Information technology sector
> - Nuclear reactors, materials, and waste sector
> - Transportation systems sector
> - Water and wastewater systems

FIGURE 13-3 Types of Critical Infrastructure Assets

There is substantial consternation over the role of local agencies in protecting local assets. However, we must "think globally and act locally."[23] Essentially, attacks on a local asset can come from anywhere in the world, but local authorities will assume a large amount of the responsibility to prevent an attack and mitigate it if an attack does in fact occur.

Local agencies must develop strategies and policies to deal with homeland security. Currently, it appears that the states and local units of government are engaged in four homeland security activities:

1. Threat assessment via intelligence gathering (intelligence-led policing)
2. Critical infrastructure identification
3. Partnerships between law enforcement and critical infrastructure security personnel
4. Public education

Next, we briefly discuss each of these activities.

Intelligence-Led Policing and Threat Assessment

To address threat assessment at the local level, local police departments must become involved in identifying potential terrorists and suspect activities. Currently, police departments are improving their intelligence capacity through **intelligence-led policing** (discussed briefly in Chapter 1), which essentially is the enhancement of police intelligence gathering capability. Most major police departments already have some form of intelligence gathering capabilities. In the past, these efforts have been aimed at collecting information about organized crime, drug trafficking, and gangs. Intelligence-led policing dictates that departments not only begin collecting information about possible terrorists and possible targets but also that they should enhance their intelligence gathering and usage skills. It is logical to include possible terrorists and terrorist activities, especially considering that narcotics trafficking is extensively used to finance terrorism.[24] Of course, one of the major difficulties for local departments in collecting terrorist intelligence is that unlike other organized crime groups, little is known about who might be a terrorist and their potential activities. For the most part, there is an absence of baseline data or information to guide intelligence and investigative activities. Rhetorically, it is too late to gather information about possible terrorists once they have been identified as terrorists. Nonetheless, departments are encouraged to begin gathering information on "persons of interest" who fit some profile of terrorists. As witnessed with the 9/11 attacks, one undiscovered attack can result in the loss of thousands of lives.

Intelligence-led policing is compatible with and complementary to community policing. Police officers across the country are now working more closely with citizens and communities. These relationships provide a vast reservoir of "eyes and ears" for the police, which not only enhances problem solving but also provides a way to collect intelligence about suspicious persons and activities in a community. Intelligence gathered in the community can be collated and compared to other intelligence to provide a clearer picture of the activities in a jurisdiction. It is important for police managers and supervisors to reinforce this mandate.

Fusion Centers

An innovation in intelligence collection is fusion centers. A number of cities and counties have partnered with the FBI to form terrorism early warning groups or fusion centers.[25] The **fusion center** provides overarching coordination of all response and counter-terrorism elements within a community or metropolitan area. As information or intelligence is gathered by local and federal agencies it is fed into the fusion center where it is analyzed. The fusion center is a comprehensive approach in that it allows for the analysis of information from a variety of sources. It is the most comprehensive manner by which to collect and analyze data for a particular geographical area. Once analyzed, terrorist threat or activity information is generated and supplied to affected constituents. The fusion centers include medical personnel and fire department personnel as well as law enforcement personnel. The medical personnel can act as an early warning system for a biological attack by providing the fusion center with information about suspicious diseases or illnesses, and the firefighter personnel can provide information about suspicious fires or chemical problems. The fusion center also allows for more comprehensive planning and a better-coordinated response should a terrorist event occur. Where possible, police administrators should ensure that their departments are involved in fusion centers.

Critical Infrastructure Identification

Police departments need to take inventory of the critical infrastructure within their jurisdictions. This requires that the police identify all potential terrorist targets. This is especially important given the numerous potential targets that may exist and that attacks on different types of targets present dissimilar challenges to the police and other first responders. Local police departments must create a catalog or database of all possible terrorist targets in the jurisdiction, especially those that would result in significant damage or public danger if attacked. This process serves two functions. First, the database allows the department to comprehensively develop response plans for the various identified targets. A police department should have a response plan in place for all of these locations. Second, it results in focusing attention on areas that are of interest to possible terrorists. Once assets are identified, the police department should focus intelligence operations near and around the locations. It is very likely that if a terrorist plans to attack an asset, he or she will conduct reconnaissance. Due vigilance may result in the terrorist being identified before the act.

As police departments develop their critical infrastructure asset database, they should remember that there are all sorts of assets that must be considered. They range from areas with a large concentration of people, such as shopping malls and sporting events, to medical facilities and petrochemical facilities. Also included are transportation corridors, such as railways and roadways, and airports. Smaller, less obvious facilities or businesses such as gun shops, government buildings, and tourist attractions should also be included in any such database. The police department should develop a contingency plan for an attack on each of the critical assets in the community.

Partnering with Private Security

Each year more funding is devoted to private security than on public police, and the private sector employs larger numbers of personnel than do public police departments.[26] Private security is a significant force in the public safety arena. Public policing and private security are not necessarily mutually exclusive domains. For example, Green has defined the role of **private security** as "those individuals, organizations, and services other than public law enforcement and regulatory agencies that are engaged primarily in the prevention and investigation of crime, loss, or harm to specific individuals, organizations, or facilities."[27] There is, therefore, substantial overlap between private security and the police. Because private security secures a number of potential terrorist targets, it can be an important asset for a department in its efforts to develop a comprehensive homeland security plan.

Historically, there has been little cooperation or communication between the police and private security personnel even though they endeavor to achieve the same goals. The police often saw areas or facilities that were guarded by security personnel as "dead zones." That is, they were areas that did not require police services unless called upon. However, in an effort to better protect the community from the threat of terrorism and the need to secure critical infrastructure, the police must develop close working relationships with private security firms. Often security personnel have more information about the critical asset than the police. For example, many of these facilities have controlled access and activities, and therefore, security personnel are more likely to observe people and actions that are out of the ordinary or suspicious, and independently, or in cooperation with the police, investigate them. At a minimum, the police should be aware of those facilities that are target-hardened through private security, and strengthen relationships with the private security personnel who monitor them. Such relationships would (1) improve joint response to critical incidents, (2) coordinate infrastructure protection, (3) improve communications and the interpretation of data, (4) bolster information and intelligence sharing, (5) prevent and investigate high-tech crime, and (6) devise responses to workplace violence.[28]

FOCUS ON: DES MOINES HOMELAND SECURITY BUREAU

The Des Moines Police Department, like many other police departments, established a homeland security bureau. The bureau is charged with (1) information analysis and sharing, (2) preparedness and response, and (3) prevention and protection. The bureau provides several important functions in the City of Des Moines. It contains a special tactics and response team that can quickly respond to incidents. The bureau's bomb squad is prepared to respond to any explosive devices. Finally, the bureau works closely with the FBI's fusion center that is located in Des Moines. Additionally, the bureau works closely with other agencies such as the fire department and the Polk County Sheriff's Department. The Des Moines homeland security bureau has a structure that is similarly used in departments across the nation. In larger cities, their homeland security unit may include other functions, but it is paramount that these types of units be prepared for any terrorist, natural, or man-made incident.

Source: Adapted from Homeland Security Bureau, https://www.dmgov.org/Departments/Police/Pages/HomelandSecurity.aspx

Public Education

On May 9, 2007, the FBI arrested six suspects who had planned to attack and kill soldiers at Fort Dix in New Jersey. The initial investigative lead was supplied by an alert photography store clerk who was asked to copy a video cassette onto a DVD. The cassette contained footage of the suspects training for their attack. The alert store clerk notified the police, which resulted in an extended FBI investigation and subsequent arrests. This incident exemplifies how law enforcement can obtain valuable intelligence information from the general public.

Community policing necessitates that the police work closely with communities. One of the programs that resulted from this partnering is public education about a variety of crime and safety issues. Jurisdictions must develop programs that produce results similar to those experienced in the New Jersey case. The police should employ education programs that encourage citizens to observe for and report suspicious persons and activities.[29] These programs are similar to some of the drug and crime citizen reporting systems that have been used for decades. Lyon advises that the police should develop programs in communities or neighborhoods that are likely to engender support for the police and the reduction of terrorist activities.[30]

PREPARING FOR THE WORST: A NATIONAL INCIDENT MANAGEMENT SYSTEM

We have described local law enforcement's role in homeland security; now we examine how this role is operationalized. In 2003, the DHS created the **National Incident Management System (NIMS)**.[31] The purpose of this system is to provide a consistent nationwide approach for federal, state, and local governments to work effectively together to prepare for, prevent, respond to, and recover from disasters and domestic incidents. The NIMS is a comprehensive document addressing response to critical incidents. By adopting a national consistent response protocol, agencies at all levels have a standard set of procedures when responding to an event. Since police departments are the first responders to an event, the procedures outlined in the NIMS should be integrated into police departments' policies. The following discussion is limited to some of its primary components, with primary emphasis placed on the **Incident Command System (ICS)**.

Command and Management

The **Incident Command Center (ICC)** is created to provide unity of command when responding to an event. This is particularly important when responding to large events or events that encompass large periods of time such as barricaded persons, large fires, mass shootings, and tornados. The ICC may be simple in some cases depending on the event, while in other cases it may be large and complex. The ICC serves to coordinate response personnel. They may be from a single agency or personnel from more than one agency or teams from more than one jurisdiction. The NIMS has been adopted to help local police agencies respond to disasters, critical incidents, and terrorist incidents.

A key strength of ICS is its unified command component, which is composed of four sections: operations, planning, logistics, and finance. Under ICS, all functions are housed in the same location and establish a unified command post.[32] The most critical period of time for controlling a crisis is those initial moments when first responders arrive at the scene. They must quickly contain the situation, analyze the extent of the crisis, request

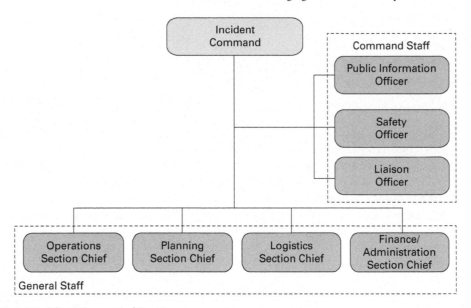

FIGURE 13-4   Incident Command System
Source: DHS, *National Incident Management System* (Washington, DC: 2008): 53.

additional resources and special teams if needed, and communicate available information and intelligence to head-quarters. Their initial actions provide a vital link to the total police response, and will often determine its outcome.

In terms of **command**, the command staff, particularly the ICS commander, is responsible for over-all management of the incident. When an incident occurs within a single jurisdiction, without any overlap, a single incident commander should be designated with overall incident management responsibility, to develop the objectives on which an actual action plan will be based. This ensures that the response is coordinated and controlled. When this does not occur, it substantially increases the probability that a misstep will occur.

The **unified command** (UC) concept is used in multi-jurisdictional or multi-agency incidents, to provide guidelines for agencies with different legal, geographic, and functional responsibilities to coordinate, plan, and interact effectively. The composition of the UC will depend on the location(s) and type of incident. Nonetheless, all directives emanating from the ICC should be coordinated. Under the UC concept, the following planning objectives must be considered:

- Responsibilities for incident management
- Incident objectives
- Resource availability and capability
- Limitations
- Areas of agreement and disagreement between agencies[33]

The **operations section** is responsible for all activities focused on reduction of the immediate hazard, saving lives and property, establishing control of the situation, and restoring normal operations. Resources for this section might include specially trained, single-agency personnel and equipment, and even special task forces and strike teams. The nature of the incident dictates the composition of the operations section. For example, if a department is responding to a barricaded person, a number of police units may be used: patrol officers may be used to surround or otherwise contain the situation; traffic enforcement officers may be used to restrict and control traffic; a hostage negotiator may be called upon to negotiate with the suspect; and a SWAT team may be present to breach the structure or to neutralize the suspect. Units from other agencies may be called upon. Fire department equipment may be present should there be a fire as a result of the situation, and EMT personnel may be present should there be a need to transport any injured persons to a hospital.

Larger incidents will require personnel from a larger number of agencies. For example, a terrorist event such as a mass shooting or bombing will involve a number of federal agencies such as the FBI, ATF, and home-land security. Ancillary agencies will also be involved, including fire, emergency medical personnel, hospitals, gas and electric utility personnel, and so on. Their efforts will be coordinated through a unified ICC.

The **planning section** collects, evaluates, and disseminates incident situation information and intelligence to the incident commander or unified command, prepares status reports, displays situation information, and maintains status of resources assigned to the incident. It basically records and evaluates the actions taken at the scene.

YOU DECIDE...

The state director of homeland security recently issued a policy directing all cities to prepare a comprehensive terrorist or major event response plan. He advised that the plan should concentrate on two areas: prevention and response. Although officials in the department were acutely aware of the need to move resources into homeland security, the department had not done so. In essence, the department must build its plan from the ground up. The police chief appointed you to the new position of Police Homeland Security Director.

Questions for Discussion

1. What areas should you address?
2. How should you address the city's infrastructure?
3. What new departmental standard operating procedures should be developed?
4. How should you attempt to involve officers from patrol and other operational units in homeland security, especially when responding to a critical incident?

Note that you may wish to incorporate your answers to the box on page 239.

In terms of planning, large incidents are extremely complex. They often require multiple tactics or actions. Moreover, circumstances can change frequently requiring adjustments in an incident response. For example, a multiple structure fire may continue to spread resulting in the need for more fire equipment and personnel and more police officers to evacuate people and prevent people from entering the area. The planning section continuously monitors the situation and makes recommendations to the incident commander about incident requirements.

Since many incidents involve a crime, it is important that all evidence be collected and well documented. This is a function that is coordinated by the planning section. Although individual law enforcement agencies are directly involved in evidence collection and documentation, these efforts must be coordinated to ensure that they examine the total area to ensure that nothing is missed.

The **logistics section** is responsible for all support requirements needed to facilitate effective incident management: facilities, transportation, supplies, equipment maintenance and fuel, food services, communications and technology support, and emergency medical services. Obviously, small events do not require a great deal of logistical support, but in some cases medical, fire, and other governmental support agencies are required. A 2017 school shooting in San Bernardino, California, where a teacher and an elementary school student were killed and another student wounded required the police to procure a staging area where students could be evacuated.

Larger incidents require substantially more logistical support. For example, a flood may require the police department to obtain watercraft to evacuate citizens and animals. The procurement and managed deployment of the watercraft can be extremely complex depending on the magnitude of the flood. This situation would also require that shelters for evacuated people be established, and they would need to be provided food and water. Incidents can become extremely complex, requiring that a range of supplies be obtained.

The **Finance/Administration** section is not required at all incidents, but will be involved where incident management activities require finance and other administrative support services—compensation/claims, determining costs, procurement, and so on. In large-scale incidents where FEMA has been called in, FEMA will handle most of these duties as they will be covered by FEMA. Nonetheless, law enforcement executives should also create budget line-item codes and emergency purchase orders before such an event, so they will be readily available and accessible. Moreover, police managers should keep track of all expenditures when responding to an incident. This allows departments to show city and county officials the costs of the incident and allows them to request additional funding. In some cases, the federal government or state government will reimburse the city or county for those expenditures, so an accurate accounting is important.

In addition, to the operational units within the ICC, there are three support units: public information officer, safety officer, and liaison officer. The **public information officer** is responsible for informing the public about the incident and the progress being made to resolve it. The public information officer is responsible for communicating timely and accurate information to the public during crisis or emergency situations. The answer to the question, "How much do we tell the public?" is a simple one: you tell them everything that does not need to be safeguarded for valid reasons of security. Openness and candor are essential, and keeping the public informed will render good results; keeping the public informed is essential in gaining their cooperation. For example, when there is the possibility of a flood, a public information officer should advise people who live in the area to evacuate and where they can find shelter. When there is a major crime scene, the public information officer should advise the public about traffic issues. The public information officer is key to moving people out of harm's way and gaining their cooperation. Public information officers should use all sorts of media, including radio, television, and social media.

1. Animal Health Emergency Support
2. CBRNE Detection
3. Citizen Preparedness and Participation
4. Citizen Protection: Evacuation and/or In-Place Protection
5. Critical Infrastructure Protection
6. Critical Resource Logistics and Distribution
7. Economic and Community Recovery
8. Emergency Operations Center Management
9. Emergency Public Information and Warning
10. Environmental Health and Vector Control
11. Explosive Device Response Operations
12. Fatality Management
13. Firefighting Operations/Support
14. Food and Agriculture Safety and Defense
15. Information Collection and Threat Recognition
16. Information Sharing and Collaboration
17. Intelligence Fusion and Analysis
18. Interoperable Communications
19. Isolation and Quarantine
20. Mass Care (Sheltering, Feeding, and Related Services)
21. Mass Prophylaxis
22. Medical Supplies Management and Distribution
23. Medical Surge
24. On-Site Incident Management
25. Planning
26. Public Health Epidemiological Investigation and Laboratory Testing
27. Public Safety and Security Response
28. Restoration of Lifelines
29. Risk Analysis
30. Search and Rescue
31. Structural Damage Assessment and Mitigation
32. Terrorism Investigation and Intervention
33. Triage and Pre-Hospital Treatment
34. Volunteer Management and Donations
35. WMD/Hazardous Materials Response and Decontamination
36. Worker Health and Safety

FIGURE 13-5 Possible Actions Taken by Responders at a Large-Scale Event
Source: DHS, *Interim National Preparedness Goal* (Washington, DC: Author, 2005): 7.

The **safety officer** is responsible for monitoring rescue and recovery operations to ensure that they are conducted in a safe manner. They attempt to ensure the safety of responders as well as citizens. They attempt to ensure that responders have the necessary equipment and that it is used safely. They ensure that responders and citizens are provided with adequate food, water, and shelter. They monitor the situation for unsafe conditions to ensure that improper recovery procedures are not used. They ensure that responders are not working in unsafe environments. Even though emergency situations call for drastic actions, they should be performed in a safe manner.

Finally, the **liaison officer** represents the point of contact for coordinating government and nongovernment agencies. When there is a significant incident, there generally is a large number of nongovernment organizations (NGOs) that volunteer and provide a variety of support services. These services must be coordinated. Coordination includes providing locations for these agencies to set up and provide their services. It requires the liaison officer to ensure that all services are being provided. The liaison officer must have the authority to guide the NGOs so that they can adequately provide their services in a safe manner.

These sections have outlined how the NIMS is used to respond to an incident whether it is a terrorist attack or a natural or man-made disaster. We have discussed some of the actionable areas that must be included. Figure 13-5 provides a comprehensive listing of the activities that potentially could occur in a large event.

Summary

This chapter examines homeland security and the response to a critical event. A critical event can be a man-made or natural disaster as well as a terrorist attack. Natural and man-made disasters are included within homeland security since FEMA is based in the DHS. The DHS and the FBI have primary responsibility for terrorism within the United States. This includes prevention and investigation. Federal agencies have intervened in a number of attacks and plots.

We define terrorism and identify some of the primary international groups involved in terrorist activities. Although we mention a few, there literally are hundreds of these groups across the world. Many of the attacks and

plots in the United States have been perpetrated by lone wolf terrorists who sympathize with international terrorist groups. Lone wolf terrorists are examined as well as the radicalization process that moved them to plot to attack America. It is important to note that there are a number of right-wing groups and environmental groups that have also launched attacks.

Weapons of mass destruction are examined in this chapter. The three primary categories of WMDs are nuclear or radiological, biological, and chemical, with nuclear or radiological WMDs being the most destructive. The DHS and other federal departments have extensive programing to prevent them from falling into terrorists' hands, and these agencies have developed a number of response protocols should one be used. Nonetheless, the most common weapons being used are conventional weapons, firearms, and, more recently, vehicles.

The DHS is examined in this chapter. The department has a number of support agencies as well as enforcement agencies. The support agencies primarily conduct research on equipment that can be used to better identify a potential attack. The enforcement agencies have different responsibilities ranging from immigration and border protection to executive protection. These agencies work closely with other federal agencies as well as with state and local law enforcement.

The National Infrastructure Protection Plan is discussed. It provides an outline as to how critical infrastructure is identified and protected. Local police agencies are engaged in a variety of homeland security operations, including threat assessment, critical infrastructure identification, partnerships with private security, and public education. The 9/11 attacks and other attacks and plots have resulted in police leaders reorganizing their departments to carry out these new responsibilities.

Finally, the National Incident Management System (NIMS) is discussed. The NIMS was developed by the DHS to standardize responses to critical incidents. Standardization results in responder agencies knowing the procedures and activities that occur at a critical incident. This results in a more effective response.

Discussion Questions

1. List some of the terrorist organizations operating internationally and in the United States.
2. Describe the categories of weapons of mass destruction and provide examples of each.
3. What are some of the agencies in the Department of Homeland Security, and what are their functions?
4. List the actions that a local police department should take as part of its homeland security program.
5. What is the primary purpose of the National Incident Management System, and what are its primary component parts?
6. Define what is meant by *Incident Command System* as well as its component parts.
7. What are the kinds of natural and man-made disasters that can occur?

Internet Investigations

FEMA, "National Incident Management System"
https://www.fema.gov/national-incident-management-system

Department of Homeland Security, "Critical Infrastructure Security"
https://www.dhs.gov/topic/critical-infrastructure-security

FBI, "Terrorism"
https://www.fbi.gov/investigate/terrorism

U.S. State Department, "Country Reports on Terrorism"
https://www.state.gov/j/ct/rls/crt/2015/

PBS, Lone Wolf Terrorism"
http://www.pbs.org/wgbh/frontline/article/lone-wolf-attacks-are-becoming-more-common-and-more-deadly/

Department of Homeland Security, "State and Major Urban Area Fusion Centers"
https://www.dhs.gov/state-and-major-urban-area-fusion-centers

In the Police Toolkit: Essentials for the Tasks

CHAPTER 14

Technologies for the Tasks: Tools for Today's Police Leaders

STUDENT LEARNING OUTCOMES

As a result of reading this chapter, the student will:

- be able to delineate the five core technologies for police
- understand how to know which technologies to select, by examining types of functions performed
- be able to list the use of technologies for crime analysis, mapping, and problem solving
- understand the application of databases for crime mapping, real-time crime centers, crime management (e.g., predictive and intelligence-led policing; CompStat), and fingerprinting
- comprehend the debate surrounding police use of body-worn cameras and license plate readers
- know the status of several selected technologies, including drones, social media, facial recognition, robots, and apps for crime-fighting
- be able to review some legal, moral, and practical considerations involving technologies in policing
- know what is on the horizon with what is termed the Internet of Things

KEY TERMS AND CONCEPTS

- Apps
- Automatic License Plate Recognition
- Biometrics
- Body-worn cameras
- Cold cases
- Command and control systems
- Community policing and problem solving
- Computer-aided dispatch (CAD)
- Crime mapping
- Drone (unmanned aerial vehicle)
- Electronic control device (ECD)
- Facial recognition
- Fingerprinting

- Geographic information system (GIS)
- Information technology
- Internet of Things
- Management information systems
- Operations information systems
- Proactive policing
- Reactive policing
- Real-time crime center
- Records management system
- Robots
- Smartphones
- Social media
- Support functions

INTRODUCTION

Including a chapter on police technologies for this or any other textbook is, inherently, a risky undertaking. The advancement of technologies in the automotive, television, aeronautic, and other industries demonstrates that there is constant and rapid change in technology. Moreover, several factors—for example, the ongoing research and rapid development of computer hardware, software, and databases; legislative and federal court decisions; the national economy; and the social and political acceptance of technologies—can radically cause the landscape of technologies that are in use or planned today to soon be outdated.

Still, because of the impact and importance of technologies in all of criminal justice, and especially in policing, we must attempt to provide a snapshot of how, why, and which tools are selected and used for crime-fighting. Current and potential police leaders must absolutely understand the nature and capabilities of today's technologies, especially information technologies (IT) which deal with data, analysis, and the inherent privacy concerns.

Furthermore, since the Great Recession forced the funding to decline for most police agencies, police leaders have had to police smarter and more efficiently; certainly technologies can serve as a "force multiplier." And while many police administrators may believe it difficult to afford or justify new or existing technologies in this fiscal environment, it can also be argued that it is certainly unwise to cut technology investments and support staff. As a RAND report noted, technologies can improve the effectiveness of operations and generate cost savings.[1] And as policing budgets begin to increase and return to their pre-Recession state, it would be wise to likewise increase the agency's IT capabilities to the extent possible.

This chapter begins by reviewing five broad categories of police technologies, while focusing on those that involve analytics and sensor/surveillance technologies. Included here are tools for police in their problem-oriented policing efforts (mapping, real-time crime centers, crime management, and fingerprinting tasks). Included are discussions of whether or not police should be compelled to use body-worn cameras and the controversies surrounding license plate readers and drones. Then we look at some means by which one can determine which technologies to use for different police functions, and next is a discussion of how social media and civic apps are being used to better communicate with the general public and address crime and disorder. Robots, apps that assist with crime-fighting, and addressing cold cases are then examined, followed by some caveats: legal, moral, and practical considerations involving technologies in policing. Finally, we discuss a relatively new concept termed the Internet of Things (IoT). The chapter then concludes with a summary, discussion questions, and Internet investigations. A number of case studies, "you decide" scenarios, and examples of technology applications are disseminated throughout the chapter.

CORE TECHNOLOGIES FOR POLICING: FIVE TYPES

The term technology is broadly used to include anything from new computers, a management information system, or sophisticated software for data analysis.[2]

Our chapter discussions of some of the technologies now found in use will be organized around five general categories of technologies that now exist in policing: (1) information technology, (2) analytic technology, (3) communication technology, (4) sensor and surveillance technology, and (5) identification technology.

Information Technology: Computers and Telecommunications

This category of technologies includes the use of computers and telecommunications to store, retrieve, transmit, and manipulate data; this comprises record management systems, computer-aided dispatch systems (CAD), databases, and mobile computer and data terminals. Management information systems (MIS) consist of various databases, such as officer productivity, citizen complaints (see discussion of early intervention systems in Chapter 6), and inventory; it is designed to aid managers and executives in carrying out their administrative duties. MIS captures, maintains, and analyzes all police agency and incident-related information and is vital for tracking and managing criminal and noncriminal events, investigations, and personnel information.

Also included in this category might be records, the FBI's National Crime Information Center, mobile computers, cellular phones, and so on. These were designed to supply police officers and detectives with raw data on such topics as calls for service (CFS), persons, property, and vehicles. Mobile computing allows officers to work in a "mobile office," to query local, state, and national databases; receive and initiate CAD events; view unit status; send e-mail; prepare and file incident reports; issue citations; capture field interview information; access department policies and procedures; research penal codes; and perform many other functions.

Figure 14-1 shows the various categories relating to law enforcement information technology.

Police technologies include computers and telecommunications to store, retrieve, transmit, and manipulate data, including record management systems, various databases, and mobile computer and data terminals.
Courtesy of Federal Bureau of Investigation, USA

Analytic Technology: Discerning Crime Patterns for Problem Solving

This area of police technology encompasses the accumulation and use of large amounts of data along with the employment of systematic methods and techniques for use in identifying crime patterns and relationships. Here we focus on IT for community policing and problem solving, which includes crime analysis, crime mapping, and real-time crime centers. We also consider technologies in another critical policing function: fingerprinting.

The value of employing computers for community policing and problem solving (discussed in Chapter 10) efforts quickly became evident as soon as this philosophy began to surface. As one major city police chief put it, "The use of high-technology equipment and applications is essential to the efficient practice of community policing. Without high technology, officers would find it difficult to provide the level and quality of services the community deserves."[3]

To do their jobs effectively, law enforcement professionals at all levels depend on information. According to one estimate, "roughly 92 percent of an officer's time is spent acquiring, coalescing, or distributing information in one form or another."[4]

More modern, sophisticated policing approaches (e.g., CompStat, predictive policing, intelligence-led policing, and smart policing, discussed in earlier chapters) are even more information-intensive and dependent. They involve not just information on crimes and perpetrators but also data on community conditions, priorities, and other factors that could shape crime prevention and responses. Next, we briefly discuss those interrelated strategies.

Under CompStat, police employ technologies to allow them to think proactively about ways to deal with crime in terms of suppression, intervention, and prevention. Commanders must proactively respond to crime problems, and explain what tactics they have employed to address crime patterns, what resources they have and need, and with whom they have collaborated. Follow-up by top administrators further ensures accountability.

To accomplish intelligence-led policing, many police agencies have both crime analysts and intelligence analysts. Crime analysts use technologies to keep their fingers on the pulse of crime in the jurisdiction: which crime trends are up, which ones are down, where the hot spots are, what type of property is being stolen, and so on. As noted in Chapter 10, *crime analysis* allows police to understand the "what, when, and where," while *intelligence analysis* provides an understanding of the "who"—crime networks and individuals.

With respect to predictive policing (see Chapter 10), the next generation of police problem solving could combine existing technologies like computers, crime analysis, and police reports with a few newer technologies such as artificial intelligence. The future may well bring technologies that can predict crimes before they happen—with predictive analytics acting as a force multiplier that are focused on problem solving.[5] Of course, high-tech tools alone cannot solve crimes, but when trained crime analysts and police management combine the tools with their ingenuity, anything is possible in this high-tech world.

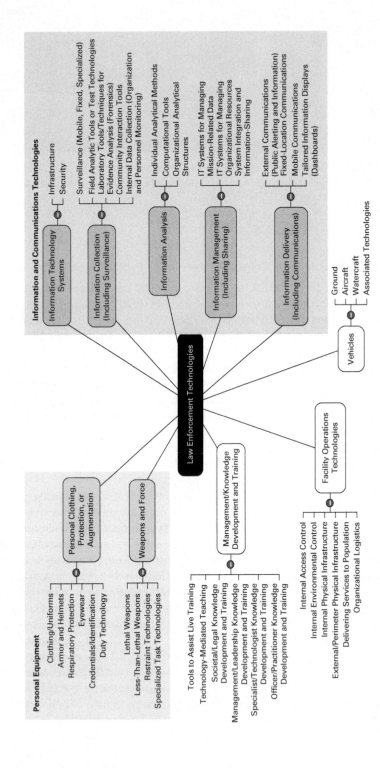

FIGURE 14-1 Categories of Law Enforcement Information Technology

Source: John S. Hollywood, John E. Boon, Jr., Richard Silberglitt, Brian G. Chow, and Brian A. Jackson, *High-Priority Information Technology Needs for Law Enforcement*, RAND Corporation, 2015. Used with permission from RAND Corporation

Compstat meetings rely on strategic problem solving in order to allow police agencies to focus on identifying problems and developing solutions.
Source: Splash News/Alamy Stock Photo

Vestiges of each of the above three strategies can be found in what is now generally termed smart policing initiatives (SPI; see Chapter 10), which contains a research partnership. SPI uses in-depth problem analysis and definition to guide police efforts.

Regarding crime mapping, police leaders, criminologists, sociologists, and other professionals understand that geography has a major influence on crime; indeed, crime is often highest where living conditions are at their worst. Therefore, combining geographic data with police report data and then displaying the information on a map is an effective way to analyze and predict where, how, and why crime occurs. The features and characteristics of cityscapes and rural landscapes can make it easier or more difficult for crime to occur. The placement of alleys, buildings, and open spaces, for example, affects the likelihood that a criminal will strike.

Community policing and problem solving thus looks to simultaneously address the relationship between people and their environments—particularly those places where social ills cause real problems. Geographic analysis can help to reveal crime patterns in places, such as examining where past victims and offenders lived and where crimes occurred.[6] With Geographic Information Systems (GIS), analysts map where crime occurs, combine the resulting visual display with other geographic data (such as location of schools, parks, and industrial complexes), analyze and investigate the causes of crime, and develop responses. Recent advances in statistical analysis make it possible to add more geographic and social dimensions to the analysis.[7] Computerized crime mapping combines geographic information from global positioning satellites with crime statistics gathered by the department's CAD system and demographic data provided by private companies or the U.S. Census Bureau. The result is a picture that combines disparate sets of data for a whole new perspective on crime. Maps can thus paint a picture for crime analysts, who in turn inform officers where they need to focus their patrols. Maps of crimes can also be overlaid with maps or layers of causative data: unemployment rates in the areas of high crime, locations of abandoned houses, population density, reports of drug activity, or geographic features (such as alleys, canals, or open fields) that might be contributing factors. Furthermore, the hardware and software are now available to nearly all police agencies for a few thousand dollars.

The National Institute of Justice's Mapping and Analysis for Public Safety (MAPS) program supports research that helps agencies use GIS to enhance public safety. (See, for example, NIJ's "Mapping and Analysis for Public Safety," at: http://www.nij.gov/topics/technology/maps/pages/welcome.aspx.)[8]

Real-time Crime Centers

Related to crime mapping and analysis is another relatively new approach, the real-time crime center (RTCC), which has the purpose of using technologies to reduce officers' reliance on paper reports and nonintegrated databases to identify crime patterns. By collecting vast amounts of crime-related data—arrest records, mug shots, and warrant information—and providing it rapidly to officers and investigators in the field, these facilities can help in investigations and protect officer safety. Soon, RTCCs may become as ubiquitous as CompStat and other such strategies.

Essentially, with RTCC police use a new information hub containing many years of voice, video, and crime data, which is translated into actionable intelligence that shows criminal activity unfolding in real time. Resembling a "mission control" center, it allows crime analysts and commanders to track the police calls as they are occurring citywide. The RTCC allows staff to notice patterns and spikes in certain activity so commanders can deploy patrol officers and detectives where they're most needed at any given time.[9]

Seattle, Washington, Police Chief Kathleen O'Toole called RTCC "agile policing," combining the work of police officers and crime analysts so as to adapt to the changes in the city's criminal activity.[10] The initiative can also include daily morning meetings among neighboring police agencies to share information on what anomalies or spikes they are observing. Commanders and crime analysts look at a dashboard illuminating a large screen on the wall that shows how many calls police are responding to, the priority level of each call, the nature of the calls, and where on a city map each call is coming from. The information is drawn from 911 dispatch calls, crime data, radio traffic, and vehicle information data and allows the staff to visualize the call data so commanders can make operational decisions on how to deploy officers. Agencies hope this practice will allow police to halt crime sprees as they happen and stop crimes and incidents before they become more serious.[11]

Patrol officers and detectives receive information from the RTCC via radio and the computers in their patrol cars. The crime center consolidates the agency's Criminal Intelligence Section, Data Driven Policing Section, and Crime Analysis detectives into a new Intelligence and Analysts Section.[12]

The accompanying "Focus On" box describes how the New York and Houston police departments established and use RTCC.

Fingerprinting: Expanding Tech and Databases

The FBI's Integrated Automated Fingerprint Identification System, or IAFIS, is the largest criminal fingerprint database in the world, housing the fingerprints and criminal histories for more than 70 million subjects in its criminal master file. Included in its criminal database are fingerprints from 73,000 known and suspected terrorists processed by the U.S. or by international law enforcement agencies.

In this same connection, a biometrics finger reader exists that allows end users the ability to simultaneously capture a fingerprint and finger vein pattern with a single scan; the reader can prevent forgery and

---

FOCUS ON: NEW YORK AND HOUSTON REAL-TIME CRIME CENTERS

The New York Police Department's RTCC system, launched in 2005 (and recently expanded beyond homicides and firearms-related crimes to include robberies, rapes, missing persons, and other serious crimes), can comb through 120 million criminal complaints, arrests, and 911 call records dating back a decade; five million criminal records and parole files maintained by the state; and more than 31 million records of crime committed nationwide. RTCC also made it possible for officers to receive photographs of individuals via handheld devices, and the technology to transmit photographs to the police car laptops also became available.[13]

In Houston, for 15 years police officers lacked the ability to regularly and quickly employ databases containing huge volumes of crime and related information. Another challenge was to make the data accessible in real time. Working with a private concern, HPD developed an RTCC that makes critical information—derived from crime, jail booking, probation, and other databases—immediately available to officers responding to calls. Now, when a call comes in, integration technologies feed the incident information to the RTCC crime analysts. A report is run, pulling related historical information from the various law enforcement databases. Analysts then cross-reference that information with the details of emergency calls. Additional data on persons, vehicles, and property is pulled from internal officers' notes, as well as external government databases. All this information can then be communicated to the responding officers while enroute to the crime scene. For example, officers sent to a domestic violence incident will know if the husband is a repeat offender, has spent time in prison for similar crimes, or is permitted to carry a concealed weapon—all of which will impact the way the officer responds.[14]

Information Builders, "Houston Police Department Creates Real-Time Crime Center," n.d., http://www.informationbuilders.com/applications/houston.

spoofing (a type of scam where one attempts to gain unauthorized access to a another person's system or information by pretending to be the user). Furthermore, it has been certified by the FBI as achieving what is termed "personal identity verification (PIV).

This same technology has been integrated into the latest smartphones, which include a touch fingerprint sensor. Denver, Colorado, police use this technology, and initial results are that the technology works with 99 percent accuracy, providing verification in less than 30 seconds, and identifying gang members, car thieves, and sex offenders.

Communication Technology: The Ability to Talk Across Disciplines and Jurisdictions

In this category, the radio remains the primary means of communication technology in law enforcement agencies. A major issue here is interoperability: the ability to talk across disciplines and jurisdictions via radio communications networks on demand, in real time. Simply put, a lot of systems do not work well together, as many police leaders who purchase a new radio system soon learn after implementation.[15] They must ensure that, to the extent possible, the infrastructure on which the systems run is carefully selected. For example, if local police departments, sheriff's office, state highway patrol, and other first responders (fire and emergency medical services) are on different radio frequencies and unable to communicate with each other directly, the results may be catastrophic in the case of a critical incident, disaster, or terrorist attack.

Sensor and Surveillance Technology: Body Cameras, Drones, Other Applications

These technologies include closed circuit televisions (CCTVs), which, if used properly, can provide benefits by reducing fear of crime, aiding police investigations, managing crime-ridden locations, and gathering information.[16] Body-worn cameras (BWC), which are being adopted to improve evidence collection, strengthen officer performance and accountability, enhance agency transparency, and investigate and resolve complaints about officer-involved incidents are a relatively new surveillance technology. Similarly, license plate readers (LPRs), which read vehicle license plates and compare these to a database of wanted offenders or stolen vehicles is now being used more extensively. Unmanned aerial vehicles (or unmanned aircraft systems, also known as drones) are increasing in popularity. In this section we discuss BWC, LPR, and drones.

The Cry Heard Round the Nation: "Wear Body Cameras!"

Body-worn cameras (BWC) were discussed briefly in Chapter 9. Here we examine them in more detail, in terms of potential assets and liabilities.

Two national ramifications of the recent rash of controversial police shootings across the United States (also discussed in Chapter 9) have been an examination of police methods and an emphasis on greater police transparency—both of which include a cry for BWC. With peoples' cellphones often recording what appears to many people to be questionable cases of police use of force, many politicians and activists argue that all officers should be compelled to use BWC.

As is often the case with the implementation of new criminal justice policies and procedures, however, "the devil is in the details." Putting such a practice into effect carries a number of hidden issues and problems.

Indeed, according to Cindy Shain, Director of the Southern Police Institute, University of Louisville, the following issues accompanying BWC must be addressed[17]:

1. Legal issues (privacy): many kinds of potentially sensitive images can be captured, of both citizens and police officers. Should videos be made that are publicly embarrassing, such as people who are being arrested or are intoxicated? Would videos be made of strip searches and interviews of suspects? Of innocent child victims, witnesses, confidential informants, and bystanders? People who are suspects but not yet charged with a crime? What about officers' reasonable right to privacy, such as during bathroom visits or lunch breaks or in private conversations? Finally, who should be allowed to view the videos?[18]
2. Storage and related costs: as one expert put it, the "800-pound gorilla in the room" with BWC is that, unless state laws are changed, the ability of and cost for police to dedicate personnel and equipment to store, redact, and provide videos for all open-records requests (to include those by defense attorneys) would be extremely challenging if not impossible. If recording is to be continual during a shift, many hours of editing might be required. Therefore, body cameras can carry tremendous costs—not only from the equipment itself but also from the time required to store and edit the videos. A related issue is that Freedom of Information Act (FOIA) requests are often from individuals or companies wishing to post police activity on YouTube and sell advertising space.[19]
3. Personnel considerations: relating to the above cost considerations is the added—possibly exorbitant— cost of increased staffing to handle all the evidence, redaction, preparing evidence for court, Open Records requests, and so on..

The use of body-worn cameras by police involves a number of issues that police leaders must address.
Source: David McNew/Getty Images News/Getty Images

4. Policies and procedures concerning the equipment: directives must be established; at minimum, they should include where the cameras will be worn (e.g., hat, sunglasses, chest); who will maintain, charge, and issue new cameras; training to be provided on when to activate and deactivate cameras; where data will be stored and safeguarded; how to protect and document the chain of custody; and the process for releasing recorded data to the public (including redaction processes).[20]
5. Community acceptance/understanding/involvement in decision making: certainly, for all of the foregoing legal, financial, and other reasons, it is important to begin the conversation about BWC early with elected leaders, community members, and with the police union.

License Plate Readers

License plate readers (also known as Automatic License Plate Recognition, or ALPR) are a surveillance technology that can be mounted to patrol cars and capture license plate numbers during an entire patrol shift. When a suspect license plate number is read, audible and visual alarms alert the officer. To demonstrate its power, in two months' time the Denver police department processed 835,000 license plate images, which led to 17,000 hits for warrants, stolen vehicles, and other violations.[22]

For obvious reasons, this technology is rapidly becoming popular as a tool. However, the "You Decide" box below describes a legal conundrum that exists with regard to the use of license plate readers.

FOCUS ON: CELLPHONES TO SOON REPLACE BODY CAMERAS?

Perhaps not surprisingly, a new smartphone app has been announced as a solution for police agencies seeking more accessible and inexpensive means for officers to record audio and video. In mid-2017, the Jersey City, New Jersey, Police Department announced it was testing the app with 250 officers.

The officers simply download the app on a smartphone, strap the phone onto their chest, and simply push a button to begin recording; the video is streamed live to supervisors who can monitor the recording from their offices. The entire encounter is then saved onto a server, saving officers having to download all of their shift video at end of shift. The app is free to any police department, thus offsetting a major barrier to body camera use: the cost. Test runs of the app already performed in Rio de Janeiro, South Africa, and Bulgaria show that officers are quick to adapt to the app.[21]

YOU DECIDE...

LAWSUITS ARGUING FOR/AGAINST LICENSE PLATE READERS

For many people ALPR has too little regulation against invasion of privacy. For example, the American Civil Liberties Union (ACLU) argues that ALPRs collect a lot of data that is sometimes pooled into regional sharing systems; as a result, enormous databases of innocent motorists' location information are rapidly growing. This information is often retained for years, or even indefinitely, with few or no restrictions to protect privacy rights. While not calling for a complete ban, the ACLU believes that as ALPR technology spreads, legislation and law enforcement agency policies should be adopted that will respect personal privacy and prevent the government from tracking our movements on a massive scale.[23]

Conversely, a Utah law prohibiting the use of such automated high-speed cameras to photograph license plates is being challenged in a lawsuit filed in federal court by two ALPR manufacturing firms. According to the lawsuit, the Utah Automatic License Plate Reader System Act infringes on constitutionally protected speech of the First Amendment. It is also argued that license plates are public by nature and contain no sensitive or private information. Five states have already enacted legislation that is identical or similar to the Utah act.[24]

In related litigation, in what appeared to be the first legal challenge by a private individual, in May 2015 a Virginia man sued the Fairfax County (Virginia) Police Department for collecting images of his license plate and storing them in its massive database. After learning that his license plate had been scanned by an ALPR twice in the previous year and stored in a police database, he opted to sue.[25]

According to the RAND Corporation, because the use of ALPR is legal in most states, it is unlikely that any lawsuit attacking their use would result in civil liability; however, because of their privacy implications, it is recommended that agencies establish clear policies regarding data retention, access, to help address some of the privacy concerns.[26]

Should police be permitted to deploy license plate readers? Or, conversely, do they pose an unacceptable threat to our right to privacy?

Rules and Restriction on Drones

Drones, or unmanned aerial vehicles, are proliferating; indeed, nearly 300,000 drone owners registered their small aircraft during the initial 30 days after the Federal Aviation Administration (FAA) introduced an online registration system in December 2015, for a mere $5 fee. Indeed, for the first time in U.S. history, in order for children to play with the new drone received as a Christmas or birthday gift, the "toy" must first be registered with an agency of the federal government.

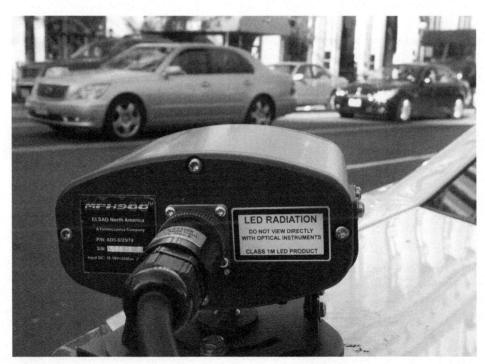

To many people, policies should be adopted for use of license plate readers that will respect personal privacy and prevent the government from tracking people on a massive scale.
Source: Paul J. Richards/Afp/Getty Images

Given that, drones are rapidly beginning to cause a number of problems—such as the (apparently intoxicated) operator whose drone crashed onto the White House lawn in early 2015 as well as legal challenges; in the latter regard, some attorneys are already becoming specialized in drone law (see, e.g., Drone.law.pro and Dronelaw.com).

State-legislated rules for and restrictions over drones have become necessary (see box below); accordingly, in February 2015 President Barack Obama issued an executive memorandum concerning how federal agencies will use drones of all sizes. During that same month, the FAA promulgated rules allowing small commercial drones weighing up to 55 pounds and flown within sight of their remote pilots during daylight hours. The aircraft must stay below 500 feet in the air and fly less than 100 mph. People flying drones would need to be at least 17 years old, pass an aeronautics test, and be vetted by the Transportation Security Administration.

Finally, as a possible harbinger of things to come, in early 2016 a bill was introduced in the California legislature that would require drone hobbyists to obtain a physical or electronic license plate for identification purposes; pay a small insurance fee at the time of purchase for any future damage or injury associated with the drone; and have some drones be equipped with GPS and emergency shutoff capabilities. The goal is to make drones identifiable and owners financially responsible in the event of injuries, improper handling, or property damage.

These actions represent major progress in integrating drones into U.S. airspace—which is particularly critical because the Association for Unmanned Vehicle Systems International projects the industry will create 70,000 jobs with $13.6 billion in economic activity immediately after drones fully share the skies with other aircraft. The FAA has been granting certificates for drone flight to police departments for years.

As a final note, the U.S. government now patrols nearly half the Mexican border by drones in areas where there are no agents, camera towers, ground sensors, or fences. It plans to expand the strategy to include the Canadian border. A Predator B drone (which operates up to 50,000 feet, carries a 3,850-pound payload, and is twice as fast as the original Predator) can sweep remote mountains, canyons, and rivers with a high-resolution video camera and return within three days for another video in the same spot. The two videos are then overlaid for analysts who use sophisticated software to identify tiny changes, such as the tracks of immigrants who entered the country illegally or a drug-trafficker's vehicle. The government has operated about 10,000 drone flights under the strategy, known internally as "change detection," since it began in March 2013. In the future, drones might also be used for seeking out and surveilling persons who are planning or involved in terroristic activities. However, this use of drones is not without controversy; Congressional hearings in early 2013 on drone surveillance of U.S. citizens whose behavior conforms to a particular profile would indicate that politicians and Americans are very suspicious of such uses of drones in this country.

Identification Technology: Facial Recognition

This area includes technologies for facial recognition and DNA analysis (rape kits, not discussed here, might also be included).[27]

Facial recognition software is being rapidly adopted by police across the country. The software can identify 16,000 points on a person's face—determining the distance between the eyes or the shape of the lips, for instance—and compare them with thousands of similar points in police booking or other photos at a rate of more than one million faces a second. However, as with several of the IT tools discussed above, this technology is being

---

FOCUS ON: OREGON'S DRONE SURVEILLANCE LAW

In July 2013, Oregon enacted legislation limiting the police use of drones to prevent mass and/or suspicionless surveillance. The law prohibits the use of drones by law enforcement except in the following circumstances:

- A warrant specifically authorizing the use of a drone
- Exigent circumstances that make it unreasonable for law enforcement to first get a warrant
- Consent
- Search and rescue

- Assisting an individual in a life-or-death emergency
- State of emergency declared by governor
- Reconstruction of a crime scene

The law makes clear that information gathered via drones in violation of this act will not be admissible in court nor used as reasonable suspicion or probable cause. The law also requires enforcement to register their drones with the Oregon Department of Aviation and provide annual report detailing the frequency and purpose of use during the previous year.

Lawmakers in a number of states are considering legislation that would impose limitations on police use of drones.
Source: alxpin/E+/Getty Images

often used with few guidelines and little oversight; thus, questions regarding privacy and concerns about potential misuse arise. For example, when Aaron Harvey was stopped by San Diego police while driving, an officer searched his car and also took his photograph; it was run through the software to try to confirm his identity and determine whether he had a criminal record. In another case, a retired San Diego firefighter was ordered to sit on a curb while police took his photo and ran it through the software, and then used a cotton swab to collect a DNA sample from inside his cheek. (At the time, the San Diego Police Department did not require police officers to file a report when using the facial recognition technology but not making an arrest. Rather, it was viewed as a pilot program, and thus the department did not have a written policy regulating facial recognition software.)

Concerns are that officers are collecting a great deal of information that could impact a lot of completely innocent people, and there is very little oversight of the equipment. Indeed, police in Boston tested facial recognition technology but decided not to adopt it, saying it crossed an ethical line.

However, the Federal Bureau of Investigation believes in the future of facial recognition systems, continuing its $1 billion program known as Next Generation Identification (NGI), begun in 2008 and now allowing police agencies to search more than 20 million images available in its database, in addition to fingerprints, for their investigations.

YOU DECIDE...

You are captain of the agency's traffic division and recently attended a national conference where the benefits of red light and speed cameras were presented by a major vendor of the technology. Vendor representatives cited reduced intersection accidents, lower number of red light and speed violations, and decreased pedestrian fatalities as the benefits. You also learn of significant revenues coming to the city—a major selling point for the city manager and council.

You present this proposal at an executive staff meeting, seeking approval to move forward with their acquisition. However, your peers and executives express concerns about how the cameras may impact public opinion as well as the agency's community policing efforts. The chief of police opts to table the issue until the next meeting so she can have more time to consider both sides of the issue.

Questions for Discussion:

1. What other questions would the chief likely have before arriving at a decision concerning your proposal?

2. What would you consider benefits and drawbacks to this technology?

3. Will this technology likely have a negative impact on the department's community policing efforts? If so, how? Is there a way to implement this technology and not impact community policing?

WHICH IT TOOLS TO USE? CONSIDER THE TYPE OF TASK INVOLVED

A primary consideration for police leaders is which technologies they should invest their time and effort in, so as to develop a comprehensive acquisition plan. One way for them to approach this question is to categorize police activities by types of functions performed. Such a classification was developed by Hoey,[28] whose three broadly defined areas were as follows:

1. *Support* functions, including communication, coordination, administrative, and oversight functions, such as dispatch, personnel management, surveillance, and in-service training. Specific types of IT investments supporting these functions include:
   a. Administrative systems, including records management
   b. Communications systems, including computer-aided dispatch (a software system for call handling and dispatching, crime mapping (discussed below), data reporting and analysis, and so on) and in-car mobile data terminals
   c. Surveillance systems, including CCTV and gunshot detection systems.
4. *Reactive policing* functions, including responding to citizens' CFS, responding to emergencies, and conducting investigations. Specific types of related IT investments included systems intended to help law enforcement with criminal investigations, such as an Integrated Automated Fingerprint Identification System terminal; and
5. *Proactive policing* functions, including intelligence-driven operations, such as hotspot patrols, community-oriented engagement, and data sharing with other federal and state agencies, businesses, and partner organizations. IT investments in this area include use of intelligence systems (e.g., hot spot analysis), problem analysis, and sharing information with other state, federal, and local repositories and intel centers.

These three categories reflect key differences in strategies. They also demonstrate that before a police agency can realize any value from its IT investments, it must first understand the kinds of activities those tools are intended to assist.

This is most readily seen with proactive policing techniques: for example, while IT-based, predictive crime-pattern tools might be valuable for a department deeply involved in community policing and problem solving, an agency that chooses to only engage in reactive answering of calls for service would find such an investment to be a waste of scarce resources. Therefore, the above classification scheme allows agencies to separate activities by the different potential effects of IT in terms of desired outcomes, and also to determine whether benefits would even be expected from particular IT investments, given departmental strategies and officer allocation decisions.[29]

YOU DECIDE...

1. Your chief executive has tasked you, the agency's technology specialist, with bringing your agency into "the next decade" by examining technologies that should be acquired. Using information and descriptions of the technologies presented in this chapter, select and prioritize five new technologies (either extant or in development) that you believe your agency should minimally acquire and use, justifying each in terms of its capabilities.

2. More local law enforcement agencies are using or considering the use of drones, but many questions remain concerning their use and privacy issues. Respond to the following questions, and defend your answers:

   • Do you support police use of drones for surveillance purposes involving serious offenses? If so, for what crime-related purposes?

   • Should police be allowed to use drones for Fourth Amendment (searches and seizures) types of operations, if legal conditions have been met?

   • Do you endorse using drones for lower-level functions, such as catching traffic speeders?

   • Would you be in favor of arming the drones with bullets or tear gas?

   • Should drones be used, without prior consent from U.S. courts or other oversight body, to kill persons whose "profile" indicates they pose a dangerous threat to security?

   Assume that a major motorcycle rally of approximately 50,000 bikers is coming to your jurisdiction soon. These rallies are known to be frequented by opposing gang and club members, resulting in violence in other cities. Your police chief has tasked you with planning efforts in preparing and staffing for the bikers' arrival. Accordingly, what kinds of information would you want to obtain, databases would you consult, and which outside agencies would you contact in order to develop a strategy for policing this large gathering?

What Police Leaders Must Know

It is beyond the intended purpose, scope, and audience of this textbook to discuss the comprehensive and complex aspects of technologies planning, acquisition, and implementation—all of which must be cognized by police leaders; rather, we succinctly depict these various steps or phases in Figure 14-2.

In this chapter section we will merely review two important aspects of technologies that must be understood by these individuals: the need for tech interface and the use of social media.

Knowing which police technology to use depends on the type of problem to be addressed and functions performed.
Courtesy of Federal Bureau of Investigation, USA

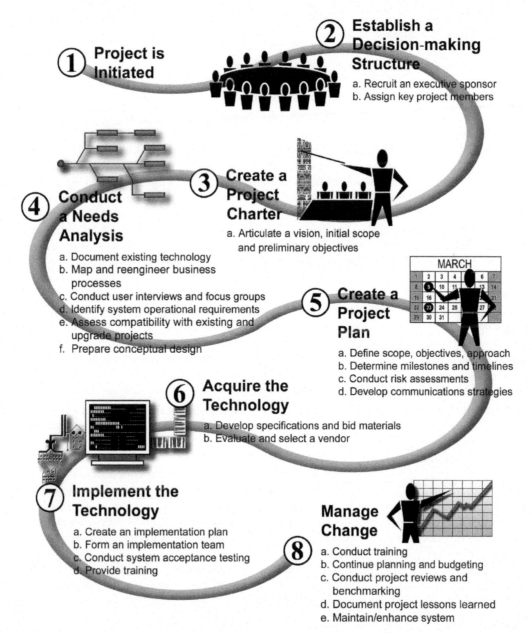

FIGURE 14-2 Planning for, Acquiring, Implementing Law Enforcement IT Projects: A Roadmap
Source: U.S. Department of Justice, Office of Community Oriented Policing Services, Law Enforcement Tech Guide: How to Plan, Purchase and Manage Technology (Successfully!), 2002, p. 8, http://www.search.org/files/pdf/TECHGUIDE.pdf.

The Need for Tech Interface

The challenge for police leaders is to ensure that the departments' technology framework ensures that all IT programs are fully interfaced with one another. This means Computer Aided Dispatch (CAD), Records Management System (RMS), Jail Management System (JMS), Mobile Data and Report Writing System, Fire reporting, Mapping and GIS and Personnel and Resources are fully integrated and accessible to functional areas of police, courts, and correctional agencies with access to the IT. These systems allow officers and staff to perform a number of functions, including voiceless dispatch and wants and warrants checks using mobile data terminals in police vehicles, crime analysis and mapping using CAD and RMS data, photo lineups for investigations using JMS programs, and automated report writing for officers in vehicles or at a computer in the station using RMS programs. The integration of these primary functions significantly improves efficiencies and effectiveness by eliminating duplicate entry of data and information in each of the programs.

Employing Social Media

The term social media has come to denote a vast array of Internet-based tools and platforms that increase and enhance the sharing of information, both in the public and private sectors. Social media can involve the transfer of text, photos, audio, video, and information in a general fluid manner among Internet users. Furthermore, social media platforms have created online communities where people and information can be easily shared, searched, promoted, disputed, and created.[30]

In this section, we discuss social media use in the context of policing, focusing on the Boston Marathon bombing of 2013 and the use of social media by officers themselves.

Lessons from Boston's Marathon Bombing

In April 2013, two bombs exploded during Boston's annual Marathon, killing three people and injuring more than 260 others. What ensued was an extraordinary manhunt and massive use of social media by law enforcement to keep the media and frightened citizens accurately informed about what was going on, via its official Twitter account. In sum, the practice was very simple and yet effective.[31]

Today, some police agencies employ full-time civilian personnel who are in charge of social media and to direct public relations through the various channels—Twitter, Facebook, YouTube—in a real-time manner. The scope of social media continues to grow, with social media also allowing police to have two-way conversations with the community, to include receiving messages from citizens about crime and disorder (including anonymous tips). It can also be used to conduct virtual "ride-alongs," with live tweeting during an entire shift from an officer's patrol car. This gives the public a view of what police do and what is going on.[32]

Police agencies now commonly use social media for investigations, including evidence collection (people bragging about their actions on social media sites); location of suspects (investigators "friend" suspects and track their locations); and criminal network investigations (again, gangs are prone to boast about their actions on social media sites). A good example of this use is the Albuquerque, New Mexico, Police Department, which works with private security partners to monitor tweets containing certain keywords, in order to intercept rival gangs. In one instance, police prevented the gangs from causing disruptions at a major amusement park.[33]

A Concern: When Police Use Facebook

A Brooklyn police officer arrested a burglary gang by adding gang members as friends on Facebook. The officer tracked the gang members to their location, where they photographed the young men committing a burglary, and then arrested them.

For years, social media have been used to track criminal networks. Police methods are becoming more sophisticated, however: by combining social media, databases, and network analysis tools, police can keep track of gang activities. They not only see the status updates of youths but also view photos to determine who might be a witness in a particular case. Bystanders (potential witnesses) can also be identified from background photos that are posted, and a time-stamped photo can be relevant in an investigation. Social media also helps in identifying suspects who were friends or associates of other suspects in a crime; all of them can be brought in to be interviewed and possibly convicted of crimes.

Some teens' families complain that their kids are being unfairly labeled as criminal affiliates because of their social media connections. There have been cases where the description of a shooter was given ambiguously, for example, as "a tall light-skinned black man in a hoodie," leading to an arrest being labeled in a database as a gang member or affiliate. Also, two siblings, one who is law-abiding and the other a criminal, can be lumped together because of their computer's social connections, entered into a database of suspected criminals, and be viewed as criminals.

YOU DECIDE...

You, a lieutenant, are recently assigned to manage a regional gang task force comprised of law enforcement agencies in a large metropolitan area. You are immediately surprised to learn that the task force lacks any technology to track gang members, which severely hampers the ability to identify potential offenders and gang affiliations. Also severely lacking in funding, you are assigned a sergeant who is familiar with how to establish such a database.

However, you are informed that the issue of gang databases has recently come under legislative scrutiny (e.g., the State of Washington legislature enacted RCW 423.43.762, which provides agencies guidelines for operating a gang database;

see https://app.leg.wa.gov/rcw/default.aspx?cite=43.43.762 in preparation for addressing the following questions), and must take into account such challenges.

Questions for Discussion:

1. What advantages may the database provide the regional task force?
2. After reading the Washington legislation, what issues concerning the database must you be concerned with?
3. How will you ensure compliance with the legislation and obtain the technology needed?

UPDATES ON SELECTED TECHNOLOGIES

Next, we consider what seems to be the current state of two IT tools for police: robots and relatively new apps for crime-fighting.

Uses of Robots

Robots are playing an increasingly important role in our lives. Consider the patrol officer's vehicle was at least partially assembled by robots, people have robot vacuum cleaners in their homes, NASA's probes are interplanetary robots, and of course the police are finding many uses of the big and small varieties.[34] Robots are now fitted with odor sensors, video capability (including night vision), and a camera for photographing crime scenes; an ECD; and even the ability to engage in two-way communications.[35]

One of the most notable uses of robots was after James Eagan Holmes committed one of the worst mass shootings in American history, killing 12 people and wounding 58 at an Aurora, Colorado, movie theater in July 2012. Being informed that his apartment was booby-trapped, police officers and bomb-squad experts sent in a bomb-removal robot to disarm a tripwire guarding the apartment's front door. The robot then neutralized potential explosive devices, incendiary devices, and fuel found near the door.[36]

The largest robot in the police arsenal is one used by the Los Angeles police; at 39,000 pounds, the remote-controlled vehicle can be used to lift cars and tear into buildings. With a hydraulic arm extending up to 50 feet and equipped with a claw, a forklift, or a bucket, the $1 million robot can be used for both barricade and bomb incidents. Another large robot is a vehicle that carries a shield capable of protecting 12 officers and can be used for breaching.

Submersible drones can now operate under water at depths of up to 330 feet. Equipped with a wide-angle camera, they are used by police to make fixed lawn mower-style sweeps of wide areas for body and evidence recovery.

Helpful Apps for Crime-fighting

Recently, the City of Chicago released to the public a large amount of city data for public consumption, including up-to-date crime incident data. This release of data helped citizens to better understand the police and crime. This helped to merge the needs for safe communities with law enforcement's efforts to fight crime and improve public safety.

"Hacking" has understandably become a dirty word for most Americans and governments. However hacking is not always bad. Hacking can be a positive approach to problem solving. Here, civic hacking for the public's benefit is defined as

> hands-on, citizen-driven action which produces civic innovation—it could be contributing code to an open-source civic app...or conducting a workshop with city officials to discuss how new policy could improve a neighborhood.[37]

In 2013, Chicago city officials sponsored a "safe communities" hackathon, where participants were to use new methods to query crimes, wanted lists, and mug shots, as well as graffiti problems, vacant building code violations, and even police beat boundaries. The result was a wave of apps that Chicagoans could use to track crime and improve public safety. The success of this crime hackathon spawned other such practices, some of which included contests for the best civic app. One of the winners was a mobile app that allows an injured or lost person to send out a distress notice to anyone designated as a recipient. A second companion app sends out continuous updates on the location of the individual in trouble.[38]

A smartphone and tablet app now is capable of making facial composites from witness descriptions. The officer chooses the various facial features from a sliding menu that appears below the main screen. Each feature can be moved and resized individually, and the completed composite looks like a pencil sketch. Once complete, the composite is saved as an image file and can be printed or emailed as necessary.

Inexpensive apps are also available for people who work complicated schedules, so users can tell in the future when they will be on- or off-duty or flag comp time, vacation, training, or court appearances.[39] Another app is a report-writing aid, where users enter information such as times, dates, locations, names, notes, and so on into fields, and the app organizes them by case. The file can then be e-mailed as a PDF or just stored in "the cloud."[40]

Solving Cold Cases

South San Francisco's Police Department (SSFPD) was asked to reopen a cold case known as the Gypsy Hill murders, which involved five homicides in multiple Bay Area locations. SSFPD was tasked with spearheading a multi-jurisdictional task force that included four cities as well as the FBI, and to canvass four widely dispersed neighborhoods in three separate cities. Because of the large scope of this investigation, SSFPD needed a sophisticated tool. The city's IT department was approached and asked to help develop a tool that would allow officers to visualize reports from the field and thus expedite the collection and coordination of the investigation. A desktop app was created to track where officers in the field had visited. Key information (e.g., time and status of contact) could then be entered. An interactive map was automatically updated so an entire room of officers could visually follow the investigation.

Using these and other techniques, eventually the Gypsy Hill killer was identified as Rodney Halbower, who had spent most of his life in prison. In January 2015, Halbower was charged with two of the murders when DNA evidence was believed to link him to the crimes.[41]

SOME CAVEATS: LEGAL, MORAL, AND PRACTICAL CONSIDERATIONS

If police leaders or students of criminal justice are looking to the courts for clear-cut guidance in the use of new technologies, particularly in the area of privacy rights, they will likely come away wanting: the law seems to be "all over the place" regarding this subject.

As an example, a U.S. District Judge in Wisconsin ruled that it was reasonable for Drug Enforcement Administration agents to enter rural property without permission or a warrant to install multiple "covert digital surveillance cameras" in hopes of uncovering evidence that 30 to 40 marijuana plants (reasoning that the drug was being grown in "open fields" and thus could be searched without warrants because they're not protected by the Fourth Amendment).[42] However, the United States Supreme Court held in 2012 that police attaching a Global Positioning System (GPS) device to a suspect's vehicle without a search warrant does violate the Fourth Amendment.[43]

Police use of new technologies thus poses a wide range of unresolved issues in terms of legality. First, many technology tools (including the use of robots and drones, which do not fall under the IT category) are so new that the courts have not had time to rule on their constitutionality. Furthermore, in some jurisdictions different state and federal courts have handed down conflicting rulings. This means that police are often experimenting with little or no guidance from the courts about the constitutionality of their actions. In the near future, many of these constitutional questions (many of which will involve citizens' right to privacy) will be taken up by lower courts and eventually reach the U.S. Supreme Court.[44] Meanwhile, police leadership is free to test different technologies that appear to be the most useful, cost-effective.[45]

Another touchy technology issue concerns the matter of legitimacy in the eyes of the communities as they regard privacy issues. Even within a given city or county, people in different neighborhoods or regions may differ in their opinions about how to balance privacy concerns and crime-fighting.

There are a number of legislative issues that must be decided as well; oftentimes, the laws governing their use were written decades ago and do not reflect current realities. For example, most wiretap laws were written in the era of land-line telephones, and many Freedom of Information laws were intended to govern the release of written documents, not video footage from police cameras.[46]

ON THE HORIZON: THE INTERNET OF THINGS

Now technology is about to diverge into a new direction, called the Internet of Things (IoT). What is IoT? It is still an ambiguous term, but in sum, IoT is a relatively new term generally describing interconnected computing devices, mechanical and digital machines, objects, animals, or people that have the ability to transfer data over a network without requiring human-to-human or human-to-computer interaction.[47] In other words, with sensors, code, and infrastructure, any object—from a car, to a cat, to a barcode—can become networked. Therefore, IoT is essentially a system of machines or objects that are specially outfitted so that those objects can communicate with one another.[48]

In the past, technologies had to be programmed by and interact with humans in order to function. With IoT, such is not the case. For example, it's possible for a doctor to monitor someone's heart activity through an Internet connection; people can set their home's thermostat or to check on security while they are away. Here, devices in one's home are connected to the Internet and that connection can be used to monitor them.

One of the potential uses of IoT involves wearable technologies, and the U.S. Department of Homeland Security (DHS) is now supporting their development—while also compelling public safety agencies to think about a future where mobile sensors, communications, materials, and visualization technologies can enhance the safety of the public and its responders.[49] With wearable technologies, sensors can be integrated into police and firefighters' uniforms, making it possible to deliver vital data on their status as a critical incident unfolds. This is a rapidly growing area that could soon include

- puncture-detection sensors woven into fabric, so that if an officer is shot, a 911 call would go out automatically
- fabrics that generate electricity by the body's own movements, keeping devices charged without the need to carry extra batteries and chargers
- a mouth guard that can channel signals through the teeth and jawbone, conveying sound even in a noisy environment[50]
- wireless camera and video capabilities built into eyewear.

Summary

This chapter demonstrated for police leaders how technologies have become an essential prerequisite to effective policing and crime-fighting. Since computers first came to the field in the 1970s, their use and potential for crime-fighting has grown exponentially, and it would seem that their application is only limited by the budgets and creativity of police. Certainly, just a few years ago, one could not have conceived of police technologies that could engage in addressing crime and disorder to the extent they are today. And, as amounts of data and numbers of available databases continue to increase, the police will only become more astute in addressing crime and disorder. Soon, the real-time crime centers, discussed in this chapter, may be as commonplace as computers in patrol cars and officers with smartphones. Certainly, technologies—along with the ability of all police personnel to use their creativity in its practical application, make this a most exciting time to be employed in the law enforcement field.

Discussion Questions

1. How do police determine which technologies are most helpful by types of functions performed?

2. Why and how is IT suited for problem-oriented policing?

3. What are some of the promises and pitfalls involved with equipping police with body-worn cameras?

4. What are some of the purposes and practical applications of crime mapping? Real-time crime centers?

5. How can social media and civic apps be used to address crime and disorder?

6. How are technologies assisting with various traffic-related functions?

7. What must be done in terms of planning and application in order for IT to improve policing?

8. How would you describe some of the legal, moral, and practical considerations involving the use of IT in policing?

9. How can technologies assist in addressing the issue of texting while driving?

10. What do studies indicate concerning the safety of electronic control devices?

11. What is the legal and practical status of drones, facial recognition, fingerprinting, robots, and apps for crime-fighting?

12. What is the Internet of Things, and what promise does it hold for public safety?

Internet Investigations

Center for Evidence-based Crime Policy, George Mason University, "Police Technology"
http://cebcp.org/evidence-based-policing/what-works-in-policing/research-evidence-review/police-technology/

Ibid., "Realizing the Potential of Technology in Policing"
http://cebcp.org/wp-content/technology/ImpactTechnologyFinalReport.pdf

National Institute of Justice, "Law Enforcement Equipment and Technology"
http://www.nij.gov/topics/law-enforcement/technology/pages/welcome.aspx

Police Technology, "History of Police Technology"
http://www.police-technology.net/id59.html

Advice That Has Stood the Test of Time: Some Practical Counsel

LAO-TZU'S VIEWS

This book has covered many facets of police leadership in its 14 chapters. Perhaps at its simplest level, the book is saying that a successful leader influences others by example and gains the willing obedience, confidence, respect, and loyalty of subordinates. This characteristic of leadership was recognized in the sixth century B.C. by Lao-Tzu, when he wrote:

> The superior leader gets things done
>
> With very little motion.
>
> He imparts instruction not through many words
>
> But through a few deeds.
>
> He keeps informed about everything
>
> But interferes hardly at all.
>
> He is a catalyst.
>
> And although things wouldn't get done as well
>
> If he weren't there,
>
> When they succeed he takes no credit.
>
> And because he takes no credit
>
> Credit never leaves him.
>
> (quoted in Bennett and Hess, 2001:56)

ANALECTS OF CONFUCIUS AND MACHIAVELLI

The writings of two other major figures have stood the test of time. The analects (or brief passages) of Confucius (551–479 B.C.) and the writings of Machiavelli (A.D. 1469–1527) are still popular today. Many college and university students in a variety of academic disciplines have analyzed the writings of both, especially Machiavelli's *The Prince*, written in 1513. Both of these philosophers tended to agree on many points regarding the means of governance, as the following will demonstrate. After reading some quotations from each philosopher, we consider their application to police leadership.

Confucius often emphasized the moralism of leaders, saying, "He who rules by moral force is like the pole-star, which remains in its place while all the lesser stars do homage to it. Govern the people by regulations, keep order among them by chastisements, and they will flee from you, and lose all self-respect. Govern them by moral force, keep order among them...and they will...come to you of their own accord. If the ruler is upright, all will go well even though he does not give orders. But if he himself is not upright, even though he gives orders, they will not be obeyed." (Waley, 1938:88, 173)

Confucius also believed that those people whom the leader promotes are of no small importance: "Promote those who are worthy, train those who are incompetent; that is the best form of encouragement" (Waley, 1938:92). He also believed that leaders should learn from and emulate good administrators:

> In the presence of a good man, think all the time how you may learn to equal him. In the presence of a bad man, turn your gaze within! … Even when I am walking in a party of no more than three I can always be certain of learning from those I am with. There will be good qualities that I can select for imitation and bad ones that will teach me what requires correction in myself. (Waley, 1938:105, 127)

Unlike Confucius, Machiavelli is often maligned for being cruel; the "ends justify the means" philosophy imputed to him even today has cast a pall over his writings. Although often as biting as the "point of a stiletto" (Machiavelli, 1992:xvii) and seemingly ruthless at times ("Men ought either to be caressed or destroyed, since they will seek revenge for minor hurts but will not be able to revenge major ones," and "If you have to make a choice, to be feared is much safer than to be loved" (Machiavelli, 1992:7, 46)), he, like Confucius, often spoke of the leader's need to possess character and compassion. For all of his blunt, management-oriented notions of administration, Machiavelli was prudent and pragmatic.

Like Confucius, Machiavelli believed that administrators would do well to follow examples set by other great leaders (we would encourage the reader to take some literary license with Machiavelli's writings and substitute "leader" and/or "manager" for "prince"):

> Men almost always prefer to walk in paths marked out by others and pattern their actions through imitation. A prudent man should always follow the footsteps of the great and imitate those who have been supreme…a prince should read history and reflect on the actions of great men. (Machiavelli, 1992:15, 41)

On the need for developing and maintaining good relations with subordinates, he wrote:

> If … a prince … puts his trust in the people, knows how to command, is a man of courage and doesn't lose his head in adversity, and can rouse his people to action by his own example and orders, he will never find himself betrayed, and his foundations will prove to have been well laid. The best fortress of all consists in not being hated by your people. Every prince should prefer to be considered merciful rather than cruel…. The prince must have people well disposed toward him; otherwise in times of adversity there's no hope. (Machiavelli, 1992:29, 60)

As police organizations struggle with the complexities of a rapidly changing world and ever-demanding workforce, their leaders might do well to heed the analects of Confucius and the work of Machiavelli, as well as other, more contemporary observers.

CUES FOR TODAY'S POLICE LEADERS

Several implications for contemporary police leaders come from these philosophers. First, they must lead by example, including by appearance, and occupy several roles. Lao-Tzu tells us that the successful leader is one who keeps informed, does not rant and rave, and prefers to "condemn in private, praise in public." Confucius tells us that one who leads must, above all, be moral and upright, advance subordinates, and try to learn something from each human contact.

Machiavelli also teaches us that today's leaders should emulate others who have been successful; recruit and train competent subordinates; be able, upon newly assuming a leadership role, to maintain an adequate amount of professional distance between themselves and their subordinates, some of whom were formerly good friends and may now attempt to see how far they can "push the envelope"; and be able to say "no" to underlings while being compassionate toward them.

References

Machiavelli, N. (1992). *The Prince.* R. M. Adams, trans. New York: Norton. (Original work published in 1513.)
Waley, A., trans. (1938). *The Analects of Confucius.* London: Allen and Unwin.

CHAPTER 1

1. J. Kerr, "Leader or Manager? These 10 Important Distinctions Can Help You Out." *Inc.* http://www.inc.com/james-kerr/leading-v-managing-ten-important-distinctions-that-can-help-you-to-become-better.html.

2. J. Bueermann, "Preparing the Police for an Uncertain Future: Four Guiding Principles," in D. McCullough and D. Spence eds., *American Policing in 2022: Essays on the Future of a Profession* (Washington, DC: COPS Office, n.d.), pp. 17–22.

3. New York City Police Department, *NYPD New York's Finest, 2016.* http://www.nyc.gov/html/nypd/html/faq/faq_police.shtml#1.

4. S. P. Robbins, *Organization Theory: Structure, Design, and Applications* (Englewood Cliffs, NJ: Prentice-Hall, 1990).

5. J. Skinner, "The Future of Policing Can Be Found in the Past," in D. McCullough and D. Spence eds., *American Policing in 2022: Essays on the Future of a Profession* (Washington, DC: COPS Office, n.d.), pp. 7–10.

6. C. Roberts, D. Roberts, and D. Bisson, *A History of England: A Prehistory to 1714* (Englewood Cliffs, NJ: Prentice-Hall, 2002).

7. C. Reith, *A Blind Eye of History* (Montclair, NJ: Patterson-Smith, 1975).

8. A. Germann, F. Day, and R. Gallati, *Introduction to Law Enforcement and Criminal Justice* (Springfield, IL: Charles C. Thomas, 1973).

9. L. Gaines and V. Kappeler, *Policing in America* (Waltham, MA: Anderson, 2011), p. 94.

10. Ibid., pp. 92–96.

11. V. Kappeler and L. Gaines, *Community Policing: A Contemporary Perspective* (New York: Routledge, 2015).

12. Ibid., Chapter 1.

13. M. Davis, "Community Building as Crime Control," in D. McCullough and D. Spence eds., *American Policing in 2022: Essays on the Future of a Profession* (Washington, DC: COPS Office, n.d.), pp. 29–32.

14. M. Peterson, *Intelligence-Led Policing: The New Intelligence Architecture* (Washington, DC: U.S. Department of Justice, 2005).

15. BJA, *Reducing Crime through Intelligence-Led Policing* (Washington, DC: Author).

16. L. Sherman, "The Rise of Evidence-Based Policing: Targeting, Testing and Tracking," *Crime and Justice* 42 (2013): 377–451.

17. D. Weisburd, C. Telep, J. Hinkle, and J. Eck, "Effects of Problem-Oriented Policing on Crime and Disorder," *Campbell Systematic Reviews* 4 (14) (November 2008), p. 6, https://www.ncjrs.gov/pdffiles1/nij/grants/224990.pdf.

18. B. Pearsall, "Predictive Policing: The Future of Law Enforcement," *NIJ Journal#* 266, June 2010, https://www.nij.gov/journals/266/pages/predictive.aspx.

19. Ibid., p. 17.

20. Ibid.

21. L. Gaines and J. Worrall, *Police Administration* (Clifton Park, NJ: Delmar, 2003).

22. Los Angeles Police Department, *The Mission Statement of the LAPD.* http://www.lapdonline.org/inside_the_lapd/content_basic_view/844.

23. Tucson Police Department Strategic Plan 2013–2018. https://www.tucsonaz.gov/files/police/SPFinal.pdf.

24. Ibid., pp. 16–18.

25. Ibid., p. 16.

26. W. Lowery, "Aren't More White People than Black People Killed by the Police? Yes, but No," *The Washington Post.* https://www.washingtonpost.com/news/post-nation/wp/2016/07/11/arent-more-white-people-than-black-people-killed-by-police-yes-but-no/?utm_term=.8a8a2bb539a2.

27. M. Berman, "Charlotte Police Officer Who Fatally Shot Keith Scott 'Acted Lawfully,' Won't Be Charged," *The Washington Post.* https://www.washingtonpost.com/news/post-nation/wp/2016/11/30/charlotte-police-officer-wont-be-charged-for-fatal-shooting-that-set-off-days-of-unrest-prosecutor-says/?utm_term=.8f149e8a2a97.

28. T. Tyler, *Why People Obey the Law* (Princeton, NJ: Princeton University Press, 2006).

29. J. Sunshine and T. Tyler, "The Role of Procedural Justice and Legitimacy in Shaping Public Support for Policing," *Law & Society Review* 37 (2003): 513–548.

30. L. Mazerolle, E. Antrobus, S. Bennett, and T. Tyler, "Shaping Citizen Perceptions of Police Legitimacy: A Randomized Field Trial of Procedural Justice," *Criminology* 51 (2013): 33–63.

31. Ibid., Bueermann, "Preparing the Police for an Uncertain Future," p. 20.

32. P. Kraska, "Militarization and Policing—Its Relevance to the 21st Century Police," *Policing* 1 (2007): 501–513.

33. M. White, *Police Officer Body-Worn Cameras* (Washington, DC: Office of Justice Programs, 2014).

34. B. Ariel, W. Farrar, and A. Sutherland, "The Effect of Police Body-Worn Cameras on Use of Force and Citizens' Complaints against the Police: A Randomized Controlled Trial," *Journal of Quantitative Criminology* 31 (2015): 509–535.

35. Mesa, Arizona Police department, *On-Officer Body Camera System: Program Evaluation and Recommendations* (Mesa, AZ: Author, 2013).

36. D. Rosenbaum, A. Schuck, S. Costello, D. Hawkins, and M. Ring. "Attitudes toward the Police: The Effects of Direct and Vicarious Experience," *Police Quarterly* 8 (2005): 343–365.

37. C. Telep and D. Weisburd, "Policing," in D. Weisburd, D. Farrington, and C. Gill eds., *What Works in Crime Prevention and Rehabilitation* (New York: Springer, 2016), pp. 137–168.

CHAPTER 2

1. L. Gaines and J. Worrall, *Police Administration*, 3rd ed. (Clifton Park, NY: Delmar, 2012).

2. F. Taylor, *The Principles of Scientific Management* (New York: Harper & Bros., 1911).

3. D. Guyot, "Bending Granite: Attempts to Change the Rank Structure of American Police Departments," *Journal of Police Science and Administration* 7 (1979): 253–284.

4. M. Hickman and B. Reaves, *Local Police Departments, 2003* (Washington, DC: Bureau of Justice Statistics, 2006).

5. L. Gaines and C. Swanson, "Empowering Police Officers: A Tarnished Bullet?" in L. Gaines and G. Cordner eds., *Policing Perspectives* (Los Angeles, CA: Roxbury, 1999), pp. 363–371.

6. M. Crozier, *The Bureaucratic Phenomenon* (Chicago, IL: University of Chicago Press, 1964).

7. M. Weber, *The Theory of Social and Economic Organizations*, trans. A. Henderson and T. Parsons (New York: Free Press, 1947), p. 337.

8. L. Gaines and C. Swanson, "Empowering Police Officers: A Tarnished Bullet?".

9. E. Bittner, *The Functions of the Police in a Modern Society* (Washington, DC: Government Printing Office, 1970).

10. T. Johnson, G. Misner, and L. Brown, *The Police and Society: An Environment for Collaboration and Confrontation* (Englewood Cliffs, NJ: Prentice-Hall, 1981).

11. K. Gray, J. Bodner, and N. Lovrich, "Community Policing and Organizational Change Dynamics," in Q. Thurman and E. McGarrell eds., *Community Policing in a Rural Setting* (Cincinnati, IL: Anderson, 1997), pp. 41–48; V. Kappeler and L. Gaines, *Community Policing: A Contemporary Perspective*, 7th ed. (New York: Routledge, 2015).

12. L. Gaines and C. Swanson, "Empowering Police Officers: A Tarnished Bullet?".

13. E. Maguire, "Structural Change in Large Municipal Police Organizations during the Community Policing Era," *Justice Quarterly* 14 (1997): 547–576.

14. L. Gulick and L. Urwick, *Papers on the Science of Administration* (New York: Institute of Public Administration, 1937).

15. M. Weber, *The Theory of Social and Economic Organizations* (New York: Free Press, 1947).

16. M. Sparrow, M. Moore, and D. Kennedy, *Beyond 911: A New Era for Policing* (New York: Basic Books, 1990).

17. T. Lane, *The Police Manager: Professional Leadership Skills* (Englewood, NJ: Prentice-Hall, 1986).

18. L. Gaines and J. Worrall, *Police Administration*, 3rd ed.

19. G. Alpert and W. Smith, "Developing Police Policy: An Evaluation of the Control Principle," in L. Gaines and G. Cordner eds., *Policing Perspectives* (Los Angeles, CA: Roxbury, 1999), pp. 353–362.

20. S. Walker, *Taming the System* (New York: Oxford Press, 1993).

21. T. Reddin, "Are You Oriented to Hold Them? A Searching Look at Police Management," *The Police Chief* 3 (1966): 17.

22. L. Gaines and C. Swanson, "Empowering Police Officers: A Tarnished Bullet?", pp. 363–371.

23. J. Greenberg and R. Baron, *Behavior in Organizations: Understanding and Managing the Human Side of Work* (Englewood, NJ: Pearson, 2003).

24. Ibid.

25. H. More and W. Wegener, *Behavioral Police Management* (New York: Macmillan, 1992).

26. J. Tenzel, L. Storms, and H. Sweetwood, "Symbols and Behavior: An Experiment in Altering the Police Role," *Journal of Police Science and Administration* 4 (1976): 21–27.

27. R. Likert, *New Patterns of Management* (New York: McGraw Hill, 1961).

28. L. Gaines, "Overview of Organizational Theory and Its Relation to Police Administration," in L. Gaines and T. Ricks eds., *Managing the Police Organization* (St. Paul: West, 1978), pp. 151–178.

29. F. Luthans, *Organizational Behavior* (New York: McGraw-Hill, 1986), p. 9.

30. S. Certo, *Principles of Modern Management: Functions and Systems*, 4th ed. (Boston, MA: Allyn & Bacon).

31. E. Maguire, "Structural Change in Large Municipal Police Organizations during the Community Policing Era," *Justice Quarterly* 14 (1997): 547–576; L. Gaines and C. Swanson, "Empowering Police Officers: A Tarnished Bullet?".

32. M. Wycoff, *Community Policing Strategies*, unpublished report (Washington, DC: Police Foundation, 1994).

33. S. Robbins, *The Administrative Process* (Englewood Cliffs, NJ: Prentice-Hall, 1976).

34. L. Gaines and J. Worrall, *Police Administration*.

35. J. Crank, *Understanding Police Culture* (Cincinnati, OH: Anderson, 2004).

36. L. Gaines and C. Swanson, "Empowering Police Officers: A Tarnished Bullet?".

37. V. Kappeler and L. Gaines, *Community Policing*.

38. J. Worrall and L. Gaines, "The Effect of Police-Probation Partnerships on Juvenile Arrests," *Journal of Criminal Justice* 34 (2006): 579–589.

39. D. Webster, J. Whitehill, J. Vernick, and F. Curriero, "Effects of Baltimore's Safe Streets Program on Gun Violence: A Replication of Chicago's Cease Fire Program," *Journal of Urban Health* 90 (2013): 27–40.

CHAPTER 3

1. W. Bennis and B. Nanus, *Leaders* (New York: Harper & Row, 1985), p. 5.
2. S. Certo, *Principles of Modern Management: Functions and Systems*, 4th ed. (Boston: Allyn & Bacon, 1989), p. 351.
3. P. Hersey and K. Blanchard, *Management of Organizational Behavior* (Upper Saddle River, NJ: Prentice Hall, 1988), p. 86.
4. J. Stoner and R. Freeman, *Management*, 5th ed. (Upper Saddle River, NJ: Prentice-Hall, 1992), p. 472.
5. C. Bernard, *The Functions of the Executive* (Cambridge, MA: Harvard University Press 1938).
6. R. Katz, "Skills of an Effective Administrator," *Harvard Business Review* 52 (1974): 90–101.
7. Ibid., p. 63.
8. Ibid., p. 65.
9. T. Gove, "Empowerment and Accountability: Tools for Law Enforcement Leaders," *FBI Law Enforcement Bulletin* (September 2007): 8–13.
10. T. Wuestewald, "Can Empowerment Work in Police Organizations?" *The Police Chief* (January 2006): 48–55.
11. T. Gove, "Empowerment and Accountability: Tools for Law Enforcement Leaders," *FBI Law Enforcement Bulletin* (September 2007): 8–13.
12. Ibid.
13. Ibid., p. 10.
14. H. Mintzberg, "The Manager's Job: Folklore and Fact," *Harvard Business Review* 53 (July–August, 1975): 49–61.
15. L. Herocleous, "Strategic Thinking or Strategic Planning?" *Long Range Planning* 31 (1998): 481–487.
16. E. Lawrence, *Strategic Thinking: A Discussion Paper.* Ottawa, Ontario, Can.: Public Service Commission of Canada, Research Directorate, Policy, Research, and Communications Branch, April 27, 1999.
17. K. Charrier, "The Role of the Strategic Manager," *The Police Chief* (June 2004): 60.
18. K. Peak and R. Glensor, *Community Policing and Problem Solving: Strategies and Practices*, 5th ed. (Upper Saddle River, NJ: Prentice Hall, 2008).
19. J. Greenberg and R. Baron, *Behavior in Organizations* (Upper Saddle River, NJ: Prentice Hall, 1995), p. 126.
20. A. Maslow, *Motivation and Personality* (New York: Harper & Row 1954).
21. C. Argyris, *Personality and Organization* (New York: Harper & Bros 1957).
22. F. Herzberg, "One More Time: How Do You Motivate Employees?" *Harvard Business Review* 46 (January/February 1968): 53–62.
23. S. Certo, *Principles of Modern Management: Functions and Systems*, 4th ed. (Boston: Allyn & Bacon, 1989).
24. D. McClelland, *The Achieving Society* (Princeton, NJ: Van Nostrand Reinhold, 1964).
25. J. Adams, "Toward an Understanding of Inequity," *Journal of Abnormal Psychology* 67 (1963): 422.
26. V. Vroom, *Work and Motivation* (New York: Wiley, 1964).
27. W. Bennis and B. Nanus, *Leaders* (New York: Harper & Row, 1985), p. 21.
28. Ibid., p. 92.
29. Ibid.
30. Ibid., pp. 80–81.
31. P. Whisenand and F. Ferguson, *The Managing of Police Organizations* (Upper Saddle River, NJ: Prentice Hall, 1996), p. 13.
32. R. Davis, *Industrial Organization and Management* (New York: Harper & Bros., 1940).
33. R. Tannenbaum and I. Weschler, *Leadership and Organization: A Behavioral Science Approach* (New York: McGraw-Hill, 1961).
34. W. Bennett and K. Hess, *Management and Supervision in Law Enforcement* (Belmont, CA: Wadsworth, 2001).
35. S. Sales, "Supervisory Style and Productivity: Review and Theory," in L. Cummings and W. Scott eds., *Readings in Organizational Behavior and Human Performance* (Homewood, IL: Richard D. Irwin, 1969).
36. C. Swanson and L. Territo, "Police Leadership and Interpersonal Communications Styles," in J. Greene ed., *Police and Police Work* (Beverly Hills: Sage, 1982).
37. M. Hitt, C. Miller, and A. Colella, *Organizational Behavior: A Strategic Approach* (New York: Wiley, 2006), p. 286.
38. P. Hersey and K. Blanchard, *Management of Organizational Behavior*, p. 86.
39. Ibid.
40. Ibid.
41. T. Burns and G. Stalker, *The Management of Innovation* (London: Tavistock, 1961); J. Woodward, *Industrial Organization: Theory and Practice* (London: Oxford University Press, 1965).
42. F. Fieldler, "Engineer the Job to Fit the Manager," *Harvard Business Review* 43 (September/October, 1965): 115–122.
43. W. Plunkett, *Supervision: The Direction of People at Work* (Dubuque, IA: Wm. C. Brown, 1983).
44. T. Burns and G. Stalker, *The Management of Innovation* (London: Tavistock, 1961); J. Woodward *Industrial Organization: Theory and Practice* (London: Oxford University Press, 1965); W. Plunkett, *Supervision: The Direction of People at Work* (Dubuque, IA: Wm. C. Brown, 1983).

45. R. Likert, *New Patterns of Management* (New York: McGraw-Hill, 1961).

46. H. Toch, "The Democratization of Policing in the United States: 1895–1973," *Police Forum* 7 (1997): 1–8.

47. J. Witte, L. Travis, and R. Langworthy, "Participatory Management in Law Enforcement: Police Officer, Supervisor, and Administrator Perceptions." *American Journal of Police* 9 (1990): 1–24.

48. R. Engel, "Supervisory Styles of Patrol Sergeants and Lieutenants," *Journal of Criminal Justice* 29 (2001): 341–355.

49. R. Heifetz, *Leadership without Easy Answers* (Cambridge, MA: The Belknap Press of Harvard Press, 1994).

50. Ibid.

51. J. Schmerhorn, *Management* (New York: Wiley, 2008).

52. Ibid.

53. K. Lewin, "Defining the Field at a Given Time," *Psychological Review* 50 (1943): 292–310.

54. S. Brown, "Fatal Errors Managers Make: And How You Can Avoid Them," *Police Leadership Report, The National Law Enforcement Leadership Institute, Safety Harbor, Florida* 1 (1989): 6–7.

CHAPTER 4

1. L. Mayo, *Analysis of the Role of the Police Chief Executive* (Ann Arbor: University Microfilms, 1983).

2. H. More and W. Wegener, *Effective Police Supervision*, 2d ed. (Cincinnati: Anderson, 1996).

3. T. Von der Embse, *Supervision: Managerial Skills for a New Era* (New York: Macmillan, 1987).

4. J. Greenberg and R. Baron, *Behavior in Organizations*, 5th ed. (Upper Saddle River, NJ: Prentice Hall, 1995), p. 330.

5. R. Lussier, *Human Relations in Organizations: Applications and Skill Building* (New York: McGraw-Hill, 1999).

6. D. Katz, and R. Kahn, *The Social Psychology of Organizations* (New York: Wiley, 1996).

7. J. Schermerhorn, J. Hunt, and R. Osborn, *Managing Organizational Behavior*, 5th ed. (New York: Wiley, 1994).

8. T. Peters and R. Waterman, *In Search of Lessons from America's Best-Run Companies* (New York: Warner Books, 1983).

9. D. Van Fleet and T. Peterson, *Contemporary Management*, 3rd ed. (Boston: Houghton Mifflin, 1994).

10. G. Garner, "Handling Bad Press," *Law and Order* (September, 2004): 22–24.

11. C. Dolon-Cotton, "Model Media Policy," *Law and Order* (October, 2005): 18–19.

12. D. Rosenbaum, L. Graziano, C. Stephens, and A. Schuck, "Understanding Community Policing and Legitimacy-Seeking Behavior in Virtual Reality: A National Study of Municipal Police Websites," *Police Quarterly* 14 (2011): 25–47.

13. J. Lieberman, D. Koetzle, and M. Sakiyama, "Police Departments' Use of Facebook: Patterns and Policy Issues," *Police Quarterly* 16 (2013): 438–462.

14. J. Crump, "What Are the Police Doing on Twitter? Social Media, the Police and the Public," *Policy & Interest* 3 (2011): 1–27.

15. E. Davis, A. Alves and D. Sklansky, "Social Media and Police Leadership: Lessons from Boston," *Australasian Policing* 6 (2014): 10–16.

16. J. Donnelly, J. Gibson, and J. Ivancevich, *Fundamentals of Management*, 9th ed. (Chicago: Irwin, 1995), p. 433.

17. J. Schermerhorn, *Management*, 5th ed. (New York: Wiley, 1996).

18. H. Cohen, *You Can Negotiate Anything* (Toronto: Bantam Books, 1980).

19. J. Stoner and R. Freeman, *Management*, 5th ed. (Upper Saddle River, NJ: Prentice Hall, 1992).

20. J. Schermerhorn, J. Hunt, and R. Osborn, *Managing Organizational Behavior*, 5th ed. (New York: Wiley, 1994).

21. J. Greenberg and R. Baron, *Behavior in Organizations*, 5th ed. (Upper Saddle River, NJ: Prentice Hall, 1995).

22. K. Thomas, "Conflict and Negotiation Processes in Organizations," in M. Dunnette and L. Hough eds., *Handbook of Industrial and Organizational Psychology*, 2d ed., Vol. 3 (Palo Alto: Consulting Psychologists Press, 1992), pp. 651–718.

23. J. Greenberg and R. Baron, *Behavior in Organizations*, 5th ed. (Upper Saddle River, NJ: Prentice Hall, 1995).

24. J. Schermerhorn, *Management*, 5th ed. (New York: Wiley, 1996).

CHAPTER 5

1. G. Starling, *Managing the Public Sector* (Belmont, CA: Wadsworth, 2008), p. 442.

2. *Griggs v. Duke Power Co.*, 401 U.S. 424, 433 (1971).

3. *Vanguard Justice Society v. Hughes*, 471 F. Supp. 670 (D. Md. 1979).

4. *Washington v. Davis*, 96 S.Ct. 2040 (1976).

5. B. Reaves, *Local Police Departments, 2013: Personnel, Policies, and Practices* (Washington, DC: Bureau of Justice Statistics, 2015).

6. M. White and G. Escobar, "Making Good Cops in the Twenty-first Century: Emerging Issues for the Effective Recruitment, Selection and Training of Police in the United States and Abroad," *International Review of Law Computers and Technology* 22 (2008): 119–134.

7. L. Gaines and V. Kappeler, *Policing in America*. 8th ed. (Waltham, MA: Anderson, 2015).

8. C. Kilgannon, "A Race for the Jobs in Police Depts. On Long Island," *The New York Times* (May 22, 2007): www.nytimes.com/2007/05/22/nyregion/22cops.html.

9. M. White and G. Escobar, "Making Good Cops in the Twenty-first Century: Emerging Issues for the Effective Recruitment, Selection and Training of Police in the United States and Abroad," *International Review of Law Computers and Technology* 22 (2008): 119–134.

10. Ibid., 14.

11. D. Orrick, "Common Interview Questions for Police Candidates" (December, 2013).

12. *City of Canton v. Harris*, 57 U.S.L.W. 4263 (1989).

13. Darrel L. Ross, "Emerging Trends in Police Failure to Train," *Journal of Police Strategies and Management* 23 (2000): 169–193.

14. Michale Birzer, "The Theory of Andragogy Applied to Police Training," *Policing: An International Journal of Police Strategies and Management* 26 (2003): 29–42.

15. J. Violanti, "What Does High Stress Police Training Teach Recruits? An Analysis of Coping," *Journal of Criminal Justice* 21(1993): 411–417.

16. G. Post, "Police Recruits. Training Tomorrow's Workforce," *FBI Law Enforcement Bulletin* 61 (1992): 19–24.

17. Brian Reaves, Local Police Departments, 2013: *Personnel, Policies, and Practices* (Washington, DC: Bureau of Justice Statistics, 2015), p. 14.

18. R. Mathis and J. Jackson, *Human Resource Management* (St. Paul: West Publishing, 1997), p. 343.

19. F. Landy and C. Goodin, "Performance Appraisal." In *Police Personnel Administration.*

20. International Association of Chiefs of Police and the Police Foundation. *Police Personnel Practices in State and Local Governments* (Washington, DC: Police Foundation, 1973).

21. D. Cederblom, "Promotability Ratings: An Under-used Promotion Method for Public Safety Organizations, *Public Personnel Management Journal* (1991): 27–34.

22. D. Gorby, "Police Performance and the Rise of Broader Measures of Performance," *Policing* 7 (2013): 392–400.

23. D. Lilley and S. Hinduja, "Officer Evaluation in the Community Policing Context," *Policing: An International Journal of Police Strategies & Management* 29 (2006): 19–37.

24. S. Falkenberg, L. Gaines, and G. Cordner, "An Examination of the Constructs Underlying Police Performance Appraisals," *Journal of Criminal Justice* 19 (1991): 351–359.

25. V. Kappeler and L. Gaines, *Community Policing: A Contemporary Perspective* (New York: Routledge, 2015).

26. T. Oettmeier and M. Wycoff, *Personnel Performance Evaluation in the Community Policing Context* (Washington, DC: Community Policing Consortium, 1997).

27. D. Lilley and S. Hinduja, "Officer Evaluation in the Community Policing Context," *Policing: An International Journal of Police Strategies & Management* 29 (2006): 19–37.

28. L. Coutts and F. Schneider, "Police Officer Performance Appraisal Systems: How Good Are They?" *Policing: An International Journal of Police Strategies & Management* 27 (2004): 67–81.

29. *Mentor Savings Bank v. Vinson,* 474 U.S. 1047 (1986).

30. *Hall v. Gus Construction Co.* 842 F.2d 1010 (8th Cir. 1988).

31. *Mentor Savings Bank v. Vinson,* 474 U.S. 1047 (1986).

32. *Harris v. Forklift Systems* 114 S.Ct. 367 (1993).

33. K. Lonsway, R. Raynich, and J. Hall, "Sexual Harassment in Law Enforcement: Incidence, Impact, and Perception," *Police Quarterly* 16 (2013): 177–210.

34. C. Archbold, *Police Accountability, Risk Management, and Legal Advising* (El Paso: LFB Scholarly Publications, 2004).

35. G. Gallagher, "Risk Management for Police Administrators," *The Police Chief* (June, 1990): 18–29.

CHAPTER 6

1. W. W. Schmidt, "Peace Officers Bill of Rights Guarantees: Responding to Union Demands with a Management Sanctioned Version," *Law Enforcement Executive Forum*, March 2005, http://www.aele.org/pobr-iacp.pdf.

2. K. M. Keenan and S. Walker, "An Impediment to Police Accountability? An Analysis of Statutory Law Enforcement Officers' Bills of Rights," *Public Interest Law Journal* 14 (2005): 185–244.

3. *Muller v. Conlisk*, 429 F.2d 901 (7th Cir. 1970).

4. See *Connick v. Myers*, 1983; *Jones v. Dodson* (1984).

5. *Kelley v. Johnston*, 425 U.S. 238 (1976).

6. *Katz v. United States*, 389 U.S. 347 (1967).

7. *People v. Tidwell*, 266 N.E.2d 787 (Ill. 1971).

8. *McDonell v. Hunter*, 611 F.Supp. 1122 (S.D. Iowa, 1985), affd. as mod., 809 F.2d 1302 (8th Cir., 1987).

9. *Biehunik v. Felicetta*, 441 F.2d 228 (1971).

10. *Gabrilowitz v. Newman*, 582 F.2d 100 (1st Cir. 1978).

11. California Government Code, Section 3307.

12. D. L. Schofield, "Freedom of Religion and Law Enforcement Employment: Recent Court Decisions," *FBI Law Enforcement Bulletin* 64(6) (June 1995): 28–32.

13. *U.S. v. City of Albuquerque,* 12 EPD 11, 244 (10th Cir. 1976); also see *Trans World Airlines v. Hardison,* 97 S.Ct. 2264 (1977).

14. P. M. Stinson, Sr., J. Liederbach, S. L. Brewer, Jr., B. E. Mathna, "Police Sexual Misconduct: A National Scale Study of Arrested Officers," *Criminal Justice Policy Review* 26(7): 665–690.

15. Ibid.

16. *McCarthy v. Philadelphia Civil Service Commission,* 424 U.S. 645, 96 S. Ct. 1154 (1976).

17. See *Brenckle v. Township of Shaler,* 281 A.2d 920 (Pa. 1972); *Cox v. McNamara,* 493 P.2d 54 (Ore. 1972); *Flood v. Kennedy,* 239 N.Y.S.2d 665 (1963); and *Hopwood v. City of Paducah,* 424 S.W.2d 134 (Ky. 1968).

18. *Lally v. Department of Police,* 306 So.2d 65 (La. 1974).

19. Codified as 18 USC § 926B and USC § 926C,

20. *Marusa v. District of Columbia,* 484 F.2d 828 (1973).

21. *Sager v. City of Woodlawn Park,* 543 F.Supp. 282 (D. Colo., 1982).

22. *Bonsignore v. City of New York,* 521 F.Supp. 394 (1981).

23. *Popow v. City of Margate,* 476 F.Supp. 1237 (1979).

24. *Hester v. Milledgeville,* 598 F.Supp. 1456, 1457. (M.D.Ga. 1984); *Krolick v. Lowery,* 302 N.Y.S.2d. 109 (1969), p.115.

25. *National Treasury Employees Union v. Von Raab,* 489 U.S. 656, 1989: 38.

26. T. Dees, "Can Cops Smoke Marijuana in States Where It Has Been Legalized?" Quora (n.d.), https://www.quora.com/Can-Cops-Smoke-marijuana-in-states-where-it-has-been-legalized.

27. Med-Health.Net, "How Long Is THC Detectable in Urine?" December 14, 2016, http://www.med-health.net/How-Long-Is-Thc-Detectable-In-Urine.html.

28. J. Kaminsky, "Seattle Police Department Loosens Rules On Marijuana Use For Recruit," February 18, 2013, http://www.huffingtonpost.com/2012/12/19/seattle-police-marijuana-rules_n_2333912.html.

29. K. Rector, "Davis wants to Relax Restrictions on Past Marijuana Use for Police Recruits in Maryland," *The Baltimore Sun,* December 13, 2016, http://www.baltimoresun.com/news/maryland/crime/bs-md-ci-police-marijuana-standard-20160721-story.html

30. *Brady v. Maryland,* 373 U.S. 83 (1963).

31. J. Van Derbeken, "Police with Problems Are a Problem for the DA," *San Francisco Chronicle,* May 16, 2010, http://www.sfgate.com/cgi-bin/article.cgi?f=/c/a/2010/05/15/MNKC1DB57E.DTL.

32. See R. Lisko, "Agency Policies Imperative to Disclose *Brady v. Maryland* Material to Prosecutors," *The Police Chief* 77(3) (March 2011), http://www.policechiefmagazine.org/magazine/index.cfm?fuseaction=display_arch&article_id=2329&issue_id=32011.

33. Lisko, "Agency Policies Imperative to Disclose *Brady v. Maryland* Material to Prosecutors"; also see Val Van Brocklin, "*Brady v. Md* Can Get You Fired," Officer.com (August 16, 2010), http://www.officer.com/article/10232477/brady-v-md-can-get-you-fired.

34. J. Ryan, "Police Officers May Be Liable for Failure to Disclose Exculpatory Information under the Brady Rule Managing Risks," Policelink (n.d.), http://police-link.monster.com/training/articles/2123-police-officers-may-be-liable-for-failure-todisclose-exculpatory-information-under-the-brady-rulemanaging-risks.

35. S. Rothlein, "*Brady v Maryland*: Do You Understand Your Obligations?" Public Agency Training Council, http://www.patc.com/weeklyarticles/bradyvmaryland.shtml.

36. L. Morris, *Incredible New York* (New York: Bonanza, 1951).

37. J. A. Inciardi, *Criminal Justice* 5th ed. (Orlando, FL: Harcourt Brace, 1996).

38. V. McLaughlin and R. Bing, "Law Enforcement Personnel Selection," *Journal of Police Science and Administration* 15(1987): 271–276.

39. Adapted from Pine Bluff, Arkansas, Police Department, *Pine Bluff Police Department Policy & Procedures Manual,* Policy No. 1100, http://www.pbpd.org/Policies/Chapter-XI/Microsoft%20Word%20-%20POL-1100%20_Standards%20of%20Conduct_.pdf.

40. For a listing of jurisdictions with citizen review boards, see National Association of Civilian Oversight of Law Enforcement, http://www.nacole.org/police_oversight_by_jurisdiction_usa.

41. Quoted in Martin Kaste, "Police Are Learning to Accept Civilian Oversight, But Distrust Lingers," http://www.npr.org/2015/02/21/387770044/police-are-learning-to-accept-civilian-oversight-but-distrust-lingers.

42. Ibid.

43. Ibid.

44. Jeff Rojek, S. H. Decker, and A. E. Wagner, "Addressing Police Misconduct: The Role of Citizen Complaints," in Roger G. Dunham and Geoffrey P. Alpert, eds., *Critical Issues in Policing: Contemporary Readings.* 7th ed. (Prospect Heights, IL: Waveland, 2015), pp. 162–183.

45. Jon Arnold, "Internal Affairs Investigation: The Supervisor's Role," *FBI Law Enforcement Bulletin* (January 1998): 11–16.

46. S. Walker, S. O. Milligan, and A. Berke, *Supervision and Intervention within Early Intervention Systems: A Guide for Law Enforcement Chief Executives,* Office of Community Oriented Policing Services, December 2005, http://www.policeforum.org/assets/docs/Free_Online_Documents/Early_Intervention

_Systems/supervision%20and%20intervention %20within%20early%20intervention%20 systems%202005.pdf; also see S. Walker, *Early Intervention Systems for Law Enforcement Agencies: A Planning and Management Guide*, Office of Community Oriented Policing Services, 2003, https:// chicagopatf.org/wp-content/uploads/2016/02 /EarlyInterventionSystemsLawEnforcement.pdf.

47. Ibid.

48. *Parish v. Luckie*, 963 F.2d 201 (1992).

49. *Gutierrez-Rodriguez v. Cargegena*, 882 F.2d 553 (1st Cir., 1989).

50. *Bordanaro v. McLeod*, 871 F.2d 1151 (1989).

51. *Ramos v. City of Chicago*, 707 F.Supp. 345 (1989).

52. Z. Elinson and D. Frosch, "Police-misconduct Costs Soar: Data from Big Cities Show Rising Payouts for Settlements and Court Judgments; Video Affects Cases," *Wall Street Journal* (July 16, 2015): A1.

53. M. Yang, "Chicago Police Settlements Cost Taxpayers $210 Million Plus Interest," *The Huffington Post*, July 14, 2016, http://www.huffingtonpost.com/entry /chicago-police-settlement-misconduct-210-million _us_5787f6a6e4b03fc3ee500a88.

54. Rolando v. del Carmen, "Civil Liabilities of Police Supervisors," *American Journal of Police* 8(1) (1989): 107–136.

55. Ibid.

56. *Lenard v. Argento*, 699 F.2d 874 (7th Cir. 1983).

57. *Grandstaff v. City of Borger*, 767 F.2d 161 (5th Cir. 1985).

58. Victor E. Kappeler, *Critical Issues in Police Civil Liability* 4th ed. (Long Grove, IL: Waveland, 2005).

59. *Fielder v. Jenkins*, 833 A.2d 906 (NJ Super. A.D. 1993).

60. *Thomas v. Williams*, 124 S.E.2d 409 (Ga. App. 1962).

61. *Guice v. Enfinger*, 389 So.2d 270 (Fla. App. 1980).

62. *Davis v. City of Detroit*, 386 N.W.2d 169 (Mich. App. 1986).

63. *Penilla v. City of Huntington Park*, 115 F.3d 707 (9th Cir., 1997).

64. *Scott v. Harris*, 550 U.S. 372 (2007).

65. *Seide v. State of Rhode Island*, 875 A.2d 1259 (2005).

CHAPTER 7

1. Bureau of Labor Statistics, "Union Members Summary," https://www.bls.gov/news.release/union2.nr0 .htm, January 28, 2017.

2. G. Ronald DeLord and Jerry Sanders, *Understanding the Crosswinds from the Community as They Affect Law Enforcement*. In U.S. Department of Justice, Office of Community Oriented Policing Services, *Police Labor-Management Relations Vol. I* (2006), pp. 7–12, https://ric-zai-inc.com /Publications/cops-p110-pub.pdf.

3. J. H. Burpo, *The Police Labor Movement: Problems and Perspectives* (Springfield, IL: Charles C. Thomas, 1971), pp. 3–4.

4. M. J. Levine, "A Historical Overview of Police Unionization in the United States," *Police Journal*, 61(4): 334–343.

5. Ibid., p. 335.

6. D. Ziskind, *One Thousand Strikes of Government Employees* (New York: Ayer, 1940), p. 49.

7. Ibid.

8. Criminal Justice Research, "Unionization of Police Officers" (n.d.), http://criminal-justice.iresearchnet .com/system/unionization-of-police-officers/.

9. Ibid.

10. Bureau of Justice Statistics, *Local Police Departments, 2013: Personnel, Policies, and Practices* (May 2015), p. 5, https://www.bjs.gov/content/pub /pdf/lpd13ppp.pdf.

11. Adapted from Police Officers Research Association of California, "About," http://porac.org/.

12. R. G. DeLord, *American Policing: Launched in Controversy and Still Controversial Today.* In U.S. Department of Justice, Office of Community Oriented Policing Services, *Police Labor-Management Relations* (Vol. I) (2006), pp. 13–18, http://www .cops.usdoj.gov/mime/open.pdf?Item=1856.

13. Ibid., p. 17.

14. W. Aitchison, *The Rights of Law Enforcement Officers* (Portland, OR: Labor Relations Information System, 2004).

15. U.S. Office of Community Oriented Policing Services and Police Executive Research Forum, *Collaborating to Address Key Challenges in Policing* (Washington, DC: Authors, 2015), pp. 9–13.

16. Ibid., p. 9.

17. Ibid.

18. DeLord, *American Policing*, p. 17.

19. L. Hoover, J. L. Dowling, and G. Blair, (2006). *Management and Labor in Community Policing: Charting a Course*. In U.S. Department of Justice, Office of Community Oriented Policing Services, *Police Labor-Management Relations (Vol. I): Perspectives and Practical Solutions for Implementing Change, Making Reforms, and Handling Crises for Managers and Union Leaders*, http://www.cops.usdoj.gov /mime/open.pdf?Item=1856, pp. xix–xxix.

20. Adapted from A. Cheng, "Police Union Disputes New Firearm Training Policy," *Yale News*, October 28, 2016, http://yaledailynews.com/blog/2016/10/28 /police-union-disputes-new-policy/.

21. Adapted from R. G. DeLord, "Ten Things That Law Enforcement Unions and Managers Do to Run Aground," in U.S. Department of Justice, Office of Community Oriented Policing Services, *Police Labor-Management Relations (Vol. I): Perspectives and Practical Solutions for Implementing Change Making Reforms, and Handling Crises for Managers and Union Leaders,* August 2006, pp. 153–157, http://www.cops.usdoj.gov/files/ric/Publications /e07063417.pdf.

CHAPTER 8

1. Bureau of Justice Statistics, *Local Police Departments, 2013: Personnel, Policies, and Practices* (May 2015), p. 1, http://www.bjs.gov/content/pub/pdf/lpd13ppp.pdf.
2. Quoted in C. R. Swanson, L. Territo, and R. W. Taylor, *Police Administration: Structures, Processes, and Behavior*, 6th ed. (Upper Saddle River, NJ: Prentice Hall, 2005), p. 682.
3. J. M. Wilson and A. Weiss, *A Performance-based Approach to Police Staffing and Allocation* (Washington, DC: Office of Community Oriented Policing Services (August 2012), http://a-capp.msu.edu/sites/default/files/files/041218461_Performance_Based_Approach_Police_Staffing_FINAL100112.pdf.
4. C. K. Coe and D. Lamm Weisel, "Police Budgeting: Winning Strategies," *Public Administration Review* 61(6), pp. 718–727.
5. See Ibid.; also see J. McCabe, *An Analysis of Police Department Staffing: How Many Officers Do You Really Need?* (Washington, DC: International City/County Management Association, n.d.).
6. Police Executive Research Forum, *Policing and the Economic Downturn: Striving for Efficiency Is the New Normal* (December 2013), pp. 5–9. http://www.policeforum.org/assets/docs/Critical_Issues_Series/policing%20and%20the%20economic%20downturn%20-%20striving%20for%20efficiency%20is%20the%20new%20normal%202013.pdf.
7. Coe and Weisel, "Police Budgeting," p. 725.
8. Ibid., p. 723.
9. G. Gascón and T. Foglesong, *Making Policing more Affordable: Managing Costs and Measuring Value in Policing* (Washington, DC: U.S. Department of Justice, National Institute of Justice) December 2010), pp. 3–5. https://www.ncjrs.gov/pdffiles1/nij/231096.pdf.
10. Ibid.
11. Note that while this Web site focuses on police agencies, most if not all of the recommendations and steps in the process will apply to courts and corrections agencies as well. See: Policegrantshelp.com, "Grants 101: A Beginner's Guide to Helping Your Department Get Grants," http://www.policegrantshelp.com/grants101/.
12. "Civilianization May Improve Police Effectiveness in the Face of Budget Crisis," Envisage Technologies, March 29, 2016, http://www.envisagenow.com/civilianization-may-improve-police-effectiveness-in-face-of-budget-crisis/.
13. Ibid.
14. Coe and Weisel, "Police Budgeting," p. 719.
15. L. Heracleous, "Strategic Thinking or Strategic Planning?" *Long Range Planning* 31 (1998): 481–487.
16. Ibid.
17. Internet Nonprofit Center, "What Is Strategic Planning?" (San Francisco, CA: Author, 2000), p. 1.
18. U.S. Department of Justice, *Strategic Plan, Fiscal Years 2014–2018* (n.d.), https://www.justice.gov/sites/default/files/jmd/legacy/2014/02/28/doj-fy-2014-2018-strategic-plan.pdf.
19. Police Executive Research Forum, *Policing and the Economic Downturn*, pp. 13–19, http://www.policeforum.org/assets/docs/Critical_Issues_Series/policing%20and%20the%20economic%20downturn%20-%20striving%20for%20efficiency%20is%20the%20new%20normal%202013.pdf.
20. J. C. Snyder, "Financial Management and Planning in Local Government," *Atlanta Economic Review* (November–December 1973): 43–47.
21. A. Wildavsky, *The Politics of the Budgetary Process*, 2nd ed. (Boston: Little, Brown, 1974), pp. 1–4.
22. O. K. Cope, "Operation Analysis—The Basis for Performance Budgeting," in *Performance Budgeting and Unit Cost Accounting for Governmental Units* (Chicago: Municipal Finance Officers Association, 1954), p. 8.
23. L. R. Bittel, *The McGraw-Hill 36-Hour Management Course* (New York: McGraw-Hill, 1989).
24. Ibid., p. 187.
25. R. Townsend, *Further Up the Organization: How to Stop Management from Stifling People and Strangling Productivity* (New York: Alfred A. Knopf, 1984), p. 2.
26. R. N. McKean, *Public Spending* (New York: McGraw-Hill, 1968), p. 1
27. S. Kenneth Howard, *Changing State Budgeting* (Lexington, KY: Council of State Governments, 1973), p. 13.
28. M. C. Thomsett, *The Little Black Book of Budgets and Forecasts* (New York: AMACOM, American Management Association, 1988), p. 38.
29. Quoted in V. A. Leonard and Harry W. More, *Police Organization and Management,* 7th ed. (Mineola, NY: Foundation Press, 1987), p. 212.
30. Swanson et al., *Police Administration,* p. 693.
31. Adapted, with some changes, from Wildavsky, *Politics of the Budgetary Process,* pp. 63–123.
32. L. L. Moak and K. W. Killian, *A Manual of Techniques for the Preparation, Consideration, Adoption, and Administration of Operating Budgets* (Chicago: Municipal Finance Officers Association, 1973), p. 5, with changes.
33. L. M. Knighton, "Four Keys to Audit Effectiveness," *Governmental Finance* 8 (September 1979): 3.
34. The Comptroller General of the United States, *Standards for Audit of Governmental Organizations, Programs, Activities, and Functions* (Washington, DC: General Accounting Office, 1972), p. 1.

35. Ibid.
36. P. F. Rousmaniere (ed.), *Local Government Auditing* (New York: Council on Municipal Performance, 1979), Tables 1 and 2, pp. 10, 14.
37. Swanson et al., *Police Administration,* p. 707.
38. A. Schick, *Budget Innovation in the States* (Washington, DC: Brookings Institution, 1971), pp. 14–15. Schick offers 10 ways in which the line-item budget fosters control.
39. Adapted from T. Sells, "City Council Budget Meeting: Lots of Ideas, No Easy Solutions," Scripps International Paper Group–Online, June 18, 2014, http://www .commercialappeal.com/news/2014/jun/18/city -council-budget-meeting-lots-of-ideas-no-/; also see L. Moore, "Memphis' Financial Woes Impact All of Shelby County," Scripps International Paper Group —Online, June 18, 2014, https://www.commercialappeal .com/news/2014/jun/18/memphis-financial-woes-impact -all-of-shelby/?print=1.
40. M. L. Watlington and S. G. Dankel, "New Approaches to Budgeting: Are They Worth the Cost?" *Popular Government* 43 (Spring 1978): 1.
41. J. Burkhead, *Government Budgeting* (New York: Wiley, 1956), p. 11.
42. L. K. Gaines, J. L. Worrall, M. D. Southerland, and John E. Angell, *Police Administration,* 2nd ed. (New York: McGraw-Hill, 2003), p. 519.
43. Swanson et al., *Police Administration,* p. 710.
44. Ibid., p. 711.
45. Gaines et al., *Police Administration,* p. 519.
46. Ibid.
47. D. Novick (ed.), *Program Budgeting* (New York: Holt, Rinehart and Winston, 1969), p. xxvi.
48. Ibid., p. xxiv.
49. Council of State Governments, *State Reports on Five-Five-Five* (Chicago: Author, 1968).
50. International City Management Association, *Local Government Budgeting, Program Planning and Evaluation* (Washington, DC: Author, 1972), p. 7.
51. Democracy Arsenal, "Increasing Our Security by Cutting Military Spending" (May 27, 2010), http:// www.democracyarsenal.org/2010/05/increasing-our -security-by-cutting-military-spending.html.
52. A. Schick, "The Road to PPBS: The Stages of Budget Reform," *Public Administration Review* 26 (December 1966): 244.
53. Ibid.
54. Swanson et al., *Police Administration*, p. 712.
55. P. A. Phyrr, "Zero-Base Budgeting," *Harvard Business Review* (November–December 1970): 111–121; see also E. A. Kurbis, "The Case for Zero-Base Budgeting," *CA Magazine* (April 1986): 104–105.
56. J. S. Wholey, *Zero-Base Budgeting and Program Evaluation* (Lexington, MA: Lexington Books, 1978), p. 8.

CHA PTER 9

1. R. E. Kania, "Police Acceptance of Gratuities," *Criminal Justice Ethics* 7(2) (1988): 37–49.
2. J. Kleinig, *The Ethics of Policing* (New York: Cambridge University Press, 1996), p. 55.
3. T. J. Martinelli, "Unconstitutional Policing: The Ethical Challenges in Dealing with Noble Cause Corruption," *The Police Chief* (October): 150.
4. J. P. Crank and M. A. Caldero, *Police Ethics: The Corruption of Noble Cause* (Cincinnati: Anderson, 2000).
5. Martinelli, "Unconstitutional Policing," p. 151.
6. Quoted in President's Task Force on 21st Century Policing, *Interim Report of the President's Task Force on 21st Century Policing* (Washington, DC: Office of Community Oriented Policing Services, April 2015), p. 9.
7. Quoted in Ibid., p. 10.
8. Quoted in Police Executive Research Forum, *Constitutional Policing as a Cornerstone of Community Policing* (Washington, DC: Author, April 2015), p. 18.
9. Quoted in Ibid., p. 2.
10. President's Task Force on 21st Century Policing, *Interim Report of the President's Task Force on 21st Century Policing*, Office of Community Oriented Policing Services, p. 1, http://www.cops.usdoj.gov/ pdf/taskforce/Interim_TF_Report.pdf. Accessed March 4, 2015.
11. Adapted from L. Kunard, and C. Moe, *Procedural Justice for Law Enforcement: An Overview* (Washington, DC: Office of Community Oriented Policing Services, 2015), p, 7.
12. Adapted from Ibid., pp. 5–10.
13. St. Louis County, Missouri, Police Department, "Values: Our Mission Statement and Codes of Ethics," http://www.stlouisco.com/LawandPublicSafety/ PoliceDepartment/AboutUs/Values
14. Adapted from Kunard and Moe, *Procedural Justice for Law Enforcement*, p. 5.
15. T. Barker and D. Carter, "'Fluffing Up the Evidence and Covering Your Ass': Some Conceptual Notes on Police Lying," *Deviant Behavior* 11 (1990): 61–73.
16. J. Kuykendall, "The Municipal Police Detective: An Historical Analysis," *Criminology* 24(1) (1986): 175–201.
17. *Illinois v. Perkins,* 110 S.Ct. 2394 (1990).
18. Barker and Carter, "Fluffing Up the Evidence and Covering Your Ass," p. 70.
19. Ibid.
20. J. L. Skolnick, "Deception by Police," *Criminal Justice Ethics* 1(2) (1982): 27–32.
21. Kania, "Police Acceptance of Gratuities," p. 39.
22. *Knapp Commission Report on Police Corruption.* (New York: George Braziller, 1972).

23. D. Carter, "Theoretical Dimensions in the Abuse of Authority." In T. Barker and D. Carter, eds., *Police Deviance* (Cincinnati: Anderson, 1994), pp. 269–290.

24. C. Joyner and C. Basile, "The Dynamic Resistance Response Model," *FBI Law Enforcement Bulletin* (September 2007): 15–20.

25. J. Fyfe, *Police Personnel Practices* (Washington, DC: International City Management Association, 1986).

26. Human Rights Watch, *Shielded from Justice: Police Brutality and Accountability in the United States* (New York: Author, 1998).

27. D. A. Smith and C. Visher, "Street-level Justice: Situational Determinants of Police Arrest Decisions," *Social Problems* 29 (1981): 167–178.

28. R. J. Friedrich, "The Impact of Organizational, Individual, and Situational Factors on Police Behavior," Ph.D. dissertation, Department of Political Science, University of Michigan, 1997; also see D. Black and A. Reiss, "Police Control of Juveniles," *American Sociological Review* 35 (1967): 63–77.

29. L. W. Brooks, "Determinants of Police Orientations and their Impact on Police Discretionary Behavior." Unpublished Ph.D. dissertation. Institute of Criminal Justice & Criminology, University of Maryland, 1986.

30. Ibid.; also see Smith and Visher, "Street-level Justice: Situational Determinants of Police Arrest Decisions."

31. Friedrich, "The Impact of Organizational, Individual, and Situational Factors on Police Behavior"; also see Smith and Visher, "Street-level Justice: Situational Determinants of Police Arrest Decisions."

32. Brooks, "Determinants of Police Orientations and their Impact on Police Discretionary Behavior"; also see Smith and Visher, "Street-level Justice: Situational Determinants of Police Arrest Decisions."

33. T. Barker, "An Empirical Study of Police Deviance Other than Corruption," *Journal of Police Science and Administration* 6(3) (September 1978): 264–272.

34. A. D. Sapp, "Sexual Misconduct by Police Officers," in T. Barker and D. Carter, eds., *Police Deviance*. (Cincinnati: Anderson, 1994), pp. 187–200.

35. Ibid.

36. R. Kennedy, "Suspect Policy," *The New Republic* (September 13, 1999): 30–35.

37. S. M. Cox, "Racial Profiling: Refuting Concerns about Collecting Race Data on Traffic Stops," *Law and Order* (October 2001): 61–65.

38. G. Voegtlin, "Bias-based Policing and Data Collection," *The Police Chief* (October 2001): 8.

CHAPTER 10

1. C. Beck, "Predictive Policing: What Can We Learn from Wal-Mart and Amazon about Fighting Crime in a Recession?" *The Police Chief* 76(11) (November 2009): 18–24.

2. L. Robinson, "Predictive Policing Symposium: Opening Remarks" (speech given at the Predictive Policing Symposium in Los Angeles, California, November 18, 2009), www.nij.gov/topics/law-enforcement/strategies/predictive-policing/symposium/opening-robinson.htm.

3. R. W. Glensor and K. J. Peak, "New Police Management Practices and Predictive Software: A New Era They Do Not Make," in *American Policing in 2022: Essays on the Future of a Profession* (Washington, DC: U.S. Department of Justice, 2012), pp. 11–17.

4. S. Fuller, quoted in D. Diamond and D. Mead Weiss, *Community Policing: Looking to Tomorrow* (Washington, DC: U. S. Department of Justice, Office of Community Oriented Policing Services, May 2009), p. 19.

5. L. Mayo, quoted in in eds. D. R. Cohen McCullough and D. L. Spence, *American Policing in 2022: Essays on the Future of a Profession* (Washington, DC: U.S. Department of Justice Office of Community Oriented Policing Services, 2012), p. 35.

6. See Bureau of Justice Statistics, *Local Police Departments, 2013: Personnel, Policies, and Practices*, p. 8, https://www.bjs.gov/content/pub/pdf/lpd13ppp.pdf. Accessed May 2015.

7. Ibid.

8. Bureau of Justice Statistics, *State and Local Law Enforcement Training Academies, 2013* p. 7, https://www.bjs.gov/content/pub/pdf/slleta13.pdf. Accessed July 2016.

9. S. Miletich, "Police Academy 2.0: Less military training, more empathy," *Seattle Times*, http://www.seattletimes.com/seattle-news/police-academy-20-less-military-training-more-empathy/. Accessed July 13, 2013.

10. Ibid.

11. G. Kemerling, "Plato: The State and the Soul," The Philosophy Pages, 2001, http://www.philosophypages.com/hy/2g.htm.

12. Miletich, "Police Academy 2.0: Less military training, more empathy."

13. Adapted from R. W. Glensor and K. J. Peak, "Implementing Change: Community-Oriented Policing and Problem Solving," *FBI Law Enforcement Bulletin* 7 (July 1996): 14–20.

14. An excellent resource for police leaders to use for implementation of community policing and problem solving is: M. S. Scott and S. Kirby, *Implementing POP: Leading, Structuring, and Managing a Problem-Oriented Police Agency* (Washington, DC: Center for Problem-Oriented Policing, 2012).

15. Quoted in Office of Community Oriented Policing Services, "Are toxic leaders derailing your community policing efforts?" *Community Policing Dispatch*, http://cops.usdoj.gov/html/dispatch/03-2014/toxic_leaders_derailing_your_cp.asp. Accessed March 2014.

16. Ibid.

17. M. Tharp and D. Friedman, "New Cops on the Block," *U.S. News & World Report* (August 2, 1993): 23.

18. Ibid.

19. J. Q. Wilson, "Six Things Police Leaders Can Do About Juvenile Crime," Subject to Debate (September/October 1997): 1.

20. W. A. Geller and G. Swanger, *Managing Innovation in Policing: The Untapped Potential of the Middle Manager* (Washington, DC: Police Executive Research Forum, 1995), p. 105.

21. Ibid., p. 131.

22. Ibid., p. 109.

23. Ibid., p. 112.

24. Ibid., pp. 137–138.

25. G. L. Kelling and W. J. Bratton, "Implementing Community Policing: The Administrative Problem," *Perspectives on Policing* 17 (1993): 11.

26. H. Goldstein, Problem-Oriented Policing (New York: McGraw-Hill, 1990), p. 29.

27. Geller and Swanger, *Managing Innovation in Policing*, p. 41.

28. P. Pritchett and R. Pound, A Survival Guide to the Stress of Organizational Change (Dallas, TX: Pritchett and Associates, 1995), p. 12.

29. D. DeLorenzi, J. M. Shane, and K. L. Amendola, "The CompStat Process: Managing Performance on the Pathway to Leadership," *The Police Chief* 73, http://www.policechiefmagazine.org/magazine/index.cfm?fuseaction=display&article_id=998&issue_id=92006. Accessed September 2006.

30. Ibid.

31. H. B. Grant and K. J. Terry, *Law Enforcement in the 21st Century* (Boston: Allyn & Bacon, 2005), pp. 329–330.

32. Information concerning the origins and initial grant-funded test sites for SPI was obtained from the following sources: J. R. Coldren Jr., A. Huntoon, and M. Medaris, "Introducing Smart Policing: Foundations, Principles, and Practice," *Police Quarterly* 16(3) (September 2014): 275–286; and N. M. Joyce, C. H. Ramsey, and J. K. Stewart, "Commentary on Smart Policing," *Police Quarterly* 16(3) (September 2014): 358–368. This special issue of *Police Quarterly* contains a number of other, site-specific articles that discuss SPI.

33. U.S. Department of Justice, Office of Justice Programs, Bureau of Justice Statistics, *Intelligence-Led Policing: The New Intelligence Architecture* (Washington, DC: Author, 2005), p. 9.

34. Ibid., p. 3.

35. Ibid.

36. U.S. Department of Justice, National Institute of Justice, "Predictive Policing Symposium: The Future of Prediction in Criminal Justice," http://www.nij.gov/topics/law-enforcement/strategies/predictive-policing/symposium/future.htm.

37. E. Perlman, "Policing by the Odds," *Governing*, www.governing.com/article/policing-odds. Accessed December 1, 2008

38. Ibid.

39. These case studies are adapted from J. E. Eck, *Assessing Responses to Problems: An Introductory Guide for Police Problem-Solvers* (Washington, DC: U.S. Department of Justice, Office of Community Oriented Policing Services, August 2011), pp. 11–13.

40. Ibid., pp. 15–18.

41. Ibid.

42. Quoted in Diamond and Mead Weiss, *Community Policing: Looking to Tomorrow*, p. 20.

43. Ibid.

44. M. C. de Guzman, "Future Impact of Community Policing on Terrorism," in Kenneth J. Peak ed., *Encyclopedia of Community Policing and Problem Solving* (Thousand Oaks, CA: SAGE, 2013), pp. 403–405.

45. Ibid.

46. G. F. Treverton, M. Wollman, E. Wilke, D.Lai, *Moving Toward the Future of Policing* (Santa Monica, CA: RAND, 2011), p. 98.

47. A. A. Harnish, "Cybercrime and Community Policing," in Kenneth J. Peak ed., *Encyclopedia of Community Policing and Problem Solving* (Thousand Oaks, CA: SAGE, 2013), pp. 111–113.

48. Ibid.

49. D. Weisburd and P. Neyroud, *Police Science: Toward a New Paradigm* (Washington, DC: National Institute of Justice, and Harvard Kennedy School, January 2011), pp. 2–3.

50. Ibid., p. 4.

51. Ibid., pp. 11–12.

52. G. Witkin and D. McGraw, "Beyond 'Just the Facts, ma'am,' " *U.S. News and World Report* (August 2, 1993), p. 28.

CHAPTER 11

1. From the Gilbert & Sullivan opera "Pirates of Penzance" (1879).

2. W. Westley, *Violence and the Police: A Sociological Study of Law, Custom, and Morality* (Cambridge, MA: MIT Press, 1970), p. 3.

3. University of Albany, *Sourcebook of Criminal Justice Statistics Online*, Table 3.154, http://www.albany.edu/sourcebook/pdf/xt31542012.pdf.

4. See Federal Bureau of Investigation, "Law Enforcement Officers Killed and Assaulted, 2001–2010," https://ucr.fbi.gov/leoka/leoka-2010/tables/table01-leok-feloniously-region-division-state-01-10.xls.

5. National Law Enforcement Officers Memorial, "Facts and Figures," January 2017, http://www.nleomf.org/facts/.

6. Center for the Study of Law Enforcement Officers Killed and Assaulted, January 2017, https://leoka.org/.

7. Bureau of Justice Assistance, BJA Fact Sheet, "Officer Safety Initiatives," September 2015, p. 1, https://www.bja.gov/Publications/OfficerSafetyFS.pdf.

8. J. B. Kuhns, E. R. Maguire, and N. R. Leach, *Health, Safety, and Wellness Program Case Studies in Law Enforcement* (Washington, DC: Office of Community Oriented Policing Services, 2015), p. 1.

9. M. L. Fiedler, *Officer Safety and Wellness: An Overview of the Issues* (Washington, DC: Office of Community Oriented Policing Services, 2011), p. 9.

10. Kuhns, et al., *Health, Safety, and Wellness Program: Case Studies in Law Enforcement*, p. 2.

11. S. Weichselbaum and B. Schwartzapfel, "When veterans become cops, some bring war home," *The Marshall Project*, http://www.usatoday.com/story/news/2017/03/30/when-veterans-become-cops-some-bring-war-home/99349228/. Accessed March 30, 2017

12. The International Association of Chiefs of Police and U.S. Department of Justice, *Employing Returning Combat Veterans as Law Enforcement Officers*, September 2009, p. 14, http://www.theiacp.org/portals/0/pdfs/iacpreturningcombatveteransfinal2009-09-15.pdf.

13. Weichselbaum and Schwartzapfel, "When veterans become cops, some bring war home." The Marshall Project, http://www.usatoday.com/story/news/2017/03/30/when-veterans-become-cops-some-bring-war-home/99349228/. Accessed March 30, 2017

14. J. Hill, S. Whitcomb, P. Patterson, D. W. Stephens, and B. Hill, *Making Officer Safety and Wellness Priority One: A Guide to Educational Campaigns* (Washington, DC: Office of Community Oriented Policing Services, 2014), p. 15–17.

15. Adapted from Hill, et al., *Making Officer Safety and Wellness Priority One*, pp. 18–34.

16. Thomas Connelly, "Perspective: Risk Management and Police Training," *FBI Law Enforcement*, March 2010, https://leb.fbi.gov/2010/march/perspective-risk-management-and-police-training.

17. Fiedler, *Officer Safety and Wellness*, p. 8.

18. Bureau of Justice Assistance and Police Executive Research Forum, "*The BJA/PERF Body Armor National Survey: Protecting the Nation's Law Enforcement Officer*" (Washington, DC: Authors, August 2009), p. 19.

19. Fiedler, *Officer Safety and Wellness*, p. 4.

20. Ibid., p. 5.

21. Ibid., p. 7.

22. E. L. Sanberg, C. Solé Brito, A. Morrozoff Luna, and S. M. McFadden, *A Guide to Occupational Health and Safety for Law Enforcement Executives*, Bureau of Justice Assistance and Police Executive Research Forum, p. 4, www.bja.gov/publications/perf_le_occhealth.pdf. Accessed September 2010.

23. Ibid., pp. 4–5.

24. Ibid., p. 6.

25. Ibid., p. 9; *Parker v. District of Columbia*, 271 U.S. App. D.C. 15, 850 F.2d 708 (1988).

26. Ibid., pp. 9–10.

27. Also see D. Stephens, M. L. Fiedler, S. M. Edwards, *OSW Annual Summary, 2011–2012: Issues and Recommendations Discussed for Improving the Well-being of Police Officers* (Washington, DC: Office of Community Oriented Policing Services, September 2012).

28. President's Task Force on 21st Century Policing, *Interim Report of the President's Task Force on 21st Century Policing*, Office of Community Oriented Policing Services, p. 1, http://www.cops.usdoj.gov/pdf/taskforce/Interim_TF_Report.pdf. Accessed March 4, 2015,

29. Ibid., pp. 61–68.

30. Ibid., p. 61.

31. Ibid., p. 63.

32. Adapted from Hill, et al., *Making Officer Safety and Wellness Priority One*, p. 17.

33. Ibid., p. 26.

34. Ibid., p. 34.

35. Ibid., p. 45.

36. Kuhns, et al., *Health, Safety, and Wellness Program Case Studies in Law Enforcement*, pp. 23–33.

37. See, for example, works by one who has been termed the "father" of police stress research, Hans Selye, such as *Stress Without Distress* (Philadelphia, PA: Lippincott, 1981).

38. Ibid.

39. J. P. Crank and M. Caldero, "The Production of Occupational Stress in Medium-sized Police Agencies: A Survey of Line Officers in Eight Municipal Departments," *Journal of Criminal Justice* 19 (1991): 339–349.

40. S. Zhao, Ne Hi, and N. P. Lovrich, "Predicting Five Dimensions of Police Officer Stress: Looking More Deeply into Organizational Settings for Sources of Police Stress," *Police Quarterly* 5 (2002): 43–62.

41. L. W. Brooks and N. Leeper Piquero, "Police Stress: Does Department Size Matter?" *Policing: An International Journal of Police Strategies and Management* 21(1) (1998): 600–617.

CHAPTER 12

1. See D. Weisburd, A. Wooditch, S. Weisburd, and S. Yang. "Do Stop, Question, and Frisk Practices Deter Crime?" *Criminology & Public Policy* 15 (2016): 31–56.

2. G. Kuper. "Productivity: A National Concern." in J. Wolfe and J. Heaphy eds., *Readings on Productivity in Policing* (Washington, DC: Police Foundation, 1975).

3. J. Schermerhorn, *Management.* (New York: John Wiley & Sons, 1996): p. 6.

4. L. Gaines, C. Famega, and G. Bichler. *Police Response to Burglar Alarms Study: San Bernardino County.* Report to the San Bernardino County Police and Sheriff's Association (California State University, San Bernardino, California, 2007).

5. J. Hepburn "Crime Control, Due Process, and Measurement of Police Performance." *Journal of Police Science and Administration* 9 (1981): 88–98.

6. V. Kappeler and L. Gaines. *Community Policing.* 7th ed. (New York: Routledge, 2015).

7. Ibid.

8. M. Moore. "The Bottom Line in Policing: What Citizens Should Value and Measure" In M. Moore and A. Braga, eds., *Police Performance* (Washington, DC: Police Executive Research Forum, 2003).

9. L. Gaines and V. Kappeler. *Policing in America.* 7th ed. (Cincinnati: Anderson, 2011).

10. W. Walsh. "Patrol Officer Arrest Rates: A Study of the Social Organization of Police Work." *Justice Quarterly* 2 (1985): 271–290.

11. W. Spelman. *Beyond Bean Counting: New Approaches for Managing Crime Data* (Washington, DC: Police Executive Research Forum, 1988).

12. National Institute of Justice. *Measuring What Matters (Part Two): Developing Measures of What the Police Do* (Washington, DC: Author, 1997).

13. Law Enforcement Assistance Administration. *Criminal Justice Planning Workbook* (Washington, DC: Author, 1975).

14. L. Gaines and J. Worrall. *Police Administration.* 3rd ed. (New York: Delmar, 2012).

15. Tucson Police Department Strategic Plan 2013–2018. https://www.tucsonaz.gov/files/police/SPFinal.pdf. Accessed December 1, 2016.

16. Ibid.

17. M. Moore and A. Braga. "Measuring and Improving Police Performance: The Lessons of CompStat and Its Progeny." *Policing: An International Journal of Police Strategies & Management* 26 (2003): 439–453.

18. W. Wells, J. Horney, and E. Maguire "Patrol Officer Responses to Citizen Feedback: An Experimental Analysis." *Police Quarterly* 8 (2005): 171–205.

19. J. Willis, S. Mastrofski and D. Weisburd. "CompStat and Bureaucracy: A Case Study of Challenges and Opportunities for Change." *Justice Quarterly* 21 (2004):463–496.

20. B. Bond and A. Braga. "Rethinking the Compstat Process to Enhance Problem-Solving Responses: Insights from a Randomized Field Experiment." *Police Practice & Research* 16 (2015): 22–35.

21. J. Eterno and E. Silverman. "The New York City Police Department's Compstat: Dream or Nightmare?" *International Journal of Police Science & Management* 8 (2006): 218–231.

22. San Francisco Police Department. *Data.* http://sanfranciscopolice.org/data#demographics. Accessed February 2, 2017.

23. Sacramento Police Department. *2015 Annual Report* (Sacramento: Author, 2016).

24. Ibid.

25. M. Levine and J. McEwen. *Patrol Deployment* (Washington, DC: U.S. Department of Justice, 1985).

26. Ibid.

27. Ibid.

28. Sacramento Police Department. *2015 Annual Report* (Sacramento: Author, 2016).

29. K. Amendola, M. Slipka, E. Hamilton, and M. Soelberg. *Law Enforcement Shift Schedules: Results of a 2009 Random National Survey of Police Agencies* (Washington, DC: Police Foundation, 2011).

30. K. Amendola, D. Weisburd, E. Hamilton, G. Jones, M. Slipka, A. Heitmann, J. Shane, C. Ortiz, and E. Tarkghen. *The Impact of Shift Length in Policing on Performance, Health, Quality of Life, Sleep, Fatigue, and Extra-Duty Employment* (Washington, DC: National Institute of Justice, 2012).

31. Ibid.

32. V. Kappeler and L. Gaines. *Community Policing: A Contemporary Perspective 7th ed.* (New York: Routledge, 2015).

33. M. Golden and C. Almo. *Reducing Gun Violence: An Overview of New York City's Strategies* (New York City: Vera Institute, 2004).

34. E. Piza and B. O'Hara. "Saturation Foot-Patrol in a High-Violence Area: A Quasi-Experimental Evaluation." *Justice Quarterly* 31 (2014): 693–718.

35. J. Wood, E. Sorg, E. Groff, J. Ratcliffe and C. Taylor. "Cops as Treatment Providers: Realities and Ironies of Police Work in a Foot Patrol Experiment." *Policing and Society: An International Journal of Research and Policy,* 24 (2014): 362–379.

36. G. Kelling, T. Pate, D. Dieckman, and C. Brown. *The Kansas City Preventive Patrol Experiment: A Summary Report* (Washington, DC: The Police Foundation, 1974).

37. L. Sherman and D. Weisburd. "General Deterrent Effects of Police Patrol in Crime 'Hot Spots': A Randomized Controlled Trial." *Justice Quarterly* 12 (1995): 625–648.

38. D. Weisburd and L. Green. "Policing Drug Hot Spots: The Jersey City Drug Market Analysis Experiment," *Justice Quarterly,* 12 (1995): 711–736.

39. L. Sherman and D. Rogan, "Deterrent Effects of Police Raids on Crack Houses: A Randomized Controlled Experiment," *Justice Quarterly* 12 (1995): 755–782.

40. M. McCampbell, "Robbery Reduction through Directed Patrol." *The Police Chief* 50 (1983): 39–41.

41. A. Braga, D. Weisburd, L. Mazerolle, W. Spellman and F. Gajewski, "Problem-Oriented Policing in Violent Crime Places: A Randomized Controlled Experiment" *Criminology* 37 (1999): 541–580.

42. L. Gaines and V. Kappeler. *Policing in America.* 7th ed. (Cincinnati: Anderson, 2011).

43. R. Davis and A. Lurigio, *Fighting Back: Neighborhood Anti-drug Strategies* (Thousand Oaks, CA: Sage, 1996).

44. A. Weiss and E. McGarrell, "Traffic Enforcement and Crime: Another Look." *The Police Chief* 60 (1999): 25–28.

45. T. Caeti, *Houston's Targeted Beat Program: A Quasi-Experimental Test of Police Patrol Strategies* (Ann Arbor, MI: University Microfilms International, 1999).

46. M. Scott, *The Benefits and Consequences of Police Crackdowns* (Washington, DC: Office of Community Oriented Policing Services, 2003).

47. L. Sherman, "Crackdowns: Initial and Residential Deterrence." In M. Tonryand N. Morris eds., *Crime and Justice: A Review of Research* (Vol. 12). (Chicago: University of Chicago Press, 1990).

48. *Terry v. Ohio*, 392 U.S. 1 (1968).

49. D. Weisburd, C. Telep, and B. Lawton, "Could Innovations in Policing Have Contributed to New York City's Crime Drop Even in a Period of Declining Police Strength?': The Case of Stop, Question and Frisk as a Hot Spots Policing Strategy." *Justice Quarterly*, 30 (2013): 1–25.

50. Kansas City Police Department Organization, http://kcmo.gov/police/wp-content/uploads/sites/2/2014/02/investbureaublue8.1.16.pdf. Accessed February 8, 2017.

51. J. Kuykendall. "The Municipal Police Detective: An Historical Analysis." *Criminology* 24 (1986): 173–201; W. Sanders. *Detective Work* (New York: Free Press, 1977).

52. P. Greenwood, J. Chaiken, and J. Petersillia. *The Investigative Process* (Lexington, MA: Lexington Books, 1977).

53. J. Eck. *Solving Crimes: The Investigation of Burglary and Robbery* (Washington, DC: Police Foundation, 1983); L. Gaines, B. Lewis and R. Swanagin. "Case Screening in Criminal Investigations: A Case Study of Robbery." *Police Studies* 6 (1983): 22–29.

54. J. Eck. *Managing Case Assignments: The Burglary Investigative Decision Model Replication* (Washington, DC: Police Foundation, 1979).

55. G. DeAngelo and B. Hansen. "Life and Death in the Fast Lane: Police Enforcement and Traffic Fatalities." *American Economic Journal: Economic Policy* 6 (2014): 231–257.

56. J. Fell, G. Waehre, R. Voas, A. Auld-Owens, K. Carr and K. Pell. "Effects of Enforcement Intensity on Alcohol Impaired Driving Crashes." *Accident Analysis & Prevention* 73 (2014): 181–186.

57. O. Ryeng. "The Effect of Sanctions and Police Enforcement on Drivers' Choice of Speed." *Accident Analysis & Prevention* 45 (2011): 446–454.

58. J. Greene. "Sobriety Checkpoints and Saturation Patrols Provide Law Enforcement Agencies with Two Powerful Ways to Curb Drunk Driving Incidents." *The FBI Law Enforcement Bulletin* 72 (2003): 1–9.

CHAPTER 13

1. L. Gaines and V. Kappeler, *Homeland Security* (New York: Pearson, 2012).

2. B. Schatz, "Meet the Terrorist Group Playing the Long Game in Syria." *Mother Jones* (August 5, 2016), http://www.motherjones.com/politics/2016/08/syria-al-qaeda-nusra-battle-aleppo.

3. U.S. Department of State, *Country Reports on Terrorism, 2015* (Washington, DC: Author 2016).

4. Ibid.

5. M. Potok, "The Year in Hate and Extremism." *Intelligence Report* (Spring 2017): 37–54.

6. J. White, *Terrorism and Homeland Security* (Belmont, CA: Wadsworth-Cengage, 2009).

7. G. Martin, *Understanding Terrorism: Challenges, Perspectives, and Issues* (Thousand Oaks, CA: Sage, 2003).

8. E. Bakker and B. de Graaf, "Lone Wolves: How to Prevent This Phenomenon?" *International Centre for Counter-Terrorism* (November 2010), https://www.icct.nl/download/file/ICCT-Bakker-deGraaf-EM-Paper-Lone-Wolves.pdf.

9. P. Bergen, A. Ford, A. Sims, and D. Sterman, *Terrorism in America after 9/11* (New York: New America, 2017).

10. M. Hamm and R. Spaaj, *Lone Wolf Terrorism in America: Using Knowledge of Radicalization Pathways to Forge Prevention Strategies* (Washington, DC: U.S. Department of Justice, 2015).

11. J. Stern, "Radicalization to Extremism and Mobilization to Violence: What Have We Learned and What Can We Do about It?" *Annals, AAPSS* 668 (2016): 102–117.

12. H. Mirahmadi, "Building Resilience against Violent Extremism: A Community-Based Approach, Annals," *AAPSS* 668 (2016): 129–144.

13. J. Horgan, "Leaving Terrorism Behind: An Individual Perspective." In Andrew Silke ed., *Terrorists, Victims and Society: Psychological Perspectives on Terrorism and its Consequences* (New York: Wiey, 2003).

14. C. Allen, "The Threat of Islamic Radicalization to the Homeland." *Testimony before the U.S. Senate Committee on Homeland Security and Governmental Affairs* (March 14, 2007), https://www.investigativeproject.org/documents/testimony/270.pdf.

15. G. Selim, "Approaches for Countering Violent Extremism at Home and Abroad." *Annals, AAPSS* 668 (2016): 94–101.

16. H. Mirahmadi, "Building Resilience against Violent Extremism: A Community-Based Approach," *Annals, AAPSS* 668 (2016): 129–144.

17. Stern, "Radicalization to Extremism and Mobilization to Violence," 102–117.

18. V. Henry and D. King, "Improving Emergency Preparedness and Public–Safety Responses to Terrorism and Weapons of Mass Destruction." *Brief Treatment and Crisis Intervention* 4 (2004): 11–35.

19. L. Gaines and V. Kappeler, *Homeland Security* (New York: Pearson, 2012).

20. M. Hamm and R. Spaaj, *Lone Wolf Terrorism in America: Using Knowledge of Radicalization Pathways to Forge Prevention Strategies* (Washington, DC: U.S. Department of Justice, 2015).

21. Department of Homeland Security, *National Infrastructure Protection Plan* (Washington, DC: Author, 2006).

22. Ibid, p. 30.

23. D. Carter, *Law Enforcement Intelligence: A Guide For State, Local, and Tribal Law Enforcement Agencies* (Washington, DC: Office of Community Oriented Policing Services, no date).

24. M. Kleiman, "Illicit Drugs and the Terrorist Threat: Causal Links and Implications for Domestic Drug Control Policy." *CRS Report to Congress* (Washington, DC: Congressional Research Service, 2004); and B. McCaffrey and J. Basso. "Narcotics, Terrorism, and International Crime: The Convergence Phenomenon." In Howard, R. and Sawyer, R. eds., *Terrorism and Counterterrorism: Understanding the New Security Environment* (Guilford, CN: Dushkin, 2004). pp. 206–221.

25. J. Sullivan, "Terrorism Early Warning Groups: Regional Intelligence to Combat Terrorism." In Howard, R., Forest, J., and Moore, J. eds., *Homeland Security and Terrorism* (New York: McGraw-Hill, 2006): pp. 235–245.

26. A. Morabito and S. Greenberg, *Engaging the Private Sector to Promote Homeland Security: Law Enforcement-Private Security Partnerships* (Washington, DC: Bureau of Justice Assistance, 2005).

27. G. Green, *Introduction to Security* (Stoneham, MA: Butterworth, 1981).

28. Ohlhausen Research Inc. (2004). *Private Security/Public Policing: Vital Issues and Policy Recommendations* (Alexandria, VA: International Association of Chiefs of Police, 2004).

29. International Association of Chiefs of Police, *Using Community Policing to Counter Violent Extremism: Five Key Principles for Law Enforcement* (Washington, DC: Office of Community Oriented Policing Services, 2014).

30. W. Lyon, "Partnerships, Information, and Public Safety." *Policing* 25 (2002): 530–543

31. DHS, *National Incident Management System* (Washington, DC: Author, 2008).

32. J. Buntin, "Disaster Master." *Governing* (December 2001): 34–38.

33. DHS, *National Incident Management System* (Washington, DC: 2008): p. 51.

CHAPTER 14

1. B. A. Jackson, V. A. Greenfield, A. R. Morral, and J. S. Hollywood, *Police Department Investments in Information Technology Systems* (Santa Monica, CA: RAND Corporation, 2014), p. 2.

2. Bureau of Justice Assistance, *Acquisition of New Technology* (n.d.), p. 1, http://www.theiacp.org/portals/0/pdfs/BP-NewTechnology.pdf.

3. Lee Brown, quote in Seaskate, Inc., "The Evolution and Development of Police Technology," http://www.police-technology.net/id59.html#.

4. Jackson et al., *Police Department Investments in Information Technology Systems*, p. 3.

5. Ibid., p. 63.

6. National Institute of Justice, "Mapping and Analysis for Public Safety," May 22, 2013, http://www.nij.gov/topics/technology/maps/pages/welcome.aspx.

7. Ibid.

8. In addition, a full catalog of NIJ mapping tools and databases is available at: http://www.nij.gov/topics/technology/pages/software-tools.aspx#maps; also see NIJ's "MAPS: How Mapping Helps Reduce Crime and Improve Public Safety," http://www.nij.gov/topics/technology/maps/Pages/reduce-crime.aspx.

9. L. Burton, "New SPD 'crime center' shows city's activity unfolding in real time," *Seattlepi.com*, October 7, 2015, http://www.seattlepi.com/local/crime/article/New-SPD-crime-center-shows-city-s-activity-6556969.php.

10. Quoted in Ibid.

11. Ibid.

12. Ibid.

13. Joseph D'Amico, "Stopping Crime in Real Time," *The Police Chief*, November 2015, http://www.policechiefmagazine.org/magazine/index.cfm?fuseaction=display&article_id=995&issue_id=92006.

14. Ibid.

15. J. Facella, "Communications Interoperability: What a Chief Has to Know," August 2007, http://www.hendonpub.com/resources/article_archive/results/details?id=4245.

16. See the Center for Problem Oriented Policing, "How CCTV Aims to Prevent Crime," http://www.popcenter.org/responses/video_surveillance/3.

17. C. Shain, personal communication, October 11, 2015.

18. Adapted from D. Smith, Police Departments Consider Discontinuing Use of Body Cameras Due To Expense of Public Disclosure Requirements, Jonathan Turley, http://jonathanturley.org/2014/11/22/police-departments-consider-discontinuing-use-of-body-cameras-due-to-expense-of-public-disclosure-requirements.

19. R. N. Holden, "The Technology Cycle and Contemporary Policing," paper presented at the annual meeting of the Academy of Criminal Justice Sciences, March 5, 2015, Orlando, Florida.

20. Bureau of Justice Assistance, "Body Worn Camera Toolkit: Training," https://www.bja.gov/bwc/Topics-Training.html.

21. A. Gomez, "Who needs body cameras? Police testing cellphone cameras," *USA Today*, June 25, 2017, https://www.usatoday.com/story/news/world/2017/06/25/who-needs-body-cameras-police-testing-cellphone-cameras/426859001/.

22. M. W. Tobias, "Police Cars Can Now Identify Criminals While on Patrol," *Forbes*, June 25, 2015, http://www.forbes.com/sites/marcwebertobias/2015/06/25/denver-police-cars-that-identify-criminals/#284669426e48.

23. American Civil Liberties Union, "Automatic License Plate Readers," 2015, https://www.aclu.org/issues/privacy-technology/location-tracking/automatic-license-plate-readers

24. B. Shockley, "Lawsuit Challenges State of Utah Ban on License Plate Readers as Unconstitutional Censorship of Photography and Violation of 1st Amendment," *Vigilant Solutions*, http://vigilantsolutions.com/press/drn_vigilant_utah_lpr_federal_lawsuit.

25. K. Zetter, "Virginia Man Sues Police Over License Plate Database," *Wired*, May 6, 2015, http://www.wired.com/2015/05/virginia-man-sues-police-license-plate-database/.

26. K. Gierlack, S. Williams, T. LaTourrette, J. M. Anderson, L. A. Mayer, and J. Zmud, *License Plate Readers for Law Enforcement: Opportunities and Obstacles* (Santa Monica, CA: RAND Corporation, 2014), p. 46, https://www.ncjrs.gov/pdffiles1/nij/grants/247283.pdf.

27. Office of Community Oriented Policing Services, "Comprehensive Law Enforcement Review: The Importance of Technology in Policing," (n.d.), https://cops.usdoj.gov/pdf/taskforce/01-31-2015/Tech-and-Social-Media-Review.pdf.

28. Quoted in Jackson et al., *Police Department Investments in Information Technology Systems*, p. 7.

29. Ibid., p. 9.

30. Social Media Defined, "What is Social Media," 2014, http://www.socialmediadefined.com/what-is-social-media/.

31. T. Newcombe, "Social Media: Big Lessons from the Boston Marathon Bombing," *Government Technology* (September 24, 2014); see also Edward F. Davis III, Alejandro A. Alves, and David Alan Sklansky, *Social Media and Police Leadership: Lessons from Boston* (Washington, DC: National Institute of Justice, 2014).

32. Ibid.

33. Ibid.

34. D. Griffith, "Police Robots on Land and Sea," *Police*, December 28, 2015, http://www.policemag.com/channel/technology/articles/2015/12/police-robots-on-land-and-sea.aspx.

35. B. Huber, "Wis. Police Get Robo-Cop's Help," PoliceOne.com, November 14, 2006, www.policeone.com/police-technology/robots/articles/1190983.

36. J. Ingold, "James Holmes faces 142 counts, including 24 of first-degree murder," *The Denver Post*, July 30, 2012, http://www.denverpost.com/breakingnews/ci_21191265/hearing-underway-man-suspected-killing-12-aurora-theater.

37. J. Levitas, "Defining Civic Hacking," *Code for America*, http://www.codeforamerica.org/blog/2013/06/07/defining-civic-hacking/.

38. T. Newcombe, "Civic Apps: Can They Help Fight Crime?" *Government Technology*, September 25, 2014, http://www.govtech.com/public-safety/Civic-Apps-Can-They-Help-Fight-Crime.html.

39. T. Dees, "4 helpful police smartphone apps for Android," *PoliceOne.com*, December 12, 2014, https://www.policeone.com/police-products/police-technology/articles/6645023-4-helpful-police-smartphone-apps-for-Android/.

40. Ibid.

41. J. Brown, "App Helps Police Manage 'Gypsy Hill' Cold Case Murder Investigation," *Government Technology*, August 6, 2015, http://www.govtech.com/applications/App-Helps-Police-Manage-Gypsy-Hill-Cold-Case-Murder-Investigation.html.

42. D. McCullagh, "Court OKs Warrantless Use of Hidden Surveillance Cameras," *CNET*, October 30, 2012, http://www.cnet.com/news/court-oks-warrantless-use-of-hidden-surveillance-cameras/.

43. *U.S. v. Jones*, 565 U.S. ____, 132 S. Ct. 945, (2012)

44. Police Executive Research Forum, *Constitutional Policing as a Cornerstone of Community Policing* (Washington, DC: Office of Community Oriented Policing Services, 2015), p. 29, http://ric-zai-inc.com/Publications/cops-p324-pub.pdf.

45. Ibid., p. 30.

46. Ibid., p. 31.

47. Margaret Rouse, "Internet of Things (IoT)," n.d., http://internetofthingsagenda.techtarget.com/definition/Internet-of-Things-IoT.

48. B. Botelho, "Explained: What Is the Internet of Things?" IoT Agenda (n.d.), http://internetofthingsagenda.techtarget.com/feature/Explained-What-is-the-Internet-of-Things; see also Internet Society, *The Internet of Things*, October 2015, https://www.internetsociety.org/sites/default/files/ISOC-IoT-Overview-20151014_0.pdf.

49. U.S. Department of Homeland Security, "Dr. Brothers Will Speak at Internet of Things World 2015," (n.d.), https://www.dhs.gov/science-and-technology /internet-things-world-2015.

50. A. Stone, "Next-Generation Public Safety," *Government Technology*, March 2, 2016, http://www .emergencymgmt.com/disaster/A-New-World-in -Public-Safety.html?utm_medium=email&utm _source=Act-On+Software&utm _content=email&utm_campaign=What%27s%20 Next%20in%20Public%20Safety%20Response&utm_ term=Next-Generation%20Public%20Safety.

INDEX